Hospitality Management and Digital Transformation

Hospitality managers are at a critical inflection point. Digital technology advancements are ramping up guest expectations and continuing to introduce nontraditional competitors that threaten to disrupt the whole industry. The hospitality managers whose organizations are to thrive need to get their organizations into a position where they can effectively leverage digital technologies to simultaneously deliver breakthroughs in efficiency, agility, and guest experience.

Hospitality Management and Digital Transformation is a much-needed guidebook to digital disruption and transformation for current and prospective hospitality and leisure managers. The book:

- Explains digital technology advancements, how they cause disruption, and the implications of this disruption for hospitality and leisure organizations.
- Explains the digital business and digital transformation imperative for hospitality and leisure organizations.
- Discusses the different digital capabilities required to effectively compete as a digital business.
- Discusses the new and/or enhanced roles hospitality and leisure managers need to play in effecting the different digital capabilities, as well as the competencies required to play these roles.
- Discusses how hospitality and leisure managers can keep up with digital technology advancements.
- Unpacks more than 36 key digital technology advancements, discussing what they are, how they work, and how they can be implemented across the hospitality and leisure industry.

This book will be useful for advanced undergraduate and postgraduate students studying strategic management, IT, information systems, or digital business–related courses as part of degrees in hospitality and leisure management, as well as practitioners studying for professional qualifications.

Richard Busulwa researches and teaches in the Business School at Swinburne University of Technology, home to Australia's first fully immersed Industry 4.0 facility. His digital business research explores different digital technology advancements, how they drive disruption, and their implications for particular industries, business functions, and professions. He is the author of *Strategy Execution and Complexity: Thriving in the Era of Disruption* and *Start-Up Accelerators: A Field Guide*. Before entering academia, Richard worked as managing director, COO, CFO, divisional manager, and sales executive in the hospitality, IT, telecommunications, and healthcare industries. He is co-founder of Leapin Digital Keys, the world's first NBIoT smart lock platform.

Nina Evans is Associate Professor of STEM at the University of South Australia. She also holds a professorial lead position in the STEM academic unit. Nina has had a long career in ICT and STEM education leadership that has included time as vice dean, associate head of teaching and learning, and industry liaison manager. Nina started her career as a chemical engineer and completed undergraduate and postgraduate studies in computer science/IT, education, an MBA and a PhD. Her research and teaching interests are in digital innovation, ICT leadership, information/knowledge management and governance.

Aaron Oh is a professional hotelier, general manager, and hospitality management educator. He has more than 12 years' experience in operations management and property development of independent and boutique hotels such as the five-star Mayfair Hotel, The Point Brisbane Hotel, and Adabco Boutique Hotel. Aaron teaches hospitality property development, hospitality information systems management, and strategic management at the International College of Hotel Management, the only affiliate school of the Swiss Hotel Association in the Asia Pacific region.

Moon Kang is a hospitality management educator with nearly two decades of experience as a frontline manager, middle manager, senior manager, and strategic leader within the hotel industry in the Asia Pacific. This includes stints as food and beverage director with the Shangri-la (Sydney), food and beverage director with the Grand Intercontinental COEX and Grand Intercontinental (Seoul), executive assistant manager with the Sheraton Maldives, and frontline manager and middle manager with Westin Hotels and Resorts. Moon teaches guest experience creation and delivery and food and beverage management at the International College of Hotel Management.

Business and Digital Transformation

Digital technologies are transforming societies across the globe, the effects of which are yet to be fully understood. In the business world, technological disruption brings an array of challenges and opportunities for organizations, management and the workplace.

This series of textbooks provides a student-centred library to analyse, explore and critique the evolutionary effects of technology on the business world. Each book in the series takes the perspective of a key business discipline and examines the transformational potential of digital technology, aided by real world cases and examples.

With contributions from expert scholars across the globe, the books in this series enable critical thinking students to excel in their studies of the new digital business environment.

Strategic Digital Transformation
A Results-Driven Approach
Edited by Alex Fenton, Gordon Fletcher and Marie Griffiths

Hospitality Management and Digital Transformation
Balancing Efficiency, Agility and Guest Experience in the Era of Disruption
Richard Busulwa, Nina Evans, Aaron Oh and Moon Kang

For more information about the series, please visit www.routledge.com/Routledge-New-Directions-in-Public-Relations – Communication-Research/book-series/BAD

Hospitality Management and Digital Transformation

Balancing Efficiency, Agility and Guest Experience in the Era of Disruption

Richard Busulwa, Nina Evans, Aaron Oh and Moon Kang

LONDON AND NEW YORK

First published 2021
by Routledge
2 Park Square, Milton Park, Abingdon, Oxon OX14 4RN

and by Routledge
52 Vanderbilt Avenue, New York, NY 10017

Routledge is an imprint of the Taylor & Francis Group, an informa business

British Library Cataloguing-in-Publication Data
A catalogue record for this book is available from the British Library

Library of Congress Cataloging-in-Publication Data
A catalog record for this book has been requested

ISBN: 978-0-367-34352-1 (pbk)
ISBN: 978-0-367-34354-5 (hbk)
ISBN: 978-0-429-32520-5 (ebk)

Typeset in Bembo
by Apex CoVantage, LLC

Visit the eResources: www.routledge.com/9780367343521

Contents

10 Role of hospitality and leisure managers in cybersecurity, information privacy, and digital ethics

11 Role of hospitality and leisure managers in digital leadership, accelerated change and transformation, digital risk management, and digital governance

16 Video analytics, computer vision, and virtual reality technologies   175

17 Robotics, drones, and 3D/4D printing technologies   187

Figures

Tables

Part I

Digital technology advancements, digital disruption, and digital business transformation

1 Introduction and need for this book

Introduction

Information systems researchers have established that growing advancements in digital technologies (e.g. cloud computing, the internet of things [IoT], artificial intelligence [AI], and blockchain) are resulting in disruptions to industries, organizations, and professions.[1] Often referred to as digital disruption,[2,3] these disruptions manifest themselves in a variety of ways, including as changes to the way value is created, changes to the competitive landscape, changes to customer expectations, and changes to the basis of competition.[4] Incumbent organizations can turn a blind eye to digital disruption, deny its existence, or accept it but change too slowly; in such cases, they often end up sowing the seeds of their destruction (consider the fate of businesses like Blockbuster and Kodak, or industries such as the taxi industry). Alternatively, incumbent organizations in an industry can leverage and exploit digital technologies to adapt to disruption and to recreate themselves as digital businesses that leverage digital technologies for breakthroughs in efficiency, customer value, adaptability, and agility.[5,6,7,8] This process of organizations adapting to digital disruption and recreating themselves as digital businesses is most specifically referred to as digital business transformation,[9] although the more slippery term digital transformation is commonly used.[10] Notwithstanding that digital transformation is a slippery term, we use both terms interchangeably in this book, since digital transformation is a more commonly used term in most literature. We strictly mean digital business transformation each time we use either term.

Hospitality and leisure organizations have not been immune to digital disruption. Industry participants have faced nontraditional industry entrants such as Airbnb and online travel agencies (OTAs).[11] They have also faced increased pressure from traditional competitors leveraging digital technologies for a competitive edge.[12] Thus digital technology advancements and the resultant disruption risk they create require hospitality and leisure firms to reexamine their businesses from end to end and to redesign them so as to leverage digital technologies for breakthroughs in efficiency, differentiated customer value, adaptability, and agility.[13] But doing so requires hospitality and leisure managers at all levels (i.e. board, executive, middle management, and frontline managers across all functions) to effectively participate in digital business transformation. In turn, this requires that hospitality and leisure managers understand different digital technologies and their implications for hospitality operations and strategy, make sense of related critical digital technology issues (e.g. privacy and digital ethics, cybersecurity, scalability and interoperability, sourcing, digital ecosystems, digital innovation, digital business models)[14,15] and lead the hospitality and leisure workforce in transforming their organizations into and competing as a digital business.

Need for this book

The computing field (comprising the disciplines of information systems, information technology, computer science, computer engineering, and software engineering) is renowned for its specialized terminology, jargon, acronyms, and abbreviations. These can often make it challenging, even for professionals within the field, to clearly understand critical issues. Unfortunately, the growing proliferation in digital technologies and related terminology only compounds this challenge; consider the specialized and slippery terminology related to blockchain, cloud computing, and artificial intelligence technologies. Despite this challenge, within many of the hospitality and leisure management curriculums we reviewed, courses related to management information systems or information technology tended to focus on traditional information systems and IT concepts (e.g. traditional hardware, software, networks, operating systems, enterprise resource planning systems, decision support systems). In doing so, we contend that they miss opportunities to help hospitality and leisure managers make sense of the slippery terminology related to digital business and digital transformation, to help them understand the different digital technologies and their implications for digital business transformation and digital business, to provide them with a framework for understanding the digital capabilities required by organizations and the resultant managerial roles and competencies required, and to provide them with a framework for learning how to keep up with accelerating digital technology advancements. Seizing these missed opportunities is critical to hospitality and leisure managers having the required knowledge and skills to effectively participate in digital transformation and digital business, and thus to maximizing their managerial effectiveness and their organizations' long-term survival.

Filling these gaps, then, is the need for and the focus of this book. That is, the book focuses on the implications of digital technology advancements, digital transformation, and digital business for the hospitality and leisure industry and for the practice of hospitality and leisure management. It unpacks the concepts of digitalization, digital business, digital business capabilities, and digital transformation. It explains how these concepts can be shaped by the use of different digital technologies to optimize hospitality and leisure organization strategy and operations. As a part of this, the book unpacks more than 36 key digital technology advancements (e.g. IoT, blockchain, smart infrastructure, artificial intelligence, augmented reality) and explains their implications for digital transformation strategy and digital business strategy. The book then explains the role that hospitality managers can play in leveraging digital technology advancements to enable their organizations to simultaneously pursue efficiency, guest experience, adaptability, and agility so as to gain a competitive edge today and also to guard against disruption tomorrow. To conclude, a framework is provided that hospitality managers can use to keep up with digital technologies and to develop the technology skills they need to effectively lead in the digital era.

A range of industry-specific case studies and exercises is also provided to enable current and future managers to practically engage with the concepts. In using this book, we expect readers to understand the relationship between traditional information systems/information technology concepts, digital business/digital transformation concepts, the more than 36 key digital technology advancements we unpack, and any future digital technologies that may emerge. We expect them to understand the digital capabilities required by their organizations and the managerial roles to play in order to effect and optimize these capabilities. We expect them to understand which new technology related managerial competencies to develop and how to develop them. And we expect them to be able to test and reinforce their different understandings through a range of industry application examples, curated online search activities, and discussion question exercises. Used fully, the book will position hospitality and leisure managers to effectively lead in the digital era and or to effectively support senior managers at their organizations to lead digital transformation efforts.

Research for this book

The research for this book consisted of five stages. In stage 1 we undertook a review of the relevant and seminal information systems research on digital technology advancements, digital disruption, digital transformation, and digital business. The purpose of this stage was to understand the implications of these concepts for organization strategy and operations in general and for hospitality and leisure organizations and hospitality managers in particular. In stage 2 we reviewed key hospitality and leisure industry practitioner literature on digital technologies, digital transformation, digital business, and digital strategy. The aim of this stage was to understand how hospitality and leisure organizations were undertaking digital transformation, what digital strategies and digital business models they were pursuing, what digital capabilities they were building, and how they were safeguarding themselves against disruption risks. In stage 3 we sought out industry case studies of organizations successfully leveraging digital technologies, digital transformation strategies, and digital business strategies. The aim of this stage was to provide practical examples of digital technologies, concepts, and strategies in practice within the hospitality and leisure industry. In stage 4 we reviewed relevant and seminal hospitality and leisure management research on required digital technology capabilities of organizations and associated competencies required of hospitality and leisure managers. Noticing potential competency gaps, we extended this literature review to incorporate the broader information systems research on required digital transformation and digital business organization capabilities and corresponding management competencies. Still noticing potential capability and gaps, we further extended the literature review to include entrepreneurship, innovation, change management, and general management literature focusing on accelerated change and transformation. We reasoned that these literatures may have additional digital transformation–related competencies, given they typically study change in rapidly changing or high-velocity environments.[16] Finally, in stage 5 we reviewed the curriculums of hospitality and leisure management degrees and programs around the world. The purpose of this review was to explore the extent to which these programs and courses covered digital transformation and digital business–related organization capabilities and managerial competencies. See Table 1.1 for a summary of the types of literatures reviewed at each stage of the research process.

How to use this book

This book is organized into five parts. Part I discusses the nature of digital technology advancements and how they drive digital disruption, the threats and opportunities of digital disruption, and the digital business and digital transformation imperatives. This part links contemporary digital business and digital transformation concepts to traditional information technology and information systems concepts. Part II discusses the impact of digital disruption in the hospitality and leisure industry, how the industry has adapted to this disruption, what digital transformation initiatives organizations in the industry have undertaken to date, and the effectiveness of these initiatives. Part III discusses how hospitality and leisure organizations can leverage digital technologies to thrive in the digital era and what roles this requires hospitality and leisure managers to play. It identifies digital

Table 1.1 Key literatures reviewed at each research stage for this book and the focus of each literature review

Research Stage	Research Activity
Stage 1	Review of the *information systems academic research* for discussions of: • The relationship between traditional information systems concepts and contemporary digital business concepts • The link between digital technology advancements and digital disruption • The need for digital transformation and digital business • The capabilities required for digital transformation and digital business • The managerial competencies required for digital transformation and digital business
Stage 2	Review of the *hospitality and leisure industry practitioner literature* discussing: • The relationship between traditional information systems concepts and contemporary digital business concepts • The link between digital technology advancements and digital disruption • The need for digital transformation and digital business • The capabilities required for digital transformation and digital business • The managerial competencies required for digital transformation and digital business
Stage 3	Review of hospitality and leisure *industry case studies* focusing on: • Digital transformation initiatives • Building digital business capabilities • Required digital business managerial competencies • Digital transformation and digital business challenges, benefits, and lessons learned
Stage 4	Review of *hospitality and leisure academic research* on: • Digital technology advancements • Digital transformation • Digital business and digital business capabilities • Digital business and digital transformation managerial competencies
Stage 5	Review of hospitality and leisure IT/IS/technology degrees and courses around the world for: • Key topics taught • Presence of contemporary digital technologies • Presence of digital disruption concepts/issues • Presence of digital transformation concepts/issues • Presence of digital business concepts/issues • Presence of digital business capabilities • Presence of digital business competencies

capabilities required by hospitality and leisure organizations for digital transformation and digital business, it identifies what roles hospitality and leisure managers need to play to effect and sustain each capability, and it identifies what new or enhanced competencies hospitality and leisure managers require to play these roles. Part IV discusses the challenge of keeping up with digital technology advancements, the risks of not doing so, and what strategies hospitality and leisure managers can adopt to keep up with digital technologies. Finally, Part V unpacks more than 36 digital technologies, explaining what they are and how they work, their implications for hospitality and leisure operations and strategy, current and future industry use cases, and implications for hospitality and leisure managers.

Managers

The book, if read from end to end, will provide a great understanding of the inter-relationships between IT, information systems, digital technologies, digital disruption, digital transformation, digital business, digital business capabilities, and managerial roles and competencies. However, it has been written in such a way that each chapter can be read on its own. Thus hospitality and leisure managers seeking an explanation of digital disruption can go straight to Chapter 3, and managers only seeking to understand a particular digital business capability can go straight to the chapter on that capability. Alternatively, managers who already have a good understanding of digital transformation and digital business and who only need a reference book explaining different digital technologies (e.g. blockchain, mixed reality, IoT, data science) and their implications for the industry can skip to the chapter on that specific digital technology in Part V. Readers should notice that we have unpacked each part and chapter extensively in the table of contents to enable them to efficiently search for and locate the information they need (concepts, case studies, diagrams, questions, vendors).

Instructors

Instructors can use this book as the principal book for information systems, information technology, and digital business–related courses in hospitality and leisure degrees at the postgraduate and undergraduate levels, in order to give those courses a strong digital transformation and digital business foundation. For example, each of the first 12 chapters can form a topic to be covered over a 12-week study period. And each week, a specific set of digital technologies (i.e. a chapter from Part V) can also be covered in parrallel. Used this way, the book will provide future hospitality and leisure managers with a comprehensive, practical, and integrated understanding of important digital transformation and digital business concepts, as well as a working knowledge of key groups of digital technologies. Alternatively, instructors can use the book as a supplementary text in any hospitality and leisure management course that may need to cover a particular digital technology (e.g. augmented reality), a particular digital technology issue (e.g. digital ethics), or a particular digital transformation and digital business issue (e.g. digital business models). The book can also be a reference book for definitions of slippery terms and concepts.

Students

Students doing assessments on digital technology, digital transformation, or digital business–related issues will find this an invaluable reference book. It explains key terms, concepts, and issues in simple terms from the perspective of a hospitality manager. Students can use the book as a resource for understanding specific digital technologies when these come up in an assessment exercise (e.g. researching how the IoT works and the implications of IoT technologies for guest experience). For more interested and proactive students, a cover-to-cover read of the book would provide a useful framework for understanding digital technologies, digital transformation, and digital business. This is critical to future managerial performance and career mobility.

Researchers

Finally, researchers investigating a particular digital technology or a particular digital transformation and digital business issue from the perspective of the hospitality and leisure industry may find this book an helpful starting point. The book provides a plain language explanation and an integrated picture of how that technology or issue fits with other technologies and issues and with the broader strategic and operational aims of the industry. Researchers may also find the review of different technologies invaluable for identifying unresolved research questions at the intersection between hospitality and leisure management and digital business.

Notes

1 Vial, G. (2019). Understanding Digital Transformation: A Review and a Research Agenda. *The Journal of Strategic Information Systems*, 28(2), 118–144. https://doi.org/10.1016/j.jsis.2019.01.003
2 Karimi, J., & Walter, Z. (2015). The Role of Dynamic Capabilities in Responding to Digital Disruption: A Factor-based Study of the Newspaper Industry. *Journal of Management Information Systems*, 32(1), 39–81.
3 Digital Disruption. (2019). Gartner. Retrieved November 26, 2019, from www.gartner.com/en/information-technology/glossary/digital-disruption
4 Vial, G. (2019). Understanding Digital Transformation: A Review and a Research Agenda. *The Journal of Strategic Information Systems*, 28(2), 118–144. https://doi.org/10.1016/j.jsis.2019.01.003
5 Vial, G. (2019). Understanding Digital Transformation: A Review and a Research Agenda. *The Journal of Strategic Information Systems*, 28(2), 118–144. https://doi.org/10.1016/j.jsis.2019.01.003
6 Gupta, S. (2018). *Driving Digital Strategy: A Guide to Reimagining Your Business*. Harvard Business Press.
7 Busulwa, R., Tice, M., & Gurd, B. (2018). *Strategy Execution and Complexity: Thriving in the Era of Disruption*. Routledge.
8 Hoffman, R., & Sullivan, T. (2016). Blitzscaling. *Harvard Business Manager*, 27(6), 32–41.
9 Digital Business Transformation. (2019). Gartner. Retrieved November 25, 2019, from www.gartner.com/en/information-technology/glossary/digital-business-transformation
10 Digital Transformation. (2019). Gartner. Retrieved November 25, 2019, from www.gartner.com/en/information-technology/glossary/digital-transformation
11 The Airbnb Effect: Cheaper Rooms for Travelers, Less Revenue for Hotels. (2018). HBS Working Knowledge. Retrieved November 26, 2019, from https://hbswk.hbs.edu/item/the-airbnb-effect-cheaper-rooms-for-travelers-less-revenue-for-hotels
12 Lessons in Digital Transformation from the Hotel Industry. (2017). INSEAD Knowledge. Retrieved November 26, 2019, from https://knowledge.insead.edu/marketing/lessons-in-digital-transformation-from-the-hotel-industry-5123
13 The Digital Imperative. (2015). www.bcg.com. Retrieved November 26, 2019, from www.bcg.com/publications/2015/digital-imperative.aspx
14 Heltzel, P. (2019). The 11 Biggest Issues IT Faces Today. CIO. Retrieved November 26, 2019, from www.cio.com/article/3245772/the-12-biggest-issues-it-faces-today.html
15 Lenkenhoff, K., Wilkens, U., Zheng, M., Süße, T., Kuhlenkötter, B., & Ming, X. (2018). Key Challenges of Digital Business Ecosystem Development and How to Cope with Them. *Procedia CIRP*, 73, 167–172.
16 Davis, J. P., Eisenhardt, K. M., & Bingham, C. B. (2009). Optimal Structure, Market Dynamism, and the Strategy of Simple Rules. *Administrative Science Quarterly*, 54(3), 413–452.

2 IT, information systems, strategic information systems, and digital technologies

Introduction

Although they differ significantly and have important interrelationships, the terms information technology (IT), information systems (IS) and digital technology are often used interchangeably as umbrella terms for computer- or software-related products and solutions. This often results in misunderstandings, trivialization of the importance of one or all terms, and feelings of overwhelm for some stakeholders outside of (and at times even within) the IT and IS professions. It is these misunderstandings of the slippery and overlapping terms that often drives some hospitality managers to trivialize, or to only see a part of, the importance and value of IS and digital technologies to business operations and strategy. In turn, this leads them to misunderstand their role in IS and digital technology issues and therefore sideline them, or to see such issues as ones that can be relegated to the IT/IS/technology function. This misunderstanding and the resultant attitudes and actions can be a risk to managers' careers and to the fates of their organizations. In this chapter we unpack these terms, delineate the boundaries between them, explain how they interrelate and interact, and explain their importance. We finish the chapter by explaining the important and growing role of hospitality and leisure managers in information systems and digital technology issues.

Information systems

An information system is a collection of interrelated components (hardware, software, data, networks, processes, and people) that work together to perform specific roles for an organization. These roles include the collection, storage, organization, and transformation of data into information and knowledge, and the distribution of that information and knowledge throughout the organization.[1] The distributed information and knowledge plays a crucial role in the operations and strategy of an organization (e.g. supporting decision making and supporting coordination and control at all levels and in all parts of an organization).[2]

Components of an information system

The hardware component of an information system includes all the physical components used by an organization for collecting, storing, organizing, transforming, and distributing data and information. For example, hardware includes physical computers and computer components, smartphones, servers and server components, sensors, physical robots, drones, and more. The software component of information systems refers to sets of instructions, software algorithms, or code for controlling or telling the hardware what to do. Software includes systems software, which operates the hardware and coordinates instructions between application software and the hardware. Examples of systems software are operating system software, utilities software, compilers, assemblers, debuggers, and drivers. Popular operating system software include Microsoft Windows, Mac, Linux, and Android. The software component also includes application software, the software most people are familiar with and interact with to perform tasks or work. Examples of application software are word processing software, spreadsheets, and other applications (or apps). The data component of information systems refers to what data is collected or created (e.g. text, videos, images), how that data is stored (e.g. in what systems/databases, in which locations), how it is organized, how it is transformed into information, how it is presented for understandability, and how it is distributed throughout the organization. For more information, see the chapter on data and data management technologies in Part V of this book. The network component of information systems refers to the technology that enables devices and other entities within an information system to communicate with each other, and for communication between different information systems to occur. The network component includes networking hardware and software (e.g. servers, coaxial cables, network interface cards, hubs, routers, local area network cables, network operating systems). Figure 2.1 visually represents the components of an information system.

Although many people tend to focus on the technology aspects of information systems (i.e. hardware, software, data, and network technology), the process and people components are also important aspects of information systems that should not be overlooked. Regarding the process component, organizations have a range of processes for getting organization work done and meeting organizational objectives. Examples of these are product development processes, procurement processes, customer acquisition processes, customer support processes, accounting processes, marketing processes, human resources (HR) processes, strategy-making processes, governance processes, and risk management processes. Technology is increasingly becoming integrated into these processes and is used

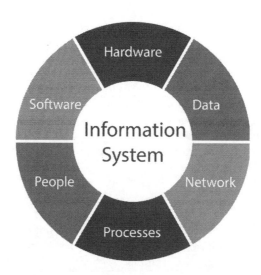

Figure 2.1 Components of an information system

to design, facilitate, manage, and optimize processes. For example, hardware and software are used to detect when particular processes have not occurred or to trigger particular processes to occur (e.g. sensors can detect an unsafe change in temperature and initiate building evacuation processes; video monitoring hardware and software may spot vandalism and automatically request security or police attendance). Hardware and software are also used to provide the data used to perform many processes (e.g. data-driven operational decisions), to alert people to events that have occurred or failed to occur (e.g. patients missed during ward rounds at a hospital), to orchestrate or perform processes (e.g. driving vehicles), to provide the platforms on which people perform processes (e.g. workflow management platforms), to automate processes (e.g. robotic process automation or workflow automation), and more. Used in the right processes and in the right ways, both software and hardware can optimize process efficiency (speed and cost), effectiveness (customer satisfaction, stakeholder satisfaction, and competitive advantage), adaptability (the ability to adapt processes to unexpected internal and external events), and agility (the capacity for flexibility and speed in sensing and responding to external changes).

Regarding the people component of information systems, people are creators of information systems (imagining, designing, and developing information systems); people are typically the operators of information systems (implementing, troubleshooting, maintaining, training and supporting users); people are the administrators of information systems (undertaking upkeep, configuration, and maintenance); and people are typically the managers of information systems (overseeing governance, performance management, risk management, project management). And it is also people who are typically the users of information systems, who experience the benefits or challenges of using information systems, and who are ultimately served by the outputs of information systems. The people aspect of information systems is typically concerned with the different formal and informal roles involved in the creation, operation/administration, management, use, and value of information systems. Examples of information systems creation roles include systems analysts, systems architects, systems engineers, programmers, software engineers, hardware engineers, and network engineers. Examples of systems operators include hardware technicians, help desk analysts, security analysts/engineers, IS product managers, and IS trainers. Examples of information systems administration roles include systems administrators, database administrators, and network administrators. Examples of managers of information systems include chief information officer (CIO), chief technology officer (CTO), chief digital officer (CDO), IS functional or specialist managers (application managers, network services managers, desktop support managers, systems design and development managers, ERP managers, IS security managers, IS project managers, and digital risk managers). As we noted earlier, the people component of information systems is also concerned with users of information systems. An important focus of this aspect is how users adopt new information systems. Frameworks such as Everett Rogers' diffusion of innovations categorize user adoption behavior or approaches into innovators, early adopters, early majority, late majority, and laggard adoption behaviors or adoption approaches. Understanding the different types of adopters, adoption approaches, and adoption behaviors is often instrumental in planning the speed and effectiveness with which information systems can be implemented.

Roles of information systems

Information systems play three key roles in organizations. First, as we noted earlier, the components of an information system work together to capture data, store it, organize it,

transform it into information, and organize that information into organizational knowledge. Second, the information and knowledge produced by information systems is distributed throughout the organization to support decision making (day-to-day operational
decisions and more long-term strategic decisions). Examples of operational decisions are
how much inventory to buy and from whom, who to put on what shifts, and which customers to serve and when. Examples of strategic decisions are what business models and
revenue models to use, what technology infrastructure to use, and how to combine business models and technology infrastructure to optimize competitiveness, adaptability, and
agility. Third, information systems facilitate operational and strategic processes (enabling
a range of organization processes and workflows such as product development, procurement, customer acquisition, customer support, accounting, marketing, HR, strategy
making, risk management, and governance). Almost all organization work is informed,
facilitated, and or supported by information systems.

Types of information systems

The term information systems is often combined with other terms to refer to subsets of
information systems or particular types of information systems. These subsets, or typologies, are usually based on what technologies are used or not used, which processes those
information system subsets focus on, which stakeholders the specific information systems
subsets serve in the organization hierarchy, or which specific organization functions the
information systems subsets focus on. Subsets or types of information systems focusing
on the technologies used or not used include computer-based information systems and
manual-based information systems. Computer-based information systems are information systems that use computer hardware and software to capture data, store it, organize it,
transform it into information, organize that information into organizational knowledge,
and disseminate it throughout the organization. In contrast, manual-based information
systems are information systems that perform the role of information systems without
computer hardware and software (using paper, filing cabinets, human memory). Types
of information systems focusing on stakeholders in the organization hierarchy include
transaction processing systems (those used by operational level employees to serve customers), management information systems and decision support systems (those used by
middle managers and senior managers to monitor and manage performance), and executive information systems (those used by the top management team or executive team to
monitor organization-wide performance and risk and to inform strategic decision making). Types of information systems focusing on specific organization processes/activities
include data warehousing systems, enterprise resource planning systems, and office automation systems. Types of information systems focusing on specific organization functions include hospitality information systems, property management systems, customer
relationship management systems, marketing information systems, accounting information systems, HR information systems, and procurement systems. Figure 2.2 provides a
summary of types of information systems and the most-intensive users of that type of
information system.

Information systems specialists typically study curriculums in information systems
that focus on systems design and development methodologies, enterprise information
management, enterprise architecture and governance, database systems and information
modeling, business process management, project and change management, IS security,
and IS strategy and governance. They often specialize in areas such as IS infrastructure

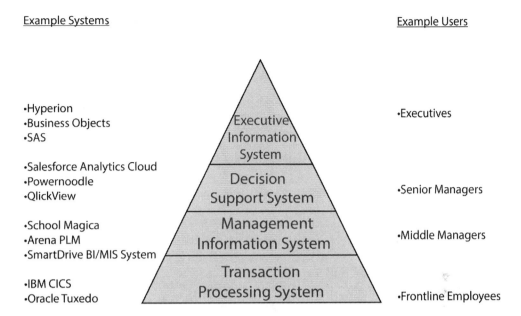

Example Systems   Example Users

•Hyperion   •Executives
•Business Objects
•SAS

•Salesforce Analytics Cloud
•Powernoodle   •Senior Managers
•QlickView

•School Magica   •Middle Managers
•Arena PLM
•SmartDrive BI/MIS System

•IBM CICS
•Oracle Tuxedo   •Frontline Employees

Figure 2.2 Types of information systems, including example systems and example users

management, IS project and change management, business analysis, business analytics, and functional IS areas (accounting information systems, HR information systems). IS specialists may become business systems analysts, solution architects, data and analytics managers, data engineers, IS project managers, consultants, and functional system managers (finance systems manager, HR information systems managers, property information systems managers).

Information technology and information communications technology (ICT)

Although people use the terms IT and IS interchangeably, information technology is actually a subset of information systems. As a subset, it typically only focuses on the technology component of information systems. IT specialists focus on ensuring the organization has the right hardware and software products, installing them, customizing them, integrating them with existing products, maintaining them, supporting users to use them, and ensuring that the security, availability, and accessibility of each product (and of the information system as a whole) is optimized. IT specialists typically require degrees in information technology or computer science. Within such degrees, they often specialize in hardware and/or software areas such as network design, hardware design, software design, software development, cybersecurity, artificial intelligence, and the internet of things (IoT). They enter jobs such as network architects, software developers, IT systems analysts, security analysts, web developers, systems administrators, software product managers, and IT managers.

The term information communications technology (ICT) is sometimes used interchangeably with IT. It refers to the convergence or integration of IT with audiovisual technologies and telephone networks (e.g. media broadcasting technologies, audio and video transmission, and telephony). Thus ICT can be thought of as an extended synonym for IT.

Strategic information systems and digital technologies

Strategic information systems

Strategic information systems are information systems that can significantly transform the strategic position of an organization in its external environment. Such transformation can be in the form of breakthroughs in efficiency, differentiation, innovation, adaptability, or agility. Efficiency breakthroughs include dramatically speeding up or enabling cost leadership in processes such as product and service delivery processes, customer engagement and support processes, and strategy execution processes. For example, in its early days, Dell Technologies leveraged web/internet technology to be able to offer custom, built-to-order computers to customers at a cost of 10% of its revenue.[3] In contrast, dominant industry competitors such as Hewlett-Packard, Gateway, and Cisco could only do this at a cost of 20% to 50% of their revenue.[4] This improved Dell's strategic position (i.e. Dell had cost leadership as a competitive advantage), enabling it to grow into a dominant player in the industry. Differentiation breakthroughs include being able to offer products and services that, relative to competitors, have unique benefits that are important to customers. For example, Apple has leveraged a closed technology ecosystem and greater investment in product design to differentiate its products from those of its competitors. As a result, Apple is able to charge two to three times as much as competitors for its products and also enjoys strong customer loyalty. Innovation breakthroughs relate to the rate at which new and better products/services are created and delivered. For example, Amazon's first product was an online bookstore platform, but it has since leveraged its information systems (technology infrastructure, processes, and people) to globally deliver a consistent stream of products including Kindle, Amazon Web Services, Amazon Prime, Amazon Publishing, and Amazon Robotics. These innovation breakthroughs have propelled Amazon to become a leader in a range of industries. Adaptability refers to an organization's ability to adapt its operations to surprising events in its external environment (financial crises, pandemics, disruptive competition). Agility refers to an organization's capacity for flexibility and speed in sensing and responding to external changes. Companies such as Google and Intel configure their information systems to enable them to maximize their adaptability and agility. For example, Google uses its sophisticated information systems to sense changes in its external environment (collect and interpret data on search patterns and online ad performance) and then uses the insights to drive operational responses to external events.[5] Furthermore, both Google and Intel use investment arms (Google Ventures and Intel Capital) to discover and profit first from the next breakthrough product and market innovations.[6,7] Thus when they are designed or configured appropriately, information systems (different combinations of technology, networks, people, and business processes) can be very powerful strategic weapons capable of transforming the fortunes of organizations.

Digital technologies

The term digital technologies refers to combinations of information (or data), computing (or computation), communication, and connectivity technologies.[8] Digital technologies include all types of electronic hardware and software that use information in the form of binary code (information represented by strings of 0s and 1s). Digital technologies include electronic tools, systems, devices, personal computers, calculators, traffic light controllers, mobile telephones, satellite technology, high-definition television, the internet and other networks, software applications, email, and mobile apps. Digital technologies generate, receive, store, process, transmit, and even act on data. Increasingly, digital technologies are enabling all manner of things (people, organizations, physical products, physical infrastructure, software) to capture data within and around them, to communicate that data with other things locally or globally, to receive information from other things, to use sophisticated computation/algorithms to gain insights from that information (e.g. spot patterns, understand instructions), and to use combinations of algorithms and robotics capabilities to act on that information in the same way that a person can (e.g. call the police on capturing or receiving information that a known fugitive is nearby).

We noted earlier that, used the right way, information systems can become very powerful strategic weapons capable of conferring often insurmountable strategic advantages. The right digital technologies can supercharge this strategic power of information systems by drastically enhancing how efficiently and effectively such information systems function. For example, the right combination of digital technologies can speed up the rate at which data flows between hardware, software, networks, business processes, and people, making it near instant. The right combination of digital technologies can transform all of an organization's infrastructure (buildings, machinery, furniture, cars, stationery, etc.) into smart things capable of collecting data, communicating data, and acting on data insights, and doing all of these things autonomously. The right combination of digital technologies can enable an organization's employees to work from anywhere in the world, to collaborate with any of the organization's infrastructure and other physical things, and to serve large numbers of customers globally in real time, irrespective of their location. The right combination of digital technologies can enhance the efficiency and effectiveness of interactions between people, technology, and processes. These examples only scratch the surface of the power of digital technologies to supercharge the strategic power of information systems. Microsoft, Google, Amazon, and other global giants are leveraging combinations of digital technologies and breakthroughs in these digital technologies to create strategic information systems that enable them to efficiently and effectively serve billions of people globally every day. Doing so has conferred significant wealth and global influence on the owners, employees, and strategic partners of these organizations.

Implications for hospitality and leisure managers

So far, we have unpacked the terms IT, IS, strategic information systems, and digital technologies. We have delineated the boundaries and overlaps between them. We have also explained the importance of digital technologies to information systems and how they can supercharge the efficiency, effectiveness, and strategic value of information systems. Ensuring the effective design, implementation, operation, maintenance, and optimization of information systems is not just the responsibility of the IT/IS or similar function, but it is a shared responsibility of hospitality managers and leaders at all levels. For example, hospitality and leisure managers can play an important role in ensuring that the right digital technologies are used, that the right operational and strategic processes are in place, that these processes leverage digital technologies for optimal efficiency and effectiveness, that the right job roles exist with the right capabilities to ensure information systems function optimally, that the right strategic partnerships are in place to optimize the strategic value of IS, and that employees throughout the organization continuously upgrade their technology skills and keep up with digital technologies. In order to deliver on this responsibility, hospitality and leisure managers must first make sense of the often-confusing terminology and acronyms related to information systems and digital technologies. This will enable them to make clear sense of what they read or hear about different digital technologies and their implications for information systems (what they read in product brochures, consultant proposals, white papers, books; what they hear in meetings and conferences) and to constructively engage in conversations with stakeholders about digital technologies and information systems (stakeholders such as strategic leaders, employees, IT/IS professionals, IT/IS consultants, IT/IS vendors, and strategic partners). They will then be in a position to leverage resultant insights to spot opportunities for improving their organizations' information systems and to effectively participate in and play a leadership role in necessary IS-related changes.

Google and reflect

To improve your comfort with IT/IS/digital technology terminology, perform an internet search on the following terms to find an explanation that makes clear sense to you:

Chief information officer (CIO), chief technology officer (CTO), chief digital officer (CDO), IT manager, IS manager, digital strategist, business systems analyst, ERP system, IT strategy, information systems strategy, information systems governance, information systems assurance, information systems security, digital technology device, digital technology platform, digital convergence.

Discussion questions

To test your understanding of the concepts covered in this chapter, please provide or discuss concise answers to the following questions:

1 What is the difference between IT and ICT?
2 What is the difference between IT and information systems?
3 Is information systems a part of IT, or is IT a part of information systems? Does it matter which is a part of which?
4 What is the best metaphor you can think of to explain the interrelationship between digital technologies and information systems?
5 Are digital technologies a part of IT, or is IT a part of digital technologies?
6 What is the role of digital technologies in information systems?
7 What are five different types of digital technologies?
8 Assuming that an organization is not already using the digital technologies you identified in question 7, how could using them improve each component of an information system?
9 Assuming that an organization is not already using the digital technologies you identified in question 7, how could using them improve the functioning of its information systems (e.g. how would using them impact efficiency, effectiveness, and strategic position)?
10 What are strategic information systems? How can they transform the strategic positioning of an organization? Identify five ways they can transform it.

11 Identify two organizations that are exemplars of using information systems as powerful strategic weapons.
12 What is the role of hospitality and leisure managers in the efficient and effective functioning of information systems?
13 Identify five actions that hospitality and leisure managers can take to improve the effectiveness and efficiency of information systems at their organizations.

Notes

1 Bourgeois, D. (2014). *Information Systems for Business and Beyond*. The Saylor Foundation.
2 Laudon, K. C., & Laudon, J. P. (2019). *Management Information Systems: Managing the Digital Firm*. Pearson.
3 The Power of Virtual Integration: An Interview with Dell Computer's Michael Dell. (1998, March). Retrieved April 21, 2020, from Harvard Business Review website: https://hbr.org/1998/03/the-power-of-virtual-integration-an-interview-with-dell-computers-michael-dell
4 What You Don't Know About Dell. (2003, November 3). Retrieved April 21, 2020, from Bloomberg. com website: www.bloomberg.com/news/articles/2003-11-02/what-you-dont-know-about-dell
5 Adaptability: The New Competitive Advantage. (2011, July). Retrieved April 21, 2020, from Harvard Business Review website: https://hbr.org/2011/07/adaptability-the-new-competitive-advantage
6 Rowley, J. (2018, February 17). A Peek Inside Alphabet's Investing Universe. Retrieved April 21, 2020, from TechCrunch website: https://techcrunch.com/2018/02/17/a-peek-inside-alphabets-investing-universe/
7 Burgelman, R. A., & Grove, A. S. (2007). Let Chaos Reign, then Rein in Chaos – Repeatedly: Managing Strategic Dynamics for Corporate Longevity. *Strategic Management Journal*, 28(10), 965–979.
8 Bharadwaj, A., El Sawy, O., Pavlou, P., & Venkatraman, N. (2013). Digital Business Strategy: Toward a Next Generation of Insights. *MIS Quarterly*, 37(2), 471–482.

3 Digital technology advancements and digital disruption

Game-changing opportunities and existential threats

Introduction

Although traditionally a physical industry, the hospitality and leisure industry has started to experience growing digital disruption. To date, this disruption has manifested itself as the introduction of new competitors like home-sharing platforms (e.g. Airbnb[1] and Vrbo), online travel agencies or OTAs (e.g. Expedia, Priceline, Booking.com, Skyscanner), hotel comparison/customer feedback platforms (e.g. TripAdvisor, Google Reviews, Facebook Reviews), and food delivery platforms (e.g. Uber Eats). Digital disruption is driven by digital technology advancements and results in both existential threats and game-changing opportunities. To be able to effectively guard against digital disruption, hospitality and leisure managers need to understand how digital disruption occurs, the nature of the existential threats it creates, and the game-changing opportunities digital technology advancements present. In this chapter, we explain how digital technology advancements cause digital disruption, the types of disruption created, the threats of not responding to this disruption effectively and in a timely manner, the types of game-changing opportunities presented by digital technology advancements, and how organizations can leverage digital technology advancements to both adapt to disruption and seize the game-changing opportunities that digital technology advancements present. The inability to guard against disruption paves the way to the fates of disrupted organizations like Kodak,[2] Blockbuster,[3] and Borders.[4] The ability to adapt to it, and to seize the opportunities offered by digital technologies, paves the way to the fates of organizations like Netflix, Caterpillar, Walmart, and Disney, who have leveraged digital technologies to thrive in the face of disruption.

Digital technology advancements and digital disruption

Digital technology advancements

In the preceding chapter, we defined digital technologies as those that combine information (or data), computing (or computation), communication, and connectivity technologies. Digital technologies include social, mobile, analytics, cloud, internet, the internet of things (IoT), software, platform, artificial intelligence, robotics, drones, satellite, blockchain, and other technologies.[5] Innovations in these technologies have been advancing and continue to advance exponentially. Such advancements include ongoing breakthroughs in processing speeds, memory capacity, number and size of pixels in digital cameras, computational capacity, network capacity, and software sophistication.[6]

Advancements also include the introduction and commercial adoption of technologies like blockchain, edge computing, 5G and 6G, brain–computer interfaces, 4D printing, neuromorphic hardware, exoskeletons, and quantum computing. Consider that all these advancements and more have occurred in just over 40 years since the introduction of the IBM PC. Thus when we refer to advances in digital technologies or digital technology innovations, we are referring to the introduction of new digital technologies or to breakthroughs in the capacity of existing digital technologies: for instance, the introduction of new digital technologies like 3D printing and 5G, or significant improvements in existing technologies like computational power, cloud computing capacity, or artificial intelligence capabilities.

Digital technology advancements as a source of digital disruption

The term disruption refers to preventing something (routines, processes, events) from continuing as usual or as expected. Put another way, it refers to interrupting the normal course of action or throwing the status quo into disorder. Digital disruption, then, refers to disruption induced by digital technology. Digital disruption is often discussed from the perspective of incumbent organizations that are heavily invested in established ways of doing things, and whose established way of operating is interrupted or made irrelevant.[7] But digital disruption can also occur at an industry, sector, or societal level.[8] That is, the established way of doing things in a whole industry, sector, or society can be disrupted. For example, the introduction of electronic health records can render obsolete hospital and medical clinic processes for storing, retrieving and transmitting patient information (an industry-level disruption); and the introduction of and improvements in telehealth can increase the availability and quality of healthcare services to rural and emerging economies, reduce the need for travel for some patients, and reduce the cost of certain types of care (an industry- and society-level disruption). Figure 3.1 shows how the use of digital technology innovations fuels digital disruptions, which then requires organization strategic responses to adapt to the disruptions. Effecting these strategic responses, in turn, relies on using digital technology innovations to achieve new breakthroughs in customer value, efficiency, adaptability agility and ambidexterity.

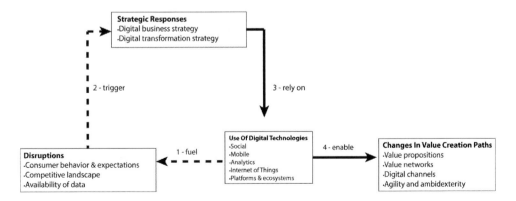

Figure 3.1 Digital technology advancements cause digital disruption but can also be leveraged to respond to disruption and recreate value offerings and capabilities[9]

Unpacking digital disruption

The introduction of new digital technologies or breakthroughs in existing digital technologies results in three types of disruptions: disruption of consumer or customer expectations and behaviors, disruption of the competitive landscape, and disruption of available data.[10] We unpack each of these disruptions in turn.

Disruption of customer expectations and behaviors

Businesses make money and are able to continue their existence if they cost-effectively provide products or services that customers want and choose to buy from them. Customers typically want and choose to buy products that they expect to provide the best cost/benefit proposition (most accessible, best quality, best brand image, most compatible with other products, and best suited for a particular job, at a particular price). Using search engines, social media, data analytics, artificial intelligence, and other digital technologies, consumers have access to an unprecedented amount of information about available product and service options and their cost/benefit differences. At the push of a button, they can see almost all available options for a particular product or service and compare their benefits and costs. In addition, consumers can easily access information on what accessibility, convenience, and other benefits are possible from substitute products/services. For example, when it comes to banking services, most consumers can easily check whether online banking, mobile banking, blockchain-based payment, email-based payment, and card-less cash withdrawal services are possible. The easy access to product/service information and the knowledge of what is possible shape consumer expectations and behavior. Continuing with the banking services example, banks that are either not competitive on price or do not provide online banking, mobile banking, blockchain-based payment, email-based payment, and card-less cash withdrawal services (for example) may gradually find themselves unable to attract new customers; they may also find their existing customers choosing to go with banks that live up to these consumer expectations. Thus digital technology advancements (the introduction of new digital technologies or improvements in existing ones) change consumer expectations.[11] They also change consumer behaviors, due to modified expectations or changes in consumer routines and habits.[12] For example, the introduction of driverless cars (a digital technology advancement) may significantly reduce consumer driving, car purchasing, car parts purchasing, and other related consumer routines. This may disrupt operations of organizations providing products and services used in those consumer routines (e.g. significantly reduced demand, inability to satisfy customers). Broadly, digital disruption manifests itself as diminishing business results (e.g. loss of customers, falling prices, diminished availability of product/service input suppliers, loss of talented staff, challenges accessing funding).

Disruption of the competitor field and bases of competition

The introduction of new digital technologies or improvements in existing digital technologies can lower barriers to entry into an industry, thereby allowing startups and existing organizations in different industries to enter that industry. For example, digital technology advancements enabled startups like Spotify (in 2006), Soundcloud (in 2007), and Tidal (in 2014) to enter and become dominant players in the music industry. Similar advancements enabled Apple (iTunes/Apple Music), Google (YouTube Music), and

Amazon (Amazon Music) to leverage the digital platforms used in different industries (cloud infrastructure, search, and device platforms) to also dominate the music industry. Digital technology advances lower barriers to new competitors entering an industry by lowering the costs to produce and distribute products and to acquire customers, support them, and manage relationships with them. For example, by leveraging cloud infrastructure to record and stream music, new entrants in the music industry were able to offer music to customers instantly (instead of waiting for physical CD delivery), to offer it at a better price (since cost was low and they unbundled the album or enabled single song purchase), and offer it to almost everyone with an internet connection (significantly expanded distribution). They were able to have significantly greater margins, as digital technologies enabled them to circumvent costly activities traditionally associated with music production and distribution (signing artists, managing artists, operating recording venues, promoting artists, setting up and managing live shows, producing CDs, packaging, marketing and distributing artist music, and manually managing intellectual property rights).

Digital technologies also disrupt incumbent organizations' bases (or sources) of competitive advantage.[13,14] For example, over a long period of time, incumbent organizations dominating the music industry had established competitive advantages such as locking in key strategic partners (companies offering services such as artist scouting, recording, live venue management, packaging, marketing, and distribution), cost leadership (from using their size to negotiate the lowest fees for artists, recording, packaging, marketing, and distribution), and brand differentiation (being more attractive to top artists due to their brands being more recognized, better financed, and having greater album sales capability). Digital technology advancements removed the potency of these advantages by making them much less relevant to music sales. By leveraging digital technology infrastructure, new competitors could circumvent the need for traditional strategic partners (companies providing recording, packaging, marketing, and distribution services); they could also reach anyone around the world with an internet connection, minimizing the need to rely on the established sales infrastructure of traditional record labels. New competitors then leveraged search engine optimization (SEO), social media, artificial intelligence, mobile, and other digital technologies to acquire customers, provide them with the songs they wanted instantly, and do all this at a fraction of the cost that traditional record labels provided their music for. The bases or sources of competitive advantage then evolved to include, for example, the quality and availability of digital music platforms, the number of consumers active on those platforms, and the ease with which artists could get their music onto those platforms.

Disruption of data availability

Organizations that leverage new or improved digital technologies are able to capture and have access to more data (about consumers and consumption experiences, about processes for creating and providing products/services, and about the market dynamics of their industries).[15] This data provides them with additional strategic advantages. For example, they can monetize it by selling it to third parties (e.g. Facebook and Google monetize their user data by selling user-targeted advertising; Amazon uses its data for targeted ads and dynamic product pricing). Outside such monetization, organizations can employ sophisticated analytics for optimizing consumer experience, operational efficiency, and effectiveness, and for strategic sensing of market and other external environment trends. They can also use collected data in combination with sophisticated artificial intelligence algorithms to provide automated consumer experiences. For example, Google and Apple leverage their data, along with sophisticated artificial intelligence, to offer chatbot and virtual assistant products like Siri and Google Assistant. In the hotel industry, organizations like Hilton augment their customer service with robots like Connie, the robot concierge. The data available from digital technologies includes data captured by the organization and data captured by external organizations (e.g. governments, suppliers, platform vendors). Savvy competitors can clean, store, organize, and integrate external and internal data and then leverage it for real-time operational insights and for strategic insights. By doing so, they have an additional basis of competitive advantage. The additional data availability that digital technologies enable disrupts existing ways of doing things by necessitating that organizations change what data they are capturing themselves, what data they are pulling in from external sources, how they integrate this data, and how they optimize the insights available to operational and strategy processes. That is, organizations can't continue as they have been, as they risk losing competitive positioning.

Existential threats and game-changing opportunities

The introduction of new digital technologies and/or improvements in existing digital technologies creates existential threats for organizations, but it also offers game-changing opportunities.[16] In the paragraphs that follow, we unpack the nature of the existential threats and the game-changing opportunities for alert and proactive organizations.

Existential threats

By disrupting customer expectations and behaviors, disrupting the competitor makeup and bases of competition, and disrupting the data available to be used, digital technology advancements create an "adapt or risk your survival" ultimatum for incumbent organizations in an industry. This survival risk is the existential threat. If organizations continue to do what they have always done (or only make token changes), and don't adapt their product and service offering to changed customer expectations and behaviors, existing customers will start going to other organizations with better value or more convenience. In addition, organizations that continue to operate the way they always have will struggle to attract new customers. In less extreme cases, the effect of disruption may play out as gradual customer attrition, gradual price erosion, gradual decline in revenue, decreasing margins, and loss of profitability – until a point at which it is no longer worth sustaining the business. In more extreme cases, the effect of disruption can manifest itself much more rapidly, resulting in sudden and significant financial losses that bring about heavy layoffs, fire sale acquisition, or even insolvency. This can occur for particular organizations, it can occur for an industry, or it can occur for a whole sector or geography. For example, digital technology advancements brought about the slow but eventual demise of Kodak (Figure 3.2 shows how Kodak failed to effectively respond to disruption from digital cameras and smartphones, despite creating the technology behind them— Kodak invented the first digital camera in 1975).[17] In contrast, digital disruption brought about the sudden demise of many organizations in the taxi industry.[18] Organizations can ignore or deny the existential threat created by digital technology advancements, or they can leverage digital technologies to reconfigure their product and service offerings, to redesign their operational processes, and to reform their medium and long-term strategies for continuous adaptation to certain future disruption. For example, Walmart has

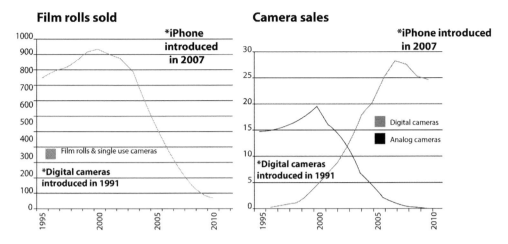

Figure 3.2 Kodak failed to effectively respond to disruption from digital cameras and smartphones, despite creating the technology behind them (Kodak invented the first digital camera in 1975)[19]

managed to adapt to the disruption of retail by leveraging digital technologies to transform both its products/services, its distribution approach, and its customer relationships and experiences.[20] Other retailers, such as Borders,[21] either ignored, denied, or were not quick enough to understand and leverage the power of digital technologies to adapt to the disruption of retail.[22,23,24]

Game-changing opportunities

Proactive organizations can leverage new digital technologies or improvements in existing digital technologies to seize three common types of game-changing opportunities. Effectively seizing one or more of these opportunities can safeguard their market position for a period or enable them to leapfrog competitors to become a market leader. The first type of game-changing opportunity is leveraging digital technologies to introduce new or significantly enhanced products and services that meet or that exceed customer expectations.[25] Netflix's business model was originally based on renting out movies stored on physical media (VHS, DVDs, Blu-ray). The company recognized the game-changing opportunities in internet and cloud computing digital technologies. Netflix leveraged these digital technologies to transform its product offering into a video streaming service. Blockbuster, the industry leader with more than 10,000 retail stores and a turnover of more than $5 billion, clung to its established business model until it was untenable. It eventually attempted to leverage digital technologies to revamp its offering, but by then it was too late. In 2010 the industry leader declared bankruptcy and today it no longer exists. Netflix, in the meantime, has gone from strength to strength, continuing to embrace digital technologies such as mobile streaming, personalized recommendation algorithms based on artificial intelligence, set-top boxes, smart TVs, game consoles (Xbox/PlayStation/Wii), and virtual private networks. Netflix also leveraged the data collected from different digital technologies to better understand what consumers like to watch, when they like to watch it, and how they like to watch it. This, in turn, continuously feeds its programming and service delivery. Today Netflix has turnover of more than $20 billion and annual income/profit of more than $2 billion.

Other proactive organizations are leveraging digital technologies to transition from product to platform organizations. That is, rather than just being sellers of products, they provide the infrastructure that other entities (businesses, contractors, consumers) can use to create, market, sell, or enhance their products and customer experiences more conveniently and at lower cost. For example, Caterpillar, the heavy equipment manufacturer, leveraged digital technologies to offer a vehicle management platform that users of its equipment can draw on for vehicle utilization, health, location, servicing, and longevity insight.[26] In addition to quality equipment, such a platform makes it difficult for customers to switch from Caterpillar in the absence of breakthrough competitor offerings.

The second type of game-changing opportunity available to proactive organizations is leveraging digital technologies to bypass intermediaries and interact directly with consumers,[27,28] to enhance collaboration and coordination between strategic partners in the value chain,[29] or to create and manage an ecosystem-based business model.[30,31] Microsoft had traditionally distributed its hardware and software through resellers but has recently started to also sell its surface hardware and cloud services direct to consumers.[32,33,34] This direct interaction with customers enables greater understanding of the customer, greater control of the customer experience, and greater customer engagement opportunities.[35] Organizations can also leverage digital technologies for more effective and faster collaboration and coordination with strategic value chain partners.[36] For instance, organizations integrate aspects of their information systems with those of strategic partners and have shared systems for collaboration and coordination that draw on the data from both sets of systems. This can improve data visibility, workflow visibility, engagement, incentives, and more. Organizations can also leverage digital technologies to create and manage an ecosystem of suppliers, consumers, and other stakeholders.[37] For example, Uber continues to build and manage an evolving ecosystem of transportation made up of self-employed drivers, restaurants, hospitals and medical clinics, end consumers, certifiers, and other stakeholders.

Digital technologies expand the number of possible consumer engagement channels from traditional physical mail, phone, and email to online live chat, social media, mobile, mobile app, IoT devices, and more. These expanded engagement channels bring about opportunities to engage with customers via their dominant or preferred engagement channels, and improved engagement can lead to better customer acquisition and retention.

Finally, the third type of game-changing opportunity available to organizations is leveraging digital technologies to improve their adaptability, agility, and ambidexterity. We defined adaptability in the previous chapter as the ability to reconfigure routines, processes, and practices to suit the demands of unexpected internal and external changes: for example, reconfiguring an organization's product development and delivery processes to suit changes in customer expectations and behaviors, as Netflix did. We defined agility as the capacity for flexibility and speed in sensing and responding to external changes. For example, through sophisticated data analytics and their Google Ventures and Intel Capital arms, Google and Intel are highly agile organizations able to continuously adapt and thrive in industries characterized by an extraordinary rate of change, unpredictability, growing convergence, and an assault on technology standards.[38,39,40] In contrast to adaptability and agility, ambidexterity is concerned with having processes to ensure existing process efficiency in parallel with processes to undertake exploratory activities so as to discover new products and services. For example, for a long time Intel has undertaken both efficiency and exploratory activities. Efficiency activities have enabled it to maximize revenue and profitability from its existing products and processes. Exploratory activities have enabled the company to discover the next breakthrough products before the decline of their existing core products.[41,42] Organizations can leverage digital technologies to configure their operations and strategy for optimal adaptability, agility, and ambidexterity.

Implications for hospitality and leisure managers

The disruption experience to date in the hospitality and leisure industry is just the beginning,[43] in the same way that early disruptions of the video rental, taxi,[44] and photography industries were just the beginning. Accelerating digital technology advancements will continue to raise customer expectations and change customer behaviors, to introduce new competitors, to raise the capabilities of existing competitors, and to change the bases of competition. To remain competitive and ensure their continued existence, hospitality and leisure organizations must keep up with evolving digital technologies and find ways to leverage them to satisfy changing customer expectations, to counter changes in competitor capabilities, and to adapt to unexpected changes in the external environments. This requires hospitality managers to continuously make sense of evolving digital technologies and to continuously explore how they can be used for breakthroughs in product/service offerings, in operations, and in strategy.

Google and reflect

Business ecosystem, disruptive technology, disruptive innovation, digital disruption, digital innovation, digital platform, digital technology infrastructure, cloud infrastructure, bimodal IT, operational backbone, digital backbone, SEO, adaptability, agility, ambidexterity, online travel agency (OTA).

Discussion questions

1 What is the difference between the terms digital disruption, disruptive technology, and disruptive innovation?
2 How do digital technology advancements cause disruption?
3 What are the three types of disruption caused by the introduction of new digital technologies or breakthroughs in existing ones?
4 What are the different ways digital disruption manifests itself in an organization's financial performance?
5 Which digital technology advancement has had the most disruptive impact on the hospitality and leisure industry in the last ten years?
6 Which digital technology advancement is likely to have the most disruptive impact on the hospitality and leisure industry in the next ten years?
7 What are the three common types of game-changing opportunities that can be seized by leveraging digital technology advancements?
8 What is the difference between adaptability, agility, and ambidexterity?

9   How can an organization use digital technologies to enhance its adaptability?
10 How can an organization use digital technologies to enhance its agility?
11 How can an organization use digital technologies to enhance its ambidexterity?
12 What is the role of hospitality and leisure managers in guarding against digital disruption at their organizations?
13 In an entry-level role, what can a hospitality and leisure management graduate do to contribute to the adaptability, agility, and ambidexterity of their organization?

Notes

1   Gerdeman, D. (2018). The Airbnb Effect: Cheaper Rooms for Travelers, Less Revenue for Hotels. Retrieved April 26, 2020, from HBS Working Knowledge website: https://hbswk.hbs.edu/item/the-airbnb-effect-cheaper-rooms-for-travelers-less-revenue-for-hotels

2   Satell, G. (2018). How Blockbuster, Kodak and Xerox Really Failed (It's Not What You Think). Retrieved April 25, 2020, from Inc.com website: www.inc.com/greg-satell/pundits-love-to-tell-these-three-famous-innovation-stories-none-of-them-are-true.html

3   Downes, L., & Nunes, P. (2013). Blockbuster Becomes a Casualty of Big Bang Disruption. Retrieved April 26, 2020, from Harvard Business Review website: https://hbr.org/2013/11/blockbuster-becomes-a-casualty-of-big-bang-disruption

4   Frazier, M. (2011). The Three Lessons of the Borders Bankruptcy. Forbes. Retrieved April 25, 2020, from www.forbes.com/sites/myafrazier/2011/02/16/the-three-lessons-of-the-borders-bankruptcy/#3c1218242a1a

5   Vial, G. (2019). Understanding Digital Transformation: A Review and a Research Agenda. *The Journal of Strategic Information Systems*, 28(2), 118–144. https://doi.org/10.1016/j.jsis.2019.01.003

6   Roser, M., & Ritchie, H. (2013). Technological Progress. Retrieved April 23, 2020, from Our World in Data website: https://ourworldindata.org/technological-progress

7   Skog, D. A., Wimelius, H., & Sandberg, J. (2018). Digital Disruption. *Business & Information Systems Engineering*, 60(5), 431–437. https://doi.org/10.1007/s12599-018-0550-4

8   Skog, D. A., Wimelius, H., & Sandberg, J. (2018). Digital Disruption. *Business & Information Systems Engineering*, 60(5), 431–437. https://doi.org/10.1007/s12599-018-0550-4

9   Vial, G. (2019). Understanding Digital Transformation: A Review and a Research Agenda. *The Journal of Strategic Information Systems*, 28(2), 118–144. https://doi.org/10.1016/j.jsis.2019.01.003

10 Vial, G. (2019). Understanding Digital Transformation: A Review and a Research agenda. *The Journal of Strategic Information Systems*, 28(2), 118–144. https://doi.org/10.1016/j.jsis.2019.01.003

11 Vial, G. (2019). Understanding Digital Transformation: A Review and a Research Agenda. *The Journal of Strategic Information Systems*, 28(2), 118–144. https://doi.org/10.1016/j.jsis.2019.01.003

12 Vial, G. (2019). Understanding Digital Transformation: A Review and a Research Agenda. *The Journal of Strategic Information Systems*, 28(2), 118–144. https://doi.org/10.1016/j.jsis.2019.01.003

13 Vial, G. (2019). Understanding Digital Transformation: A Review and a Research Agenda. *The Journal of Strategic Information Systems*, 28(2), 118–144. https://doi.org/10.1016/j.jsis.2019.01.003

14 Reeves, M., & Deimler, M. (2009). New Bases of Competitive Advantage. Retrieved April 26, 2020, from www.bcg.com website: www.bcg.com/en-au/publications/2009/business-unit-strategy-new-bases-of-competitive-advantage.aspx

15 Vial, G. (2019). Understanding Digital Transformation: A Review and a Research Agenda. *The Journal of Strategic Information Systems*, 28(2), 118–144. https://doi.org/10.1016/j.jsis.2019.01.003

16 Vial, G. (2019). Understanding Digital Transformation: A Review and a Research Agenda. *The Journal of Strategic Information Systems*, 28(2), 118–144. https://doi.org/10.1016/j.jsis.2019.01.003

17 Satell, G. (2018). How Blockbuster, Kodak and Xerox Really Failed (It's Not What You Think). Retrieved April 25, 2020, from Inc.com website: www.inc.com/greg-satell/pundits-love-to-tell-these-three-famous-innovation-stories-none-of-them-are-true.html

18 Goldstein, M. (2018). Dislocation and Its Discontents: Ride-Sharing's Impact on the Taxi Industry. Forbes. Retrieved from www.forbes.com/sites/michaelgoldstein/2018/06/08/uber-lyft-taxi-drivers/#6a5415559f0d

19 Alley. (2011). You Press the Button. Kodak Used to Do the Rest. Retrieved June 18, 2020, from MIT Technology Review website: www.technologyreview.com/2011/12/09/189254/you-press-the-button-kodak-used-to-do-the-rest/

20　Danziger, P. N. (2018). Walmart Doubles Down on Its Transformation into a Technology Company. Forbes. Retrieved from www.forbes.com/sites/pamdanziger/2018/10/22/walmart-doubles-down-on-its-transformation-into-a-technology-company/#408a349b404c

21　Frazier, M. (2011). The Three Lessons of the Borders Bankruptcy. Forbes. Retrieved April 25, 2020, from www.forbes.com/sites/myafrazier/2011/02/16/the-three-lessons-of-the-borders-bankruptcy/#3c1218242a1a

22　Frazier, M. (2011). The Three Lessons of the Borders Bankruptcy. Forbes. Retrieved April 25, 2020, from www.forbes.com/sites/myafrazier/2011/02/16/the-three-lessons-of-the-borders-bankruptcy/#3c1218242a1a

23　Streitfeld, D. (2017). Bookstore Chains, Long in Decline, are Undergoing a Final Shakeout. The New York Times. Retrieved April 25, 2020, from www.nytimes.com/2017/12/28/technology/bookstores-final-shakeout.html

24　Abramovich, G. (2017). 5 Ways Amazon Has Disrupted Retail – So Far. Retrieved April 25, 2020, from CMO.adobe.com website: https://cmo.adobe.com/articles/2017/10/two-ways-amazon-is-disrupting-retail-and-advice-for-the-way-forward.html#gs.4zgb8m

25　Vial, G. (2019). Understanding Digital Transformation: A Review and a Research Agenda. *The Journal of Strategic Information Systems*, 28(2), 118–144. https://doi.org/10.1016/j.jsis.2019.01.003

26　Vial, G. (2019). Understanding Digital Transformation: A Review and a Research Agenda. *The Journal of Strategic Information Systems*, 28(2), 118–144. https://doi.org/10.1016/j.jsis.2019.01.003

27　Calder, N., Parvarandeh, S., & Brady, M. (2018). Building a Direct-to-Consumer Strategy Without Alienating Your Distributors. Retrieved April 26, 2020, from Harvard Business Review website: https://hbr.org/2018/12/building-a-direct-to-consumer-strategy-without-alienating-your-distributors

28　Vial, G. (2019). Understanding Digital Transformation: A Review and a Research Agenda. *The Journal of Strategic Information Systems*, 28(2), 118–144. https://doi.org/10.1016/j.jsis.2019.01.003

29　Vial, G. (2019). Understanding Digital Transformation: A Review and a Research Agenda. *The Journal of Strategic Information Systems*, 28(2), 118–144. https://doi.org/10.1016/j.jsis.2019.01.003

30　Vial, G. (2019). Understanding Digital Transformation: A Review and a Research Agenda. *The Journal of Strategic Information Systems*, 28(2), 118–144. https://doi.org/10.1016/j.jsis.2019.01.003

31　Ref, R. (2019). How Ecosystems Create Value for Their Members. Accenture. Retrieved April 26, 2020, from Accenture.com website: www.accenture.com/au-en/insights/strategy/how-ecosystems-create-value-members

32　Foley, M. (2019). Microsoft to Start Selling More Azure Services Directly Starting in March. Retrieved April 25, 2020, from ZDNet website: www.zdnet.com/article/microsoft-to-start-selling-more-azure-services-directly-starting-in-march/

33　Warren, T. (2013). Microsoft is Now Selling Its Surface Tablets Direct to Businesses. Retrieved April 25, 2020, from The Verge website: www.theverge.com/2013/3/19/4124400/microsoft-surface-business-order-site

34　Burke, S. (2013). Microsoft Partners Fuming at Surface Slight. Retrieved April 25, 2020, from CRN Australia website: www.crn.com.au/news/microsoft-partners-fuming-at-surface-slight-348654

35　Calder, N., Parvarandeh, S., & Brady, M. (2018). Building a Direct-to-Consumer Strategy Without Alienating Your Distributors. Retrieved April 26, 2020, from Harvard Business Review website: https://hbr.org/2018/12/building-a-direct-to-consumer-strategy-without-alienating-your-distributors

36　Andal-Ancion, A., Cartwright, P. A., & Yip, G. S. (2003). The Digital Transformation of Traditional Business. Retrieved April 26, 2020, from MIT Sloan Management Review website: https://sloanreview.mit.edu/article/the-digital-transformation-of-traditional-business/

37　Ref, R. (2019). How Ecosystems Create Value for Their Members. Accenture. Retrieved April 26, 2020, from Accenture.com website: www.accenture.com/au-en/insights/strategy/how-ecosystems-create-value-members

38　Eisenhardt, K. M., & Sull, D. N. (2001). Strategy as Simple Rules. *Harvard Business Review*, 79(1), 107–116.

39　Davis, J., Eisenhardt, K. M., & Bingham, C. B. (2009). Optimal Structure, Market Dynamism and the Strategy of Simple Rules. *Administrative Science Quarterly*, 54, 413–452.

40　Davis, J., Eisenhardt, K. M., & Bingham, C. B. (2009). Optimal Structure, Market Dynamism, and the Strategy of Simple Rules. *Administrative Science Quarterly*, 54, 413–452

41　Burgelman, R. A., & Grove, A. S. (2007). Let Chaos Reign, then Rein in Chaos – Repeatedly: Managing Strategic Dynamics for Corporate Longevity. *Strategic Management Journal*, 28(10), 965–979.

42 Busulwa, R., Tice, M., & Gurd, B. (2018). *Strategy Execution and Complexity: Thriving in the Era of Disruption*. Routledge.

43 Comcast. (2018). The Next Phase of Digital Transformation in Hospitality. Retrieved April 26, 2020, from Comcast.com website: https://cbcommunity.comcast.com/community/browse-all/details/the-next-phase-of-digital-transformation-in-hospitality

44 Goldstein, M. (2018). Dislocation and Its Discontents: Ride-Sharing's Impact on the Taxi Industry. Forbes. Retrieved from www.forbes.com/sites/michaelgoldstein/2018/06/08/uber-lyft-taxi-drivers/#6a5415559f0d

4 Digital business, the digital business imperative, and digital business transformation

Introduction

We noted earlier that hospitality and leisure industry organizations have not been immune to disruption, and that modern guests expect hospitality and leisure organizations to deliver on the consumer benefits and promise of digital business. These include benefits such as much higher levels of guest-centric convenience and comfort, instantaneous customer service, novel experiences, expanded entertainment possibilities, and platforms that automatically integrate with their devices/apps and follow them everywhere. Digital business offers much more scope for guest value creation and experience, operational efficiency, new market creation and scalability, adaptability and agility, and staff satisfaction. But realizing the promise and benefits of digital business requires hospitality and leisure managers to understand the vision of digital business, the nature of business transformation required to realize this vision, and how to undertake such transformation successfully and safely. In this chapter, we unpack the nature, characteristics, and promise of digital business. We then explain the imperative for hospitality organizations to become digital businesses. We discuss digital business transformation and the challenges and risks associated with the journey to becoming a digital business. Finally, we discuss the implications for hospitality managers – that is, the unique roles they can play in accelerating and enhancing the success rate of digital business transformation efforts. On completion of this chapter, we expect current and prospective hospitality and leisure managers to understand what they can do now and in future to build their digital business and digital transformation knowledge and competencies, to leverage the knowledge and competencies to effectively lead or participate in digital transformation efforts at their current and future organizations, and to leverage their knowledge, competencies, and digital leadership experiences to supercharge their career development.

Digital business

Pinning down a slippery term

World-leading IT research firm Gartner defines digital business as the creation of new business designs by blurring the digital and physical worlds.[1] Forrester, another leading technology research firm, defines digital business as the use of digital assets and ecosystems to continually improve customer outcomes while continuously increasing operational agility. Yet another IT research firm, Aragon Research, defines a digital business as an organization with business models that enable it to proactively reach, serve, and support its customers and partners from their contextual perspective (i.e. from each customer's unique setting or environment, device, timing) rather than restricting them to what is defined by the traditional infrastructure of the business.[2] Digital business has also been defined more simply as the use of digital technologies to enable major business improvements, such as enhancement of customer experience, operations optimization, and creation of new business models.[3]

Gartner's Jorge Lopez proposes that what makes digital business different from prior terms such as e-business, for example, is the presence and integration of connected and intelligent things with business processes and with people.[4] He adds that once objects ("things") start to negotiate amongst themselves and communicate with business processes and people, an entirely new world of potential becomes possible.[5] In the past, people were required to be proxies for objects at certain stages (turn them on, sense for them, transfer data to/from them, perform actions that required intelligence); but increasingly, human proxies are required less and less as things become more intelligent (using data analytics, artificial intelligence), able to sense (using a vast array of sensors), able to communicate (exchange information with other things, processes, and people via the cloud), able to take physical action (using robotic and drone capabilities), and able to be more autonomous (aware of themselves and others, aware of the environment around them, and able to independently determine the optimal actions to take).[6]

Karel Dörner, a senior partner at McKinsey & Company, proposes that the promise of digital business is a universe of applications and digitized assets that almost automatically work together to deliver value and yield competitive advantage.[7] He adds that this promise requires companies to understand where the new frontiers of value are and to be open to reexamining their entire way of doing business.[8] Forrester's Nigel Fenwick puts it another way, saying that companies must think of their businesses as being part of a dynamic ecosystem that connects digital resources inside and outside the firm to create value for customers[9] – that is, not as a set of products and services but as a personal value ecosystem that customers can assemble to suit their unique needs and desires, and that companies create greater value by increasing their role and value in customers' personal value ecosystems.[10] Either way, Karel Dörner adds that being a digital business, and realizing the promise of digital business, requires sophisticated engineering, integration, and orchestration capabilities.[11]

Digital business as a future state

Digital business is often described as a future state (i.e. how business should function once it becomes a digital business and what characteristics or capabilities it should have in order to function this way). Such characteristics and capabilities discussed to date include having a frictionless operating system (e.g. one that delivers easy communication/interaction/engagement and collaboration across the value chain and between internal and external stakeholders);[12] having a competitive digital platform strategy[13,14] (e.g. one that enables rapid value delivery, enables other stakeholders' technologies or platforms to integrate/interact with the digital platform in a simple "plug and play" manner, enables easy self-service access to data insights, enables stakeholders to run value creation improvement experiments safely, and ensures consistent/dependable customer experience); and designing products and customer experiences based on value as defined by the customer (e.g. leveraging technology to be where customers are, to do things with them, to walk in their shoes, and to understand their preferences and habits). The characteristics and capabilities of a digital business include intelligence-driven decision making or weaponization of data for competitive advantage (e.g. collecting, storing, cleaning, curating, featurizing, modeling, productionalizing, and leveraging to support operational and strategic execution). An increasingly discussed characteristic or capability of digital businesses is combining technical excellence and an engineering culture that gets things done/delivered (e.g. upgrading engineering skills and capabilities to world-class level and cultivating an engineering culture that enables engineering to be more integrated into the business).

Digital business as a change journey or change process

Digital business has also been described as a journey or process of change (i.e. what activities a business should undertake, and in what sequence, in order to become a digital business, to realize the promise of digital business, or to avert the dangers of not becoming a digital business). Such discussed required changes have included digitalizing stakeholder interactions/communications, business processes, business functions, and business models (i.e. turning them into more digital ones), and then connecting and integrating them internally and externally, and with digitalized things internal and external to the organization.

They've also included enhancing the sensing (e.g. using sensors), computational capacity (e.g. computation speed, sophistication), connectivity (e.g. connection speed, strength, distance, reliability), intelligence (e.g. using data analytics, data science, artificial intelligence), autonomy (e.g. applications and things that can sense, make decisions, and take corresponding action independently, without human intervention), and scalability of business models/processes/technology platforms (e.g. being able to serve many more customers around the world quickly and at acceptable cost and risk). More recently, they have included activities such as enhancing customer engagement across a range of platforms and channels (e.g. desktop, mobile, social, video, IoT, video), and building digital strategy and digital innovation capabilities to be able to better sense, adapt to, and capitalize on new customer expectations and preferences.

Whether viewed as a future state or a change process, most organizations' digital business capability, functioning, or change journey exists across a digital business maturity continuum. On one end are digital natives like Google, Amazon, Microsoft, and Apple, which are very advanced in their digital business capabilities and functioning. On the other end of the continuum are businesses either turning a blind eye to growing digital disruption, or realizing the need for change, but moving glacially to digitize, let alone digitalize most of their processes. The first category of organizations typically grows rapidly from strength to strength, entering new markets, disrupting dominant incumbents, making outsized profits, and expanding their influence and power. Of the second category of organizations, some are lucky enough to survive disruption when it eventually reaches them, and others experience a slow loss of relevance and finally death or sudden collapse. Most organizations are somewhere between these two extremes. A range of models exist for measuring or mapping an organization's digital business maturity, such as the one in Figure 4.1.

Benefits of being a digital business

Organizations that undertake the journey to become digital businesses and compete as digital businesses open themselves up to a range of benefits. From a customer perspective, they expand their ability to engage with their customers, understand them, have

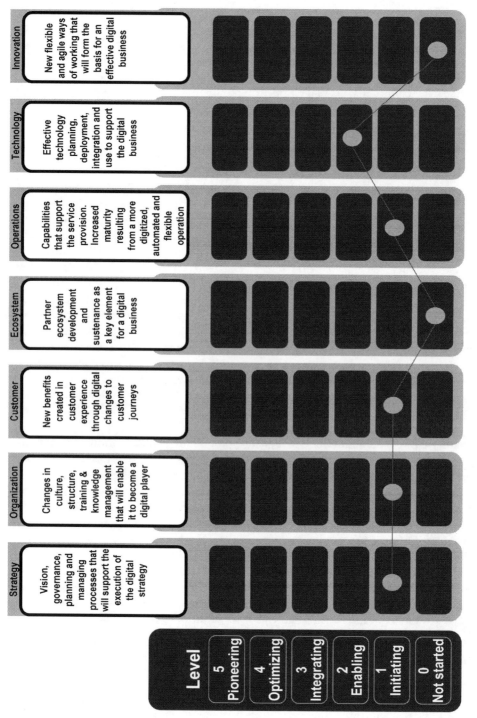

Figure 4.1 Digital business maturity models, like this one,[15] attempt to map where an organization is along various digital business capabilities or outcome areas

an expanded understanding of their needs and preferences, offer them better value, and be able to enter other markets to acquire new customers. From a product perspective, digital businesses are better able to identify and act on new product/service/value delivery opportunities or to digitally enhance existing products/services. From an operations perspective, digital businesses can realize efficiency and effectiveness breakthroughs that nondigital businesses can't dream of (e.g. a nondigital business couldn't dream of the speed to market, employee productivity, process efficiency, or asset utilization of Amazon or Google).

From a strategy perspective, digital businesses are able to employ novel, highly agile, and highly scalable business models (e.g. marketplaces, ecosystem platforms); are able to unbundle offerings to offer customization or remove nonvalue-adding aspects of a product (e.g. so customers can buy the one song they like for $2 instead of a whole album they won't listen to for $30); and are able to unconstrain supply (e.g. have access to all suppliers rather just a few). From a decision-making perspective, digital businesses are able to access massive amounts of data from within and outside of the firm, and they are able to optimally manage and use this data to make better and faster decisions (e.g. through access to real-time insights). In doing so, they weaponize data and make it a strong competitive capability. From a technology infrastructure perspective, digital businesses are able to assemble and integrate hardware, things, networks, software, and platforms to enable them to function optimally as a digital business. Finally, from a people perspective, digital businesses have enough people in the organization with the right digital mindsets (e.g. attitudes and behaviors) and skills (e.g. digital technology, digital business and communication/influencing skills) to effect a digital business culture (e.g. one with a collective appreciation of the importance and urgency of becoming a digital business).

The digital business imperative

In Chapter 3 on digital disruption, we explained how digital technology advancements disrupt customer expectations and behaviors, disrupt the competitive field and bases of competition, and disrupt data availability. We noted that this disruption creates existential threats for organizations not able to guard against it or adapt to it in a timely manner. We pointed to examples of disrupted organizations and industries such as Kodak, Blockbuster, Borders, the taxi industry, and the newspaper industry. We also explained the game-changing opportunities presented by digital technology advancements, which are essentially the promise of or opportunities available to digital businesses. We now propose that the digital business imperative is a four-pronged ultimatum for businesses. The first such ultimatum is to guard against and have the capacity to adapt to disruption (e.g. like Intel, Disney, and Caterpillar) or face certain death.[16,17,18] The second is to become a digital business and realize the promise of digital business, or risk becoming sidelined by competitors who do so (ultimately leading to certain death).[19,20,21] The third is to continuously and sufficiently upgrade and leverage digital business capabilities to become the disruptor, or still risk disruption from companies with superior digital business capabilities[22,23,24] – this is despite being a digital business. Finally, even though businesses may initiate efforts to guard against disruption, to build their capacity to adapt to disruption, to become digital businesses, and to leverage their digital business capabilities in order to become a disruptor, if they can't do it fast enough (relative to the speed of technology changes and/or the speed of existing competitors and new entrants), they may still risk disruption and death.[25,26]

Digital business transformation

Defining digital business transformation

Like digital business, the term digital business transformation, often used interchangeably with digital transformation, is also a term that is difficult to define. Gartner defines it as:

> the process of exploiting digital technologies and supporting capabilities to create a robust new business model.[27]

Synthesizing the extant definitions of digital business transformation, University of Montreal Assistant Professor Gregory Vial defined it as:

> a process that aims to improve an entity by triggering significant changes to its properties through combinations of information, computing, communication, and connectivity technologies.[28]

Michael Wade, professor of innovation and strategy and Cisco Chair in Digital Business Transformation at IMD Business School, and Donald Marchand, professor of strategy execution and information management, offer a simpler definition of digital business transformation as being:

> organizational change through the use of digital technologies to materially improve performance.[29]

ZDNet's Mark Samuels adds that although the idea is to use digital technologies to make processes more efficient and effective, it's not just replicating those processes into digital form, rather, it is transforming them and, in turn, transforming the product's or the business's offering into something significantly better.[30]

Salesforce, a leading cloud CRM platform, proposes this definition of digital transformation:

> Digital transformation is the process of using digital technologies to create new – or modify existing – business processes, culture, and customer experiences to meet changing business and market requirements. This reimagining of business in the digital age is digital transformation.[31]

Digital business transformation is not just about digital technologies

Bringing together the preceding definitions and the earlier definition of digital business, we put it yet another way and propose that digital business transformation is the process of transforming to or becoming a digital business – thus realizing the promise of being a digital business. Digital transformation researchers and practitioners point out that the transformation to a digital business is not just about changes to the digital technologies used. It is also about changes to an organization's strategy (e.g. business models, bases of competition, strategy execution, adaptability, and agility), changes to its structure (e.g. organization hierarchy, business functions, roles and responsibilities), changes to its processes (operational, functional, and strategic processes), changes to its workforce at all levels (e.g. hiring and retention choices, roles and responsibilities, and cultivation of appropriate competencies, attitudes, and behaviors), and changes to its culture (collective attitudes and behaviors).[32]

Challenges and risks of digital business transformation

In general, such all-encompassing change and transformation efforts have a low success rate, with management consultancy firm McKinsey estimating this success rate at about 30%. This means up to 70% of such change and transformation efforts fail to deliver. McKinsey further points out that the success rate of digital transformation efforts is even lower, at about 16%. A range of potential causes for this low success rate have been discussed. These include unspoken disagreement among senior managers about the goals and approach to digital transformation,[33] organizations not having the supporting digital capabilities to support the transformation (e.g. appropriately skilled people, technology infrastructure),[34] lack of a clear strategy and CEO sponsorship of it,[35] falling into the "let's wait and see" trap with change initiatives, not understanding what needs to change and how to go about it, challenges getting the right technology and/or the right talent to operate the technology, employee resistance to change or employee efforts to undermine the change, obsession with technology tools that don't meaningfully improve customer value, not changing fast enough, challenges sourcing top talent (e.g. technology leaders, digital strategists, designers, DevOps engineers, data scientists, artificial intelligence specialists),[36] and not dealing with employees' fears of being replaced.[37]

Successful digital transformation is the barrier between the existential threats of disruption and the promise or benefits of being a digital business. Thus, despite the low success rate, organizations invest in digital business transformation and navigate the obstacles and challenges because the alternative, digital disruption, has little upside. Figure 4.2 summarizes how the use of digital technologies combines with structural changes to overcome organization barriers to digital business transformation and enable changes in value creation paths. It also shows examples of the benefits and risks associated with these changes.

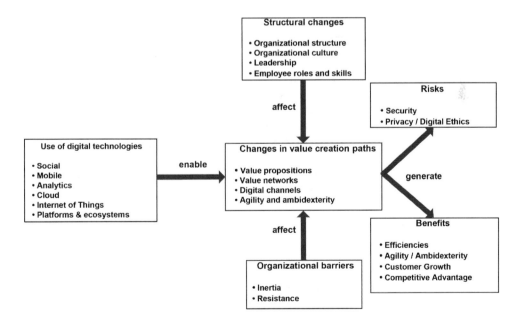

Figure 4.2 Digital business transformation is not just about using digital technologies; it is also about changing organization structures, overcoming change barriers, and managing both digital risks and change risks

Implications for hospitality managers

Hospitality and leisure managers are a vital link between the top management team and frontline employees. They translate top management team intentions to frontline and other employees. They translate top management team strategic initiatives into day-to-day action. They are responsible for hiring, performance development, and retention choices that impact organization culture and competencies within the organization. And they are responsible for modeling attitudes and behaviors aligned with top management team intentions. They also typically have a more intimate knowledge of internal processes, products/services, and customer relationships. Given this vital position they occupy and the roles they play, they are critical to the success of digital transformation efforts. Through their actions (or lack thereof) they can significantly enhance the chance of success or significantly derail it.

To leverage their important role to significantly enhance the probability of success of digital transformation efforts, hospitality and leisure managers can develop their digital transformation related competencies and then leverage these competencies to support digital transformation efforts. To develop their digital transformation competencies, hospitality and leisure managers need to do the ongoing work to understand and keep up with digital technologies (e.g. cloud, IoT, AI, blockchain, robotics, drones, low-power wide-area networks [LPWAN], low Earth orbit satellites) and with digital business and digital transformation concepts/practices (e.g. digital business characteristics, digital business strategy, digital business models, successful digital transformation approaches and case, digital transformation leadership roles and responsibilities). They also need to do the work to understand and keep up with change and transformation methodologies (e.g. agile, lean, change management). Armed with this understanding, they can then build relevant digital technology, digital business, and digital transformation competencies (e.g. deep and broad technical technology and data skills, strategic technology skills, digital leadership skills, strategic thinking skills, cross-functional leadership and change management skills). Further, they can build informal networks vertically and across the organization that are important for accelerating change and transformation.

Having developed the aforementioned digital business and digital transformation competencies, hospitality and leisure managers can leverage these competencies to accelerate and improve the odds of success for digital transformation efforts. For example, they can use their digital transformation and digital business knowledge and skills to cultivate the digital business and digital transformation competencies of their direct reports and of other people across the organization. They can shape appropriate digital business and digital transformation attitudes and behaviors, thus helping nurture the digital culture to support digital business transformation efforts. They can ensure the hiring of direct reports and other employees with appropriate digital business and digital transformation attitudes and skills. They can leverage their digital business and digital transformation knowledge/skills to take on and successfully carry out one or more key digital transformation leadership roles (e.g. chief digital officer, project/program manager, operating model lead, customer engagement lead, digital product manager, ethics compliance lead, user experience [UX] designer, change and transformation specialist).[38] They can leverage their informal networks to accelerate implementation of transformation initiatives, and to encourage frontline staff to understand and accept transformation-related changes. Finally, they can leverage their technology and data skills to work hand in hand with technologists, service delivery staff, and senior executives to accelerate and minimize the risks of transformation efforts.

The alternative to building and leveraging the digital business and digital transformation knowledge and competencies we've described is for hospitality managers to become one more of the bottlenecks or barriers to digital transformation efforts (e.g. by lacking the digital business and digital transformation knowledge and competencies to understand and support transformation). Hospitality and leisure managers in the latter category are likely to find themselves disrupted by those in the former category.

Google and reflect

Digitization, digitalization, digital business, digital business transformation, digital transformation, digital business capabilities, digital business competencies, digital platforms, digital strategy, omnichannel strategy, scalability, digital customer engagement, digital customer experience, agile methodologies, lean methodologies, digital accelerator, user story, customer touch point, digital business imperative, digital transformation imperative, user-centered design.

Discussion questions

1 What is the difference between the terms digital transformation and digital business transformation?
2 What is the difference between the terms digital business and digital business transformation?
3 Which of the definitions of digital business transformation makes more sense to you? Why?
4 What does the common assertion that "digital transformation is not just about technology" mean?
5 Are any businesses you know of fully digital businesses? If not, how can they become fully digital businesses?
6 Once an organization becomes a digital business, does it have any need for digital transformation?
7 What is meant by the assertion that digital business is "a change process or a journey"?
8 What is meant by the assertion that digital business is "a future state"?
9 What are the top four benefits of being a digital business? Why are they more important than other benefits?
10 What is the digital business imperative?
11 People often talk about the digital business imperative and the digital transformation imperative. Are these the same or different?
12 What are some challenges and risks of digital business transformation?
13 What is the success rate for transformation efforts in general? What is the success rate for digital transformation efforts? Why is the success rate for digital transformation efforts much worse?
14 What are two important implications of digital business and digital business transformation for hospitality and leisure managers?
15 What are five things hospitality and leisure managers can do to maximize their organizations' odds of succeeding at digital transformation?

Notes

1 Gartner Inc. (2014). Digital Business. Retrieved April 28, 2020, from Gartner website: www.gartner.com/en/information-technology/glossary/digital-business

2 Aragon Research. (2020). Defining Digital Business – Business and IT Glossary. Retrieved May 20, 2020, from Aragon Research website: https://aragonresearch.com/glossary-digital-business/

3 Chaffey, D. (2015). *Digital Business and E-Commerce Management: Strategy, Implementation and Practice*, 6th edn. Financial Times/Prentice Hall.

4 Lopez, J. (2014). Digital Business is Everyone's Business. Forbes. Retrieved from www.forbes.com/sites/gartnergroup/2014/05/07/digital-business-is-everyones-business/#636bd0da7f82

5 Lopez, J. (2014). Digital Business is Everyone's Business. Forbes. Retrieved from www.forbes.com/sites/gartnergroup/2014/05/07/digital-business-is-everyones-business/#636bd0da7f82

6 Lopez, J. (2014). Digital Business is Everyone's Business. Forbes. Retrieved from www.forbes.com/sites/gartnergroup/2014/05/07/digital-business-is-everyones-business/#636bd0da7f82

7 Dörner, K., & Edelman, D. (2015). What "Digital" Really Means. Retrieved April 28, 2020, from McKinsey & Company website: www.mckinsey.com/industries/technology-media-and-telecommunications/our-insights/what-digital-really-means

8 Dörner, K., & Edelman, D. (2015). What "Digital" Really Means. Retrieved April 28, 2020, from McKinsey & Company website: www.mckinsey.com/industries/technology-media-and-telecommunications/our-insights/what-digital-really-means

9 Sacolick, I. (2017). *Driving Digital: The Leader's Guide to Business Transformation Through Technology*. Amacom.

10 Fenwick, N. (2015). Unleash Your Digital Predator. Retrieved May 22, 2020, from Forrester website: https://go.forrester.com/blogs/15-12-09-unleash_your_digital_predator/

11 Dörner, K., & Edelman, D. (2015). What "Digital" Really Means. Retrieved April 28, 2020, from McKinsey & Company website: www.mckinsey.com/industries/technology-media-and-telecommunications/our-insights/what-digital-really-means

12 Swords, J. (2020). Becoming a Modern Digital Business in 2020. Thoughtworks. Retrieved May 22, 2020, from Thoughtworks.com website: www.thoughtworks.com/perspectives/edition8-modern-digital-business-article

13 Swords, J. (2020). Becoming a Modern Digital Business in 2020. Thoughtworks. Retrieved May 22, 2020, from Thoughtworks.com website: www.thoughtworks.com/perspectives/edition8-modern-digital-business-article

14 Gupta, S. (2018). *Driving Digital Strategy: A Guide to Reimagining Your Business*. Harvard Business Press.

15 Valdez-de-Leon, O. (2016). A Digital Maturity Model for Telecommunications Service Providers. *Technology Innovation Management Review*, 6(8).

16 Stanek, R. (2018). Council Post: Why It's Important to Make Your Company the Disruptor, Not the Disrupted. Forbes. Retrieved from www.forbes.com/sites/forbestechcouncil/2018/06/04/why-its-important-to-make-your-company-the-disruptor-not-the-disrupted/#4ddb3e8331a6

17 Vial, G. (2019). Understanding Digital Transformation: A Review and a Research Agenda. *The Journal of Strategic Information Systems*, 28(2), 118–144. https://doi.org/10.1016/j.jsis.2019.01.003

18 Schadler, T., & Fenwick, N. (2017). The Digital Business Imperative. Retrieved May 22, 2020, from Forrester.com website: www.forrester.com/report/The+Digital+Business+Imperative/-/E-RES115784

19 Schadler, T., & Fenwick, N. (2017). The Digital Business Imperative. Retrieved May 22, 2020, from Forrester.com website: www.forrester.com/report/The+Digital+Business+Imperative/-/E-RES115784

20 Stanek, R. (2018). Council Post: Why It's Important to Make Your Company the Disruptor, Not the Disrupted. Forbes. Retrieved from www.forbes.com/sites/forbestechcouncil/2018/06/04/why-its-important-to-make-your-company-the-disruptor-not-the-disrupted/#4ddb3e8331a6

21 Vial, G. (2019). Understanding Digital Transformation: A Review and a Research Agenda. *The Journal of Strategic Information Systems*, 28(2), 118–144. https://doi.org/10.1016/j.jsis.2019.01.003

22 Stanek, R. (2018). Council Post: Why It's Important to Make Your Company the Disruptor, Not the Disrupted. Forbes. Retrieved from www.forbes.com/sites/forbestechcouncil/2018/06/04/why-its-important-to-make-your-company-the-disruptor-not-the-disrupted/#4ddb3e8331a6

23 Fenwick, N. (2015). Unleash Your Digital Predator. Retrieved May 22, 2020, from Forrester website: https://go.forrester.com/blogs/15-12-09-unleash_your_digital_predator/

24 Stanek, R. (2018). Why It's Important to Make Your Company the Disruptor, Not the Disrupted. Forbes. Retrieved from www.forbes.com/sites/forbestechcouncil/2018/06/04/why-its-important-to-make-your-company-the-disruptor-not-the-disrupted/#4ddb3e8331a6

25 Ross, J. (2018). Digital is about Speed – But It Takes a Long Time. Retrieved May 22, 2020, from MIT Sloan Management Review website: https://sloanreview.mit.edu/article/digital-is-about-speed-but-it-takes-a-long-time/

26 Brown, S. (2020). Strategy at the Speed of Digital. Retrieved May 22, 2020, from McKinsey & Company website: www.mckinsey.com/business-functions/strategy-and-corporate-finance/our-insights/strategy-at-the-speed-of-digital

27 Gartner. (2018). Gartner Glossary: Digital Business Transformation. Retrieved May 22, 2020, from Gartner website: www.gartner.com/en/information-technology/glossary/digital-business-transformation

28 Vial, G. (2019). Understanding Digital Transformation: A Review and a Research Agenda. *The Journal of Strategic Information Systems*, 28(2), 118–144. https://doi.org/10.1016/j.jsis.2019.01.003

29 Marchand, D. A., & Wade, M. R. (2014). Digital Business Transformation: Where is Your Company on the Journey. Retrieved May 22, 2020, from IMD business school website: www.imd.org/research-knowledge/articles/digital-business-transformation-where-is-your-company-on-the-journey/

30 Samuels, M. (2018). What is Digital Transformation? Everything You Need to Know about How Technology is Reshaping Business. Retrieved May 22, 2020, from ZDNet website: www.zdnet.com/article/what-is-digital-transformation-everything-you-need-to-know-about-how-technology-is-reshaping/

31 Salesforce. (2018). What is Digital Transformation? A Definition by Salesforce. Retrieved May 22, 2020, from Salesforce.com website: www.salesforce.com/products/platform/what-is-digital-transformation/

32 Vial, G. (2019). Understanding Digital Transformation: A Review and a Research Agenda. *The Journal of Strategic Information Systems*, 28(2), 118–144. https://doi.org/10.1016/j.jsis.2019.01.003

33 Sutcliff, M., Narsalay, R., & Sen, A. (2019). The Two Big Reasons that Digital Transformations Fail. Harvard Business Review. Retrieved May 22, 2020, from Harvard Business Review website: https://hbr.org/2019/10/the-two-big-reasons-that-digital-transformations-fail

34 Sutcliff, M., Narsalay, R., & Sen, A. (2019). The Two Big Reasons that Digital Transformations Fail. Harvard Business Review. Retrieved May 22, 2020, from Harvard Business Review website: https://hbr.org/2019/10/the-two-big-reasons-that-digital-transformations-fail

35 Boulton, C. (2019). 12 Reasons Why Digital Transformations Fail. CIO. Retrieved May 22, 2020, from CIO website: www.cio.com/article/3248946/12-reasons-why-digital-transformations-fail.html

36 Boulton, C. (2019). 12 Reasons Why Digital Transformations Fail. CIO. Retrieved May 22, 2020, from CIO website: www.cio.com/article/3248946/12-reasons-why-digital-transformations-fail.html

37 Tabrizi, B., Lam, E., Girard, K., & Irvin, V. (2019). Digital Transformation is Not About Technology. Harvard Business Review. Retrieved May 22, 2020, from Harvard Business Review website: https://hbr.org/2019/03/digital-transformation-is-not-about-technology

38 Boulton, C. (2018). 8 Essential Roles for a Successful Digital Transformation. Retrieved May 22, 2020, from CIO website: www.cio.com/article/3258767/8-essential-roles-for-a-successful-digital-transformation.html

Part II

Digital disruption and digital transformation in the hospitality and leisure industry

5 Digital disruption and digital transformation in the hospitality and leisure industry

Introduction

As digital technologies have advanced, within the hospitality industry they have driven disruptions in guest expectations and behaviors, disruptions in available data, and disruptions in the competitive landscape and bases of competition. New industry entrants, as well as incumbents recreating themselves, have rearranged the industry and, in many cases, inserted themselves as value chain intermediaries. As a result, the industry has become much more complex for most participants. In this chapter, we unpack these types of disruptions and discuss how they have played themselves out in the industry. We then discuss how hospitality and leisure organizations have adapted to or reacted to disruptions, and how they have started their digital transformation journeys. Current and future hospitality and leisure managers may find themselves involved in leading a new digital transformation effort, reinvigorating one that has stalled, and/or resuscitating one that has failed. In either case, it will pay to have a good understanding of the nature of disruption dynamics, the types of adaptation strategies, and the challenges of digital transformation in the industry. This chapter provides a starting point and a lens for viewing digital disruption and understanding adaptation and transformation strategies. We expect current and prospective hospitality and leisure managers will use this lens to seek out, interpret, understand, and be able to use emerging industry thought leadership on effective digital transformation and digital business strategies and practices. This is critical to their effective participation in helping their organizations navigate persistent disruptive forces.

Digital disruption in the hospitality and leisure industry

Disruption of guest expectations and behaviors

Not too long ago, hospitality and leisure organizations had voluminous binders of information for operations, had printed pamphlets or brochures for guests, and manually calculated/recorded/retrieved information. Guests had to endure queues to book flights and tours, to check in and out of hotels, and to make dinner reservations. Digital technology advancements changed all that. Today, digital technologies enable guests to do everything almost instantaneously with a few clicks on their smart devices – from finding and booking tours or restaurants, to checking in and unlocking their door, and even to virtually experiencing key tourism destinations.[1] Guests also have access to unprecedented amounts of information about available product/service options and their quality. This makes them aware of what accessibility, convenience, experience, value, or other benefits are possible. As a result, guest expectations are not what they used to be. Changes in digital tools available to guests are transforming their habits/routines; their expectations about service/experience/price; and how they respond to hospitality and leisure organizations that don't live up to their expectations. Not only are these expectations much higher, but they are also much broader, and they continue to grow.

For example, depending on the hospitality and leisure service being offered, these expectations may include that hospitality and leisure organizations provide guests with the option to manage their entire trip on their smartphones (without ever having to talk to a human being if they choose),[2] that they deliver guests real-time information on what to do, where to eat, and how to get there (e.g. through AI-driven e-concierge chatbot apps that they can access anytime and from anywhere); that they provide them with next level accommodation conveniences (e.g. voice-activated chatbots that set the temperature, open the curtains, order room service, and book transport);[3] that organizations use guests' past travel/stay data to personalize and optimize their experiences (e.g. saving them a spot on that tour, allocating them their preferred attendant, delivering them a meal by that chef, having that custom pillow there for them); that they have the option to virtually preview their hospitality and leisure experience; that they have gamified augmented reality games for kids or adults; and that they enable payment in cryptocurrency.

Although these examples are overly technology centric, digital technology advancements have also driven changes nontechnology-centric expectations and behaviors. For example, personalization is taking a greater precedence and becoming a greater key to success than ever before,[4] guests want more unique and authentic experiences,[5] there is a greater expectation of instant gratification,[6] guests are placing a greater emphasis on wellness/well-being and social/environmental sustainability than materialism,[7] there is a greater diversity in the makeup of travelers and thus their wants and needs, there is a greater desire for experiencing local lifestyles and a sense of community, and there is a greater desire for serendipitous experiences and different forms of hospitableness.[8] Although these expectations don't seem technology centric, sustainably delivering on them requires leveraging digital technologies.

Digital technology advancements have disrupted or driven changes in guest expectations and behaviors, in turn pushing hospitality and leisure organizations to either rethink what the travel experience means to the customer and reconfigure their operations to live up to the changed expectations or to become sidelined in the industry and disparaged in online reviews/conversations.[9] Figure 5.1 shows how a few digital technology advancements (robotics and artificial intelligence) enable automation of particular guest value creation activities, which in turn enables hospitality and leisure staff to focus on higher value-added activities for guests (e.g. meaningful engagement, memorable experiences, service speed/efficiency/reliability). The overall effect of this is a shift in customer expectations toward higher value-added activities for most hospitality and leisure organizations.

Disruption of the competitive landscape and bases of competition

Digital technology advancements have introduced nontraditional competitors into the hospitality and leisure industry like home-sharing platforms (e.g. Airbnb, Vrbo, Homestay, FlipKey), other sharing economy platforms (e.g. Uber, Uber Eats), OTAs (e.g. Expedia, Priceline, Booking.com, Agoda, Hotel.com, TripAdvisor), and previously obscure or invisible competitors (e.g. independent and boutique hotels, emerging economy brands). While not previously considered competition by traditional hospitality and leisure

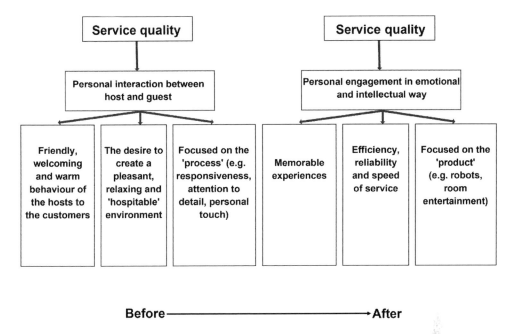

Figure 5.1 Example of how robots, artificial intelligence, and service automation technologies change the type of guest service that can be delivered, and thus guest service expectations[10]

organizations, these competitors have leveraged digital technologies to scale their operations globally, grow at near exponential rates, and establish almost insurmountable strategic positions in the industry. Airbnb, for example, has grown at a cumulative annual rate of more than 100% since 2011 to become one of the largest competitors in the industry. It has leveraged its digital business capabilities to deliver high personalization, a sense of community, serendipitous experiences, hospitableness, entertainment, a sense of aesthetic, and ease of travel that is starting to outperform traditional industry competitor offerings.[11] Home-sharing platforms have now started to move into core segments of traditional industry competitors. For example, through Airbnb Plus and Airbnb Experiences, Airbnb has started to move into the business traveler and luxury traveler segments that are an important core of traditional industry competitors.

The new industry entrants have limited incumbent organizations' abilities to set prices (e.g. to make up for low demand periods by charging high prices during peak travel times). Organizations like OTAs, online review/comparison sites, search engines and social media platform providers have made data on pricing, experience, aesthetics, service, and other offerings transparent to customers and comparable at the click of a button. As a result, previously small or obscure organizations providing great value have come to the attention of customers. These organizations have, in turn, leveraged digital technologies to scale their operations and become formidable competitors. Many of the new entrants have firmly placed themselves between travel experience seekers and traditional hospitality and leisure organizations, further shrinking traditional hospitality organizations' margins. For example, OTAs can charge up to 30% of the price for a booking to a traditional hospitality and leisure organization that is made through one of their platforms.

The combination of new entrants, strategic reactions by industry incumbents, and heightened customer expectations has shifted the bases of competition from brand, geographical availability, and standardized customer service to technology capabilities (digital business capabilities, digital marketing capabilities, digital customer engagement capabilities, digital innovation capabilities), enhanced guest experience (e.g. beyond delivering good customer service), privacy, personalization, differentiation/positioning, ethics and sustainability consciousness, operational and cost efficiencies, online presence and reputation, and adaptability/agility/ambidexterity capabilities. Digital technology-driven disruption has expanded the bases of competition beyond the old brand, service, and size bases. Needless to say, delivering on the expanded bases of competition requires making the most of digital technologies, not only for becoming a digital business but for upgrading digital business capabilities to world-class level and leveraging them for a competitive edge. Figure 5.2 shows how hospitality and leisure industry customer journey and value creation activities are being dominated by a range of new digitally capable entrants and traditional competitors leveraging digital technologies.

Disruption of data availability

Digital technology advancements have changed the data available to hospitality and leisure organizations, to their consumers, and to their competitors. From a consumer perspective, guests have push-button access to almost all available offerings, prices, deals and discounts, reviews and ratings, media coverage, and much more. They also have push-button access to information about what experience and value hospitality and leisure

Source: World Economic Forum/Accenture analysis

Figure 5.2 New entrants and established organizations have leveraged digital technologies to reorganize the industry configuration and customer journey

organizations should be able to offer. This ready accessibility to information places significant power in the hands of customers and pushes hospitality and leisure organizations to provide competitive value and experiences that live up to expectations. If they don't, they risk falling to the bottom of the competitive heap and risk negative online brand reviews that may compound the situation.[12]

Similarly, digital technology advancements enable competitors to collect an unprecedented level of information on customer demographics, customer preferences, customer experiences, customer moods and emotions, customer journeys, customer aspirations, customer wealth, customer spending patterns, customer social and professional networks, and more. Competitors can leverage data analytics and artificial intelligence technologies to weaponize this data; that is, to use it in such a way as to drive optimal strategic and operational decisions about business and revenue model design and about how to best create personalization, a sense of community, serendipitous experiences, hospitableness, entertainment, aesthetics, and ease of travel. For example, Airbnb has built a massive data set on travel characteristics (e.g. guests, destinations, hosts, accommodation sites, travel durations, online behaviors, satisfaction levels, host interactions). It leverages this massive data set as a formidable strategic weapon in the industry to drive optimization of cost leadership, differentiation, product/service innovation, pricing, accommodation site availability, host management, and guest management decisions.

The disruption or change in data available to customers and competitors means that, even unbeknownst to them, hospitality and leisure organizations who don't get their act together on the data collection, data analytics, and artificial intelligence fronts put themselves at a significant disadvantage in consumer interactions and strategic positioning.

Digital transformation in the hospitality and leisure industry

Adapting to disruption

The majority of hospitality and leisure organizations' response to digital disruption has evolved over time from ignoring it, to denying it, to attacking new entrants, to finally adapting to the disruption and to the new bases of competition.[13] The attacks of new entrants have been largely in the form of political lobbying efforts. For example, in 2016, the American Hotel and Lodging Association (AHLA) started undertaking extensive efforts to lobby political institutions and regulators to impose taxes and regulations on Airbnb in order to level the competitive playing field.[14] And in 2017, the AHLA was engaged in efforts to lobby the Federal Trade Commission (FTC) to intervene in what it contended were monopolistic powers and unfair trade practices by OTAs.[15] Incumbents' efforts to adapt to digital disruption and the new bases of competition have included mergers/acquisitions and brand expansions (e.g. Marriott's $13.6 billion merger with Starwood Hotels to bring together Starwood's Sheraton, Westin, W Hotels, and St. Regis properties with its Marriott, Courtyard, and Ritz-Carlton brands[16] – giving Marriott more than 30 brands and making it the largest hotel chain in the world as at 2016).[17] Incumbent's efforts have also included investing in brand loyalty programs, further enhancing and differentiating on the human aspects of service (e.g. proactive and useful concierges, warm and friendly reception, great food and beverage and room service staff), cutting costs, forming strategic partnerships, and leveraging digital technologies like search engine optimization, social media, cloud, and mobile.

Digital transformation efforts to date and their impact

Most hospitality and leisure organizations have recognized the importance of digital transformation to their survival and competitiveness. Many have been making big but targeted investments in digital transformation efforts to increase guest satisfaction/loyalty, operational efficiency and effectiveness, and revenue growth. For example, in 2018 improving digital customer engagement and guest loyalty was a top priority for many hotel and lodging organizations.[18] These transformation initiatives have been and continue to target areas such as services–rich mobile apps, comprehensive and smart in-room services, sophisticated back–office data analytics, home-sharing-like attributes and experiences, virtual/augmented/mixed reality capabilities and offerings, cloudification of enterprise information systems, hybrid cloud and on-premise architectures, and omni channel presence and engagement. Enabling these investments has first required investments in structural, cultural, and people transformations. Organizations succeeding with their digital transformation efforts have been seeing competitive improvements in guest experience and value, efficiency and effectiveness breakthroughs, improved adaptability and agility, enhanced ability to disrupt the disruptors, and strong gains in competitive positioning.

Implications for hospitality and leisure managers

The hospitality and leisure industry has grappled with digital disruption and continues to do so. The organizations that have adapted to disruption and remain in a strong strategic position in the industry have embraced it and continue their pursuit of becoming world-class digital businesses. Early career and prospective hospitality and leisure managers will likely enter organizations partway through these transformations. They may find successful, stalled, or failed transformations. They may have the opportunity to bring new energy and capabilities to participate in successful transformations, to supercharge stalled efforts, or to reengage their teams around a new transformation vision. In either case, the digital technology, digital business, and digital transformation knowledge and skills they develop now will be critical to their careers and the survival and longevity of their organizations.

Google and reflect

AI-driven e-concierge chatbot app, OTAs, hyper-personalization, SEO, dynamic pricing algorithm, Airbnb Plus, Airbnb experiences, online review platforms, experience economy, localness, hospitableness, ethical consumerism.

Discussion questions

1 How do digital technology advancements cause disruptions in guest expectations and behaviors?
2 Identify four changed guest expectations and three changed behaviors as a result of digital technology advancements.
3 Identify three digital technologies that hospitality and leisure organizations can leverage to live up to the guest expectations identified in question 2.
4 Identify two hospitality and leisure organizations that offer prospective guests a virtual preview of their potential experiences.

5 Identify one or more hospitality and leisure organizations differentiating on localness and sense of community.

6 How have digital technology advancements caused disruptions in the competitive field and in the bases of competition in the hospitality and leisure industry?

7 Do you agree that new industry entrants like home-sharing platforms and OTAs have had an unfair competitive advantage? Should the government intervene to make it a level playing field?

8 Where do the biggest home-sharing platform and the biggest OTA organization rank in a list of the biggest organizations in the hospitality and leisure industry? How long has it taken such organizations to reach this size and market position?

9 How have digital technology advancements driven margin erosion in the hospitality and leisure industry? Can such margin erosion be reversed?

10 What are the current key bases of competition in the hospitality industry? Are these different from what they have traditionally been?

11 How do digital technology advancements disrupt data availability? How does the disruption of data availability create survival and competitive threats for hospitality and leisure organizations?

12 Identify three or more approaches hospitality and leisure organizations have taken to adapt to digital disruption.

13 Do you believe hospitality and leisure organizations have been successful at digital business transformation?

14 Thinking about digital technology advancements, digital business, and digital business transformation, what do you think remains still to be done by hospitality and leisure organizations?

15 Is there or can there be an end to digital business transformation?

Notes

1 Newman, D. (2018). Top 6 Digital Transformation Trends in Hospitality and Tourism. Forbes. Retrieved from www.forbes.com/sites/danielnewman/2018/01/02/top-6-digital-transformation-trends-in-hospitality-and-tourism/#356723ae67df

2 Newman, D. (2018). Top 6 Digital Transformation Trends in Hospitality and Tourism. Forbes. Retrieved from www.forbes.com/sites/danielnewman/2018/01/02/top-6-digital-transformation-trends-in-hospitality-and-tourism/#356723ae67df

3 Newman, D. (2018). Top 6 Digital Transformation Trends in Hospitality and Tourism. Forbes. Retrieved from www.forbes.com/sites/danielnewman/2018/01/02/top-6-digital-transformation-trends-in-hospitality-and-tourism/#356723ae67df

4 Newman, D. (2018). Top 6 Digital Transformation Trends in Hospitality and Tourism. Forbes. Retrieved from www.forbes.com/sites/danielnewman/2018/01/02/top-6-digital-transformation-trends-in-hospitality-and-tourism/#356723ae67df

5 Mody, M., & Gomez, M. (2018). Airbnb and the Hotel Industry: The Past, Present, and Future of Sales, Marketing, Branding, and Revenue Management. *Boston Hospitality Review*, 6(3). Retrieved from www.bu.edu/bhr/2018/10/31/airbnb-and-the-hotel-industry-the-past-present-and-future-of-sales-marketing-branding-and-revenue-management/

6 Mody, M., & Gomez, M. (2018). Airbnb and the Hotel Industry: The Past, Present, and Future of Sales, Marketing, Branding, and Revenue Management. *Boston Hospitality Review*, 6(3). Retrieved from www.bu.edu/bhr/2018/10/31/airbnb-and-the-hotel-industry-the-past-present-and-future-of-sales-marketing-branding-and-revenue-management/

7 Newman, D. (2018). Top 6 Digital Transformation Trends in Hospitality and Tourism. Forbes. Retrieved from www.forbes.com/sites/danielnewman/2018/01/02/top-6-digital-transformation-trends-in-hospitality-and-tourism/#356723ae67df

 8 Newman, D. (2018). Top 6 Digital Transformation Trends in Hospitality and Tourism. Forbes. Retrieved from www.forbes.com/sites/danielnewman/2018/01/02/top-6-digital-transformation-trends-in-hospitality-and-tourism/#356723ae67df

 9 Newman, D. (2018). Top 6 Digital Transformation Trends in Hospitality and Tourism. Forbes. Retrieved from www.forbes.com/sites/danielnewman/2018/01/02/top-6-digital-transformation-trends-in-hospitality-and-tourism/#356723ae67df

10 Ivanov, S., & Webster, C. (Eds.). (2019). *Robots, Artificial Intelligence, and Service Automation in Travel, Tourism and Hospitality*. Emerald Publishing Limited.

11 Newman, D. (2018). Top 6 Digital Transformation Trends in Hospitality and Tourism. Forbes. Retrieved from www.forbes.com/sites/danielnewman/2018/01/02/top-6-digital-transformation-trends-in-hospitality-and-tourism/#356723ae67df

12 Newman, D. (2018). Top 6 Digital Transformation Trends in Hospitality and Tourism. Forbes. Retrieved from www.forbes.com/sites/danielnewman/2018/01/02/top-6-digital-transformation-trends-in-hospitality-and-tourism/#356723ae67df

13 Mody, M., & Gomez, M. (2018). Airbnb and the Hotel Industry: The Past, Present, and Future of Sales, Marketing, Branding, and Revenue Management. *Boston Hospitality Review*, 6(3). Retrieved from www.bu.edu/bhr/2018/10/31/airbnb-and-the-hotel-industry-the-past-present-and-future-of-sales-marketing-branding-and-revenue-management/

14 Mody, M., & Gomez, M. (2018). Airbnb and the Hotel Industry: The Past, Present, and Future of Sales, Marketing, Branding, and Revenue Management. *Boston Hospitality Review*, 6(3). Retrieved from www.bu.edu/bhr/2018/10/31/airbnb-and-the-hotel-industry-the-past-present-and-future-of-sales-marketing-branding-and-revenue-management/

15 De Vynck, G., & Zaleski, O. (2017, May 5). Hotels Plan Lobbying Push Over Priceline-Expedia "Monopoly." Retrieved May 24, 2020, from Bloomberg.com website: www.bloomberg.com/news/articles/2017-05-05/u-s-hotels-plan-attack-on-the-priceline-expedia-monopoly

16 The Associated Press. (2016). Marriott Buys Starwood, Becoming World's Largest Hotel Chain. Retrieved May 24, 2020, from CNBC website: www.cnbc.com/2016/09/23/marriott-buys-starwood-becoming-worlds-largest-hotel-chain.html

17 The Associated Press. (2016). Marriott Buys Starwood, Becoming World's Largest Hotel Chain. Retrieved May 24, 2020, from CNBC website: www.cnbc.com/2016/09/23/marriott-buys-starwood-becoming-worlds-largest-hotel-chain.html

18 Comcast. (2018). The Next Phase of Digital Transformation in Hospitality. Retrieved May 24, 2020, from Comcast.com website: https://cbcommunity.comcast.com/community/browse-all/details/the-next-phase-of-digital-transformation-in-hospitality#fn2

6 Impact of digital disruption and digital transformation on hospitality and leisure managers

Introduction

Digital disruptions and the associated digital transformation and digital business imperatives result in disruptions of managerial work.[1,2,3] That is, they require managers to perform new or enhanced functions/roles and, subsequently, to have new or enhanced digital transformation and digital business–related competencies.[4] Managers with these new or enhanced competencies are able to accelerate the digital transformation, digital business, and adaptability/agility capabilities of their organizations. Managers lacking the new or enhanced competencies are at best limited in the value they can create for their organizations and, at worst, they are risky to the long-term survival and competitiveness of their organizations. To cultivate the new or enhanced digital transformation and digital business–related competencies, managers must first understand what these competencies are, their necessity, and their fit and interrelationship with established managerial functions/roles and competencies. In this chapter, we discuss established managerial functions/roles, and how digital technology advancements disrupt them. We then identify the new or enhanced digital transformation and digital business–related competency areas and discuss their fit and interrelationship with established managerial functions/roles. Finally, we discuss the benefits of cultivating these competencies, and the risks of not doing so, for both managers' careers and the fates of their organizations. Our aim is to provide a conceptual framework or lens for hospitality and leisure managers to understand the required new or enhanced roles and competencies, the importance of these roles and competencies to their organizations, and the value of the competencies for supercharging all other managerial functions, roles, and competencies. The subsequent chapters build on this framework with a dedicated chapter on each key digital transformation and digital business capability, hospitality and leisure managers' roles in the creation and optimization of that capability, and the corresponding competencies by hospitality and leisure managers to effectively perform those roles.

Evolution of management functions, roles, and competencies

Resilience of Fayol's management functions

Practitioners and researchers within and outside of the hospitality and leisure industry have long been interested in the job functions or roles of managers, the corresponding competencies required to carry out those functions and roles, and how both functions/roles and competencies evolve in response to the different management challenges facing organizations.[5,6,7,8] Although there have been debates about their meaningfulness and completeness, the management functions of planning, organizing, coordinating, leading, and controlling are still widely accepted.[9] These are based on adaptations and extensions of French management theorist Henri Fayol's ideas from as far back as 1916 (these functions and their interrelationships are shown in Figure 6.1).[10] The planning function involves deciding what needs to happen and how to make it happen (e.g. what objectives/steps/activities to carry out, in what order, by whom, when, with what resources).[11] It includes activities such as setting objectives, forecasting, budgeting, scheduling, and forming policies and procedures.[12] The organizing function involves allocating human and other resources, assigning work, and granting authority.[13] It includes activities such as establishing/configuring organization structures, delegating work, and building relationships.[14] It also includes staffing activities such as recruiting, training, and developing employees. The coordinating function involves aligning the actions and efforts of people

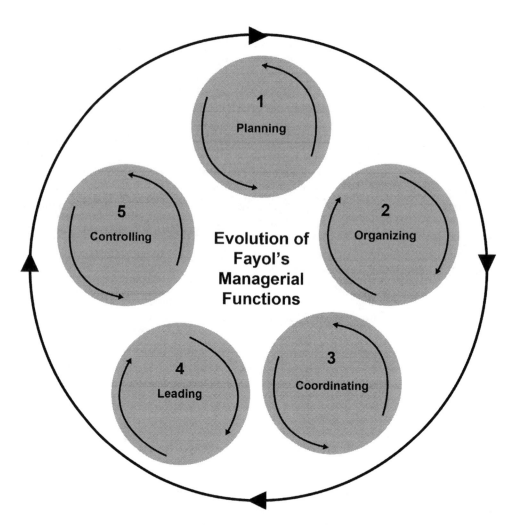

Figure 6.1 Managerial functions as commonly conceptualized today evolved from Fayol's research introduced in 1916

contributing to the plan across functional, department, and hierarchical groups.[15] The leading function involves communicating, motivating, guiding, encouraging, influencing, coaching, and mentoring[16] activities. The controlling function involves activities such as continuously monitoring performance to plan, identifying deviations, and taking corrective actions.[17,18]

Mintzberg's ten managerial roles

Contending that the functions discussed in the previous section didn't really make it clear what day-to-day roles and activities managers undertook, renowned management thinker Henry Mintzberg offered a different view of the job of manager. He proposed that managers are people vested with formal authority over a team or unit. That formal authority enables managers to have status, particular relationships, and access to particular information.[19] As a result, this formal authority gives rise to ten roles of managers. Mintzberg organized these ten roles into three categories: interpersonal, informational, and decision roles (see Figure 6.2).[20] In the interpersonal roles category, the manager fulfills figurehead, leader, and liaison roles.[21] Being a figurehead involves representational activities such as performing ceremonial or symbolic duties, signing legal documents, and greeting dignitaries. Being a leader involves traditional leadership activities like hiring, developing, and influencing and directing staff and other stakeholders.[22] Being a liaison involves facilitating and maintaining information links across formal and informal organization structures and within and outside the organization. In the informational roles category, the manager fulfills monitor, disseminator, and spokesperson roles.[23] Being a monitor involves constantly scanning the internal and external environment for information about risks and opportunities facing the team. For example, external monitoring may involve reviewing relevant information platforms for political, economic, social, technological, ethical, and legal opportunities and threats that may face the team. Internal monitoring may involve formal and informal interactions such as catch-ups with people up the hierarchy, across functions and business units, and in other subgroups. In carrying out monitoring activities, the manager may come across information about opportunities for and threats to the team and its efforts. Being a disseminator involves sharing information between team and organization members (e.g. via emails, reports, memos, meetings).[24] Being a spokesperson involves speaking on behalf of individual team members and of the team as a whole (e.g. speaking up for team members unable to do so by themselves, or speaking for the team up the hierarchy, across functions, and outside the organization).[25] In the decisional roles category, the manager fulfills entrepreneur, disturbance handler, resource allocator, and negotiator roles.[26] Being an entrepreneur involves constantly seeking out new ideas and approaches to improve the team's effectiveness and to adapt it to changing internal and external conditions.[27] Being a disturbance handler involves responding to disruptions, crises, and pressures (e.g. a key employee abruptly quits, a financial crisis or pandemic occurs, a key customer goes out of business).[28] As a resource allocator, the manager decides how to allocate time, financial, talent, attention, and other resources.[29] As a negotiator, the manager represents the team in negotiations (e.g. with senior managers, other departments, unions, other team members).[30] Managerial functions and roles discussed have also included innovation (which can be included in Mintzberg's entrepreneur role or in the leadership role), decision making (which can be included in the planning or leading functions), communicating (which can be included in the leading functions or in Mintzberg's informational roles category), and others.

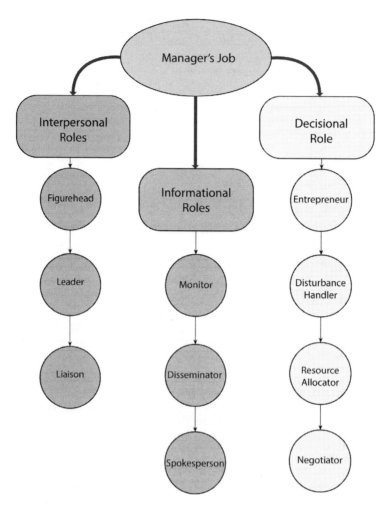

Figure 6.2 Mintzberg's ten roles of managers[31]

Role of managerial competencies in fulfilling managerial functions and roles

Along with identifying key management functions and roles, researchers and practitioners have also explored key competencies or the knowledge/skills/abilities required to effectively perform those functions and roles. To this end, they have identified management competencies such as performance management (e.g. conducting performance planning/facilitation/evaluation; setting employee goals; providing effective employee feedback; ensuring employee efforts and behaviors are aligned with organization requirements); effective communication (e.g. effective communication methods and approaches for face-to-face, virtual, written, and other modes); effective leadership (e.g. authentic, situational, inspirational, and other leadership styles and approaches); effective coaching skills; effective delegation; effective motivation; emotional intelligence; cross–cultural leadership; understanding how the different parts of an organization work together to create value and being able to collaborate with those functions (e.g. working competencies in managerial finance and accounting, marketing, HR, operations, corporate communications, procurement); influencing and negotiation skills; project management skills; strategic thinking/strategic planning/strategic leadership competencies; critical thinking skills; business analysis and problem-solving skills; team-working skills; and ethical/environmental/social responsibility consciousness/promotion or compliance. Many of these competencies/skills are now essential components of tertiary general management programs around the world.

Industry-specific management functions, roles, and competencies

The need for industry-specific managerial roles and functions

The management functions, roles, and competencies we've already discussed so far are generic (i.e. industry or sector agnostic). However, in particular industries, industry specific managerial functions, roles, and competencies may be needed to a greater degree and be more critical to success. For example, in combination with specific technical and/or functional skills, the healthcare industry tends to highly value communication, stakeholder engagement, influencing, and leadership competencies relative to other managerial competencies.[32]

Resilience of Sandwith's competency domain model in the hospitality and leisure industry

Since the early 1980s, hospitality and leisure industry researchers have been interested in identifying the management competencies uniquely required by the industry or of particular importance to success in the industry. To this end, they have identified a range of industry-specific managerial functions and competencies.[33,34,35,36,37,38,39] These typically fit into Paul Sandwith's competency domain model (see Figure 6.3)[40,41,42] – a "domain" can be thought of as a managerial function or role. This model identifies leadership, interpersonal, technical, conceptual–creative, and administrative domains. It also identifies the key competencies within those domains.[43,44,45,46,47]

The leadership domain identifies leadership competencies that are critical to managers in the industry.[48] Given the importance of customer experience in the industry, these competencies are typically customer experience oriented. The key competencies in this domain include developing positive customer relations; recognizing and solving customer problems; managing customer problems with understanding and sensitivity; operating calmly and effectively in crisis situations; cultivating professional appearance and poise; portraying enthusiasm, competence, and confidence; portraying work commitment, diligence, and initiative; maintaining a professional and ethical work environment; cultivating a climate of trust; and maintaining customer satisfaction.[49] The interpersonal domain identifies interpersonal or human interaction skills critical to managerial success in the industry.[50] Key competencies in this domain include listening, face-to-face communication, written and group presentation skills, building rapport, and developing sound working relations with important stakeholders within and outside the organization.[51] The conceptual–creative domain identifies skills in systems thinking/strategic thinking that enable managers to see how the various aspects of the

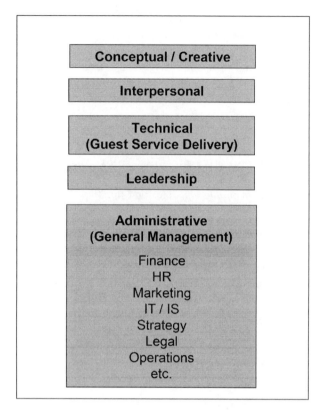

Figure 6.3 Sandwith's competency domain model[52]

organization interact to create/safeguard value as a single system, and how they can be leveraged to do so.[53] Key competencies in this domain include surfacing and nurturing new ideas and being able to adapt creatively to change.[54] The technical domain identifies specific operational activities, processes, methods, and techniques that managers need to be proficient in for success in the industry.[55] These competencies can vary by the specific unit or area that is being managed (e.g. different technical competencies may be emphasized in food and beverage, front office, reservations, housekeeping, concierge, guest services, security, communications).[56] But in general, key competencies in this domain include working knowledge of the industry, working knowledge of the organization's products/services, working knowledge of industry product/service quality assurance standards, daily room availability and room rate management, guest arrival and departure processing, dining room management, relocating/walking guests, working knowledge of credit and no-show policies and procedures, working knowledge of sanitation, cash and bank management, selling skills (e.g. promoting, upselling, crossselling, overcoming objections, closing, dealing with rejection), working knowledge of hospitality information systems, reservation and function space management, and working knowledge of property and facilities management.[57] Finally, the administrative domain is a catchall for remaining management competencies (e.g. financial, marketing, HR, procurement management).[58]

Impact of digital disruption and digital transformation on management functions, roles, and competencies

New or enhanced digital capabilities require new or enhanced managerial roles and competencies

We previously discussed how digital technology advancements disrupt customer expectations and behaviors, disrupt the competitive landscape and bases of competition, and disrupt data availability. We also noted how organizations need to respond to this disruption by undertaking digital business transformation, effectively operating as a digital business, and effectively competing on the strengths of their digital business capabilities. We referred to these required responses as the digital transformation imperative and the digital business imperative. To effectively undertake digital transformation, effectively operate as a digital business, and effectively compete on digital business capabilities, the imperatives require organizations to build and continuously upgrade particular digital transformation and digital business capabilities.[59] Information systems and strategy researchers have identified a number of these capabilities, including digital transformation strategy,[60] digital business strategy,[61] digital leadership,[62,63] digital innovation,[64,65] digital customer and stakeholder engagement,[66] digital customer experience,[67,68,69,70] leveraging key digital technologies (e.g. cloud, IoT, blockchain, artificial intelligence, edge computing), digital learning,[71] enterprise architecture, digital risk management, digital ethics, adaptability/agility,[72,73,74,75] and being able to keep up with exponential digital technology advancements.[76] An organization's capability is essentially what the organization is able to effectively do to create competitive value for its stakeholders, and the capability is derived from people's competencies within the organization. Thus an organization's digital transformation and digital business capabilities imply the need for managers to play particular roles in these capabilities and thus to have particular management competencies for building and sustaining these capabilities. That is, as the people who lead the creation and maintenance of these capabilities, managers need the corresponding knowledge, skills, and abilities (or competencies) in these capability areas. Without such knowledge, skills, and abilities, managers are unlikely to be able to lead successful digital transformation efforts, to adequately lead/manage in digital businesses, and to leverage digital technologies to optimize the adaptability and agility of their organizations.

How new or enhanced managerial functions, roles, and competencies fit with traditional managerial functions, roles, and competencies

The required digital transformation, digital business, and adaptability/agility competencies can either be thought of as catalysts for all other managerial functions/domains (and thus roles and competencies), as enhancements to or extensions of existing managerial functions/domains, or as their own new "digital transformation/digital business" managerial competency function/domain. As a catalyst for all other managerial functions/domains, managerial competencies in the digital transformation and digital business capability areas we have identified can improve the efficiency and effectiveness of managers' planning, organizing, coordinating, leading, and controlling functions. For example, working knowledge or proficiency with digital stakeholder engagement platforms like Jira, Trello, Zoom, Microsoft Teams, Zendesk, LiveChat, Slack, and Culture Amp can enable a manager to perform coordination, communication, and liaison activities more efficiently and effectively. As enhancements to or extensions of existing managerial functions, the new areas we have identified introduce digital roles and competencies to existing managerial competency categories or change the nature of those categories. For example, new digital leadership and digital innovation roles and associated competencies enhance the existing leadership functions by identifying new or existing leadership roles, activities, and competencies that best drive and support digital transformation and digital business capabilities.[77] As their own digital "transformation/digital business" managerial function, the new or enhanced role and competency areas we've identified bring together the digital aspects of managerial work into one function, eliminating debate about where they best fit and whether they replace existing roles and competencies. Whether each of the resultant new competencies can neatly fit into an existing managerial function/role, or whether a new digital transformation or digital business managerial function is needed, is likely to be subject to long debate, and is not our aim here. In this chapter, we had three key aims. First, we wanted to explain how the organization requirement for digital business transformation, digital business, and adaptability/agility capabilities disrupts managerial practice by requiring new or enhanced management roles and competencies. Second, we wanted to identify some of the specific new or enhanced managerial roles and competencies required to help organizations create and maintain the identified digital business, digital business transformation, and adaptability/agility capabilities. Third, we wanted to explain the fit of these new or enhanced roles and competencies with established managerial functions, roles, and competencies. In doing so, we hope we have gotten across to current and future managers that the new or enhanced managerial roles and competencies actually enhance existing managerial functions, roles, and competencies, thus providing the opportunity to supercharge managerial practice.[78]

In the chapters that follow, we will unpack each of the new or enhanced digital transformation and digital business capability areas and the specific new or enhanced managerial roles and competencies required. We will discuss challenges, strategies, and benefits of acquiring and using the new competencies. We will also discuss the risks of not doing so to both organizations' survival and to managerial career prospects.

Implications for current and future hospitality and leisure managers

Digital technology advancements are disrupting organizations and, in turn, disrupting managerial practice (i.e. changing required managerial roles and competencies for success).[79,80] In the past, hospitality and leisure managers could get away with relegating digital technology issues to the IT or IS function, in order to focus on people, strategic, and operational issues. Perhaps they reasoned they could create more value for their organizations by focusing on the industry-critical managerial functions, roles, and competencies we discussed earlier. But now, digital business is the main business, and digital transformation and digital business issues are arguably the most critical people, strategic, and operational issues.[81] Hospitality and leisure managers who attempt to relegate digital business and digital business transformation issues or think they can get by solely on the strengths of their other managerial competencies (i.e. with limited or no digital technology, digital transformation, digital business, and adaptability/agility competencies) put their organizations' survival (and their managerial careers) at risk. That is, without the relevant digital transformation and digital business competencies, their management/leadership capacity is severely limited, to the point that they may in fact become significant obstacles to their organizations' survival.

Google and reflect

Digital transformation strategy, digital business strategy, digital leadership, digital innovation, digital customer engagement, digital employee engagement, digital stakeholder engagement, digital customer experience, enterprise architecture, digital risk management, adaptability, agility, being able to keep up with digital technology advancements.

Discussion questions

1 Which model of managerial work best describes managerial work as you currently understand it: the one based on Henri Fayol's research, the one based on Henry Mintzberg's research, or the one based on Paul Sandwith's research?
2 How do digital technology advancements disrupt managerial work?
3 Who is more valuable to a hospitality and leisure organization: a rooms division manager with strong digital transformation/digital business competencies but average competencies in all other areas, or one with minimal digital transformation/digital business competencies but first-rate leadership/interpersonal/service skills?
4 Why isn't a good IT/IS department sufficient (i.e. why do hospitality and leisure managers have to develop digital transformation/digital business competencies on top of everything else they have to learn)?
5 What is digital customer engagement? What challenges would a manager without digital technology/digital transformation/digital business competencies face in building and optimizing competitive digital customer engagement capabilities?
6 How do digital technology/digital transformation/digital business competencies enhance the performance of all other managerial functions/roles?
7 Could a manager lead at a mature digital business like Google or Amazon without digital technology/digital transformation/digital business competencies?
8 Could a manager effectively lead the introduction of virtual assistants, customer service robots, and cobots (collaborative robots) without compromising guest experience if they did not have knowledge/skills/abilities in artificial intelligence?
9 How are organization capabilities and managerial competencies related? Could an organization have capabilities in an area but not have any managerial competencies in that area? If so, could it sustain that capability?
10 Which hospitality and leisure organizations have world-class digital business capabilities? What is the growth rate and profitability of these organizations relative to their peers who are less digital business capable?
11 Identify a hospitality and leisure organization that has successfully undertaken digital business transformation efforts and one that has undertaken disastrous ones.

Notes

1 Araujo, C. (2019, January 9). The "Future of Work" in the Digital Era May Not Be What You Think. Retrieved May 29, 2020, from CIO website: www.cio.com/article/3332203/the-future-of-work-in-the-digital-era-may-not-be-what-you-think.html
2 Gleeson, B. (2017, March 28). The Future of Leadership and Management in the 21st-Century Organization. Forbes. Retrieved from www.forbes.com/sites/brentgleeson/2017/03/27/the-future-of-leadership-and-management-in-the-21st-century-organization/#2ff06d1b218f

3 Grant, R. M. (2008). The Future of Management: Where is Gary Hamel Leading Us? *Long Range Planning*, 41(5), 469–482. https://doi.org/10.1016/j.lrp.2008.06.003

4 Weill, P. (2018, June 28). Why Companies Need a New Playbook to Succeed in the Digital Age. Retrieved May 29, 2020, from MIT Sloan Management Review website: https://sloanreview.mit.edu/article/why-companies-need-a-new-playbook-to-succeed-in-the-digital-age/

5 Giddens, A. (1981). *A Contemporary Critique of Historical Materialism* (Vol. 1). University of California Press.

6 Lynch, F. M. (1997). Management, Labour and Industrial Politics in Modern Europe: The Quest for Productivity Growth During the Twentieth Century. *Business History*, 39(2), 138–140.

7 Waring, S. P. (2016). *Taylorism Transformed: Scientific Management Theory Since 1945*. UNC Press Books.

8 Carroll, S. J., & Gillen, D. I. (1987). Are the Classical Management Functions Useful in Describing Managerial Work? *Academy of Management Review*, 12(1), 38–51.

9 Levin, J. S. (2019, April 17). Council Post: The Role of the Successful Manager in Four Simple Functions. Forbes. Retrieved from www.forbes.com/sites/forbescoachescouncil/2019/04/17/the-role-of-the-successful-manager-in-four-simple-functions/#1c1b22721b12

10 Mintzberg, H. (1990). The Manager's Job: Folklore and Fact. Harvard Business Review. Retrieved June 18, 2020, from Harvard Business Review website: https://hbr.org/1990/03/the-managers-job-folklore-and-fact

11 Peaucelle, J. L. (2015). *Henri Fayol, The Manager*. Routledge.

12 Levin, J. S. (2019, April 17). Council Post: The Role of the Successful Manager in Four Simple Functions. Forbes. Retrieved from www.forbes.com/sites/forbescoachescouncil/2019/04/17/the-role-of-the-successful-manager-in-four-simple-functions/#1c1b22721b12

13 Peaucelle, J. L. (2015). *Henri Fayol, The Manager*. Routledge.

14 Levin, J. S. (2019, April 17). Council Post: The Role of the Successful Manager in Four Simple Functions. Forbes. Retrieved from www.forbes.com/sites/forbescoachescouncil/2019/04/17/the-role-of-the-successful-manager-in-four-simple-functions/#1c1b22721b12

15 Peaucelle, J. L. (2015). *Henri Fayol, The Manager*. Routledge.

16 Levin, J. S. (2019, April 17). Council Post: The Role of the Successful Manager in Four Simple Functions. Forbes. Retrieved from www.forbes.com/sites/forbescoachescouncil/2019/04/17/the-role-of-the-successful-manager-in-four-simple-functions/#1c1b22721b12

17 Peaucelle, J. L. (2015). *Henri Fayol, The Manager*. Routledge.

18 Levin, J. S. (2019, April 17). Council Post: The Role of the Successful Manager in Four Simple Functions. Forbes. Retrieved from www.forbes.com/sites/forbescoachescouncil/2019/04/17/the-role-of-the-successful-manager-in-four-simple-functions/#1c1b22721b12

19 Mintzberg, H. (1990). The Manager's Job: Folklore and Fact. Harvard Business Review. Retrieved June 18, 2020, from Harvard Business Review website: https://hbr.org/1990/03/the-managers-job-folklore-and-fact

20 Mintzberg, H. (1990). The Manager's Job: Folklore and Fact. Harvard Business Review. Retrieved June 18, 2020, from Harvard Business Review website: https://hbr.org/1990/03/the-managers-job-folklore-and-fact

21 Mintzberg, H. (1990). The Manager's Job: Folklore and Fact. Harvard Business Review. Retrieved June 18, 2020, from Harvard Business Review website: https://hbr.org/1990/03/the-managers-job-folklore-and-fact

22 Mintzberg, H. (1990). The Manager's Job: Folklore and Fact. Harvard Business Review. Retrieved June 18, 2020, from Harvard Business Review website: https://hbr.org/1990/03/the-managers-job-folklore-and-fact

23 Mintzberg, H. (1990). The Manager's Job: Folklore and Fact. Harvard Business Review. Retrieved June 18, 2020, from Harvard Business Review website: https://hbr.org/1990/03/the-managers-job-folklore-and-fact

24 Mintzberg, H. (1990). The Manager's Job: Folklore and Fact. Harvard Business Review. Retrieved June 18, 2020, from Harvard Business Review website: https://hbr.org/1990/03/the-managers-job-folklore-and-fact

25 Mintzberg, H. (1990). The Manager's Job: Folklore and Fact. Harvard Business Review. Retrieved June 18, 2020, from Harvard Business Review website: https://hbr.org/1990/03/the-managers-job-folklore-and-fact

26 Mintzberg, H. (1990). The Manager's Job: Folklore and Fact. Harvard Business Review. Retrieved June 18, 2020, from Harvard Business Review website: https://hbr.org/1990/03/the-managers-job-folklore-and-fact

27 Mintzberg, H. (1990). The Manager's Job: Folklore and Fact. Harvard Business Review. Retrieved June 18, 2020, from Harvard Business Review website: https://hbr.org/1990/03/the-managers-job-folklore-and-fact

28 Mintzberg, H. (1990). The Manager's Job: Folklore and Fact. Harvard Business Review. Retrieved June 18, 2020, from Harvard Business Review website: https://hbr.org/1990/03/the-managers-job-folklore-and-fact

29 Mintzberg, H. (1990). The Manager's Job: Folklore and Fact. Harvard Business Review. Retrieved June 18, 2020, from Harvard Business Review website: https://hbr.org/1990/03/the-managers-job-folklore-and-fact

30 Mintzberg, H. (1990). The Manager's Job: Folklore and Fact. Harvard Business Review. Retrieved June 18, 2020, from Harvard Business Review website: https://hbr.org/1990/03/the-managers-job-folklore-and-fact

31 Mintzberg, H. (1990). The Manager's Job: Folklore and Fact. Harvard Business Review. Retrieved June 18, 2020, from Harvard Business Review website: https://hbr.org/1990/03/the-managers-job-folklore-and-fact

32 Australasian College of Health Service Management. (2020). ACHSM Management Competencies Assessment Tool. Retrieved from www.achsm.org.au/Portals/15/documents/education/internship/vic/ACHSM_Management_Competencies_Assessment_Toold6f5.pdf

33 Burgermeister, J. (1983). Assessment of the Educational Skills and Competencies Needed by Beginning Hospitality Managers. *Hospitality Education and Research Journal*, 8(1), 38–53.

34 Tas, R. F. (1988). Teaching Future Managers. *The Cornell Hotel & Restaurant Administration Quarterly*, 29(2), 41–43. https://doi.org/10.1177/001088048802900215

35 Goodman, R. J., Jr., Sprague, L. G., & Jones, W. P. (1991). The Future of Hospitality Education: Meeting the Industry's Needs. *The Cornell Hotel and Restaurant Administration Quarterly*, 32(2), 66–70. https://doi.org/10.1016/0010-8804(91)90081-2

36 Umbreit, W. T. (1992). In Search of Hospitality Curriculum Relevance for the 1990s. *Hospitality & Tourism Educator*, 5(1), 71–74.

37 Weber, M. R., Crawford, A., Lee, J., & Dennison, D. (2013). An Exploratory Analysis of Soft Skill Competencies Needed for the Hospitality Industry. *Journal of Human Resources in Hospitality & Tourism*, 12(4), 313–332. https://doi.org/10.1080/15332845.2013.790245

38 Alexakis, G., & Jiang, L. (2019). Industry Competencies and the Optimal Hospitality Management Curriculum: An Empirical Study. *Journal of Hospitality & Tourism Education*, 31(4), 210–220. https://doi.org/10.1080/10963758.2019.1575748

39 Cheung, C., Law, R., & He, K. (2010). Essential Hotel Managerial Competencies for Graduate Students. *Journal of Hospitality & Tourism Education*, 22(4), 25–32, https://doi.org/10.1080/10963758.2010.10696989

40 Burgermeister, J. (1983). Assessment of the Educational Skills and Competencies Needed by Beginning Hospitality Managers. *Hospitality Education and Research Journal*, 8(1), 38–53.

41 Tas, R. F. (1988). Teaching Future Managers. *The Cornell Hotel & Restaurant Administration Quarterly*, 29(2), 41–43. https://doi.org/10.1177/001088048802900215

42 Goodman, R. J., Jr., Sprague, L. G., & Jones, W. P. (1991). The Future of Hospitality Education: Meeting the Industry's Needs. *The Cornell Hotel and Restaurant Administration Quarterly*, 32(2), 66–70. https://doi.org/10.1016/0010-8804(91)90081-2

43 Sandwith, P. (1993). A Hierarchy of Management Training Requirements: The Competency Domain Model. *Public Personnel Management*, 22(1), 43–62.

44 Umbreit, W. T. (1992). In Search of Hospitality Curriculum Relevance for the 1990s. *Hospitality & Tourism Educator*, 5(1), 71–74.

45 Weber, M. R., Crawford, A., Lee, J., & Dennison, D. (2013). An Exploratory Analysis of Soft Skill Competencies Needed for the Hospitality Industry. *Journal of Human Resources in Hospitality & Tourism*, 12(4), 313–332. https://doi.org/10.1080/15332845.2013.790245

46 Alexakis, G., & Jiang, L. (2019). Industry Competencies and the Optimal Hospitality Management Curriculum: An Empirical Study. *Journal of Hospitality & Tourism Education*, 31(4), 210–220. https://doi.org/10.1080/10963758.2019.1575748

47 Cheung, C., Law, R., & He, K. (2010). Essential Hotel Managerial Competencies for Graduate Students. *Journal of Hospitality & Tourism Education*, 22(4), 25–32. https://doi.org/10.1080/10963758.2010.10696989

48 Porter, J. D. (2005). *Application of Sandwith's Competency Domain Model for Senior College Housing Officers in the United States*. University of Florida.

49 Kay, C., & Russette, J. (2000). Hospitality-Management Competencies. *Cornell Hotel and Restaurant Administration Quarterly*, 41(2), 52–63. https://doi.org/10.1016/S0010-8804(00)88898-9

50 Porter, J. D. (2005). *Application of Sandwith's Competency Domain Model for Senior College Housing Officers in the United States*. University of Florida.

51 Kay, C., & Russette, J. (2000). Hospitality-Management Competencies. *Cornell Hotel and Restaurant Administration Quarterly*, 41(2), 52–63. https://doi.org/10.1016/S0010-8804(00)88898-9

52 Sandwith, P. (1993). A Hierarchy of Management Training Requirements: The Competency Domain Model. *Public Personnel Management*, 22(1), 43–62.

53 Porter, J. D. (2005). *Application of Sandwith's Competency Domain Model for Senior College Housing Officers in the United States*. University of Florida.

54 Kay, C., & Russette, J. (2000). Hospitality-Management Competencies. *Cornell Hotel and Restaurant Administration Quarterly*, 41(2), 52–63. https://doi.org/10.1016/S0010-8804(00)88898-9

55 Porter, J. D. (2005). *Application of Sandwith's Competency Domain Model for Senior College Housing Officers in the United States*. University of Florida.

56 Kay, C., & Russette, J. (2000). Hospitality-Management Competencies. *Cornell Hotel and Restaurant Administration Quarterly*, 41(2), 52–63. https://doi.org/10.1016/S0010-8804(00)88898-9

57 Kay, C., & Russette, J. (2000). Hospitality-Management Competencies. *Cornell Hotel and Restaurant Administration Quarterly*, 41(2), 52–63. https://doi.org/10.1016/S0010-8804(00)88898-9

58 Porter, J. D. (2005). *Application of Sandwith's Competency Domain Model for Senior College Housing Officers in the United States*. University of Florida.

59 Westerman, G. (2012, October 29). The Digital Capabilities Your Company Needs. Retrieved May 29, 2020, from MIT Sloan Management Review website: https://sloanreview.mit.edu/article/the-digital-capabilities-your-company-needs/

60 Vial, G. (2019). Understanding Digital Transformation: A Review and a Research Agenda. *The Journal of Strategic Information Systems*, 28(2), 118–144. https://doi.org/10.1016/j.jsis.2019.01.003

61 Vial, G. (2019). Understanding Digital Transformation: A Review and a Research Agenda. *The Journal of Strategic Information Systems*, 28(2), 118–144. https://doi.org/10.1016/j.jsis.2019.01.003

62 Cortellazzo, L., Bruni, E., & Zampieri, R. (2019). The Role of Leadership in a Digitalized World: A Review. Retrieved from www.frontiersin.org/articles/10.3389/fpsyg.2019.01938/full

63 Avolio, B. J., Sosik, J. J., Kahai, S. S., & Baker, B. (2014). E-Leadership: Re-Examining Transformations in Leadership Source and Transmission. *The Leadership Quarterly*, 25(1), 105–131.

64 Demirkan, H., Spohrer, J. C., & Welser, J. J. (2016). Digital Innovation and Strategic Transformation. *IT Professional*, 18(6), 14–18.

65 Warner, K. S., & Wäger, M. (2019). Building Dynamic Capabilities for Digital Transformation: An Ongoing Process of Strategic Renewal. *Long Range Planning*, 52(3), 326–349.

66 Eigenraam, A. W., Eelen, J., Van Lin, A., & Verlegh, P. W. (2018). A Consumer-based Taxonomy of Digital Customer Engagement Practices. *Journal of Interactive Marketing*, 44, 102–121.

67 Bolton, R. N., McColl-Kennedy, J. R., Cheung, L., Gallan, A., Orsingher, C., Witell, L., & Zaki, M. (2018). Customer Experience Challenges: Bringing Together Digital, Physical and Social Realms. *Journal of Service Management*, 29(5), 776–808.

68 Nadeem, A., Abedin, B., Cerpa, N., & Chew, E. (2018). Digital Transformation & Digital Business Strategy in Electronic Commerce: The Role of Organizational Capabilities. *Journal of Theoretical and Applied Electronic Commerce Research*, 13(2), i–viii.

69 Betzing, J. H., Beverungen, D., & Becker, J. (2018). Design Principles for Co-creating Digital Customer Experience in High Street Retail. *Proceedings of the Multikonferenz Wirtschaftsinformatik, MKWI*, 18.

70 Parise, S., Guinan, P. J., & Kafka, R. (2016). Solving the Crisis of Immediacy: How Digital Technology Can Transform the Customer Experience. *Business Horizons*, 59(4), 411–420.

71 Sousa, M. J., & Rocha, Á. (2019). Digital Learning: Developing Skills for Digital Transformation of Organizations. *Future Generation Computer Systems*, 91, 327–334.

72 Cozzolino, A., Verona, G., & Rothaermel, F. T. (2018). Unpacking the Disruption Process: New Technology, Business Models, and Incumbent Adaptation. *Journal of Management Studies*, 55(7), 1166–1202.

73 Busulwa, R., Tice, M., & Gurd, B. (2018). *Strategy Execution and Complexity: Thriving in the Era of Disruption*. Routledge.

74 Burgelman, R. A. (1991). Intraorganizational Ecology of Strategy Making and Organizational Adaptation: Theory and Field Research. *Organization Science*, 2(3), 239–262.

75 Birkinshaw, J., Zimmermann, A., & Raisch, S. (2016). How Do Firms Adapt to Discontinuous Change? Bridging the Dynamic Capabilities and Ambidexterity Perspectives. *California Management Review*, 58(4), 36–58.

76 Rong, G., & Grover, V. (2009). Keeping Up-to-Date with Information Technology: Testing a Model of Technological Knowledge Renewal Effectiveness for it Professionals. *Information & Management*, 46(7), 376–387.

77 Kane, G. C. (2019, March 12). How Digital Leadership Is(n't) Different. Retrieved May 29, 2020, from MIT Sloan Management Review website: https://sloanreview.mit.edu/article/how-digital-leadership-isnt-different/

78 Kane, G. C. (2019, March 12). How Digital Leadership Is(n't) Different. Retrieved May 29, 2020, from MIT Sloan Management Review website: https://sloanreview.mit.edu/article/how-digital-leadership-isnt-different/

79 Araujo, C. (2019, January 9). The "Future of Work" in the Digital Era May Not Be What You Think. Retrieved May 29, 2020, from CIO website: www.cio.com/article/3332203/the-future-of-work-in-the-digital-era-may-not-be-what-you-think.html

80 Grant, R. M. (2008). The Future of Management: Where is Gary Hamel Leading Us? *Long Range Planning*, 41(5), 469–482. https://doi.org/10.1016/j.lrp.2008.06.003

81 Weill, P. (2018, June 28). Why Companies Need a New Playbook to Succeed in the Digital Age. Retrieved May 29, 2020, from MIT Sloan Management Review website: https://sloanreview.mit.edu/article/why-companies-need-a-new-playbook-to-succeed-in-the-digital-age/

Part III

Leveraging digital technologies to thrive in the digital era

Roles of hospitality and leisure managers

7 Role of hospitality and leisure managers in digital business transformation strategy, digital business strategy, digital innovation, digital learning, adaptability, and agility

Introduction

In the previous chapter, we identified critical organization capabilities necessary to effectively participate in digital business transformation and to compete as a digital business. We also pointed out that for hospitality and leisure organizations to effect these organization capabilities, hospitality and leisure managers have to play particular roles, and they require particular competencies to play those roles. In this chapter, we unpack a subset of the previously identified capabilities (i.e. digital business transformation strategy, digital business strategy, digital innovation, digital learning, and adaptability/agility/ ambidexterity capabilities). Specifically, we discuss what the capabilities mean, how they differ from their traditional or nondigital counterparts, and what their value is to organization performance and longevity. We then identify the key roles hospitality and leisure managers can play in building and maintaining each of these organization capabilities and what competencies they require to perform those key roles. Each of the capabilities identified be a complex area with lots of depth, interdisciplinary knowledge, slippery terms and concepts, and practice challenges. Our aim is to provide a meaningful introduction to the digital capability, required roles, and required competencies so managers can have a starting point and a contextual framework to support further and lifelong learning/competency development in these important capability areas. Figure 7.1 shows how traditional business capabilities and digital business capabilities have similar aims (e.g. improved business performance and longevity). However, they differ in their ability to deliver on those common aims. Digital transformation is required to effect digital business capabilities. And effecting digital transformation also requires particular capabilities (e.g. digital business transformation strategy, digital leadership).

Required managerial roles and competencies for digital business strategy and digital transformation strategy

Unpacking digital business strategy

Digital business strategy is strategy formed and realized by leveraging digital resources to achieve breakthroughs in efficiency, differentiation, adaptability, and agility.[1] It fuses together the domains of information systems and business strategy so that, rather than being positioned below business strategy or being a component of business strategy (like traditional IT strategy), digital business strategy becomes business strategy itself.[2] This is because digital technology advancements continue to rapidly fuse together people,

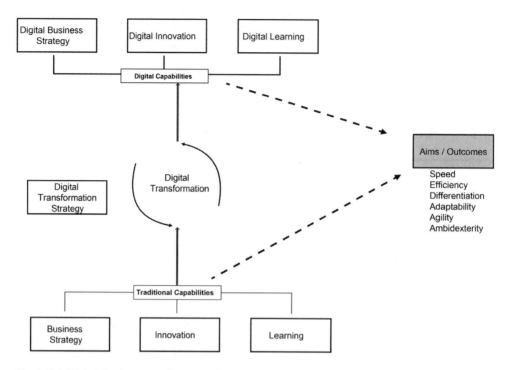

Figure 7.1 Digital business requires new organization capabilities or enhancements of traditional capabilities

Note: These new or enhanced capabilities are effected through digital transformation, which in turn requires new capabilities like digital transformation strategy. The aims of traditional and digital business are similar, although some aims become much more important to digital business.

processes, technologies, networks, and things within and outside organizations (or blur the boundaries between them) to such a degree that conceiving strategy separately is increasingly becoming counterproductive. When digital business strategy becomes the business strategy itself, it is able to be a strategic dynamic capability that enables organizations to dynamically configure and orchestrate diverse digital assets to respond to and shape changes in marketplaces.[3]

Jeanne Ross and Ina Sebastian, researchers at the MIT Center for Information Systems Research, and Cynthia Beath, emerita professor of information systems at the University of Texas, propose that a great digital business strategy sets a clear direction.[4] In doing so, it enables managers to form and lead digital initiatives, assess their progress against the set direction, and adapt their efforts as required.[5] Sunil Gupta, professor of business administration at Harvard Business School, and chair of the executive program on driving digital strategy, warns that digital business strategy shouldn't just be thought of as having an independent digital unit, or running digital experiments. That thinking of it as having an independent digital unit is like launching a speedboat to turn around a large ship (there will be lots of activity and speed but it won't turn around the ship); and just running digital experiments, without a clear roadmap, may result in proliferation of disjointed ideas that don't address fundamental strategic issues.[6] He also cautions that, while organizations should always pursue cost reduction and operational efficiency, viewing digital business strategy solely as a leveraging technology to reduce costs and improve operational efficiency ignores the potential (and high) likelihood of technology fundamentally disrupting the business and its industry.[7] This is consistent with the thinking of Ross, Sebastian, and Beath, who clarify that operational excellence (efficiency and effectiveness) is a digital business commodity, not a basis for competitive advantage. These three researchers also argue that organizations should choose between a customer engagement strategy (one that "targets superior, personalized experiences that engender customer loyalty") or a digitized solutions strategy (one that "targets information-enriched products and services that deliver new value for customers"), but should not attempt both, as they risk doing both badly.[8]

Digital business strategy is about managers determining what combination of digital assets to leverage, and how to leverage them to effectively compete as a digital business. Effectively competing as a digital business requires competing on new and evolving bases of competition: being able to rapidly flex operations up or down in response to disruptions or changes in demand (e.g. elastic cloud infrastructure);[9] benefiting from network effects and multi-sided business models;[10] being able to scale rapidly (e.g. between 1996 and 1999 Amazon grew from 151 employees, generating $5.1 million revenue to 7,600 employees generating $1.64 billion revenue);[11,12] using shared digital asset alliances and partnerships (e.g. hospitality and leisure organizations that share reservation systems, loyalty programs, and online cross-selling networks/alliances, such as Star Alliance and OneWorld); taking advantage of speed (e.g. speed to market of new products, match speed of complementary product partners and of competitors, speed of decision making, real-time customer sensing and responsiveness, speed of supply chain orchestration, speed of network formation and adaptation);[13] and expanded value creation/capture opportunities (e.g. leveraging growing data availability for product innovation, creating and capturing value from coordinating different business models in networks, building and controlling industry platforms and ecosystems).[14]

Role of digital transformation strategy in digital business strategy

Whereas digital business strategy focuses on "future states" and how to realize them, digital business transformation strategy focuses on having and effecting the blueprint for navigating the structural and cultural changes required to effectively integrate and be able to leverage digital technologies.[15] Thus digital business strategy and digital business transformation strategy differ but go hand in hand. Doing digital business strategy and digital transformation strategy right offers breakthroughs in efficiency, product/service differentiation, adaptability, and agility that just aren't possible without bringing together and orchestrating contemporary digital assets. In turn, it can shift organizations into the category of disruptors that are rewarded with a lion's share of value capture across markets, industries, and geographies. Turning a blind eye to digital business strategy and digital transformation strategy, or doing them in a token way or by half measures, is the path to loss of competitiveness, disruption, and potentially irreversible survival risks (e.g. at a certain point, Blockbuster and Kodak could not turn back time and reorient themselves).

New or enhanced managerial roles and competencies required for digital business strategy and digital transformation strategy

Given their intimate understanding of customers, markets, products/services, and operational processes, hospitality and leisure managers need to play critical roles in digital

business strategy and digital transformation strategy. These roles include leading the formation and realization of a digital business strategy (e.g. establishing a clear mission, vision,
and direction for digital business; identifying and leading digital business initiatives; motivating
people at different levels and in different parts of the organization to participate in the building
and leveraging of digital business capabilities; aligning digital business efforts). They include
participating in digital business strategy formation (e.g. contributing ideas for business model
innovations; digital assets to implement and leverage; networks/ecosystems/communities
to participate in; product/service innovations; customer experience innovations). And they
include championing and supporting digital business strategy initiatives and cultural changes
(e.g. leveraging managers' formal and informal networks to encourage employees to understand and embrace digital business strategy initiatives, ensuring managers' direct reports have
relevant knowledge and skills, and modeling appropriate attitudes and behaviors).

To effectively lead, participate in, and champion digital business strategy and digital transformation strategy efforts, hospitality and leisure managers need corresponding digital competencies. The lack of such competencies may be a key reason why managerial unwillingness
to experiment with new business models is a major barrier to incumbent organizations' digital business transformation efforts. Based on our research, we propose that the required digital
competencies include having an understanding of different digital technology advancements
and their strategic implications (e.g. what digital asset opportunities do advancements in IoT,
AI, blockchain, robotics, and drones present?); having working knowledge of the technical
aspects of these digital technologies (e.g. how do they work, what are the limitations and
issues, what is really involved in implementing and using them, what is hype and what is
reality?); having a working understanding of different digital business strategy approaches and
benefits (e.g. different business models, approaches to digital infrastructure configuration,
approaches to alliances and partnership, approaches to network and ecosystem participation,
approaches to product innovation and enhancement, approaches to adaptability and agility);
having a working understanding of digital business bases of competition and the value of
key platforms and ecosystems; and having a working understanding of digital transformation strategies and accelerated change/transformation approaches (speed is critical to digital
business strategy, so managers leading digital strategy initiatives need to understand effective approaches for rapidly implementing an instituting digital business strategy initiatives so
they aren't undermined, rejected, or killed off by the wider organization. Examples of these
approaches include agile methodologies[16,17] lean thinking principles/practices[18,19,20] lean
startup practices,[21] design thinking approaches,[22] startup accelerator practices,[23] and strategy
making processes such as the change acceleration process[24]).

Required managerial roles and competencies for digital innovation

Unpacking digital innovation

From an organization perspective, innovation refers to the introduction and application of new products, processes, and ideals that have or can have a significant and positive
net impact on organization performance.[25] This definition of innovation refers to both
the process or practice of innovating as well as the outcomes of the innovation process.
Thus, innovation discussions or efforts can be focusing on how innovation occurs (e.g.
what processes, activities, stakeholders, tools) or on what types of new products/services/
other benefits are realized from innovation efforts. Digital technology advancements,

digital transformation, and digital business change or expand the nature of innovation and the potential impact of innovation. That is, they change or expand how innovation can be done (i.e. innovation processes/practices), the nature of innovation outcomes (i.e. new products/processes/value created), and or the impact of innovation outcomes (e.g. enabling near instant global scalability to billions of consumers). The new or expanded way that innovation can occur, the types of new products/services/value creations that can occur, and the speed/scope of their impact, is what is referred to as digital innovation. Digital innovation has been formally defined by researchers as both the new products/services/business processes/models and other forms of stakeholder value created through the use of digital technologies, and as the process of using digital technologies to create (and subsequently change) these new products/services/business processes/models and other forms of stakeholder value.[26] Other formal definitions include that it is "the carrying out of new combinations of digital and physical components to produce novel products,"[27] that it is "the use of digital technologies in the process of innovating," and that it is the infusion of digital technologies into innovation outcomes and processes.[28]

Digital innovation differs from traditional innovation in four important ways. First, the nature of innovation outputs differs in that the outputs have digital or digital/physical hybrids that are programmable/reprogrammable.[29] Thus they are malleable, editable, open, transferable, and continuously shifting. They can, and often need to, continue to be improved even once they are in customer's hands. This continued evolution/improvement can even be done by customers[30] or other stakeholders outside of the organization.[31,32,33] The innovation outputs can be both products and platforms. The outputs can have several layers (e.g. device layer, network layer, service layer, content layer), with an organization competing on one or more layers but collaborating on other layers.[34] The outputs can be made to think for themselves, continue to work for their creators (e.g. collecting data), improve themselves (e.g. using AI), collaborate with other outputs (e.g. AI/IoT products), exist as orchestrated collections with other outputs, and more (e.g. Apple's iPhone can tick most of these characteristics). Second, the nature of the innovation process differs in that digital innovation processes are digitized, have blurred boundaries between stages of the innovation process (e.g. continuous iterative cycles of empathizing, defining, testing, releasing a new innovation), are much more fluid and nonlinear, and more open.[35] For example, digital innovation processes can be both intra- and/or inter-organizational and leverage community-based generativity and platform-based network effects (e.g. crowdsourcing, crowdfunding, network-centric innovation platforms). Third, digital innovation differs from traditional innovation in that the innovation actors, or the people/entities/things doing the innovation, aren't just employees. Instead, they can also include dynamic and often unexpected collections of actors (or innovation collectives) with different interests, motivations, abilities, and tools.[36,37,38] Concepts such as distributed innovation, open innovation, network-centric innovation, shared cognition, and joint sense-making reflect different approaches to facilitating innovation among diverse actors.[39,40,41] Fourth, digital innovation involves use of different tools to facilitate the innovation process and act as components in innovation outputs: for example, a broad swath of new digital technologies (e.g. 3D/4D printing, AI, blockchain, big data) and tools (e.g. crowdsourcing/crowdfunding platforms, smart devices and algorithms, data analytics/data science models) can facilitate innovation processes or be used in innovative new products.[42,43,44] Exponential growth in the number and abilities of these technologies and tools is rapidly expanding their role in facilitating innovation processes/practices and as key components of innovation outputs.[45] Fortunately for innovation leaders and innovators, digital innovation can simplify, democratize, and drastically lower the cost of innovation outputs. Table 7.1 provides examples of the different ways digital technology advancements impact digital innovation and provides examples of these impacts in action.

New or enhanced managerial roles and competencies required for digital innovation

Hospitality and leisure managers at all levels can play a range of critical roles in digital innovation. Examples of these roles include setting or clarifying the innovation vision and direction, effectively leading/managing/facilitating innovation processes, identifying/ensuring use of the right tools for optimizing innovation process and outcomes, effectively engaging innovation collectives across relevant networks and ecosystems, instituting the right mindsets and behaviors for digital innovation, building/continuously upgrading organization innovative capacity, and ensuring effective capture of organization value from innovation efforts and outputs. To play such roles, hospitality and leisure managers need to understand digital innovation, have working knowledge of different digital innovation platforms/tools/ methodologies/practices, have a working knowledge of digital innovation collectives and how to best leverage them, have working knowledge of important digital technologies to the innovation process and to innovation outputs, and have strong digital leadership skills.

Required managerial roles and competencies for digital learning

Unpacking digital learning

Organizations have long been interested in employee/workforce/workplace-based learning as a driver of competitive advantage and a safeguard to disruption or loss of competitiveness. To this end, they have commonly been interested in how to optimize learning (maximize the knowledge/skills/abilities derived by employees from learning efforts and the subsequent value created from that learning) and invested in upgrading their workforce learning capability. But for each gain they have made, digital technology advancements, in combination with unprecedented growth in complexity/uncertainty, regulation, compliance requirements, globalization, and competition, have exponentially expanded the nature and amount of learning required. This has resulted in many employees finding themselves unable to keep up with technological advances that affect their everyday work processes as their knowledge/skills become obsolete quickly and new knowledge/skill requirements are increasingly necessitated[47] (e.g. new skills with big data, data analytics and artificial intelligence). In response, companies have sought ways to close the learning gap (the gap between actual and required workforce knowledge/skills/abilities).[48] As a result, workforce learning has evolved from traditional, instructor-centered, class-style delivery to become much more online, interactive, multidisciplinary, multiplatform, multi-device, portable, user-centered/personalized, self-directed, gamified, always on anywhere/anytime/real time, immersive, social, and so forth.[49] These evolutions have largely been made possible by digital technology advancements.

Digital learning, then, is employee learning that leverages digital technologies in the learning process, learning content, and/or learning outcomes. It has been described as a both planned and/or unplanned, implicit and/or explicit, multi-technology and/or multi-device, intentional and/or unintentional, spontaneous/unconscious and/or planned/ defined, independent/autonomous and/or directed/controlled, and occurring in the

Table 7.1 Impact of digital technology advancements on digital innovation and examples of opportunities that can be leveraged[46]

Impact Type	Impact Description	Examples
Industry transformation	industry and market convergence; transformation of whole industries	Apple, Bonnier, Netflix, GM OnStar, 3D printing, digital convergence
Distinctive diffusion dynamics	standards wars, risk of stranding	VHS vs. Beta; Apple Mac vs. Windows; iPhone vs. Android; HD DVD vs. Blu-ray
Greater diversity of products and services	greater diversity of products and services developed and offered ("long tail" effect)	Netflix, Amazon, Hulu's customized ads, Zara's quicker and more localized market, social media/user-generated content
Greater personalization of products and services	greater personalization of novel processes, products, and services	Personalization, mass customization, gamification
Faster innovation cycles and processes	more rapid development and evolution of innovative processes and products	Capital One, Shinsei Bank, Enterprise IT at SYSCO, Zara's Fast Fashion, CVS
Faster/broader product diffusion	accelerated emergence and faster/broader diffusion of new products and business models	DVD players, iPhone/smartphones, tablet computers, Facebook/social networking
Product pricing and delivery flexibility	increased control over how digital products are used, when, and by whom (e.g. bundling, trials, "freemium" models); greater pricing flexibility (e.g. how much is charged, to whom, when, by what mechanism, and for what level of functionality)	Napster, Rhapsody, Hulu, YouTube
New ways to market new products	new avenues for marketing and supporting new products	Google, Facebook, Twitter
Move to smart technologies and servitization	widespread emergence of "smart" technologies; accelerated move to servitization (converting products into services) and other kinds of new business models enabled by smart technologies	Rolls-Royce "power by the hour," Progressive Insurance Snapshot program, Zipcar, RFID, smart hospitals
Move to real-time question answering systems	new organizational process and business models based on generalized real-time question answering systems	Apple Siri, streaming data analytics, IBM Watson
Creation of analytics-driven digital innovation opportunities	increased opportunities for process and product/business model innovation	Amazon, Capital One, Harrah's, business analytics
Democratized innovation	process and product innovation discovery and development becomes more open, democratized, and user-driven	Innocentive, P&G Connect and Develop, open prize competitions, Dell Ideastorm, Whirlpool's Innovation E-Space, Threadless

workplace or outside it.[50,51] It differs from traditional learning in that the nature/characteristics of the learning process are significantly transformed, the learning context is significantly transformed, the teaching methodologies are significantly transformed, the learning participants are expanded, and the learning systems and tools are significantly transformed. As noted above, the nature and characteristics of digital learning include it being much more online, interactive, multidisciplinary, multiplatform, multi-device, portable, user-centered/personalized, self-directed, gamified, always on anywhere/anytime/real time, immersive, social, and so forth. With regard to teaching methods, digital learning differs from traditional learning in that new teaching methods/approaches are used that better involve learners in the learning process and optimize learning efficiency and effectiveness.[52,53] Examples of these methodologies/approaches include project-based learning, problem-based learning; digital stories, online learning environments, digital moments, technology-integrated teaching methods, digital storytelling, educational games, and authentic learning.[54,55] Regarding learning contexts, digital learning differs from traditional learning in that learning contexts that support new and more effective pedagogical models are used. Examples of these include collaborative communities, cooperative learning, collaborative learning, digital combinational systems, digital media–based flipped classrooms, online spaces, experiential online development, open educational practice, and network participation.[56,57] Regarding learning participants, digital learning differs from traditional learning in that the participants are expanded to include collaborative community participants, cooperative/collaborative learning participants, network participants, and software algorithms.[58,59] Finally, digital learning differs from traditional learning in that it leverages a diverse collection of digital technology platforms and tools to provide/maintain the learning context, to facilitate the learning process, to support learners, and to report on the effectiveness of both learning processes and learning outcomes. Examples of such tools include web-based video applications, narrated stop–motion animation applications, augmented reality applications, webinar applications, learning management systems (LMS), YouTube, Facebook, Instagram, Wikipedia, LinkedIn, Google/other search engines, mobile learning apps, learning object repositories, Blackboard, Moodle Learning Manager, Collaborate Ultra, Zoom, Twitter, and massive open online courses (MOOCs).[60,61]

New or enhanced managerial roles and competencies required for digital learning

Effective digital learning can upskill, engage, empower, motivate, and retain employees. In turn, this can accelerate organization efficiency, adaptability, and agility, and become a strong basis for competitive advantage. Hospitality and leisure managers at all levels can play important roles in optimizing digital learning. Examples of these roles include setting or clarifying the digital learning vision and direction, effectively leading/managing/facilitating digital learning processes, identifying/ensuring use of the right tools for optimizing digital learning process and outcomes, ensuring access to the best content, identifying/ensuring use of the most effective teaching methodologies and pedagogical models, inspiring and motivating employees to make the most of available learning opportunities, instituting the right mindsets and behaviors for digital learning, building/continuously upgrading organization digital learning capacity, and ensuring effective capture of organization value from digital learning efforts and outputs. To play such roles, hospitality and leisure managers need to understand the nature and functioning of digital leaning capability, have working knowledge of different digital learning platforms/tools/methodologies/pedagogical models, have working knowledge of important digital technologies to the digital learning process and to digital learning outputs, and have strong digital leadership skills.

Required managerial roles and competencies for adaptability, agility, and ambidexterity

Unpacking adaptability, agility, and ambidexterity

We previously defined adaptability as the ability to dynamically reconfigure routines, processes and practices to suit the demands of unexpected internal and external events or disruptions. And we defined agility as the capacity for flexibility and speed in sensing and responding to such events and disruptions, especially external ones. For example, a highly agile organization is able to anticipate/spot/understand disruptions early (e.g. disruptions such as COVID-19), and is able to efficiently and effectively redeploy/redirect its resources to value creating/value capturing/value protecting activities dynamically as the situation warrants.[62] In contrast, we defined ambidexterity as having the ability to ensure efficiency/effectiveness in the organization's existing products/services while also ensuring the organization undertakes the exploratory activities necessary to discover future winning products and services.[63]

We noted that adaptability capabilities are critical to enabling organizations to reconfigure their operations and offerings to surprising internal and external events, such as the financial crisis (which in many cases resulted in lack of access to new credit, clawing back of approved credit facilities, growth in payment defaults, a sharp decline in consumer demand, and drying up working capital) or the COVID-19 pandemic (which resulted in social distancing and travel restrictions, inability of staff to attend workplaces, procurement challenges, sharp declines in many products/services, restrictions on ways in which organizations could serve customers, etc.).[64] Organizations with established adaptability capabilities would have had the relevant infrastructure, processes, talent, culture, and financial resources to enable them to reconfigure their operations in response to the surprising events or disruptions. For example, during the COVID-19 pandemic, hospitality and leisure organizations that had made significant progress with the their digital transformation efforts were able to have their workforce work from home and still undertake meaningful work that contributed to the organization's future adaptive capacity, to offer existing or new products virtually, and to do all of this without compromising customers' and employees' experience, safety, and privacy. Organizations with established agility capabilities are able to sense/anticipate surprising events and disruptions, are able to effect fast responses to seize the corresponding opportunities or react to the threats, and have the flexibility to dynamically vary their responses as the situation requires.[65] Organizations with established ambidexterity capabilities are able to build, maintain, and use their adaptability and agility capabilities without those capabilities materially compromising their established operational processes.[66]

Digital technology advancements are key drivers of the need for adaptability, agility, and ambidexterity (through driving digital disruption). But paradoxically, they also offer unparalleled opportunities to build, maintain, and optimize adaptability, agility, and ambidexterity capabilities. For example, big data/data analytics/AI technologies and tools can be used for digital scouting and digital scenario planning (approaches for anticipating disruptions and preparing to adapt to them). Cloud/AI/learning platforms can be used for digital learning and digital mindset shaping. Elastic/anywhere/anytime/any device digital infrastructure can be used to enable dynamic flexing of resources in response to customer/demand side changes or supplier/supply side changes. Combinations of digital technologies can be brought together to assemble highly efficient and scalable business models, to build smart products that can sense and report on consumer behavior changes, or to build smart and autonomous processes that can independently flex with demand and supply side changes. Combinations of digital technologies can be used to effect bimodality (e.g. operating digital infrastructure to facilitate/support established processes in parrallel with digital infrastructure to facilitate/support exploratory or experimental processes).

New or enhanced managerial roles and competencies required for adaptability, agility, and ambidexterity

Hospitality and leisure managers at all levels can play important roles in leveraging digital technologies for building, maintaining and optimizing the adaptability, agility, and ambidexterity capforilities of their organizations. Examples of these roles include setting or clarifying a vision for firm adaptability/agility/ambidexterity capabilities (e.g. clarifying what the "future state" of this capability should look like in practice), enabling the building and maintaining of both efficiency and exploratory digital infrastructure and processes, ensure the right combination of technologies are used and configured in the right way to maximize adaptability/agility/ambidexterity capabilities, institute conditions/mindsets/attitudes that provide impetus for both exploration and exploitation actions, and cultivating and modeling ambidextrous leadership styles.

Google and reflect

Discussion questions

1   How is digital business strategy different from traditional strategy?
2   Which managerial role in digital business strategy is the most critical to building and maintaining that capability? Why?
3   Which digital business strategy managerial competency is likely to have the greatest positive impact on a hospitality and leisure manager's career?
4   How is digital innovation different from traditional innovation?

Digital Capability	Common Terminology
Digital business strategy	Digital business strategy, digital transformation strategy, digital asset, network effects, elastic infrastructure, dynamic capability, digital infrastructure
Digital innovation	Crowdsourcing, crowdfunding, network-centric innovation platform, innovation collective, shared cognition, joint sense-making, design thinking, layered modular architecture
Digital learning	Digital learning context, digital learning systems/platforms, gamification, self-directed learning, immersive learning, autonomous learning, learning efficiency, multi-disciplinary knowledge, multi-disciplinary teaching, interdisciplinary teaching, pedagogical model, collaborative communities, cooperative learning, collaborative learning, digital combinational systems, flipped classroom, experiential online development, open educational practice, narrated stop-motion animation application, augmented reality application, webinar application, learning management system (LMS), learning object repository, massive open online course (MOOC)
Adaptability, agility, ambidexterity	adaptability, agility, ambidexterity, strategic sensing, bimodality

5 Which managerial role in digital innovation is the most critical to building and maintaining that capability? Why?
6 How is digital learning different from traditional learning?
7 Which managerial role in digital learning is the most critical to building and maintaining that capability? Why?
8 Which digital learning managerial competency is likely to have the greatest positive impact on a hospitality and leisure manager's career?
9 Which of the capabilities discussed in this chapter is the most important to succeeding at digital transformation and digital business?

Notes

1 Bharadwaj, A., El Sawy, O. A., Pavlou, P. A., & Venkatraman, N. (2013). Digital Business Strategy: Toward a Next Generation of Insights. *MIS Quarterly*, 471–482.
2 Bharadwaj, A., El Sawy, O. A., Pavlou, P. A., & Venkatraman, N. (2013). Digital Business Strategy: Toward a Next Generation of Insights. *MIS Quarterly*, 471–482.
3 Bharadwaj, A., El Sawy, O. A., Pavlou, P. A., & Venkatraman, N. (2013). Digital Business Strategy: Toward a Next Generation of Insights. *MIS Quarterly*, 471–482.
4 Ross, J. W. (2016, November 8). How to Develop a Great Digital Strategy. Retrieved May 31, 2020, from MIT Sloan Management Review website: https://sloanreview.mit.edu/article/how-to-develop-a-great-digital-strategy/
5 Ross, J. W. (2016, November 8). How to Develop a Great Digital Strategy. Retrieved May 31, 2020, from MIT Sloan Management Review website: https://sloanreview.mit.edu/article/how-to-develop-a-great-digital-strategy/
6 Gupta, S. (2018). *Driving Digital Strategy: A Guide to Reimagining Your Business*. Harvard Business Press.
7 Gupta, S. (2018). *Driving Digital Strategy: A Guide to Reimagining Your Business*. Harvard Business Press.
8 Ross, J. W. (2016, November 8). How to Develop a Great Digital Strategy. Retrieved May 31, 2020, from MIT Sloan Management Review website: https://sloanreview.mit.edu/article/how-to-develop-a-great-digital-strategy/
9 Bharadwaj, A., El Sawy, O. A., Pavlou, P. A., & Venkatraman, N. (2013). Digital Business Strategy: Toward a Next Generation of Insights. *MIS Quarterly*, 471–482.
10 Bharadwaj, A., El Sawy, O. A., Pavlou, P. A., & Venkatraman, N. (2013). Digital Business Strategy: Toward a Next Generation of Insights. *MIS Quarterly*, 471–482.
11 Hoffman, R., & Yeh, C. (2018, October). The Blitzscaling Basics. Retrieved June 1, 2020, from strategy+business website: www.strategy-business.com/article/The-Blitzscaling-Basics?gko=3ebb0
12 Hoffman, R., & Yeh, C. (2018). *Blitzscaling: The Lightning-fast Path to Building Massively Valuable Businesses*. Broadway Business.
13 Hoffman, R., & Yeh, C. (2018). *Blitzscaling: The Lightning-fast Path to Building Massively Valuable Businesses*. Broadway Business.
14 Hoffman, R., & Yeh, C. (2018). *Blitzscaling: The Lightning-fast Path to Building Massively Valuable Businesses*. Broadway Business.
15 Vial, G. (2019). Understanding Digital Transformation: A Review and a Research Agenda. *The Journal of Strategic Information Systems*, 28(2), 118–144. https://doi.org/10.1016/j.jsis.2019.01.003
16 Rigby, D. K., Sutherland, J., & Takeuchi, H. (2016). Embracing Agile. *Harvard Business Review*, 94(5), 40–50.
17 Busulwa, R., Tice, M., & Gurd, B. (2018). *Strategy Execution and Complexity: Thriving in the Era of Disruption*. Routledge.
18 Haque, B., & James-Moore, M. (2004). Applying Lean Thinking to New Product Introduction. *Journal of Engineering Design*, 15(1), 1–31.
19 Womack, J. P., & Jones, D. T. (1997). Lean Thinking – Banish Waste and Create Wealth in Your Corporation. *Journal of the Operational Research Society*, 48(11), 1148–1148.
20 Melton, T. (2005). The Benefits of Lean Manufacturing: What Lean Thinking Has to Offer the Process Industries. *Chemical Engineering Research and Design*, 83(6), 662–673.
21 Ries, E. (2011). *The Lean Startup: How Today's Entrepreneurs Use Continuous Innovation to Create Radically Successful Businesses*. Crown Books.

22 Martin, R., & Martin, R. L. (2009). *The Design of Business: Why Design Thinking is the Next Competitive Advantage.* Harvard Business Press.

23 Busulwa, R., Birdthistle, N., & Dunn, S. (2020). *Startup Accelerators: A Field Guide.* John Wiley & Sons.

24 Kotter, J. P. (2014). *Accelerate: Building Strategic Agility for a Faster-Moving World.* Harvard Business Review Press.

25 West, M., & Farr, J. (1989). Innovation at Work: Psychological Perspectives. *Social Behavior,* 4, 15–30.

26 Nambisan, S., Lyytinen, K., Majchrzak, A., & Song, M. (2017). Digital Innovation Management: Reinventing Innovation Management Research in a Digital World. *MIS Quarterly,* 41(1).

27 Yoo, Y., Henfridsson, O., & Lyytinen, K. (2010). Research Commentary – The New Organizing Logic of Digital Innovation: An Agenda for Information Systems Research. *Information Systems Research,* 21(4), 724–735.

28 Nambisan, S., Lyytinen, K., Majchrzak, A., & Song, M. (2017). Digital Innovation Management: Reinventing Innovation Management Research in a Digital World. *MIS Quarterly,* 41(1).

29 Nambisan, S., Lyytinen, K., Majchrzak, A., & Song, M. (2017). Digital Innovation Management: Reinventing Innovation Management Research in a Digital World. *MIS Quarterly,* 41(1).

30 Bradonjic, P., Franke, N., & Lüthje, C. (2019). Decision-Makers' Underestimation of User Innovation. *Research Policy,* 48(6), 1354–1361. https://doi.org/10.1016/j.respol.2019.01.020

31 Nambisan, S., Lyytinen, K., Majchrzak, A., & Song, M. (2017). Digital Innovation Management: Reinventing Innovation Management Research in a Digital World. *MIS Quarterly,* 41(1).

32 Yoo, Y., Henfridsson, O., & Lyytinen, K. (2010). Research Commentary – The New Organizing Logic of Digital Innovation: An Agenda for Information Systems Research. *Information Systems Research,* 21(4), 724–735.

33 Lee, J., & Berente, N. (2012). Digital Innovation and the Division of Innovative Labor: Digital Controls in the Automotive Industry. *Organization Science,* 23(5), 1428–1447.

34 Nambisan, S., Lyytinen, K., Majchrzak, A., & Song, M. (2017). Digital Innovation Management: Reinventing Innovation Management Research in a Digital World. *MIS Quarterly,* 41(1).

35 Nambisan, S., Lyytinen, K., Majchrzak, A., & Song, M. (2017). Digital Innovation Management: Reinventing Innovation Management Research in a Digital World. *MIS Quarterly,* 41(1).

36 Nambisan, S., Lyytinen, K., Majchrzak, A., & Song, M. (2017). Digital Innovation Management: Reinventing Innovation Management Research in a Digital World. *MIS Quarterly,* 41(1).

37 Yoo, Y., Henfridsson, O., & Lyytinen, K. (2010). Research Commentary – The New Organizing Logic of Digital Innovation: An Agenda for Information Systems Research. *Information Systems Research,* 21(4), 724–735.

38 Lee, J., & Berente, N. (2012). Digital Innovation and the Division of Innovative Labor: Digital Controls in the Automotive Industry. *Organization Science,* 23(5), 1428–1447.

39 Nambisan, S., Lyytinen, K., Majchrzak, A., & Song, M. (2017). Digital Innovation Management: Reinventing Innovation Management Research in a Digital World. *MIS Quarterly,* 41(1).

40 Yoo, Y., Henfridsson, O., & Lyytinen, K. (2010). Research Commentary – The New Organizing Logic of Digital Innovation: An Agenda for Information Systems Research. *Information Systems Research,* 21(4), 724–735.

41 Lee, J., & Berente, N. (2012). Digital Innovation and the Division of Innovative Labor: Digital Controls in the Automotive Industry. *Organization Science,* 23(5), 1428–1447.

42 Nambisan, S., Lyytinen, K., Majchrzak, A., & Song, M. (2017). Digital Innovation Management: Reinventing Innovation Management Research in a Digital World. *MIS Quarterly,* 41(1).

43 Yoo, Y., Henfridsson, O., & Lyytinen, K. (2010). Research Commentary – The New Organizing Logic of Digital Innovation: An Agenda for Information Systems Research. *Information Systems Research,* 21(4), 724–735.

44 Lee, J., & Berente, N. (2012). Digital Innovation and the Division of Innovative Labor: Digital Controls in the Automotive Industry. *Organization Science,* 23(5), 1428–1447.

45 Nambisan, S., Lyytinen, K., Majchrzak, A., & Song, M. (2017). Digital Innovation Management: Reinventing Innovation Management Research in a Digital World. *MIS Quarterly,* 41(1).

46 Fichman, R. G., Dos Santos, B. L., & Zheng, Z. (2014). Digital Innovation as a Fundamental and Powerful Concept in the Information Systems Curriculum. *MIS Quarterly, 38*(2), 329–A15.

47 Willyerd, K., Grünwald, A., Brown, K., Welz, B., & Traylor, P. (2016, March). A New Model for Corporate Learning. Digitalit Magazine. Retrieved June 2, 2020, from www.digitalistmag.com/executive-research/a-new-model-for-corporate-learning

48 Willyerd, K., Grünwald, A., Brown, K., Welz, B., & Traylor, P. (2016, March). A New Model for Corporate Learning. Digitalit Magazine. Retrieved June 2, 2020, from www.digitalistmag.com/executive-research/a-new-model-for-corporate-learning

49 Willyerd, K., Grünwald, A., Brown, K., Welz, B., & Traylor, P. (2016, March). A New Model for Corporate Learning. Digitalit Magazine. Retrieved June 2, 2020, from www.digitalistmag.com/executive-research/a-new-model-for-corporate-learning

50 Sousa, M. J., & Rocha, Á. (2019). Digital Learning: Developing Skills for Digital Transformation of Organizations. *Future Generation Computer Systems*, 91, 327–334.

51 Sousa, M. J., & Rocha, Á. (2019). Digital Learning: Developing Skills for Digital Transformation of Organizations. *Future Generation Computer Systems*, 91, 327–334.

52 Sousa, M. J., Cruz, R., & Martins, J. M. (2017). Digital Learning Methodologies and Tools – A Literature Review. *EDULEARN17 Proceedings*, 5185–5192.

53 Sousa, M. J., & Rocha, Á. (2019). Digital Learning: Developing Skills for Digital Transformation of Organizations. *Future Generation Computer Systems*, 91, 327–334.

54 Sousa, M. J., Cruz, R., & Martins, J. M. (2017). Digital Learning Methodologies and Tools – A Literature Review. *EDULEARN17 Proceedings*, 5185–5192.

55 Sousa, M. J., & Rocha, Á. (2019). Digital Learning: Developing Skills for Digital Transformation of Organizations. *Future Generation Computer Systems*, 91, 327–334.

56 Sousa, M. J., Cruz, R., & Martins, J. M. (2017). Digital Learning Methodologies and Tools – A Literature Review. *EDULEARN17 Proceedings*, 5185–5192.

57 Sousa, M. J., & Rocha, Á. (2019). Digital Learning: Developing Skills for Digital Transformation of Organizations. *Future Generation Computer Systems*, 91, 327–334.

58 Sousa, M. J., Cruz, R., & Martins, J. M. (2017). Digital Learning Methodologies and Tools – A Literature Review. *EDULEARN17 Proceedings*, 5185–5192.

59 Sousa, M. J., & Rocha, Á. (2019). Digital Learning: Developing Skills for Digital Transformation of Organizations. *Future Generation Computer Systems*, 91, 327–334.

60 Sousa, M. J., Cruz, R., & Martins, J. M. (2017). Digital Learning Methodologies and Tools – A Literature Review. *EDULEARN17 Proceedings*, 5185–5192.

61 Sousa, M. J., & Rocha, Á. (2019). Digital Learning: Developing Skills for Digital Transformation of Organizations. *Future Generation Computer Systems*, 91, 327–334.

62 Warner, K. S., & Wäger, M. (2019). Building Dynamic Capabilities for Digital Transformation: An Ongoing Process of Strategic Renewal. *Long Range Planning*, 52(3), 326–349.

63 Busulwa, R., Tice, M., & Gurd, B. (2018). *Strategy Execution and Complexity: Thriving in the Era of Disruption*. Routledge.

64 Busulwa, R., Tice, M., & Gurd, B. (2018). *Strategy Execution and Complexity: Thriving in the Era of Disruption*. Routledge.

65 Busulwa, R., Tice, M., & Gurd, B. (2018). *Strategy Execution and Complexity: Thriving in the Era of Disruption*. Routledge.

66 Busulwa, R., Tice, M., & Gurd, B. (2018). *Strategy Execution and Complexity: Thriving in the Era of Disruption*. Routledge.

8 Role of hospitality and leisure managers in digital customer engagement, digital stakeholder engagement, and digital customer experience

Introduction

Digital technology advancements have disrupted customer and other stakeholder expectations and behaviors. Owing to this disruption, customers increasingly expect dramatically higher personalization of experiences and interactions, anytime/anywhere responsiveness, any device/any channel service availability, respect for the value of their time in interactions with organizations, feeling valued at all times, and feeling like they are part of a community that uses the product/service or engage with the organization. Living up to these expectations requires fundamental changes in the nature of customer engagement, stakeholder engagement, and customer experience practices. These transformed practices are what are respectively referred to as digital customer engagement, digital stakeholder engagement, and digital customer experience capabilities. They offer the promise of organizations not only being able to live up to changed and rapidly changing customer/stakeholder expectations but also having important bases for building strategic differentiation, adaptability, and agility from state-of-the-art practice of the capabilities. In this chapter, we unpack each capability and discuss what it means, how it differs from its traditional counterpart, and its value to organization performance and longevity. We then identify the key roles hospitality and leisure managers can play in building and maintaining these organization capabilities, and what competencies they require to perform those roles. As with earlier capabilities, each of these capabilities can be a complex area of practice with significant depth, interdisciplinary knowledge, slippery terms and concepts to make sense of, and practical practice challenges. Our aim was to provide a meaningful introduction to each digital capability, the required roles, and the required competencies, so managers can have a starting point and a contextual framework to support further and lifelong learning/competency development in these important capability areas.

Required managerial roles and competencies for digital customer engagement and digital stakeholder engagement

Unpacking digital customer engagement

Customer engagement refers to both the process and effect of organizations or brands creating deep connections with customers that drive purchase decisions, interaction, participation, and brand advocacy.[1] Its value to profitability and competitiveness is well established and includes benefits such as improved customer experience (e.g. through more empathetic service), improved customer relations/retention (e.g. greater trust/forgiveness of organization mistakes), improved brand/product awareness and image (e.g. through word of mouth), improved product innovation (e.g. through customers providing ideas for new products or for existing product improvements), improved competitor intelligence (e.g. getting information on competitor activities from customers) and improved risk mitigation (e.g. discovering information on fatal product flaws and customer grievances from customers). Given these benefits, competitive organizations have long been interested in building and continuously upgrading their customer engagement capability (i.e. the efficiency and effectiveness of the capability).[2,3,4,5,6,7]

In previous chapters, we have noted how digital technology advancements disrupt consumer expectations and behaviors, disrupt the competitive field and the bases of competition, and disrupt data availability. From a consumer engagement perspective, these disruptions have manifested themselves as, for example, dramatically higher expectations of personalization, dramatically higher expectations of anytime/anywhere responsiveness, dramatically higher expectations of any device/any channel availability, and dramatically higher expectations of experiencing a sense of community in purchasing or brand interactions. To deliver on these dramatically higher expectations, organizations succeeding at it have transformed the nature of their customer engagement processes and practices.

The new or transformed processes and practices are collectively referred to as digital customer engagement. Digital customer engagement is the use of digital technologies and tools in the processes/practices and effect of creating deep connections with customers

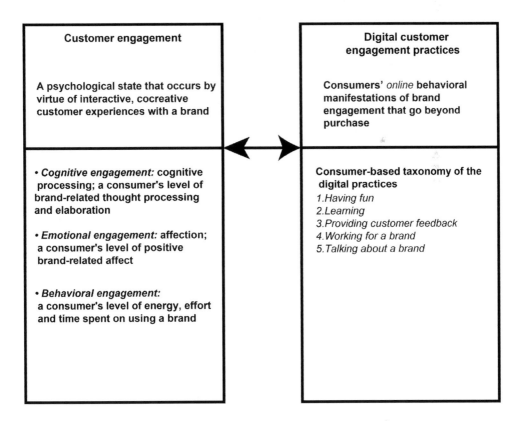

Figure 8.1 Traditional customer engagement vs. digital customer engagement[8]

that drive purchase decisions, interaction, participation, and advocacy (see figure 8.1 for a contrast of digital customer engagement practices with traditional customer engagement). Digital customer engagement deals with all the ways current and prospective customers can and do interact in relation to an organization, brand, or product across digital channels, platforms, devices, and connected or smart things.[9] Digital customer engagement has rapidly evolved to include a rich repertoire of engagement strategies/approaches and specific engagement practices.[10] Examples of these include digitally managed loyalty programs (e.g. web-based or mobile app frequent flyer programs), online brand communities (e.g. discussion board/chat-style interactions with other customers/prospective customers or with the organization, consumers solving other consumers' problems, consumers giving other consumers advice/tips), use of digital customer engagement platforms (e.g. Zendesk, Freshdesk, HubSpot, Salesforce, Mailchimp), customer co-creation (e.g. product co-creation, product improvement feedback, product testing), brand websites, consumer-generated brand stories, consumer engagement on social media (e.g. liking, commenting, sharing, posting, calling up product photographs, hash-tagging), consumer reviews (e.g. search engine reviews, review platform reviews, social media reviews), brand-consumer interactions (e.g. liking a brand on Facebook, following a brand on Twitter), purchase funnel practices, brand fan pages, mobile interactions (e.g. SMS interactions), LiveChat platforms, mobile marketing, consumer-generated advertising (e.g. consumer-generated brand videos), consumer buzz (e.g. consumer generation of content by sharing personal experiences, providing online feedback, expressing sentiments), email marketing, customers' online brand related activities (COBRAs), consumption community participation, consumer initiated mobile marketing, and consumer advocates (e.g. consumers doing remote voluntary work for the organization, acting as multiplier of brand messages, accepting invitations to company-related events, speaking up for the brand at events).[11] Figure 8.2 provides a taxonomy of business to consumer, consumer to business, and consumer to consumer engagement types, aims, and example activities.

Effectively done, digital customer engagement provides organizations with a range of other opportunities including being able to harness all their customer interactions across channels and platforms to inform decision making, developing breakthrough and market-validated products (e.g. from spotting new problems to solve for customers, liaising with customers about possible solutions, and receiving product test feedback from customers), involving more customers in digital innovation, being able to get granular in their understanding of customer behaviors across market segments, and offering significantly improved customer service and customer experience (e.g. service that leverages interaction data to anticipate and solve customer issues in real time).

Unpacking digital stakeholder engagement

In addition to customers, a range of other stakeholders are critical to an organization's performance and well-being. These include employees, suppliers and partners, government and regulatory institutions, competitors, and different local and international communities. The organization must engage effectively with these different stakeholders in order to safeguard its existence, its legitimacy, and the opportunities available to it. For example, organizations must assure governments and regulatory institutions that they are complying with relevant laws or have acceptable reasons for not doing so; they must assure competitors that they are competing fairly; and they must ensure different communities that they are not violating their social, environmental, and ethical obligations or license to operate in

Figure 8.2 A research-derived taxonomy of digital customer engagement practices[12]

those communities and environments. To effectively do this, they must communicate and transact with these stakeholders in such a way as to build positive, trusting relationships. This is the focus of stakeholder engagement. And like digital customer engagement, digital stakeholder engagement leverages digital technologies and tools to maximize the practice and outputs of stakeholder engagement. Digital technologies and tools can dramatically improve the cost, speed, scale/reach, transparency, measurability, and effectiveness of stakeholder engagement efforts. In turn, this translates into organizations enjoying greater trust, empathy, inclusion, growth, profitability, and other benefits from stakeholders.

New or enhanced managerial roles and competencies required for digital customer engagement and digital stakeholder engagement

While organizations may leverage digital technologies and tools to improve customer engagement and stakeholder engagement, this is not enough. They must also do so more effectively and efficiently than competitors that leverage the same or similar digital technologies and tools. Hospitality and leisure managers can play an important role in building and continuously upgrading digital customer and stakeholder engagement capabilities. For example, they can set or clarify the organization's digital engagement vision and strategic objectives, they can help select the right combination of digital technologies and tools to maximize engagement of different customers and stakeholders (e.g. right technologies/ platforms/tools, right configuration and integration of technologies/platforms/tools), they can promote and institute the right supporting mindsets/attitudes/behaviors for effective digital engagement (e.g. that it's not just marketing's job), they can encourage their direct reports to participate in different digital channels in order to better empathize with stakeholders, they can ensure analytics dashboards are built that leverage and integrate interaction data from all channels, they can hire/develop in-house experts across channels and forms of engagement, and much more. To play such roles, managers need to have sufficient working knowledge of digital customer and stakeholder engagement objectives, processes, and practices. They need to have working knowledge of different digital channels and of how multichannel works. They also need to understand how to capture value for the organization from its digital engagement efforts. Finally, they need the digital leadership skills to enable them to develop, continuously upgrade, and realize value from digital engagement efforts.

Required managerial roles and competencies for digital customer experience

Unpacking digital customer experience

Customer experience refers to the quality of all of a customer's encounters with an organization's products, services, and brand.[13,14] Improvements in the quality of these encounters is linked to benefits such as improved customer acquisition, improved customer loyalty, improved revenue growth, and improved profitability. Perhaps it is for this reason that optimizing customer experience has been a strategic priority for organizations from as far back as the 19th century; and today, industry leading brands such as Ritz-Carlton, Mirazur, and Singapore Airlines revolve their management strategies around customer experience optimization.[15] As with transformations of customer engagement and stakeholder engagement, digital technology advancements are changing the nature of effective customer experience management. The drivers of this change include more and more customer encounters with an organization's products/services/brand shifting to digital channels, a proliferation in digital channels (e.g. different search engines, different social media platforms, different payment platforms, different website management platforms, different computing and mobile devices, different mobile apps, different virtual/augmented/mixed reality platforms, different IoT platforms, different online video platforms, different television platforms), and significant differences in customer interaction requirements across channels. Irrespective of the digital channels they choose or their location and timing, customers want access to organizations' services and products in the most convenient way possible.[16] They are put off by having to repeat themselves from one channel to another or from one customer representative to another. They hate process and visual inconsistency across channels, as well as having to perform actions that waste their time. And they are far less patient on digital channels than they are in traditional channels (e.g. a study found that waiting 10 seconds for a page to load can result in half of customers terminating their encounter).[17]

Digital customer experience is the aggregate quality of all of a customer's encounters with an organization's products, services, and brand across all digital channels, touchpoints, and contact moments.[18] It also refers to the process of optimizing these encounters (e.g. having the right technology/platform/application infrastructure, having the right process and people, and having the right policies). By having the right supporting technologies, the right platforms/applications, the right management processes, and the right people, organizations can ensure they are available and effectively serve customers in their preferred channels, at their preferred times, in their preferred locations, and in ways that respect their time (i.e. save them all possible effort rather than externalizing more effort to them due to the organization's shortcomings). Digital customer experience optimization strategies typically focus on enhancing reachability (e.g. customers being able to use the channels available to them to interact with or about the organization, customers being aware of all of the organization's available channels), enhancing digital channel flexibility (e.g. enabling customers to switch between channels without losing context, having consistent information across channels, and ensuring customers do not have enhancing service to repeat themselves across channels), enhancing service convenience (e.g. access to clear, up-to-date information, access to quick/live support, ability to receive end-to-end support rather than being bounced across channels), enhancing purchase convenience (e.g. ability to conduct end-to-end transactions, broad payment options, ability to subscribe to new products/services, clear and up-to-date information), simplicity and ease of use (e.g. intuitive interface design, simple and guided journeys, simple and intuitive navigation), and personalization (e.g. recognizing customers as a unique individuals, having customers' personal preferences automatically met, designing experiences suited to the customers' unique context).[19] Organizations can leverage a wide range of digital technology platforms and tools to achieve these digital customer experience optimization objectives. For example, using omnichannel support platforms (e.g. Pega CRM, Five9), organizations can track, centralize, and tie together/orchestrate all interactions across channels (e.g. face-to-face, email, phone, social media, live chat), so that a customer's digital experience is integrated and smooth rather than fragmented and conflicting.

New or enhanced managerial roles and competencies required for digital customer experience

To effectively lead or participate in digital customer experience optimization efforts, hospitality and leisure managers can play roles such as setting/clarifying/communicating the organization's digital customer experience vision and strategic objectives, championing availability of the organization's offerings and support services across as many channels as possible, helping select the right combination of digital technologies/platforms/tools to maximize digital customer experience across customer preferred channels (e.g. right technologies/platforms/tools, right configuration and integration of technologies/platforms/tools), promoting and instituting the right supporting mindsets/attitudes/behaviors to maximize digital customer experience, and encouraging their direct reports to participate in different digital channels in order to better empathize with customers' experiences and needs in those channels. Hospitality and leisure managers can also ensure analytics dashboards are built that leverage and integrate digital customer experience data from all channels, they can ensure hiring/developing of in-house experts across channels, and more. To play such roles, managers need to have sufficient working knowledge of digital customer experience objectives, strategies, processes, and practices. They need to have strong working knowledge of customer journey mapping, customer journeys, and the key moments of truth in journeys across platforms. They need to have working knowledge of different digital channels and of how multichannel works. Finally, they need the digital leadership skills to enable them to develop, continuously upgrade, and realize value from digital customer experience optimization efforts.

Google and reflect

Digital Capability	Common Terminology
Digital customer engagement	Customer engagement, digital customer engagement, digital loyalty program, online brand community, digital customer engagement platform, customer co-creation, brand fan page, LiveChat platform, consumer-generated advertising, consumer buzz, customers' online brand related activities (COBRAs)
Digital stakeholder engagement	Stakeholder management, stakeholder engagement, digital stakeholder engagement, organizational legitimacy, social license to operate (SLO), corporate social responsibility (CSR)
Digital customer experience	Customer experience (CX), digital customer experience (DCX or Digital CX), customer experience management (CEM or CXM), customer experience program, customer sentiment, customer satisfaction score (CSAT), customer effort score (CES), customer delight, brand advocacy, customer lifetime value (CLV), voice of the customer (VoC), Net Promoter Score (NPS), Customer Effort Score (CES), customer experience design (CXD), customer journey mapping, digital touchpoint, digital customer experience moment of truth (MoT), omnichannel strategy, digital customer experience platform

Discussion questions

1 How is digital customer engagement different from traditional customer engagement?
2 Which managerial role in digital customer engagement is the most critical to building and maintaining that capability? Why?
3 Which digital customer engagement competency is likely to have the greatest positive impact on a hospitality and leisure manager's career?
4 How is digital stakeholder engagement different from traditional stakeholder engagement?
5 Which managerial role in digital stakeholder engagement is the most critical to building and maintaining that capability? Why?
6 How is digital customer experience different from traditional customer experience?
7 Which managerial role in digital customer experience is the most critical to building and maintaining that capability? Why?
8 Which digital customer experience managerial competency is likely to have the greatest positive impact on a hospitality and leisure manager's career?
9 Which of the capabilities discussed in this chapter is the most important to succeeding at digital transformation and digital business?

Notes

1 Sashi, C. M. (2012). Customer Engagement, Buyer–Seller Relationships, and Social Media. *Management Decision*, 50(2), 253–272. https://doi.org/10.1108/00251741211203551
2 Hueffner, E. (2020). How Digital Customer Engagement Can Boost Your Business. Retrieved June 3, 2020, from Zendesk website: www.zendesk.com/blog/digital-customer-engagement/
3 Sashi, C. M. (2012). Customer Engagement, Buyer–Seller Relationships, and Social Media. *Management Decision*, 50(2), 253–272. https://doi.org/10.1108/00251741211203551
4 Klein Wassink, B. J., & Santenac, I. (2019, February 11). How a New Digital Engagement Model Attracts and Educates Customers. Retrieved June 3, 2020, from Ey.com website: www.ey.com/en_gl/insurance/new-digital-customer-engagement-model
5 Ebrahim, S., Rabbani, U., & Rosenberg, R. (2015). Making Digital Customer Engagement a Reality. Retrieved June 3, 2020, from McKinsey & Company website: www.mckinsey.com/business-functions/marketing-and-sales/our-insights/making-digital-customer-engagement-a-reality

6 Ebrahim, S., Rabbani, U., & Rosenberg, R. (2015). Making Digital Customer Engagement a Reality. Retrieved June 3, 2020, from McKinsey & Company website: www.mckinsey.com/business-functions/marketing-and-sales/our-insights/making-digital-customer-engagement-a-reality

7 Hueffner, E. (2020). How Digital Customer Engagement Can Boost Your Business. Retrieved June 3, 2020, from Zendesk website: www.zendesk.com/blog/digital-customer-engagement/

8 Eigenraam, A. W., Eelen, J., Van Lin, A., & Verlegh, P. W. (2018). A Consumer-based Taxonomy of Digital Customer Engagement Practices. *Journal of Interactive Marketing*, 44, 102–121.

9 Hueffner, E. (2020). How Digital Customer Engagement Can Boost Your Business. Retrieved June 3, 2020, from Zendesk website: www.zendesk.com/blog/digital-customer-engagement/

10 Eigenraam, A. W., Eelen, J., Van Lin, A., & Verlegh, P. W. (2018). A Consumer-based Taxonomy of Digital Customer Engagement Practices. *Journal of Interactive Marketing*, 44, 102–121.

11 Eigenraam, A. W., Eelen, J., Van Lin, A., & Verlegh, P. W. (2018). A Consumer-based Taxonomy of Digital Customer Engagement Practices. *Journal of Interactive Marketing*, 44, 102–121.

12 Eigenraam, A. W., Eelen, J., Van Lin, A., & Verlegh, P. W. (2018). A Consumer-based Taxonomy of Digital Customer Engagement Practices. *Journal of Interactive Marketing*, 44, 102–121.

13 Borowski, C. (2015). What a Great Digital Customer Experience Actually Looks Like. Harvard Business Review. Retrieved June 4, 2020, from Harvard Business Review website: https://hbr.org/2015/11/what-a-great-digital-customer-experience-actually-looks-like

14 Meyer, C., & Schwager, A. (2007). Understanding Customer Experience. *Harvard Business Review*, 85(2), 116.

15 Klaus, P. (2014). Towards Practical Relevance – Delivering Superior Firm Performance Through Digital Customer Experience Strategies. *Journal of Direct, Data and Digital Marketing Practice*, 15(4), 306–316. https://doi.org/10.1057/dddmp.2014.20

16 Hyken, S. (2018). Customer Experience is the New Brand. Forbes. Retrieved from www.forbes.com/sites/shephyken/2018/07/15/customer-experience-is-the-new-brand/#1e586acf7f52

17 Borowski, C. (2015). What a Great Digital Customer Experience Actually Looks Like. Harvard Business Review. Retrieved June 4, 2020, from Harvard Business Review website: https://hbr.org/2015/11/what-a-great-digital-customer-experience-actually-looks-like

18 Borowski, C. (2015). What a Great Digital Customer Experience Actually Looks Like. Harvard Business Review. Retrieved June 4, 2020, from Harvard Business Review website: https://hbr.org/2015/11/what-a-great-digital-customer-experience-actually-looks-like

19 TTEC. (2020). Digital Customer Experience Strategy: Six Key Areas to Focus Your Efforts. Retrieved June 5, 2020, from TTEC website: www.ttec.com/articles/digital-customer-experience-strategy-six-key-areas-focus-your-efforts#:~:text=A%20digital%20experience%20strategy%20requires,service%20interactions%20is%20not%20sufficient.

9 Role of hospitality and leisure managers in enterprise architecture, technology sourcing, data analytics, and data management

Introduction

This chapter puts a spotlight on three capabilities that we contend are the most important building blocks for operating and competing as a digital business, besides people. The first, enterprise architecture management, relates to how the organization's technology infrastructure, information/data, and business processes are and should be configured. The second, technology sourcing, relates to how an organization goes about finding, choosing, and procuring the technologies and related services to be added as components of its enterprise architecture. The third, data management and data analytics, relates to an organization's ability to collect, validate, store, and leverage data to spur data-driven decision making. Taken together, the organization's ability to effectively build and manage these capabilities can expand or constrain its efficiency, differentiation, adaptability, and agility. This effect can be supercharged through the capacity of these capabilities to catalyze all other digital transformation and digital business capabilities. Effectively establishing and continuously upgrading the competitiveness of these capabilities requires organization-wide improvement, and cascades as an important part of managers' roles at all levels (i.e. vertically up and down the hierarchy and horizontally across functions). We unpack the types of roles leaders can play in each capability and the types of competencies required to effectively play those roles.

Required managerial roles and competencies for enterprise architecture management and technology sourcing

Unpacking enterprise architecture

Enterprise architecture (EA) refers to the design or configuration of the different elements/assets of an organization (e.g. hardware, software, networks, business processes, information systems, information, data) and the resultant levels of efficiency, effectiveness, and longevity they enable an organization to have in the pursuit of its mission within its external environment. For example, one particular design or configuration may lead to mediocre levels of efficiency and effectiveness in the pursuit of the organization's mission (e.g. perhaps due to having a random collection of disparate hardware, software, networks, business processes, and information/data that don't work well together – thus constraining connectivity, communication, collaboration, and customer experience). For an organization like the Ritz-Carlton Hotel, for example, such enterprise architecture would severely limit its mission of providing guests with the finest personalized service and experience,[1] and would, in turn, limit its longevity. Another type of design or configuration might be suited to maximizing connectivity, integrability, communication, collaboration, automation, adaptability, and customer experience, resulting in very high levels of efficiency and effectiveness. We contend that the latter is the type of enterprise architecture that leading digital businesses like Microsoft, Amazon, Google, and Netflix have. Enterprise architecture has had simpler (although perhaps less complete) definitions, including that it is the process of aligning an organization's strategic vision with its information technology,[2] that it is how information/business/technology flow together,[3] and that it is the organizing logic for how business processes and IT infrastructure should work together to meet operational requirements.[4]

Enterprise architecture is described as being layered (i.e. having business architecture, information architecture, information systems architecture, data architecture, and delivery architecture layers), as spanning the entire organization (i.e. vertically up and down the hierarchy and horizontally across business functions), as both conceptual and physical (i.e. being a visual or written logical representations or being the actual elements/assets), as iterative (i.e. built or evolving over time through iterative additions/improvements), and as both current and forward looking (i.e. that EA designs or configurations deal with both current and future business needs). According to practitioners and researchers, good enterprise architecture should enable both current and future strategy (e.g. operational effectiveness, business transformation),[5] be proactive (i.e. anticipate and prepare for the future needs of the business),[6] speed up processes (e.g. digitize, integrate, and automate key processes), enable adaptability (e.g. through plug and play digital assets that can be adapted to different internal and external systems/technologies/processes), ensure availability and accessibility of high-quality data across the enterprise to drive decision making (e.g. cleaning, standardizing, sharing, presenting data), and instantiate the organization's digital business model.[7]

Enterprise architecture management

Enterprise architecture management refers to the processes and practices of planning, implementing, maintaining, and continuously improving an organization's enterprise architecture. At a high level, it involves the continuous and iterative activities of identifying EA stakeholders and their concerns, understanding the existing EA and the value it creates, designing the target EA, planning the EA implementation, transitioning to the target EA, and ensuring effective EA governance.[8] See Table 9.1[9] providing example EA activities and tasks and the resultant artifacts (hospitality and leisure managers may be presented with and have to interpret these artifacts by EA leaders and/or consultants). The benefits from effective EA management are broad and include the capacity for improved communication and collaboration, improved decision making, improved functional and external partner alignment, improved customer satisfaction, reduced complexity, and more. EA researchers identify more than 40 benefits of effective enterprise architecture (see Table 9.2). Given the digital business transformation and digital business imperatives, a key benefit, and the one integrating all the 40 listed benefits, is successful digital business transformation and the capacity to effectively compete as a digital business. Enterprise architecture leaders can ensure the design or configuration of and transition to architectures that simultaneously deliver efficiency, differentiation, adaptability, and agility capabilities. Although previously seen as being "either/or" choices, simultaneously having these capabilities has been shown to be essential in increasingly complex business environments.[10,11]

Table 9.1 Example enterprise architecture management activities, tasks, and artifacts

EA Management Activities	EA Management Tasks	Resultant EA Management Artifacts
Identifying EA stakeholders and their concerns	Identification of stakeholders and their concerns	List of stakeholders
	Identification of project motivation	Project goals and objectives
Understanding the existing EA and the enterprise value it creates	General view of the enterprise	Business model canvas "as is"
	Identification of company goals, objectives and indicators for their measurement	Strategy map (or goal tree) Balanced scorecard
	Identification of value proposition (VP)	Tree of products/services, value curve
	Identification of the value configuration "as is"	Value creation model
	Identification of the operations architecture "as is"	Function decomposition model Process landscape Business process models (if necessary)
	Organizational structure and responsibility matrix "as is"	Organization chart Responsibility matrix (or RACI-matrix)
	IT architecture "as is" (existing information systems and technological infrastructure)	Model of application/IS usage Description of the application/IS landscape Infrastructure use model
	General idea of EA "as is"	High-level (overview) EA model
Designing the target EA (★ several alternative scenarios may be developed at this stage)	Development of target EA vision	Business model canvas "to be"
	Development of target EA with detailing of representations by layers	High-level (overview) model "to be" Particular EA models, which will be affected by changes (composition of models as in the description of the current state), "to be"
Planning and effecting the implementation and transitioning to the target EA	Planning of the transition between the EA states (current, target, transitional)	Transition planning model (linking EA changes/gaps with work packages)
	Formation of development projects portfolio	Transformation and development program cards (proposed initiatives)
	Planning for implementation and transition (see project management)	Schedule of transformation projects (for example, in MS Project)
Ensuring effective EA governance	Establishing and maintaining effective EA organization structure with clear roles and responsibilities	EA organization chart, EA function job descriptions, KPIs
	Establishing and maintaining effective EA governance practices	EA governance model
	Establishing and maintaining effective EA standards and guidelines	EA framework
	Establishing and maintaining effective EA management tools	Architecture repository

Table 9.2 Benefits of effective enterprise architecture management

EA Management Benefits	
Document knowledge on the enterprise	Improve resource quality
Identify resource dependencies	Improve return on investments
Identify resource synergies	Improve situational awareness
Identify suboptimal resource use	Improve solution development
Improve alignment with partners	Improve stability
Improve change management	Increase agility
Improve compliance	Increase economies of scale
Improve customer satisfaction	Increase efficiency
Improve decision making	Increase growth
Improve employee satisfaction	Increase innovation
Improve enterprise-wide goal attainment	Increase market share
Improve information quality	Increase resource flexibility
Improve investment management	Increase resource reuse
Improve measurement	Increase resource standardization
Improve organizational alignment	Increase revenue
Improve organizational collaboration	Provide a high-level overview
Improve organizational communication	Provide directions for improvement
Improve resource alignment	Provide standards
Improve resource consolidation	Reduce costs
Improve resource integration	Reduce complexity

New or enhanced managerial roles and competencies required for effective enterprise architecture management

Hospitality and leisure managers can play a range of roles in enterprise architecture management. First, the top enterprise architecture management role can be filled by someone from the IT/IS/technology function, but who has deep operational process and industry knowledge, or by someone from operations or another functional area but who has sufficient IT/IS/technology competencies.[12] Both individuals are likely to be challenging to find and to retain. Another option is strong collaboration between someone from the IT/IS/technology function and someone from the operations function with deep industry knowledge. So, hospitality and leisure managers can be involved in directly managing the EA function or having shared responsibility for its effectiveness.

Outside of direct or shared management of EA, hospitality and leisure managers can play other important roles. For example, they may be involved in hiring the person to directly manage the EA function, in setting or approving the EA vision and high-level objectives, in interpreting and using EA artifacts, or in identifying and/or selecting among different technology/network/hardware/software/process options. Alternatively, they may be asked to participate in EA-related discussions; they may be involved in choosing between different EA target state options; they may participate in EA governance or oversight of EA governance; or they may have to change business processes to align with chosen EA target state options. See Figure 9.1 for examples of potential hospitality and leisure manager involvement in enterprise architecture governance at different hierarchical levels of an organization. To effectively play one or more EA roles we have outlined, hospitality and leisure managers need a working understanding of enterprise architecture and enterprise architecture management (e.g. what are their aims, how do they work, what are the opportunities and challenges), they need working knowledge of EA artifacts (e.g. being

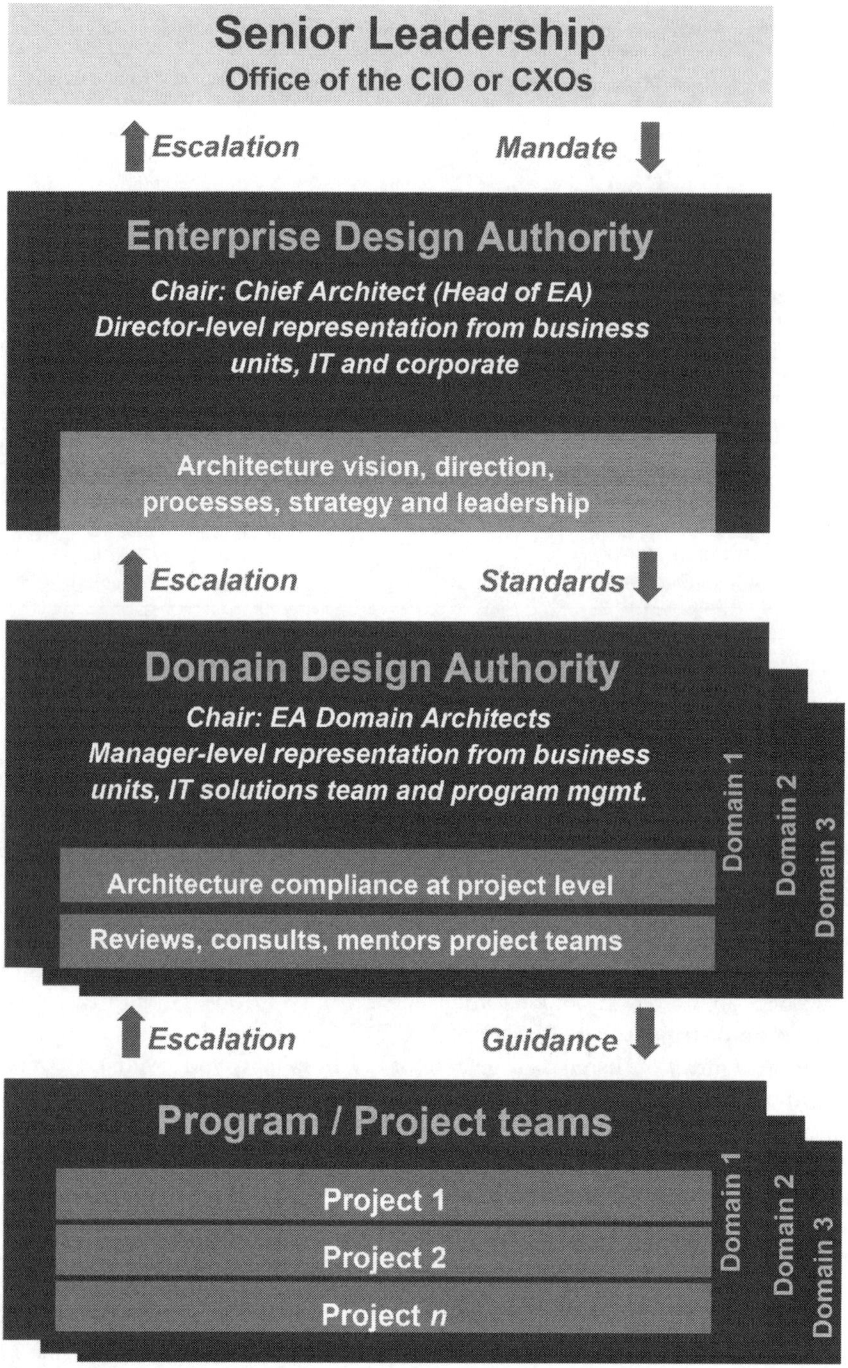

Figure 9.1 Example enterprise architecture governance model

able to read EA plans), and they need working knowledge of different digital technologies and the strategic opportunities and risks associated with those digital technologies.

Required managerial roles and competencies for technology sourcing

Unpacking technology sourcing

Technology sourcing capability refers to the effectiveness of an organization's processes/ practices for finding, choosing, and procuring technology resources required for its current and desired enterprise architectures. Digital technology advancements and digital disruption have expanded the focus of technology sourcing from cost minimization and risk mitigation to driving innovation, revenue growth, customer retention, speed, adaptability, and agility.[13] Through finding, choosing, and partnering with the right vendors, and through getting contracts right and managing the relationships appropriately, organizations can reap rewards such as having superior hardware/software/networks relative to competitors, undertaking product co-creation with vendors, vendor-induced migration to state-of-the-art practices, vendor originated to new technologies and new customers, and so forth. Through finding, choosing, and adopting breakthrough technologies and products, an organization can speed up realization of their desired enterprise architectures or exceed what they thought possible from enterprise architecture. For example, imagine an organization being one of the first companies to discover, choose, and procure Amazon's Elastic Compute Cloud back in 2006. That organization would have been able to spin up a virtual desktop, fully equipped with all of the organization's systems and data, on any computer anywhere in the world. Depending on the nature of its core products, this could have given it unfair global scalability and portability advantages relative to competitors.

New or enhanced managerial roles and competencies required for technology sourcing

Hospitality and leisure managers can play critical roles in technology sourcing including scouting for transformative technologies and vendors, building collaborative relationships with vendors, engaging in co-creation efforts with vendors,[14] sourcing informal advice from vendors, scouting for innovative business models that could be applied in the hospitality and leisure industry, scouting products/services used in the organization that are no longer needed/that need upgrading/or that have better or cheaper alternatives on the market, engaging their teams to be the organizations eyes and ears with regard to new technology breakthroughs or star vendors, and more. They can also fill formal roles such as procurement director, technology sourcing manager, vendor relationship manager, business engagement manager, and contract manager. To effectively undertake these roles, hospitality and leisure managers need to build working knowledge of the role, functioning, strategies, and potential value of the technology procurement and sourcing function. They need working understanding of different digital technologies, of related products and services, and of the vendor landscape. They also need to have an understanding of the organization's enterprise architecture and how to engage constructively with the enterprise architecture management team.

Required managerial roles and competencies for data management, data science, and data analytics

Unpacking data management

As one of their key disruption areas, digital technology advancements have made and continue to make vast quantities of internal and external data available. For example, more than 500 million tweets, 294 billion emails, 5 billion search engine searches, and 4 petabytes of Facebook data are created each day – and it is estimated that there are up to 40 times more bytes of data than there are stars in the known universe.[15] The big challenge for organizations is how to leverage the vast quantities of internal and external data to improve their efficiency, differentiation, adaptability, and agility.[16] Effective data management and data analytics, which are covered in more detail in the digital technologies deep dive section of the book, play a critical role in addressing this challenge.

Data management capabilities refer to an organization's processes and practices for collecting, validating, storing, and using data most effectively.[17] This can be a challenge, given the growing avalanche of internal and external data to manage, and the growing sources of such data. For example, data can come from software as a service (SaaS) applications, enterprise resource planning (ERP) systems, legacy systems, databases, data warehouses, and data lakes. Or it may come from the web, social media platforms, or open data and commercial data platforms. Alternatively, it may come from any number of devices including phones, computers, wearable devices, sensors, or monitoring devices. All this data has to be collected safely, validated, stored safely, and formatted and presented so that different parts of the organization can access the right information at the right time and in the right format to make the best decisions. This requires that organizations have the right technical leaders, the right technical specialists, the right technology platforms, and the right policies, procedures, and practices. The data management function typically plays a leadership role in issues such as data governance (who has what decision rights and what accountability for data quality), data architecture (what rules, policies, standards, and models are in place to determine what data is collected, how it is stored, how it is integrated, and how it is used), data modeling and design (defining and analyzing data required to support business processes), database and storage management, and data security and privacy.

Unpacking data analytics and data science

Data analytics (also referred to just as analytics)[18] is an umbrella term referring to any form of analysis of data to uncover trends, patterns, anomalies, or simply to measure performance.[19,20,21] It also includes interpretation, presentation, and communication of discovered patterns to improve decision making. Analytics approaches or methods can include descriptive analytics (using historic or current data to determine "what" happened and "how" it happened), predictive analytics (understanding the "why" or cause-and-effect relationships within data in order to be able to make accurate predictions), and prescriptive analytics (using algorithms to suggest optimal decisions based on the results of descriptive and predictive analytics). Often going hand in hand with data analytics, data science is a method for drawing insights from large data sets of structured and unstructured data. It draws on approaches, methods, techniques, and theories from disciplines such as mathematics, statistics, computer science, and information science. For example, it may draw on machine learning and deep learning techniques from the computer science field to learn from past decisions in order to improve the quality of automatically prescribed decisions. Or it may draw on statistical methods such as regression analysis and structural equation modeling to improve the reliability of information used as a basis for prescribed decisions. The role of data scientists includes activities such as collecting data, cleaning data, organizing data, making statistical inferences, building/ using machine learning or deep learning models, conducting online experiments, building customizable or personalized data products, visualizing data, and communicating findings.[22,23] Collectively, data management, data analytics, and data science have the same high level aims: leveraging internal and external data to drive optimal decisions; which may in turn drive efficiency, differentiation, adaptability and agility.

New or enhanced managerial roles and competencies required for data management, data analytics, and data science

Hospitality and leisure managers can play a range of roles in an organization's data management, data analytics, and data science efforts. For example, these include establishing a data management/data analytics/data science function, establishing data and data analytics objectives, using data insights, hiring/line managing data management/data analytics/ data science staff or service providers, sponsoring data management/data analytics/data science leaders, authorizing what systems to map and connect, getting relevant parties on board with change efforts,[24] approving funding for data investment projects, approving what data to use from inside or outside the organization, releasing function-specific data, approving procurement of particular data management technologies, and ensuring the best data is used for decision making. To effectively play one or more of these different roles, hospitality and leisure managers need to have a solid understanding of data management, data analytics, and data science (e.g. their objectives, functioning, methodologies/ tools, challenges, state-of-the-art practice, key terminology), and their related artifacts. This is in addition to earlier identified enterprise architecture management and technology sourcing competencies.

Google and reflect

Digital Capability	Common Terminology
Enterprise architecture management	Enterprise architecture, enterprise architectural planning (EAP), enterprise architecture management (EAM), Enterprise Architecture Body of Knowledge (EABOK), enterprise architect, enterprise architecture modeling (EAM), enterprise architecture framework, business architecture, information architecture, information systems architecture, data architecture, DevOps architecture, architecture repository, service-oriented architecture (SOA), backward compatibility
Technology sourcing	Procurement market intelligence, supplier co-creation, internal sourcing, partner-based sourcing, market-based sourcing, value chain sourcing, industry-university collaboration, technology scanning, technology transfer, technology licensing, technological alliance, technology acquisition, joint research and development

(*Continued*)

(Continued)

Digital Capability	Common Terminology
Data analytics and data management	Database, data mart, data warehouse, data lake, data catalog, enterprise data hub, data fabric, operational data store, data governance, data architecture, open data
	Machine learning, deep learning, neural networks, data mining, data set, data democratization, natural language processing, data anonymization, behavioral analytics, citizen data scientist, data classification, decision trees, multidimensional database (MDB), online analytical processing (OLAP), outlier, predictive modeling, Python, R (programming language), random forest, validity, reliability, decision science, association analytics, sentiment analysis, time decomposition, cluster analysis

Discussion questions

1 What is the difference between enterprise architecture, IT architecture, and technology architecture?
2 What role does enterprise architecture play in digital business capabilities?
3 Which managerial role in enterprise architecture management is the most critical to building and maintaining that capability? Why?
4 Which enterprise architecture management competency is likely to have the greatest positive impact on a hospitality and leisure manager's career?
5 What is the difference between technology sourcing and technology procurement?
6 Which managerial role in technology sourcing is the most critical to building and maintaining that capability? Why?
7 What is the difference between data management and data analytics?
8 Which is more important, data management or data analytics? Why?
9 Which data management and data analytics managerial competency is likely to have the greatest positive impact on a hospitality and leisure manager's career?
10 Which of the capabilities discussed in this chapter is the most important to succeeding at digital transformation and digital business?

Notes

1 Ritz–Carlton. (2020). Gold Standards. Retrieved June 6, 2020, from the Ritz–Carlton website: www.ritzcarlton.com/en/about/gold-standards
2 Daniel, D. (2007, March 31). The Rising Importance of the Enterprise Architect. CIO. Retrieved from www.cio.com/article/2439397/the-rising-importance-of-the-enterprise-architect.html
3 White, S. K. (2018, October 16). What is Enterprise Architecture? A Framework for Transformation. CIO. Retrieved from www.cio.com/article/3313657/what-is-enterprise-architecture-a-framework-for-transformation.html
4 Ross, J. W., Weill, P., & Robertson, D. (2006). *Enterprise Architecture as Strategy: Creating a Foundation for Business Execution.* Harvard Business Press.
5 Daniel, D. (2007, March 31). The Rising Importance of the Enterprise Architect. CIO. Retrieved from www.cio.com/article/2439397/the-rising-importance-of-the-enterprise-architect.html
6 Daniel, D. (2007, March 31). The Rising Importance of the Enterprise Architect. CIO. Retrieved from www.cio.com/article/2439397/the-rising-importance-of-the-enterprise-architect.html
7 Suer, M. F. (2018, June 26). Enterprise Architects as Digital Transformers. CIO. Retrieved from www.cio.com/article/3284475/enterprise-architects-as-digital-transformers.html
8 Kudryavtsev, D., Zaramenskikh, E., & Arzumanyan, M. (2018). The Simplified Enterprise Architecture Management Methodology for Teaching Purposes. *Lecture Notes in Business Information Processing*, 76–90. https://doi.org/10.1007/978-3-030-00787-4_6

9 Kudryavtsev, D., Zaramenskikh, E., & Arzumanyan, M. (2018). The Simplified Enterprise Architecture Management Methodology for Teaching Purposes. *Lecture Notes in Business Information Processing*, 76–90. https://doi.org/10.1007/978-3-030-00787-4_6

10 Ovans, A. (2015, May 12). What is Strategy, Again. Harvard Business Review. Retrieved June 7, 2020, from Harvard Business Review website: https://hbr.org/2015/05/what-is-strategy-again

11 Busulwa, R., Tice, M., & Gurd, B. (2018). *Strategy Execution and Complexity: Thriving in the Era of Disruption*. Routledge.

12 Daniel, D. (2007, March 31). The Rising Importance of the Enterprise Architect. CIO. Retrieved from www.cio.com/article/2439397/the-rising-importance-of-the-enterprise-architect.html

13 Pettey, C. (2018, July 16). Top Trends for the Future of IT Procurement. Retrieved June 7, 2020, from Gartner.com website: www.gartner.com/smarterwithgartner/top-trends-for-the-future-of-it-procurement/

14 Sinclair, S. (2020). What are the Future Skills of Sourcing? Aalto University. Retrieved June 8, 2020, from Aaltopro.fi website: www.aaltopro.fi/en/aalto-leaders-insight/2020/what-are-the-future-skills-of-sourcing

15 Desjardins, J. (2019, April 17). How Much Data is Generated Each Day? Retrieved June 7, 2020, from World Economic Forum website: www.weforum.org/agenda/2019/04/how-much-data-is-generated-each-day-cf4bddf29f/

16 Brylad, M. (2019). Data Literacy: A Critical Skill for the 21st Century. Tableau Software. Retrieved December 17, 2019, from www.tableau.com/about/blog/2018/9/data-literacy-critical-skill-21st-century-94221

17 "What is Data Management?" (2019). Oracle.Com. Retrieved December 9, 2019, from www.oracle.com/au/database/what-is-data-management/

18 Analytics. (2019). Gartner. Retrieved December 16, 2019, from www.gartner.com/en/information-technology/glossary/analytics

19 Comparing Business Intelligence, Business Analytics and Data Analytics. (2019). Tableau Software. Retrieved December 16, 2019, from www.tableau.com/learn/articles/business-intelligence/bi-business-analytics

20 Business Analytics: Everything You Need to Know. (2019). MicroStrategy. Retrieved December 16, 2019, from www.microstrategy.com/us/resources/introductory-guides/business-analytics-everything-you-need-to-know

21 Boulton, C. (2019). Data Analytics Examples: An Inside Look at 6 Success Stories. CIO. Retrieved December 17, 2019, from www.cio.com/article/3221621/6-data-analytics-success-stories-an-inside-look.html

22 Bowne-Anderson, H. (2018). What Data Scientists Really Do, According to 35 Data Scientists. Harvard Business Review. Retrieved December 17, 2019, from https://hbr.org/2018/08/what-data-scientists-really-do-according-to-35-data-scientists

23 What is Data Science? | Oracle. (2019). Oracle.com. Retrieved December 17, 2019, from www.oracle.com/data-science/what-is-data-science.html

24 Daniel, D. (2007, March 31). The Rising Importance of the Enterprise Architect. CIO. Retrieved from www.cio.com/article/2439397/the-rising-importance-of-the-enterprise-architect.html

10 Role of hospitality and leisure managers in cybersecurity, information privacy, and digital ethics

Introduction

Depending on how they are used, digital technologies can present significant threats to the rights and well-being of individuals and to the effective functioning of political, economic, social, environmental, and legal institutions, processes, and practices. Individuals, societies, and institutions are increasingly conscious of these threats and are apprehensive about the trust they place in organizations to safeguard against them. So, in their quest to leverage digital technologies to become and compete as a digital business, organizations must ensure they are conscious of these threats and have effective practices to safeguard against their enhancement or materialization. Organizations that don't do this can quickly find themselves in a position where they have put customers, societies, and institutions in grave danger, in addition to greatly increasing their chance of going out of business (e.g. Cambridge Analytica). In this chapter, we unpack two important capabilities for organizations in the digital era: cybersecurity capability and information privacy and digital ethics capability. We outline the meaning and need for these capabilities; the risk of not sufficiently investing in them; the functions, processes, and practices involved in establishing them; the role of hospitality and leisure managers in establishing and continuously improving these capabilities; and the competencies required to do so.

Required managerial roles and competencies for cybersecurity

Unpacking cybersecurity

At a very high level, cybersecurity refers to the state of or processes for protecting anything in the cyber realm (e.g. devices, software, things, networks, information) and recovering from cyberattacks.[1,2,3] The terms information security, IT security, ICT security, computer security, and network security are sometimes interchangeably used to refer to cybersecurity, even though there are differences in meaning.[4] Typically, these terms refer to specific subsets of cybersecurity. For example, information security is mainly focused on protecting physical and digital information from unauthorized access, use, disclosure, disruption, modification, or destruction in order to provide confidentiality, integrity, and availability.[5,6] And IT security, ICT security, and computer security tend to focus more narrowly on protecting computers, networks, and data – but what about the exploding diversity in IoT "things" and ecosystems? Given some of the limitations and slipperiness of these aforementioned terms, the term cybersecurity has emerged as a more flexible and all-encompassing term. But there have still been differences in the way practitioners and researchers have defined cybersecurity. Daniel Schatz, global head of cybersecurity at Qiagen and former director of threat and vulnerability management at Thomson Reuters, and Julie Wall, a senior researcher at the University of East London, reviewed and synthesized the various definitions to arrive at a more specific, more encompassing, and complete definition of cybersecurity. They proposed that cybersecurity is:[7]

> the approach and actions associated with security risk management processes followed by organizations and states to protect confidentiality, integrity and availability of data and assets used in cyberspace. The concept includes guidelines, policies and collections of safeguards, technologies, tools and training to provide the best protection for the state of the cyber environment and its users.

Cybersecurity may not have historically been in your consciousness as a big deal for people outside the IT or IS function. And you may be wondering what has changed to make it an issue warranting much attention from hospitality and leisure managers. If so, consider this: How much of your organization's information was indefinitely online in the past? How many devices within and outside of your organization were "plugged" into that information? How many people around the world were online and able to hack into your information systems? How sophisticated was the computation available to hackers? How fast was the internet connectivity speed? How much integration was there? As you may be starting to see, the race to digitally transform and become a digital business has meant that almost all of an organization's resources are now online and potentially accessible by billions of people anywhere in the world. On top of this, the exponentially growing proliferation of "things," external networks, and ecosystems plugging into an organization's online resources almost creates the effect of having millions, even billions, of potential front doors to your house that you may or may not be aware of. These might make it difficult to have peace of mind when not home or to be safe sleeping at night. And data flows from and to devices, from and to core systems with sensitive data, from and to external networks and devices, from and to different locations around the world, and from and to different digital ecosystems. At any point during that flow, or while it resides in a particular storage location, digitized data and information can be intercepted by sophisticated cybercriminals anywhere in the world. For example, they may intercept login details, they may steal identification information for on-selling to identity thieves, they may steal company trade secrets or key stakeholder intellectual property, they may alter company records for their own gain, they may steal sensitive key persons' information and hold it for ransom, they may steal and dump sensitive customer data online in order jeopardize the organization, and much more. Thus, the significantly expanded digitization, connectivity, integration, and ubiquity related to digital transformation and digital business means new and significantly expanded digital vulnerabilities. In fact, massive cybersecurity breaches have become almost commonplace now, with even prestige brands regularly being in attention-grabbing and alarming breach headlines.[8] For example, in early 2020 Marriott International was in one such headline.[9] A cybercriminal had hacked the login details of two employees from a franchise property and used those login details to access customer information from the app's back-end systems.[10] This impacted 5.2 million customers and included access to personal information including name, address, phone number, date of birth, gender, travel history, and travel plans.[11] It followed another incident in 2018 in which 383 million guests' details were stolen, including names, addresses, passport numbers, and credit card numbers.[12,13] Imagine how you would feel as a customer; any one of these incidents would likely undo any organization credibility or brand trust. And it could have been much worse: imagine if cybercriminals used guests' travel history and mobile information to track down key persons in remote locations and hold them hostage or sell them into human trafficking rings. In addition to ruining customers' lives, almost a century of brand building could have been brought down almost overnight, and thousands of employees could have lost their jobs. Perhaps due to the growing breaches and the significant risks customers are exposed to, a number of governments around the world have started to introduce mandatory data breach reporting laws, requiring organizations to report data breaches where personal information they hold is subject to unauthorized access or disclosure.[14,15] This makes naming and shaming through attention-grabbing headlines a certainty for organizations that fail to protect the data entrusted into their care. Finally, it goes without saying that the financial costs involved in a breach can be ruinous; these are typically exacerbated by the time it takes to discover the breach, to respond to it, and to recover from the associated disruption – to the extent this is actually possible.[16] Figure 10.1 shows the top 10 messages for leaders synthesized from the World Economic Forum's annual meeting exploring critical and emerging cybersecurity issues.

10 Messages for Global Leaders from the Annual Meeting on Cybersecurity

1 Cyberattacks are increasing in frequency and sophistication. It is hence the responsibility of public and corporate leaders to take ownership for ensuring global cybersecurity and digital trust.

2 Board and C-Suite members need to gain a better understanding of the cyber risks to which their organization is exposed and of their cyber readiness.

3 Both public and private organizations need to improve their crisis management, develop holistic response and recovery plans, including a crisis communication strategy.

4 Leaders need to create a culture of cybersecurity from the entry level to the top leadership of an organization.

5 Leaders may need to rethink organizational structures and governance to enable a more robust cybersecurity posture.

6 Innovation in cybersecurity and rapidly evolving technologies call for greater investment to stay ahead of cybercriminals who are adopting such technologies even faster and to their advantage.

7 Global cooperation across the public and the private sectors is vital. Information-sharing, business cooperation with law enforcement agencies as well as skills and capacity development to be prioritized.

8 Maintaining an open and secure internet requires a collaborative effort between the public and private sector.

9 Trusted and verified cybersecurity ratings are required for the improved assessment of an organization's cyber resilience and comparability across peers.

10 The World Economic Forum provides a neutral, trusted and globally recognized platform to facilitate cooperation and deliver tangible impact on the systemic challenge of global cybersecurity.

Figure 10.1 Ten messages for global leaders from the 2019 World Economic Forum annual meeting on cybersecurity[17]

Cybersecurity capability and cybersecurity management

Cybersecurity capability refers to how effectively an organization can protect itself and recover from cyber threats (i.e. how effective is its cybersecurity infrastructure, consisting of hardware, software, processes, and people). Cybersecurity management refers to the processes and practices of planning, implementing, maintaining, and continuously upgrading an organization's cybersecurity capability. According to the National Institute of Standards and Technology cybersecurity framework[18] (NIST CSF), cybersecurity capability consists of five core functions: identify, protect, detect, respond, and recover (see Figure 10.2). The "identify" function involves developing a clear understanding of the business' processes and environment, its supporting systems/people/assets/data/capabilities, the cyberthreats faced by these systems/people/assets/data/capabilities (e.g. ransomware, hacking, data leakage, insider threat), and the potential impact of these threats on the organization. It includes asset management, business environment, governance, risk assessment, and risk management strategy practices.

The "protect" function involves establishing and maintaining appropriate safeguards to prevent or limit the impact of a potential cybersecurity event. It includes practices such as identity management and access control, awareness training, data security, information protection processes and procedures, and use of protective technology. The "detect" function involves establishing and maintaining appropriate activities for the timely identification of cybersecurity events. It includes practice such as anomaly detection, security continuous monitoring, and detection processes. The "respond" function involves establishing and maintaining processes for containing the impact of a detected cybersecurity incident. It includes practices such as response planning, communication, analysis, migration, and improvement. Finally, the "recover" function involves establishing and maintaining resiliency and service/capability restoration plans (i.e. plans that can be effected for timely recovery

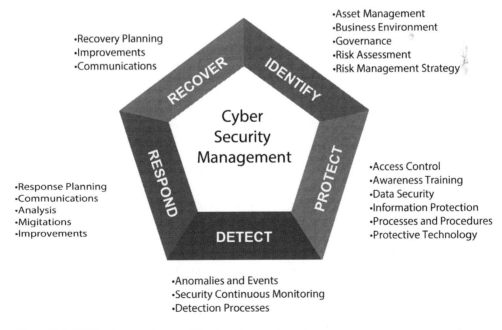

Figure 10.2 NIST cybersecurity capability functions and practices

from a disruptive cybersecurity incident). It includes practices such as recovery planning, communication, and continuous improvement. See the cybersecurity capability maturity model (C2M2) for an example of an alternative cybersecurity capability framework.[19]

New or enhanced roles and competencies for cybersecurity management

Effective cybersecurity management and an effective cybersecurity capability requires senior leadership ownership/engagement, a top–down aspect to strategy and integration of cybersecurity policies/activities into operations to ensure cyber and privacy risks are managed effectively in every part of the organization.[20,21,22] It requires leaders to cultivate and drive the cultivation of a cyber risk management culture at all levels. A hospitality and leisure manager may play the role of a senior leader with responsibility for the organization's overall cybersecurity capability (e.g. hiring the right functional leader, building the credibility and influence of this leader, and establishing cybersecurity objectives and governance mechanisms), or they may play other roles such as ensuring employee understanding of and compliance with cybersecurity policies, ensuring employees report cybersecurity breach events, and ensuring employees have adequate knowledge of and competency in cybersecurity so that they are able to avoid cybersecurity compromising behaviors.[23] In either case, a working understanding of the cybersecurity function's objectives, functioning, and challenges is essential. Similarly, an understanding of cyber risks and threats, state-of-the-art cybersecurity practices, and cybersecurity terminology is essential. Having a cybersecurity event originate from and be due to lapses within a particular line manager's team can negatively impact that manager's career.

Required managerial roles and competencies for information privacy and other digital ethics issues

Unpacking information privacy

Information privacy refers to an individual's interest and/or ability to control, or at least significantly influence, the handling of data about themselves.[24] Information privacy includes personal communication privacy, personal behavior privacy, and personal data privacy.[25] The handling of data refers to issues including what data is collected and how, the primary use of the data (the purpose for which the data is originally collected), the secondary use of the data (other data uses in addition to the primary purpose), any unauthorized secondary use, what analysis is done on the data, what improper access is it exposed to, what errors are in it, and how long the data will be kept for (e.g. does this impinge on a person's "right to be forgotten"). Although the concept of privacy existed before the advent of digital technologies,[26,27,28] the use of digital technologies results in significant privacy threats. For example, consider the expanded access to information (e.g. using big data, data analytics, search engines, social networks, triangulation algorithms), ubiquity (e.g. digital technologies are with us when we sleep, when we wake up, while we are working, while we are socializing), undetectability (e.g. cookies, location-based services, real-time video analytics, miniaturized devices), and invasiveness (e.g. implantable chips) of digital technologies. Also consider the permanency of the data they capture, the near real-time external accessibility to this data, and the ease with which it can be sold and used anywhere around the world. Unfortunately, although consumers desire privacy, they are often in a situation where they can't receive certain services without sharing personal information. Outside of leveraging privacy enhancing technologies in the purchasing process and avoiding consumption, consumers have little choice but to place their trust in particular brands and/or in regulators.

Digital ethics and digital ethics issues

Besides privacy and security, there are a range of other technology-related ethical threats that are generally collated under the umbrella of digital ethics.[29] Digital ethics considers the ethicality of the existing and potential impacts of digital technologies on political, social, economic, environmental, and legal dynamics and entities. For example, it considers and builds discussions of issues such as ethics of surveillance (e.g. when and what information can be given to the state), digital monopolies (growing concentration of power in large technology companies), uses of and regulation of artificial intelligence, automation and robotics-driven unemployment, disparities between tech-savvy and non-tech-savvy people, transparency in how data is held/where it is held/who has access to it, discrimination embedded in algorithms and big data, environmental impacts of digital technology-related waste, and more. Organizations not conscious of or not reflecting these broader digital ethics issues in their policies and conduct can quickly find themselves on the wrong side of an issue of importance to society. For example, Cambridge Analytica,[30,31] Facebook,[32] Google,[33] Twitter,[34] and Amazon[35] have recently found themselves in the crossfire in relation to one or more of these ethics issues. Thus when choosing which digital technologies to leverage and how to leverage them, in addition to security and privacy implications, organizations need to consider the broader digital ethics implications relating to use of those digital technologies.

Consumers, governments, and advocacy groups are increasingly conscious of and concerned with information privacy and other digital ethics practices of organizations. Besides the resultant ethical threats these practices can create, for some consumers the practices are also about respect – and they feel disrespected by organizations that disregard or don't take seriously their privacy and digital ethics concerns. Thus through their particular action or nonaction, organizations can alleviate the threat/disrespect concerns and enhance the trust customers have in them, or they can heighten concerns and erode this trust. Their action or nonaction, then, can have significant consequences for their brand image, profitability, and longevity.

New or enhanced managerial roles and competencies for information privacy and digital ethics

As with other digital capabilities, hospitality and leisure managers can play critical roles in their organizations' information privacy and digital ethics capabilities. For example, they can embed a culture of privacy that enables compliance (e.g. ensure staff understand their privacy responsibilities, they can assign roles and responsibilities for information privacy and digital ethics management, they can institute reporting processes to keep top management informed about evolving ethics issues and practices), they can put in place effective information privacy and digital ethics practices/procedures/systems (e.g. having an information privacy and digital ethics policy, establishing processes for receiving and responding to information privacy and digital ethics issues or complaints, integrating information privacy and digital ethics into induction and training processes), and they can evaluate and continuously improve information privacy and digital ethics practices (e.g. regularly review policies/processes/events, monitor performance to plan, establish processes to enable staff and other stakeholders to provide feedback, establish processes for staying up to date with evolving expectations/best practices in relation to information privacy and digital ethics).[36] In addition to the aforementioned roles, hospitality and leisure managers at all levels can set the tone[37] for information privacy and digital ethics through what they say, how they behave, how they handle information privacy and digital ethics situations,[38] who they reward, and who they promote. To effectively play these different roles, hospitality and leisure managers need a working understanding of information privacy and digital ethics issues and best practices. They also need to ensure they keep with changes in these issues and practices as issues and best practices evolve rapidly.

Google and reflect

Digital Capability	Common Terminology
Cybersecurity	Cyber risk, cybersecurity, cybersecurity capability, cybersecurity management, cybersecurity framework, NIST CSF, cybersecurity event, cyber resilience, identity management, access control, anomaly detection, security continuous monitoring, cyber response planning, cyber recovery planning, DevSecOps, cyber insurance, ransomware
Information privacy and digital ethics	Privacy, information privacy, information privacy threat, right to be left alone, right to be forgotten, digital ethics, privacy enhancing technologies, breach disclosure, data breach notification, privacy act, data breach reporting laws

Discussion questions

1   What is the difference between cybersecurity, IT security, and ICT security?
2   What is the difference between cybersecurity management and cybersecurity?
3   What is the difference between privacy and information privacy?
4   What is the relationship between information privacy and digital ethics?
5   What is the relationship between cybersecurity, information privacy, and digital ethics?
6   What are the top three digital ethics issues at the moment?
7   Which is most important: cybersecurity, information privacy, or digital ethics?
8   Which managerial role in information privacy and digital ethics is most important to an organization's information privacy and digital ethics capability?
9   Which cybersecurity management competency is likely to have the greatest positive impact on a hospitality and leisure manager's career?
10 Which of the capabilities discussed in this chapter is the most important to succeeding at digital transformation and digital business?

Notes

1   Cisco. (2020). What is Information Security (InfoSec)? Retrieved June 8, 2020, from Cisco website: www.cisco.com/c/en/us/products/security/what-is-information-security-infosec.html
2   Secureworks. (2017). Cybersecurity vs. Network Security vs. Information Security. Retrieved June 8, 2020, from Secureworks.com website: www.secureworks.com/blog/cybersecurity-vs-network-security-vs-information-security
3   Norton. (2020). Retrieved June 8, 2020, from Norton.com website: https://us.norton.com/internetsecurity-malware-what-is-cybersecurity-what-you-need-to-know.html

4   Schatz, D., Bashroush, R., & Wall, J. (2017). Towards a More Representative Definition of Cyber Security. *Journal of Digital Forensics, Security and Law*, 12(2), 53–74.

5   Cisco. (2020). What is Information Security (InfoSec)? Retrieved June 9, 2020, from Cisco website: www.cisco.com/c/en/us/products/security/what-is-information-security-infosec.html

6   Secureworks. (2017). Cybersecurity vs. Network Security vs. Information Security. Retrieved June 8, 2020, from Secureworks.com website: www.secureworks.com/blog/cybersecurity-vs-network-security-vs-information-security

7   Schatz, D., Bashroush, R., & Wall, J. (2017). Towards a More Representative Definition of Cyber Security. *Journal of Digital Forensics, Security and Law*, 12(2), 53–74.

8   Castelli, C., Gabriel, B., Yates, J., & Booth, P. (2017). Strengthening Digital Society against Cyber Shocks. PricewaterhouseCoopers: PwC. Retrieved June 8, 2020, from PwC website: www.pwc.com/us/en/services/consulting/cybersecurity/library/information-security-survey/strengthening-digital-society-against-cyber-shocks.html

9   Cimpanu, C. (2020, March 31). Marriott Discloses New Data Breach Impacting 5.2 Million Hotel Guests. Retrieved June 8, 2020, from ZDNet website: www.zdnet.com/article/marriott-discloses-new-data-breach-impacting-5-2-million-hotel-guests/

10 Cimpanu, C. (2020, March 31). Marriott Discloses New Data Breach Impacting 5.2 Million Hotel Guests. Retrieved June 8, 2020, from ZDNet website: www.zdnet.com/article/marriott-discloses-new-data-breach-impacting-5-2-million-hotel-guests/

11 Cimpanu, C. (2020, March 31). Marriott Discloses New Data Breach Impacting 5.2 Million Hotel Guests. Retrieved June 8, 2020, from ZDNet website: www.zdnet.com/article/marriott-discloses-new-data-breach-impacting-5-2-million-hotel-guests/

12 Fruhlinger, J. (2020, February 12). Marriott Data Breach FAQ: How Did It Happen and What Was the Impact? Retrieved June 9, 2020, from CSO Online website: www.csoonline.com/article/3441220/marriott-data-breach-faq-how-did-it-happen-and-what-was-the-impact.html

13 Cimpanu, C. (2019, January 4). Marriott Says Less than 383 Million Guests Impacted by Breach, Not 500 Million. Retrieved June 9, 2020, from ZDNet website: www.zdnet.com/article/marriott-says-less-than-383-million-guests-impacted-by-breach-not-500-million/

14 Easton, S. (2019, May 20). Almost 1000 Data Breaches in a Year, and Citizens Don't Know Who to Trust with Privacy. Retrieved June 8, 2020, from The Mandarin website: www.themandarin.com.au/108762-almost-1000-data-breaches-in-a-year-and-citizens-dont-know-who-to-trust-with-privacy/

15 Innes, K. (2019). One Year of Mandatory Data Breach Reporting: Insights and Lessons. Bradley Allen Love Lawyers. Retrieved June 8, 2020, from Bradley Allen Love Lawyers website: https://ballawyers.com.au/2019/05/28/mandatory-data-breach-reporting/

16 Swinhoe, D. (2020, May 8). What is the Cost of a Data Breach? Retrieved June 9, 2020, from CSO Online website: www.csoonline.com/article/3434601/what-is-the-cost-of-a-data-breach.html#tk.ciofsb

17 Müller, M. S., & Zwinggi, A. (2020, January 19). Global Leaders Must Take Responsibility for Cybersecurity. Here's Why. Retrieved June 19, 2020, from World Economic Forum website: www.weforum.org/agenda/2020/01/global-leaders-must-take-responsibility-for-cybersecurity-here-s-why-and-how/

18 Christopher, J. (2018, November 1). Council Post: The Cybersecurity Maturity Model: A Means to Measure and Improve Your Cybersecurity Program. Forbes. Retrieved from www.forbes.com/sites/forbestechcouncil/2018/11/01/the-cybersecurity-maturity-model-a-means-to-measure-and-improve-your-cybersecurity-program/#32e367a680bc

19 Christopher, J. (2018, November 1). Council Post: The Cybersecurity Maturity Model: A Means to Measure and Improve Your Cybersecurity Program. Forbes. Retrieved from www.forbes.com/sites/forbestechcouncil/2018/11/01/the-cybersecurity-maturity-model-a-means-to-measure-and-improve-your-cybersecurity-program/#32e367a680bc

20 Castelli, C., Gabriel, B., Yates, J., & Booth, P. (2017). Strengthening Digital Society against Cyber Shocks. PricewaterhouseCoopers: PwC. Retrieved June 8, 2020, from PwC website: www.pwc.com/us/en/services/consulting/cybersecurity/library/information-security-survey/strengthening-digital-society-against-cyber-shocks.html

21 Oltsik, J. (2019, February 19). Enterprises Need to Embrace Top-Down Cybersecurity Management. Retrieved June 9, 2020, from CSO Online website: www.csoonline.com/article/3342036/enterprises-need-to-embrace-top-down-cybersecurity-management.html

22 Dutta, A., & McCrohan, K. (2002). Management's Role in Information Security in a Cyber Economy. *California Management Review*, 45(1), 67–87. https://doi.org/10.2307/41166154

23 Dutta, A., & McCrohan, K. (2002). Management's Role in Information Security in a Cyber Economy. *California Management Review*, 45(1), 67–87. https://doi.org/10.2307/41166154

24 Bélanger, F., & Crossler, R. E. (2011). Privacy in the Digital Age: A Review of Information Privacy Research in Information Systems. *MIS Quarterly*, 35(4), 1017–1042.

25 Bélanger, F., & Crossler, R. E. (2011). Privacy in the Digital Age: A Review of Information Privacy Research in Information Systems. *MIS Quarterly*, 35(4), 1017–1042.

26 Bélanger, F., & Crossler, R. E. (2011). Privacy in the Digital Age: A Review of Information Privacy Research in Information Systems. *MIS Quarterly*, 35(4), 1017–1042.

27 Igo, S. E. (2018). *The Known Citizen: A History of Privacy in Modern America*. Harvard University Press.

28 Holvast, J. (2007). History of Privacy. In *The History of Information Security* (pp. 737–769). Elsevier Science BV.

29 de Broglie, C. (2016). We Need to Talk about Digital Ethics. Retrieved June 10, 2020, from Oecd. org website: www.oecd.org/science/we-need-to-talk-about-digital-ethics.htm

30 Facebook and Cambridge Analytica: What You Need to Know as Fallout Widens. (2018, March 19). The New York Times. Retrieved from www.nytimes.com/2018/03/19/technology/facebook-cambridge-analytica-explained.html

31 Wong, J. C. (2019). The Cambridge Analytica Scandal Changed the World – But it Didn't Change Facebook. Retrieved June 10, 2020, from the Guardian website: www.theguardian.com/technology/2019/mar/17/the-cambridge-analytica-scandal-changed-the-world-but-it-didnt-change-facebook

32 Foroohar, R. (2020). EU and US Regulators Scrutinise Big Tech and Digital "Monopoly." Retrieved June 10, 2020, from @FinancialTimes website: www.ft.com/content/f7b13372-3797-11ea-a6d3-9a26f8c3cba4

33 Novet, J. (2019). Google Cancels A.I. Ethics Panel after Uproar. Retrieved June 10, 2020, from CNBC website: www.cnbc.com/2019/04/04/google-cancels-controversial-ai-ethics-panel.html

34 Scott, M. (2020). Twitter Labels Trump Tweet as "Glorifying Violence." Retrieved June 10, 2020, from POLITICO website: www.politico.com/news/2020/05/29/twitter-labels-trump-tweet-as-glorifying-violence-288356

35 Biswas, S. (2020). Why India is Greeting Amazon's Jeff Bezos with Protests. BBC News. Retrieved from www.bbc.com/news/world-asia-india-51117315

36 Office of the Australian Information Commissioner. (2016). Privacy Management Plan Template (for Organizations). Retrieved June 10, 2020, from OAIC website: www.oaic.gov.au/privacy/guidance-and-advice/privacy-management-plan-template-for-organizations/

37 Southeastern Oklahoma State University. (2016). Why Ethics are Still Essential in Management Retrieved June 9, 2020, from Southeastern Oklahoma State University website: https://online.se.edu/articles/mba/why-ethics-are-still-essential-in-management.aspx

38 Southeastern Oklahoma State University. (2016). Why Ethics are Still Essential in Management Retrieved June 9, 2020, from Southeastern Oklahoma State University website: https://online.se.edu/articles/mba/why-ethics-are-still-essential-in-management.aspx

11 Role of hospitality and leisure managers in digital leadership, accelerated change and transformation, digital risk management, and digital governance

Introduction

Digital disruption, digital transformation, and digital business demand rapid shifts in an organization's culture and its execution speed. Effectively bringing about the required cultural shifts and execution speed requires new or adapted leadership roles and competencies that are conceptualized as "digital leadership" and juxtaposed against traditional leadership. In addition to being steep achievement challenges, the rapid shift in culture and execution capability comes with significant change risks that leaders have to manage. But although serious, these change risks are dwarfed by the new risk exposures created by digital technologies and new business models. These new and significantly expanded risk exposures demand sophisticated and fast risk management and governance practices. Fortunately, despite the new risks they create, digital technologies offer a range of sophisticated tools that can be leveraged to supercharge the effectiveness of risk management and governance practices. This is what is commonly referred to as digital risk management and digital governance. In this chapter, we introduce hospitality and leisure managers to these concepts of digital leadership, accelerated change and transformation, digital risk management, and digital governance (i.e. what are they, how do they differ from their traditional counterpart terms, what is their value proposition). We then discuss the roles and competencies they require of hospitality and leisure managers.

Required managerial roles and competencies for digital leadership

Digital leadership vs. traditional leadership

Digital disruption, digital transformation, and digital business present unique leadership challenges (e.g. the need for fast decision making and execution, the need to make rapid shifts in organization culture, the need to transform the workforce into a flexible and distributed workplace, the need for significant efficiency breakthroughs, the need to manage virtual workforces). These unique challenges require new leadership roles and/or adaptations of traditional leadership roles and activities. The augmentation of traditional leadership roles and activities with new or adapted digital technology related roles and activities is what is referred to as digital leadership (also referred to as e-leadership in academic research). Thus digital leadership refers to the new or adapted roles/activities required of leaders to effectively lead digital transformation and digital business. And it refers to the augmentation of traditional leadership roles/activities with these new or adapted roles and activities. It also refers to the effect of carrying out these roles and activities to lead in a digital environment (e.g., Figure 11.1 identifies how working in a highly digital environment differs from working in a traditional or less digital one). Digital leadership can be considered from an individual leader level (e.g. the capacity of a leader to lead digital transformation and digital business) or from an organization capability perspective (the collective ability of an organization's leaders, at all levels, to lead digital transformation and digital business. Organization digital leadership capability, then, refers to the presence and collective effectiveness of digital leaders in every part of the organization. Or, put another way, it is the effectiveness of the configuration of and abilities of an organization's digital leaders at all levels of the organization and across all parts of the value chain.

The new or adapted leadership roles of digital leadership

Several researchers and practitioners have discussed the make up of the new or adapted digital leadership roles/activities. To date, these discussions have focused on nine required roles/activity groups. First, digital leaders have to set a digital transformation/digital business vision and direction. This can be a challenging role/activity in that it requires leaders

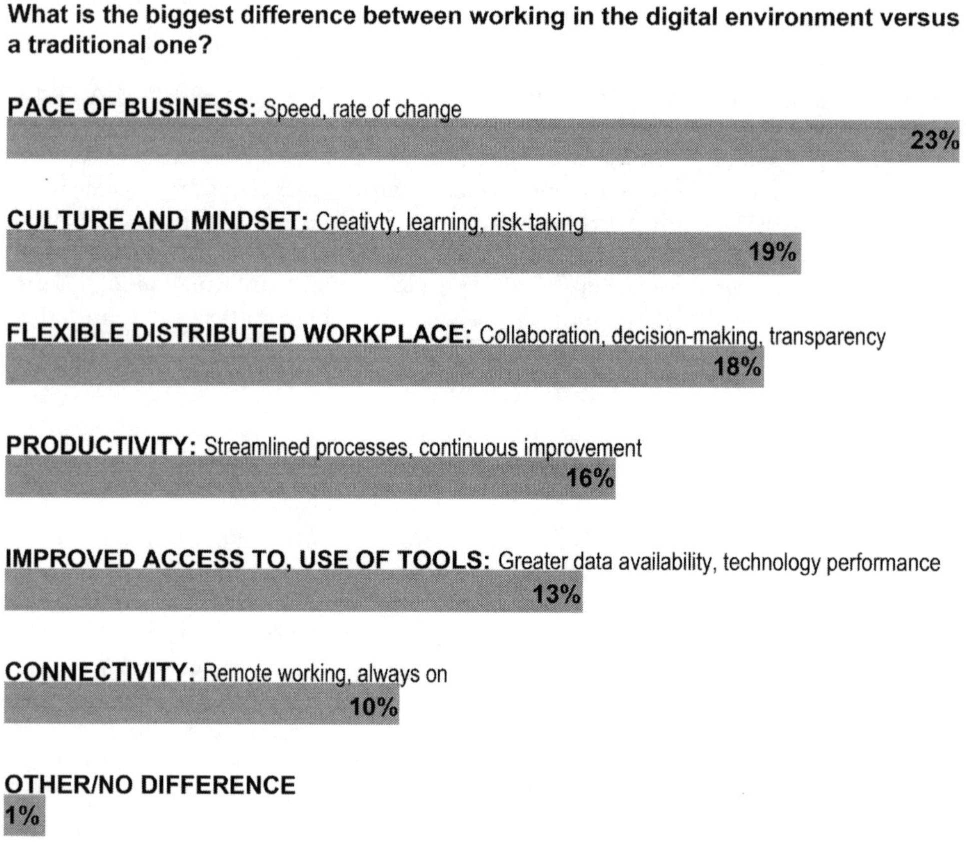

What is the biggest difference between working in the digital environment versus a traditional one?

PACE OF BUSINESS: Speed, rate of change

23%

CULTURE AND MINDSET: Creativty, learning, risk-taking

19%

FLEXIBLE DISTRIBUTED WORKPLACE: Collaboration, decision-making, transparency

18%

PRODUCTIVITY: Streamlined processes, continuous improvement

16%

IMPROVED ACCESS TO, USE OF TOOLS: Greater data availability, technology performance

13%

CONNECTIVITY: Remote working, always on

10%

OTHER/NO DIFFERENCE

1%

Figure 11.1 Results of a survey of 3,300 *MIT Sloan Management Review* readers, Deloitte Dbriefs webcast subscribers, and other interested parties regarding what is different about working in a digital business environment

to understand how digital technology advancements, digital disruption, and digital transformation may play out at the consumer, organization, industry, geographic, and societal levels,[1] before they can set the digital transformation/digital business vision and direction. The role can be viewed as an augmentation of the traditional leadership role of vision/direction setting[2] with deep digital technology, digital disruption, digital transformation, and digital business strategy knowledge/skills. For example, it is symbolically represented by the visionary digital leadership capabilities of leaders like Bill Gates (Microsoft), the late Steve Jobs (Apple), Reed Hastings (Netflix), and the late Andy Grove (Intel). Digital transformation/digital business vision or direction setting and digital technology competency are viewed as being among the top 3 leadership skills critical to success in digital workplaces (see Figure 11.2). Second, digital leaders have to be strong change agents and digital enablers who are able to push their organizations to seize the opportunities offered by digital technologies and digital disruption. These are typically fleeting opportunities with tight and closing time windows. Thus they require organizations to change their capabilities quickly and then execute fast in order to seize them. For example, Netflix was able to change itself quickly to seize the opportunities offered by the internet and then by cloud computing, whereas the opportunity window closed on Blockbuster. Digital leaders play a critical role in effectively driving the necessary rapid capability change and subsequent execution. Third, digital transformation and digital business require leaders to use much more inclusive leadership styles that involve employees in day-to-day decision

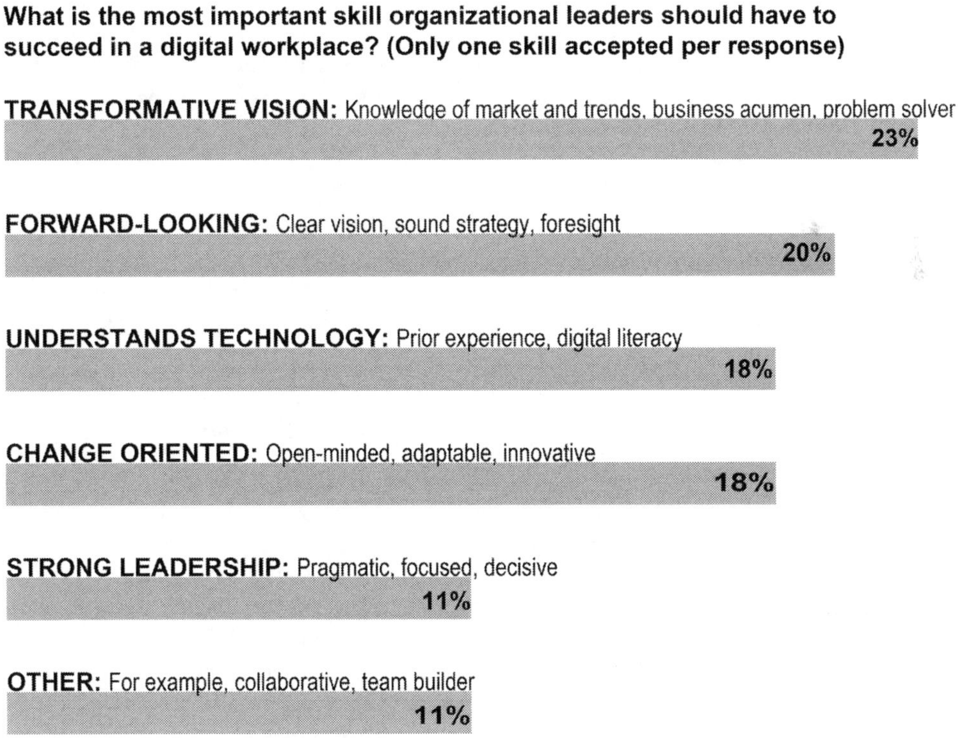

What is the most important skill organizational leaders should have to succeed in a digital workplace? (Only one skill accepted per response)

TRANSFORMATIVE VISION: Knowledge of market and trends, business acumen, problem solver

23%

FORWARD-LOOKING: Clear vision, sound strategy, foresight

20%

UNDERSTANDS TECHNOLOGY: Prior experience, digital literacy

18%

CHANGE ORIENTED: Open-minded, adaptable, innovative

18%

STRONG LEADERSHIP: Pragmatic, focused, decisive

11%

OTHER: For example, collaborative, team builder

11%

Figure 11.2 Results of a survey of 3,300 *MIT Sloan Management Review* readers, Deloitte Dbriefs webcast subscribers, and other interested parties regarding the most important skill leaders need to succeed in a digital workplace

processes (often in real time) and take into account their ideas and concerns in strategic issues.[3,4] Fourth, digital leaders need to effectively lead virtual teams and facilitate virtual teamwork. For example, this can involve leveraging the right digital technology tools to facilitate communication, workflows, and resource sharing. It can also involve effectively supporting employees with virtual work issues. Owing to virtual, remote, and autonomous work, employees can be prone to peer alienation, weak social bonds, and challenges dealing with typically greater autonomy and increased job demands. So digital leaders need to unearth these issues and support employees with them.

The fifth discussed role is that digital leaders need to proactively build an enabling digital culture (e.g. digital cultures have been described as being agile and responsive, flexible and adaptive, curious/exploratory/experimental, continuously learning, connected/networked, open, and highly collaborative).[5] Sixth, digital leaders need to build relationships with stakeholders across partner and competitor networks and ecosystems.[6] Both the way they do this and the extent to which they do it differ from networking and relationship roles/ activities associated with traditional leadership. Seventh, digital leadership plays important roles in enabling and maximizing digital innovation effectiveness. In an earlier chapter, we discussed the importance of digital innovation for effectively competing as a digital business. To drive digital innovation, digital leadership plays important roles such as creating or shaping virtual networks among internal and external communities of practice, breaking down silos, democratizing access to information, enabling the free flow of ideas, and thus enabling these communities to rapidly respond to change, solve business problems, and introduce new products/solutions.[7] Eighth, digital leaders determine how sourcing, assessment, and/ or approval of the digital technologies, platforms, and tools used in the organization occurs. The choice of technologies, platforms, and tools can significantly impact the efficiency and effectiveness of internal processes (e.g. processes such as planning and monitoring, decision making, customer engagement, collaboration) and of organization adaptability and agility efforts. For example, the use of sophisticated data tools has enabled hospitals to have real-time visibility of hospital capacity, patient flow, and patient conditions, thus dramatically improving the ability of healthcare managers to drive the efficiency and effectiveness of internal processes.[8] Ninth, digital leaders need to play an important role in building and continuously upgrading the effectiveness of their organizations' digital ethics practices. This requires a clear understanding of cybersecurity, information privacy, and other digital ethics issues to be able to identify and mitigate digital ethics risks.

New or enhanced managerial competencies required for digital leadership

Researchers and practitioners have identified a range of digital leadership competencies including adaptability/flexibility (e.g. being able to effectively respond to new/surprising work demands and events), mastery of a variety of virtual communication platforms (e.g. which platforms offer the best richness, synchronicity, speed of feedback, and ease of understanding by nonexperts – so as to maximise virtual communication effectiveness), mastery of virtual communication practices (e.g. how to set the right meeting tone, and how to communicate in a clear, organized and miscommunication free manner), management of disruptive change (e.g. being able to guide teams to effectively respond to changed consumer expectations and behaviors, changed competitors, and technological obsolescence), management of connectivity (e.g. managing intra-organizational, inter-organizational, and extra-organizational connectivity), leadership/facilitation of virtual teams (e.g. managing the forming, storming, norming, performing stages of virtual team formation), and ability to use relevant digital technologies (e.g. IoT, blockchain, edge computing, robotics, cloud).

Required managerial roles and competencies for accelerated change and transformation

One of the biggest challenges organizations face in their digital transformation and digital business efforts is the scale and speed with which the change and transformation are occurring externally, and therefore need to occur internally. This expanded scale and speed of change is incompatible with change and transformation approaches that were designed for more stable and more predictable environments. The internal and external environments organisations now face are often characterized by high dynamism, uncertainty, technological obsolescence, and disruption. Fortunately, organizations that have long existed in such environments, typically high technology firms, use a range of methodologies to effect rapid change and transformation, enabling them to adapt and thrive in such environments. We collectively refer to these methodologies as accelerated change and transformation methodologies. Examples of these accelerated change and transformation methodologies include agile innovation,[9,10,11,12] lean thinking,[13,14] lean startup,[15,16] change acceleration,[17,18,19] design thinking,[20] seed accelerators/corporate accelerators,[21,22,23] blitzscaling,[24,25,26] and hackathon methods/practices.[27,28] To effectively leverage one or more of these methodologies (e.g. to use it to facilitate transformation initiatives, to use it to drive digital innovation, to encourage particular teams to use them, or to play an effective role in catalyzing its effectiveness) hospitality and leisure managers need to have a working understanding of how these different methodologies work, the key roles and responsibilities managers can play in each methodology, and the strengths and limitations of each methodology. Armed with such understanding (i.e. both knowledge and experience), hospitality and leisure can leverage the right methodology to maximise the odds of success in digital transformation efforts. Figure 11.3 provides an example of the key management roles/activities that managers need to play in the change acceleration process (one of the accelerated change and transformation methods).

Required managerial roles and competencies for digital risk management and governance

Digital risk management and governance vs. traditional risk management and governance

Risk management is concerned with how effectively an organization detects, guards against, responds to, and recovers from risk exposures or events.[29] Governance is concerned with how effectively an organization is led, controlled, and the people operating it are held to account for the efficient, effective, and responsible pursuit of the organization's mission.[30,31,32] Effective risk management is a critical element of effective governance.[33] Digital risk management and digital governance refer to the management of the unique risk and governance issues associated with digital technologies/digital business and digital business transformation. It also refers to the leveraging of digital technologies to maximize the efficiency and effectiveness of risk management and governance functions.

Nature of digital risk and the new risk landscape

Digital technology advancements, digital transformation, and digital business bring about new risks that haven't been encountered before. They also add complexity to existing risks, thus significantly changing the risk landscape.[34] Examples of new risks and complexity introduced include inappropriate employee behaviors on social media, employees

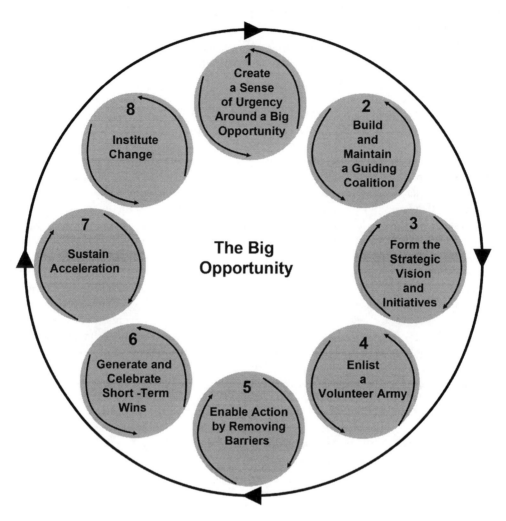

Figure 11.3 Having working knowledge of accelerated change and transformation methodologies like the Change Acceleration Process can be an invaluable tool in digital leaders' rapid change and transformation arsenal

inadvertently clicking on suspect links in emails/online or divulging sensitive corporate information, artificial intelligence product/tool algorithm–related risks (e.g. biased data, unsuitable decision models, algorithmic bias). New risks also include an expanded number of cyberattack points due to the expansion of IoT devices/platforms/networks integrating with an organization's IS infrastructure, an expanded number of cybercriminals online, cybercriminals having more sophisticated attack tools, misinformation risks (e.g. cybercriminals, nation states or other troublemakers using sophisticated digital editing and imitation technologies like machine learning, bots, and natural language generation to spread false information, incite adverse reactions, delegitimize leaders and politicians, and damage brands). The new risks further include data misuse (e.g. lack of ethics, lack of security, lack of privacy protection), the existence of ubiquitous connectivity (e.g. meaning that an attack is able to happen any time, and most likely when key security staff are offline), the growing trend of digital technology advancements outpacing laws and regulations (e.g. meaning increased of new and less legally bound competitors entering market; or risk that new business models adopted may be rendered obsolete as laws and regulations catch up), culture risk (e.g. pace of change exceeds cultural readiness resulting in destructive resistance to change, disengagement/disenfranchisement, vindictive employees/partners/contractors), and digital ethics (e.g. risk that digital technologies are used for and/or in a manner that current and future societies considers unethical).[35]

Role of digital technologies in digital risk management and governance

As just illustrated, the breadth in risk exposure and the mortal nature of the risks faced makes effective risk management and governance critical in the digital era. Fortunately, hospitality and leisure managers at all levels can leverage the same sophisticated digital technologies that drive these risk exposures to effectively detect, guard against, respond to, and recover from the diverse risk exposures or events.[36] Examples of this include leveraging robotic process automation for accelerated identity and access management, leveraging natural language generation to automate regulatory reporting, leveraging chatbots to improve understanding of policies and compliance requirements, leveraging computer vision to spot anomalies, leveraging virtual/augmented/mixed reality to simulate crisis management situations, leveraging machine learning to spot policy and ethics violations, leveraging algorithms for continuous monitoring of credit reports/court sanctions lists/search engine data in order limit third party risk exposures, leveraging blockchain-enabled proof-of-provenance to ensure verification of the origin/safety/authenticity of products, leveraging predictive analytics to anticipate and intervene in risky behaviors before the fact, and leveraging digital twins (virtual replicas of physical objects) to anticipate and mitigate risk impacts.[37]

New or enhanced managerial competencies required for digital risk management and digital governance

Hospitality and leisure managers at all levels have shared responsibility in effective digital risk management and governance. To discharge this responsibility, they can play important roles such as being establishers/maintainers/continuous improvers of risk management and governance practices, being sourcers/evaluators/procurers/vendor managers of digital risk management and governance technologies, being monitors of state-of-the-art risk management and governance practices, being monitors and testers of risk management technologies, being risk management practice auditors, and being crisis managers. Each of these roles requires an understanding of digital risk management and governance and of digital technologies and the opportunities and threats associated with them.

Google and reflect

Digital Capability	Common Terminology
Digital leadership	Leadership, digital leadership, e-leadership, digital leadership capability, digital leader, digital transformation vision, digital business vision, change agent, digital change agent, digital enabler, inclusive leadership, virtual team, virtual communication style, digital innovation
Accelerated change and transformation	Uncertainty, complexity, complicatedness, high velocity environment, fleeting opportunity, change management, organization transformation, agile innovation, lean thinking, lean startup, change acceleration, design thinking, seed accelerator, corporate accelerator, blitzscaling, hackathon

(*Continued*)

(Continued)

Digital Capability	Common Terminology
Digital risk management and digital governance	Risk management, digital risk management, governance, digital governance, governance operating model, governance structure, governance infrastructure, governance roles and responsibilities, risk exposure, risk event, biased data, algorithmic bias, attack surface, misinformation, imitation technologies, natural language generation, culture risk, digital ethics risk

Discussion questions

1 What is the difference between traditional leadership, e-leadership, and digital leadership?
2 What is the difference between risk management and digital risk management?
3 What is the relationship between risk management and governance?
4 What is the relationship between information privacy and digital ethics?
5 What is the difference between change and transformation? How do accelerated change and accelerated transformation differ?
6 What are the three most dangerous risk exposures for organizations at the moment?
7 If you were a hacker or cybercriminal, which risk surface or attack point would you find best to attack and why?
8 What are three ways digital technologies are being leveraged to enhance digital risk management?
9 Which managerial role in digital risk management and governance is most important to an organization's risk management and governance effectiveness?
10 Which competency related to risk management and governance is likely to have the greatest positive impact on a hospitality and leisure manager's career?
11 Which of the capabilities discussed in this chapter is the most important to succeeding at digital transformation and digital business?

Notes

1 Kane, G. C. (2019, March 12). How Digital Leadership Is(n't) Different. MIT Sloan Management Review. https://sloanreview.mit.edu/article/how-digital-leadership-isnt-different/
2 Cortellazzo, L., Bruni, E., & Zampieri, R. (2019). The Role of Leadership in a Digitalized World: A Review. *Frontiers in Psychology*, 10, 1938.
3 Cortellazzo, L., Bruni, E., & Zampieri, R. (2019). The Role of Leadership in a Digitalized World: A Review. *Frontiers in Psychology*, 10, 1938.
4 Schwarzmüller, T., Brosi, P., Duman, D., & Welpe, I. M. (2018). How Does the Digital Transformation Affect Organizations? Key Themes of Change in Work Design and Leadership. *MREV Management Revue*, 29(2), 114–138.
5 Cortellazzo, L., Bruni, E., & Zampieri, R. (2019). The Role of Leadership in a Digitalized World: A Review. *Frontiers in Psychology*, 10, 1938.
6 Cortellazzo, L., Bruni, E., & Zampieri, R. (2019). The Role of Leadership in a Digitalized World: A Review. *Frontiers in Psychology*, 10, 1938.
7 Cortellazzo, L., Bruni, E., & Zampieri, R. (2019). The Role of Leadership in a Digitalized World: A Review. *Frontiers in Psychology*, 10, 1938.
8 Cortellazzo, L., Bruni, E., & Zampieri, R. (2019). The Role of Leadership in a Digitalized World: A Review. *Frontiers in Psychology*, 10, 1938.
9 Gothelf, J. (2014). Bring Agile to the Whole Organization. *Harvard Business Review*, 92(11).
10 Busulwa, R., Tice, M., & Gurd, B. (2018). *Strategy Execution and Complexity: Thriving in the Era of Disruption*. Routledge.

11 Rigby, D. K., Sutherland, J., & Takeuchi, H. (2016). The Secret History of Agile Innovation. *Harvard Business Review*, 4.

12 Morris, L., Ma, M., & Wu, P. C. (2014). *Agile Innovation: The Revolutionary Approach to Accelerate Success, Inspire Engagement, and Ignite Creativity*. John Wiley & Sons.

13 Collins, D. (2016). Lean strategy. *Harvard Business Review*, 94(3), 63–68.

14 Busulwa, R., Tice, M., & Gurd, B. (2018). *Strategy Execution and Complexity: Thriving in the Era of Disruption*. Routledge.

15 Ries, E. (2011). *The Lean Startup: How Today's Entrepreneurs Use Continuous Innovation to Create Radically Successful Businesses*. Crown Books.

16 Busulwa, R., Tice, M., & Gurd, B. (2018). *Strategy Execution and Complexity: Thriving in the Era of Disruption*. Routledge.

17 Kotter, J. P. (2014). *Accelerate: Building Strategic Agility for a Faster-moving World*. Harvard Business Review Press.

18 Kotter, J. (2012). How the Most Innovative Companies Capitalize on Today's Rapid-Fire Strategic Challenges–and Still Make their Numbers. *Harvard Business Review*, 90(11), 43–58.

19 Busulwa, R., Tice, M., & Gurd, B. (2018). *Strategy Execution and Complexity: Thriving in the Era of Disruption*. Routledge.

20 Liedtka, J. (2018). Why Design Thinking Works. *Harvard Business Review*, 96(5), 72–79.

21 Busulwa, R., Birdthistle, N., & Dunn, S. (2020). *Startup Accelerators: A Field Guide*. John Wiley & Sons.

22 Say, M. (2016, February 23). Corporate Accelerators: What's in It for the Big Companies? Forbes. Retrieved from www.forbes.com/sites/groupthink/2016/02/23/corporate-accelerators-whats-in-it-for-the-big-companies/#7445a2d45f62

23 Hathaway, I. (2016). What Startup Accelerators Really Do. *Harvard Business Review*, 7.

24 Sullivan, T. (2016). Blitzscaling. *Harvard Business Review*, 94(4), 15.

25 Kuratko, D. F., Holt, H. L., & Neubert, E. (2020). Blitzscaling: The Good, the Bad, and the Ugly. *Business Horizons*, 63(1), 109–119.

26 Hoffman, R., & Yeh, C. (2018). *Blitzscaling: The Lightning-fast Path to Building Massively Valuable Businesses*. Broadway Business.

27 Spaulding, E., & Caimi, G. (2016). Hackathons Aren't Just for Coders. *Harvard Business Review*. Retrieved from https://hbr.org/2016/04/hackathons-arent-just-for-coders

28 Rosell, B., Kumar, S., & Shepherd, J. (2014). Unleashing Innovation Through Internal Hackathons. *2014 IEEE Innovations in Technology Conference*. https://doi.org/10.1109/innotek.2014.6877369

29 Iso.org. (2018). ISO 31000:2018 Risk Management – Guidelines. Retrieved June 12, 2020, from Iso.org website: www.iso.org/obp/ui/#iso:std:iso:31000:ed-2:v1:en

30 Siems, M., & Alvarez-Macotela, O. S. (2017). The G20/OECD Principles of Corporate Governance 2015: A Critical Assessment of their Operation and Impact. *Journal of Business Law*, 4, 310–328.

31 Japan Exchange Group. (2009). Principles of Corporate Governance for Listed Companies. Retrieved from www.jpx.co.jp/english/equities/listing/cg/tvdivq0000008j6d-att/principles_200912.pdf

32 Governance Institute of Australia. (2020). What is Governance? governanceinstitute.com.au. Retrieved from www.governanceinstitute.com.au/resources/what-is-governance/

33 Iso.org. (2018). ISO 31000:2018 Risk management – Guidelines. Retrieved June 12, 2020, from Iso.org website: www.iso.org/obp/ui/#iso:std:iso:31000:ed-2:v1:en

34 Marsh, J., Bhachawat, K., Maheshwari, S., & Nagpal, A. (2019). Future of Risk in the Digital Era. Deloitte. Retrieved June 12, 2020, from Deloitte Online website: www2.deloitte.com/content/dam/Deloitte/fi/Documents/risk/future-of-risk-in-the-digital-era.pdf

35 Marsh, J., Bhachawat, K., Maheshwari, S., & Nagpal, A. (2019). Future of Risk in the Digital Era. Deloitte. Retrieved June 12, 2020, from Deloitte Online website: www2.deloitte.com/content/dam/Deloitte/fi/Documents/risk/future-of-risk-in-the-digital-era.pdf

36 Marsh, J., Bhachawat, K., Maheshwari, S., & Nagpal, A. (2019). Future of Risk in the Digital Era. Deloitte. Retrieved June 12, 2020, from Deloitte Online website: www2.deloitte.com/content/dam/Deloitte/fi/Documents/risk/future-of-risk-in-the-digital-era.pdf

37 Marsh, J., Bhachawat, K., Maheshwari, S., & Nagpal, A. (2019). Future of Risk in the Digital Era. Deloitte. Retrieved June 12, 2020, from Deloitte Online website: www2.deloitte.com/content/dam/Deloitte/fi/Documents/risk/future-of-risk-in-the-digital-era.pdf

Part IV

Keeping up with digital technology advancements

12 Keeping up with digital technology advancements

Introduction

Organization digital transformation and digital business capabilities depend on managerial digital business competencies (e.g. to lead digital transformation and digital innovation efforts). These competencies, in turn, depend on managers' ability to keep up with and therefore be able to leverage digital technology advancements. Keeping up with digital technologies is increasingly becoming a critical component of "expert leadership" in digitalizing and fully digital businesses. This means it is becoming critical to all expert leaders (e.g. healthcare leaders, political leaders, engineering leaders, food and beverage leaders). As a result, keeping up with digital technologies is increasingly critical to the effectiveness of hospitality and leisure managers. In this chapter, we conceptualize keeping up with digital technologies as an accelerated learning practice. That is, hospitality and leisure managers can keep up with digital technologies to the extent that they can accelerate or align their digital technology learning rate to the rate of change in digital technologies. Accelerated learning, or learning efficiency, has individual beliefs/attitudes/traits levers that can be influenced, and it has learning strategies/practices/habits levers that can be adopted/learned. In this chapter, we unpack each of these lever types and explain how they interact together to drive the accelerated learning/learning efficiency necessary to keep up with digital technology advancements.

Importance and challenge of keeping up with digital technologies

In the preceding chapters, we outlined the threat of digital disruption, the pressing need for digital transformation, and the digital capabilities required by organizations to effectively compete as a digital business. For each of these organization digital capabilities, we highlighted required managerial competencies (knowledge, skills, abilities). A recurring theme in all organization digital capabilities is the need for hospitality and leisure managers to have sufficient technical and strategic knowledge of and proficiency with a range of different digital technologies. Without such knowledge, skills, and abilities across different digital technologies, hospitality and leisure managers can become key impediments to their organizations' digital transformation and digital business competitiveness efforts – and can also limit their own managerial careers. However, hospitality and leisure managers face challenges effectively acquiring the required working knowledge of different digital technologies and keeping it relevant. For example, the range of digital technologies to have working knowledge and skills in is broad, it's ever changing, and it seems to expand in breadth and depth at an exponential rate. As a result, keeping up with it can easily overwhelm even the most enthusiastic of managers. Managers who succeed at it recognize that technology learning is a never-ending process that combines effective technology learning habits/practices with effective strategies to maximize both what is learned and the efficiency with which it is learned.

Common strategies and practices for keeping up with digital technologies

The challenge of keeping up with digital technologies is not unique to hospitality and leisure managers. Across different industries, job functions, and professions, a range of strategies and practices are employed to keep up with digital technologies. In the remainder of this chapter, we've curated a list of commonly used strategies and practices from both academic research and from practitioners. This list is just a starting point, and what works for one manager may not work for another. Our aim in putting together this list is to start managers on the never-ending journey of seeking out effective strategies and practices to add to their repertoire and leveraging the right strategy or practice for them, at the right time, and for the right technology, to maximize their learning and learning efficiency.

Strategies and practices from the research on technological knowledge renewal effectiveness

Framing it as technological knowledge renewal effectiveness, researchers exploring challenges and drivers of effectiveness at keeping up with digital technologies have identified three individual beliefs/attitudes/traits and two technology learning strategies. The identified individual beliefs/attitudes/traits are a perceived need for digital technology competencies, sufficient appreciation of the technology learning challenge, and tolerance for ambiguity.[1] The identified technology learning strategies are learning from external experts and learning from internal experts.[2] We explain each of these below. Each of these individual beliefs/attitudes/traits and learning strategies can be thought of as a lever that can be turned one way to accelerate technology learning; or turned another way to decelerate it.

Perceived need for digital technology competencies, appreciation of the technology learning challenge, and tolerance for ambiguity

A manager's perceived need for digital technology competencies refers to a manager's belief or lack of belief that digital technology competencies materially impact their managerial job performance and career prospects.[3] People who don't believe that digital technology competencies materially impact their job performance and career prospects have been shown to lack sufficient motivation to make or sustain the necessary investments in time and effort required to learn and keep up with digital technologies. On the contrary, people who see digital technology competencies as being a significant driver of job performance and career success have been shown to have far greater motivation and persistence in pursuing these competencies. Fortunately for managers in the latter category, the research on expert leadership has reinforced the importance of technical expertise to managerial effectiveness.[4,5] For hospitality and leisure managers, this technical expertise used to mainly be expert knowledge of the industry and of hospitality and leisure operations. But with the digital transformation of products/services and operational/management processes, technical expertise now also includes technical and strategic digital technology competencies/expertise.

Managers' appreciation of the true challenge of keeping up with digital technologies refers to how accurately they understand and take seriously the rate of change in digital technologies and the resultant disruption threats.[6] The more fully managers appreciate and take seriously the rate of change, the more serious will be their approach and effort to keep up with digital technologies. Managers underestimating the nature of the challenge in front of them are anticipated make insufficient efforts to keep up with digital technologies.[7] Tolerance for ambiguity refers to a manager's tendency to perceive ambiguous situations as tolerable or even desirable.[8] For example, managers with higher tolerance for ambiguity are more willing to cope with change, modify their opinions in the face of new information, embrace new experiences, and renew their knowledge.[9] Tolerance for ambiguity has been shown to have a positive impact on the ability to learn new technology[10] and thus to keep up with digital technologies.

Hospitality and leisure managers can leverage these three research findings to enhance their motivation and that of their direct reports to keep up with digital technologies and to be resilient in the face of setbacks or overwhelm. For example, they can ensure that they and their direct reports fully understand and are continuously reminded of the value of digital technology competencies to their organizations and careers; they can ensure that they and their direct reports understand the true challenge of keeping up with digital technologies and how this challenge is evolving; and they can ensure that they continuously work on improving their tolerance for ambiguity (e.g. through work assignments and other learning activities that expand tolerance to ambiguity). For example, they can influence employees to see technological change and dynamism as an opportunity rather than a burden, and they can cultivate a culture that encourages and incentivizes employees to take on and overcome challenges, embrace change, and deal with uncertainty. Through recruiting processes, managers can ensure that they hire for ambiguity tolerance and motivation to learn and keep up with digital technologies.

Learning from external experts and learning from internal experts

Learning from external experts refers to acquiring new knowledge and skills from professional entities outside the organization. The learning activities can be in the form of reading professional literature (e.g. consulting firm research reports on a topic, professional/academic journals on a topic), attending conferences (e.g. a vendor IoT conference), attending networking events (e.g. an information ethics professionals dinner), participating in online forums and discussion boards, signing up for electronic newsletters, or some other form. The amount of time spent on such learning activities, and the choice of learning activities, are strongly associated with effectiveness in learning new digital technologies,[11] and thus with keeping up with digital technologies. In the research, learning from external experts is also referred to as "professional delegation," since the learner "delegates" the identification/curation of what to learn and how to learn it to an expert (typically a professional entity or thought leader). For example, someone wanting to learn more about artificial intelligence may seek out leading associations and vendors or research organizations in that area, and make a point of reading as much of their content (e.g. blogs, videos, reports) and attending as many of their conferences and networking events as possible. Learning from internal experts refers to acquiring new knowledge and skills from units or departments or individuals within the organization with that expertise.[12] Typically, this might be the IT/IS/technology function. So, for example, a manager may learn through informal conversations with employees from the IT/IS/technology function. Or they may learn through seeking out the support of or collaborating on projects with employees in the IT/IS/Technology function. Hospitality and leisure managers can leverage both external and internal experts in both professional and social contexts to improve what they learn and how efficiently and effectively they learn it.

Strategies and practices from practitioners

Have an evolving plan for managing information overload

The relentless torrent of information on just about any technology topic, the proliferation of information sources, the blurring boundaries between credible and non-credible information, and the growth of misinformation can leave managers feeling overwhelmed. Navigating this situation requires managers to make decisions about when to pay attention, what information to pay attention to, what information sources to trust, and when to trust both the information and the information sources. Fortunately, there is no shortage of strategies, habits, and tools that practitioners prescribe for dealing with information overload. These include filtering or explicitly deciding which information sources to pay attention to and which to ignore,[13,14,15] having a process for prioritizing and sequencing information consumption[16] (e.g. scanning selected information sources in the morning for the day's content and then curating and scheduling when important items[17] will be read and in what order), implementing automated information filtering tools[18] (e.g. recommendation engines, search tools, email inbox rules), and learning to skim-read effectively.[19] Other strategies include curating or eliminating push notification on smart devices, limiting the amount of incoming information[20] (e.g. via email, social media, push notifications, ads, search engine recommendations, smart devices, computers), and enhancing the ability to effectively process incoming information.[21] We recommend that hospitality and leisure managers devise their own plan (a combination of strategies, practices, and tools that are effective for them) and that they continuously adapt/evolve this plan to maximize its effectiveness at both enabling optimal learning and offsetting information overload–related anxiety/stress.

Continuously upgrade your learning efficiently

Learning efficiency refers to a learner's rate of learning and retention.[22] It can also be thought of as a combination of the degree of difficulty of what is being learned, the accuracy of learning, and the quantity of learning that takes place per unit of time.[23] Or, put another way, it is the amount and quality of learning that occurs per unit of time, assuming what is being learned is the same. Researchers have linked learning efficiency to attentional control,[24] working memory capacity,[25] learning strategy use (e.g. which strategy and how well it is applied),[26] curiosity,[27] and constructive self-talk.[28] In addition, "learning to learn" and "accelerated learning" are burgeoning fields with contributions from practitioners, social scientists, and educators across a range of professions and disciplines. Hospitality and leisure managers can leverage this burgeoning content to dramatically improve focus, memory, curiosity, constructive self-talk, and learning strategy literacy. In doing so, they can dramatically expand the effectiveness and speed with which they learn new digital technologies and digital technology related issues.

Choose the right learning platforms

Learning platforms continue to grow in popularity based on their ability to drive learning efficiency. They drive learning efficiency through benefits such as curation and serving up of content, personalized learning recommendations, behavioral nudges, learning analytics, and device flexibility.[29] Platforms can differ in the type of content offered, the way in which the content is delivered, cost, learner experience, certification ability, device flexibility, and more. For example, there are course-style platforms (e.g. Code-School, Udemy, Coursera, Job Ready Programmer, Pluralsight, Cloud Academy, Katacoda, DataCamp, Cybrary, Udacity, Linux Academy, Lynda, Skillshare, Code Academy, GoSkills, Edx, Future Learn), there are coaching/mentoring–oriented platforms (e.g. Masterclass, CrossKnowledge), there are technology-oriented content platforms (e.g. MIT Technology Review, ZNet, Engadget, The Next Web, Wired, Arstechnica, Tech-Crunch, Tom's Hardware, Gizmodo, Forbes), there are specialist industry technology content platforms (e.g. Revfine, hospitalitytech.com), and more. By finding and leveraging the right platforms, hospitality and leisure managers can significantly improve their ability to discover which technology concepts to learn, what issues to focus on in relation to use of that technology within and outside of the industry, what technical and strategic skills to develop, and how to develop different types of skills. In addition, the platforms can make the learning process much more enjoyable. Tables 12.1, 12.2, and 12.3 show the top learning tools/platforms by learning tool type between 2018 and 2019.

Table 12.1 Top learning tools by category and change in ranking from year to year – Part 1[30]

Ranking	Change from 2018	Tool	Learning Tool Type
181	NEW	Filtered	AI-powered learning platform
182	NEW	Docebo	AI-powered LMS
67	down 22	Powtoon	animated explainer tool
61	up 33	Audible	audiobooks platform
191	NEW	Fleeq	bite-size training video tool
116	up 74	getAbstract	book abstracts
138	down 17	Blinkist	book abstracts
165	down 15	Omnigraffle	diagramming tool
25	up 13	Evernote	digital notebook
71	down 7	Kindle App	e-books reader
6	same	Google Docs and Google Drive	file sharing and collaboration
17	down 4	Dropbox	file-sharing platform
55	down 5	OneDrive	file-sharing platform
91	down 30	Quizlet	flashcard app
164	down 3	PebblePad	learning journey platform
179	NEW	EdCast	learning platform
65	down 18	Degreed	lifelong learning platform
134	NEW	Meetup	local community events app
174	up 9	Office Lens	makes photos of whiteboards readable
158	up 4	Highbrow	micro-course platforms
39	up 12	Google Scholar	web search engine
64	down 15	Webex	webinar platform
113	NEW	Jamboard	whiteboard collaboration
197	NEW	Drafts	writing automation tool

Table 12.2 Top learning tools by category and change in ranking from year to year – Part 2[31]

Ranking	Change from 2018	Tool	Learning Tool Type
128	down 10	Axonify	micro-learning platform
170	same	Freemind	mind mapping app
133	BACK	XMind	mind mapping tool
63	up 39	Mindmeister	mind mapping app
139	down 17	Google Alerts	monitor the web
15	down 1	Feedly	news aggregator
76	up 48	Inoreader	news aggregator
183	BACK	Notability	note-taking app
151	NEW	Mind Tools	online business resources
121	down 14	CodeCademy	online coding courses
13	up 21	LinkedIn Learning (Lynda)	online courses
29	up 7	Udemy	online courses
53	down 22	Coursera	online courses
101	down 20	edX	online courses
103	down 17	FutureLearn	online courses
115	up 43	Udacity	online courses
173	up 2	Khan Academy	online courses
176	up 23	Alison	online courses
156	down 43	Pluralsight	online IT courses
24	up 6	TED Talks	online talks
54	NEW	Apple Podcasts	podcast platform
105	BACK	Pocket Casts	podcast player
146	down 16	Overcast	podcast player

Embrace omnichannel learning

Learning can take place in a variety of environments, on a variety of platforms and devices, and at a variety of times. For example, while waiting for a client to arrive, a learner may have 20 minutes to spend on learning activities. Having mobile access to the relevant learning content (e.g. Kindle book, Audible book, YouTube video, LinkedIn article) can result in seized learning opportunities. And these seized opportunities can accumulate over years to represent significant differences in time spent learning. This is a key benefit of embracing learning across a range of channels (e.g. across mobile, desktop, and other smart devices; across social and web; across email marketing; across digital and physical books). Omnichannel learning can maximize learning flexibility (e.g. there is always a right channel for the situation), it can maximize learning availability (e.g. the right content is always accessible), and it can maximize learning efficiency (e.g. the most efficient channel in a situation can be used and there are fewer wasted learning opportunities). We recommend that hospitality and leisure managers make deliberate efforts to effect and maximize omnichannel learning (e.g. signing up to platforms across a range of channels, downloading relevant apps, ensuring online/offline availability, ensuring sufficient data, ensuring access to optimal smart devices). And we recommend hospitality and leisure managers invest time in constantly improving their omnichannel learning approach (e.g. adding new tools, reconfiguring content access processes, integrating content across channels).

Build and leverage thought leaders on social networks

Besides their published works, social media provides one of the greatest vehicles to access the insights and latest thinking of digital technology, digital transformation, and digital business thought leaders. Through following digital strategy, AI, data science, and blockchain thought leaders on Twitter, LinkedIn, Facebook, and other social networks, for example, hospitality and leisure managers can access cutting-edge information directly from people shaping the evolution of these digital technologies. In contrast, this information may take decades to filter down through other information channels like published books and accredited degrees and courses. A range of strategic leaders of world-leading technology companies, technical specialists and futurists, and industry technology specialists post regularly on Twitter, LinkedIn, Facebook, and other social media sites (e.g. Bill Gates, Cathy Hackl, Michael Krigsman, QuHarrison Terry, Paul Graham, Lisa Seacat Deluca, Tom Davenport, Michael Fauscette, Brian Solis, Bill Marriott, Daniel E. Craig, Jason Q. Freed, Craig Rispin). Through regularly following the posts of these thought leaders on social networks, hospitality and leisure managers can learn first, spot technology opportunities first, and ensure their organizations profit first. For example, one early stage hospitality industry company participating in a seed accelerator to raise funding struggled to raise a million dollars in startup funding through conventional venture capitalists. In contrast, a peer company participating in the same seed accelerator acted on a tweet suggesting that there was not an easier fundraising opportunity at the time than ICOs (initial coin offerings). The startup spotting and acting on this thought leader insight spent its time setting up an ICO instead of pursuing venture capitalists; it raised millions of dollars in the course of a month without having to give up any ownership in the company.[32]

Table 12.3 Top learning tools by category and change in ranking from year to year – Part 3[33]

Ranking	Change from 2018	Tool	Learning Tool Type
155	down 22	Castro	podcast player
157	NEW	Podcast Addict	podcast player
107	BACK	Quora	Q&A website
177	BACK	Quizizz	quizzing app
178	BACK	Zotero	research management app
56	down 21	Pocket	save for later app
27	down 2	Snagit	screen capture tool
110	NEW	Loom	screen recorder
148	NEW	Screencastify	screen recorder
92	down 15	Screencast-O-Matic	screencasting app
23	up 1	Camtasia	screencasting tool
77	down 11	Google Maps	searchable/zoomable maps
32	up 17	Diigo	social bookmarking
1	same	YouTube	video platform
66	down 13	Vimeo	video platform
159	up 34	Kaltura	video platform
129	NEW	Microsoft Stream	video streaming service
99	down 16	Adobe After Effects	visual effects app
35	up 19	Google Chrome	web browser
125	up 13	Firefox	web browser
167	down 14	Microsoft Edge	web browser
81	down 21	Adobe Connect	web conferencing platform
142	BACK	Big Blue Button	web conferencing platform
94	down 24	Sway	web content app
2	up 1	Google Search	web search engine

Configure your search engines, social media, and email subscriptions

Suggested news articles, social media feeds, and subscription emails can be distractions, drawing time away from learning activities. Google's search engine app, for example, automatically suggests news articles a searcher might be interested in. And social media platforms like LinkedIn and Twitter have automatic news/post feeds that platform users see as soon as they log in. Similarly, the majority of people are likely to scroll through a bunch of subscription emails before getting to a personal or work email. But rather than being distractions, suggested news articles, social media feeds, and emails can be configured as content discovery and learning prompts. For example, Google can be configured to automatically search and suggest news articles related to desired technology learning topics (e.g. "digital business model," "digital innovation"); each time a user opens the search app, it can automatically deliver the latest news about new digital business models or digital innovation practices. Search results can also be configured to automatically be emailed monthly, weekly, or daily. For example, a user may configure weekly alerts for "new digital business model" and receive an email with links to the latest information containing those keywords as soon as such information goes online somewhere in the world. Similarly, social media feeds can be configured so that they automatically serve up information on particular learning topics. For example, on LinkedIn and on Twitter users can subscribe to or follow certain hashtags (e.g. #hospitalitytech, #hospitalitytechnology, #artificialintelligence, #digitalleadership, #digitalinnovation) to automatically receive the latest news and posts about these topics. Hashtags can also be used to filter for and follow particular thought leaders. By configuring the platforms they access most regularly, hospitality and leisure managers can ensure they have access to cutting-edge news and learning insights on technology topics; as well as near daily curiosity, reflection, and learning prompts for their targeted learning topics.

Have an effective and sustainable personal information management strategy

After configuring channels, platforms, and devices to deliver the best information, there then comes the challenge of capturing, organizing, and storing each information item and leveraging tools that can enable near instant retrieval of the desired article as and when needed. Doing so can significantly enhance learning efficiency by minimizing retrieval time and the chance that the desired information may not be found, thereby losing the learning opportunity or at least making it suboptimal. But having an effective system for storing and retrieving information can be challenging. One issue is the number of channels in which information can be sourced (e.g. social media, YouTube, search engines, email, conversations with people, conferences). For example, it can be challenging to remember in which channel the information resides, and it can be time-consuming to transfer information across channels in order to have all information on a single platform or device. Another issue is that some content requires platform-specific storage (e.g. YouTube videos may be better stored on YouTube). Yet another issue is that some platforms and devices significantly simplify the information retrieval and learning experience but are limited in their ability to integrate information from other platforms/devices. Further, settling on a particular platform or device and building learning routines around it needs careful consideration; the device or platform can be discontinued, or it may not be updated regularly enough to keep with changes across other platforms, hence limiting integrability. Fortunately, a range of personal information management platforms and tools exist. Hospitality and leisure managers can curate or architect a combination of platforms, devices, and apps that fit perfectly into their routines to maximize learning effectiveness. For example, one manager may decide on the following configuration/architecture:

- Email: Use Gmail for personal emails. Set up email folders by technology topic, and then drag and drop information into relevant folders for ease of retrieval (e.g. new digital innovation practice–related emails can be moved to a "digital innovation practices" folder, and digital business model–related emails can go in the "digital strategies" folder, etc.).
- Articles: Use Instapaper to save articles for later reading and set up folders in Instapaper (e.g. "digital innovation practices," "new digital tech to explore"). Instapaper is available on almost all devices, can be integrated into most browsers to enable single-button saving of articles, and has built-in search functionality and folder structure to enable even faster retrieval of articles.
- Video: Establish a YouTube account; follow key thought leaders' channels and set up folders for saved videos ("digital innovation practices," "digital strategies").
- Audio: Set up Audible and Blinkist to be able to listen to books and book summaries; make these apps available on mobile, desktop, and CarPlay.
- Books: Set up Kindle and Apple Books apps to be able to purchase any book and have lifetime access to it; these apps enable in-book search and have built-in note-taking functions.
- TV: Set up technology-related channels and apps on your smart TV to enable watching educational tech documentaries and other videos.
- Notes: Set up Apple Notes or Evernote to enable digital note-taking; these have highly effective built-in search functions to enable fast access to notes.
- Transcription: Set up audio recording and transcription apps on mobile and desktop (e.g. Otter Voice Meeting); integrate these with virtual meeting apps such as Microsoft Teams and Google Meet.
- Desktop/laptop: Ensure all selected platforms/apps are cloud based and can be replicated in the desktop/laptop/web environment.
- Smart device: Ensure apps are also installed on every possible smart device so that if one device is down, learning can go ahead on another device.

What we have outlined is one example of a personal information management approach; it can be configured differently to suit each individual (e.g. more or better channels, platforms, apps, devices; perhaps a better plan for integrating information across channels, devices, platforms, and apps). Most personal information management strategies/approaches can be continuously improved as users gauge their effectiveness, discover better tools, and evolve their own learning behaviors. Deliberately designing/architecting/configuring a system and continuously improving it can supercharge learning efficiency and effectiveness.

Participate in hackathons and accelerators

Hackathons originated as computer programming events in which a small group of people work intensely together, sometimes around the clock, to solve a difficult programming problem in a fixed (and often very short) amount of time.[34] For example, they could work on "hacking" or solving a complex software application or network security problem over the course of a weekend, whereas this same problem might otherwise take months or years via traditional approaches. Due to their success, hackathons have been applied to solve a range of problems across sectors, industries, and disciplines.[35] Many hackathons focus on leveraging digital technologies and digital business models to solve organization, government, community, and state problems. Many are run in a competitive format (different teams competing to solve a problem first or come up with the best solution in the time frames allowed), for a prize, and are often open to teams or to individual volunteers who are then allocated into teams by the hackathon organizers. For example, some nation states fund "Govhack"-style hackathons in which volunteer teams are formed to leverage publicly available government data to build innovative new products over the course of a weekend; these products could be mobile apps, smart devices, cloud platforms, and so forth. These particular types of hackathons usually have a big data focus, but there are others that focus on leveraging different digital technologies. Hospitality and leisure managers can build practical working knowledge of digital technologies, digital strategy, and digital innovation by participating on a hackathon team, by volunteering as hackathon organizers/facilitators, or by volunteering as judges of hackathon innovations/solutions. In either participation form, managers can gain a lot of practical knowhow about the digital technologies leveraged in that hackathon, digital innovation and digital strategy issues, and digital leadership.

In contrast to a hackathon, an accelerator (e.g. seed accelerator, startup accelerator, corporate accelerator), is a fixed-term, cohort-based, accelerated learning program that typically focuses on accelerating product development and commercialization processes.[36] An accelerator program is typically run over a 3- to 6-month period that culminates in a "Shark Tank"–style public pitch event known as "demo day."[37] Time-accelerated or compressed learning occurs through a combination of iterative experimentation, intensive mentoring and coaching, customer and investor feedback, and product/business model pitching. Accelerators usually bring together a network of investors, entrepreneurs, potential strategic partners, and potential customers that cohort companies can draw on to accelerate their learning, product development, and commercialization outcomes. Hospitality and leisure managers can participate in accelerators as volunteer organizers, industry- or function-specific coaches/mentors, demo day judges, or demo day observers. There are even hospitality tech–focused accelerators, which would expose hospitality and leisure managers to emerging industry technologies and business models, to potential areas of industry disruption, and to industry innovation challenges. Hospitality and leisure managers can also leverage the accelerator model to drive innovation at their organization (e.g. partnering with an organization such as Techstars to invite teams of internal and external people to participate in an accelerator program focused on developing innovative new products for the organization or that the organization can acquire and commercialize).

Volunteer for a startup

Similar to the learning benefits of hackathons and accelerators, hospitality and leisure managers can volunteer for the boards of technology startups. For example, a manager could join an early stage custom software development firm to provide advice about the hospitality industry or to provide other advice in a manager's specialist area of expertise. In return, that manager will likely get the opportunity to accelerate their learning of different digital technologies, digital business models, and strategic technology issues. They will also likely have an informal sounding board for their ideas or questions.

Implications for hospitality and leisure managers

This chapter had three aims. First, we sought to highlight the importance of accelerated learning or learning efficiency as an important managerial competence for keeping up with digital technologies. Second, we sought to highlight the importance of taking a strategic approach to managing accelerated learning, and to provide an example framework of such an approach in action. Finally, we wanted to provide some example strategies, practices, and habits that hospitality and leisure managers can leverage to accelerate their learning. But all this is just a starting point. Our hope is that hospitality and leisure managers use this starting point to begin the career-long process of seeking out accelerated learning practices and tools, and leveraging these to adapt and optimize their accelerated learning strategy. Doing so is crucial to keeping up with exponential advancements in digital technologies and to growing managerial performance demands.

Google and reflect

Accelerated learning, learning efficiency, learning science, content curation, expert leadership, tolerance for ambiguity, learner self-talk, constructive self-talk, experiential learning, learning platform, learning experience platform (LXP), attention control, memory capacity, learning strategy, curiosity, learning to learn, omnichannel learning, thought leader, futurist, personal information management strategy (PIM), hackathon, startup accelerator, corporate accelerator, impact accelerator, project-based learning, inquiry-based learning.

Discussion questions

1   What is accelerated learning?
2   What is learning efficiency?
3   What is the difference between accelerated learning and learning efficiency?
4   What three personal characteristics drive learning efficiency?
5   What are the top four drivers of learning efficiency?
6   What is the role of digital technologies in learning efficiency?
7   How do digital technologies enhance learning efficiency?
8   What is the relationship between digital technologies, learning efficiency, and a manager's ability to keep up with digital technologies?

Notes

1 Rong, G., & Grover, V. (2009). Keeping Up-to-Date with Information Technology: Testing a Model of Technological Knowledge Renewal Effectiveness for it Professionals. *Information & Management*, 46(7), 376–387.
2 Rong, G., & Grover, V. (2009). Keeping Up-to-Date with Information Technology: Testing a Model of Technological Knowledge Renewal Effectiveness for it Professionals. *Information & Management*, 46(7), 376–387.
3 Rong, G., & Grover, V. (2009). Keeping Up-to-Date with Information Technology: Testing a Model of Technological Knowledge Renewal Effectiveness for it Professionals. *Information & Management*, 46(7), 376–387.

4 Markman, A. (2017). Can You be a Great Leader without Technical Expertise. *Harvard Business Review*. Retrieved from https://hbr.org/2017/11/can-you-be-a-great-leader-without-technical-expertise

5 Goodall, A. H., & Pogrebna, G. (2015). Expert Leaders in a Fast-moving Environment. *The Leadership Quarterly*, 26(2), 123–142.

6 Rong, G., & Grover, V. (2009). Keeping Up-to-Date with Information Technology: Testing a Model of Technological Knowledge Renewal Effectiveness for it Professionals. *Information & Management*, 46(7), 376–387.

7 Rong, G., & Grover, V. (2009). Keeping Up-to-Date with Information Technology: Testing a Model of Technological Knowledge Renewal Effectiveness for it Professionals. *Information & Management*, 46(7), 376–387.

8 Rong, G., & Grover, V. (2009). Keeping Up-to-Date with Information Technology: Testing a Model of Technological Knowledge Renewal Effectiveness for it Professionals. *Information & Management*, 46(7), 376–387.

9 Rong, G., & Grover, V. (2009). Keeping Up-to-Date with Information Technology: Testing a Model of Technological Knowledge Renewal Effectiveness for it Professionals. *Information & Management*, 46(7), 376–387.

10 Rong, G., & Grover, V. (2009). Keeping Up-to-Date with Information Technology: Testing a Model of Technological Knowledge Renewal Effectiveness for it Professionals. *Information & Management*, 46(7), 376–387.

11 Rong, G., & Grover, V. (2009). Keeping Up-to-Date with Information Technology: Testing a Model of Technological Knowledge Renewal Effectiveness for it Professionals. *Information & Management*, 46(7), 376–387.

12 Rong, G., & Grover, V. (2009). Keeping Up-to-Date with Information Technology: Testing a Model of Technological Knowledge Renewal Effectiveness for it Professionals. *Information & Management*, 46(7), 376–387.

13 Lavenda, D. (2012). 7 Time-Proven Strategies for Dealing with Information Overload. Retrieved June 15, 2020, from Fast Company website: www.fastcompany.com/3002467/7-time-proven-strategies-dealing-information-overload

14 Asay, M. (2009). Shirky: Problem is Filter Failure, Not Info Overload. CNet. Retrieved June 15, 2020, from CNet website: www.cnet.com/news/shirky-problem-is-filter-failure-not-info-overload/

15 Beaton, C. (2017). The Single Most Effective Way to Deal with Information Overload. Retrieved June 15, 2020, from Inc.com website: www.inc.com/caroline-beaton/the-single-most-effective-way-to-deal-with-information-overload.html

16 Lavenda, D. (2012). 7 Time-Proven Strategies for Dealing With Information Overload. Retrieved June 15, 2020, from Fast Company website: www.fastcompany.com/3002467/7-time-proven-strategies-dealing-information-overload

17 Lavenda, D. (2012). 7 Time-Proven Strategies for Dealing With Information Overload. Retrieved June 15, 2020, from Fast Company website: www.fastcompany.com/3002467/7-time-proven-strategies-dealing-information-overload

18 Lavenda, D. (2012). 7 Time-Proven Strategies for Dealing With Information Overload. Retrieved June 15, 2020, from Fast Company website: www.fastcompany.com/3002467/7-time-proven-strategies-dealing-information-overload

19 Lavenda, D. (2012). 7 Time-Proven Strategies for Dealing With Information Overload. Retrieved June 15, 2020, from Fast Company website: www.fastcompany.com/3002467/7-time-proven-strategies-dealing-information-overload

20 Soucek, R., & Moser, K. (2010). Coping with Information Overload in Email Communication: Evaluation of a Training Intervention. *Computers in Human Behavior*, 26(6), 1458–1466.

21 Soucek, R., & Moser, K. (2010). Coping with Information Overload in Email Communication: Evaluation of a Training Intervention. *Computers in Human Behavior*, 26(6), 1458–1466.

22 Zerr, C. L., Berg, J. J., Nelson, S. M., Fishell, A. K., Savalia, N. K., & McDermott, K. B. (2018). Learning Efficiency: Identifying Individual Differences in Learning Rate and Retention in Healthy Adults. *Psychological Science*, 29(9), 1436–1450. https://doi.org/10.1177/0956797618772540

23 Bruce, G. S. (2004). Learning Efficiency Goes to College. In *Evidence-based Educational Methods* (pp. 267–275). Academic Press. https://doi.org/10.1016/b978-012506041-7/50016-4

24 Zerr, C. L., Berg, J. J., Nelson, S. M., Fishell, A. K., Savalia, N. K., & McDermott, K. B. (2018). Learning Efficiency: Identifying Individual Differences in Learning Rate and Retention in Healthy Adults. *Psychological Science*, 29(9), 1436–1450. https://doi.org/10.1177/0956797618772540

25 Zerr, C. L., Berg, J. J., Nelson, S. M., Fishell, A. K., Savalia, N. K., & McDermott, K. B. (2018). Learning Efficiency: Identifying Individual Differences in Learning Rate and Retention in Healthy Adults. *Psychological Science*, 29(9), 1436–1450. https://doi.org/10.1177/0956797618772540

26 Zerr, C. L., Berg, J. J., Nelson, S. M., Fishell, A. K., Savalia, N. K., & McDermott, K. B. (2018). Learning Efficiency: Identifying Individual Differences in Learning Rate and Retention in Healthy Adults. *Psychological Science*, 29(9), 1436–1450. https://doi.org/10.1177/0956797618772540

27 Andersen, E. (2016). Learning to Learn. Harvard Business Review. Retrieved June 15, 2020, from Harvard Business Review website: https://hbr.org/2016/03/learning-to-learn

28 Andersen, E. (2016). Learning to Learn. Harvard Business Review. Retrieved June 15, 2020, from Harvard Business Review website: https://hbr.org/2016/03/learning-to-learn

29 Gullotti, D. (2019, November 26). Leveraging Technology Platforms for the Best Learning Experiences. Harvard Business Publishing. Retrieved June 15, 2020, from Harvard Business Publishing website: www.harvardbusiness.org/leveraging-technology-platforms-for-the-best-learning-experiences/

30 Hart, J. (2019). Top 200 Learning Tools for 2019: Results of the 13th Annual Learning Tools Survey Published 18 September 2019. Retrieved June 20, 2020, from Toptools4learning.com website: www.toptools4learning.com/

31 Hart, J. (2019). Top 200 Learning Tools for 2019: Results of the 13th Annual Learning Tools Survey Published 18 September 2019. Retrieved June 20, 2020, from Toptools4learning.com website: www.toptools4learning.com/

32 Busulwa, R., Birdthistle, N., & Dunn, S. (2020). *Startup Accelerators: A Field Guide*. John Wiley & Sons.

33 Hart, J. (2019). Top 200 Learning Tools for 2019: Results of the 13th Annual Learning Tools Survey Published 18 September 2019. Retrieved June 20, 2020, from Toptools4learning.com website: www.toptools4learning.com/

34 Lara, M., & Lockwood, K. (2016). Hackathons as Community-Based Learning: A Case Study. *TechTrends*, 60(5), 486–495. https://doi.org/10.1007/s11528-016-0101-0

35 Lara, M., & Lockwood, K. (2016). Hackathons as Community-Based Learning: A Case Study. *TechTrends*, 60(5), 486–495. https://doi.org/10.1007/s11528-016-0101-0

36 Busulwa, R., Birdthistle, N., & Dunn, S. (2020). *Startup Accelerators: A Field Guide*. John Wiley & Sons.

37 Busulwa, R., Birdthistle, N., & Dunn, S. (2020). *Startup Accelerators: A Field Guide*. John Wiley & Sons.

Part V
Digital technologies deep dive

13 Data, data management, data analytics, and data science technologies

Introduction

Data literacy and proficiency is the unifying theme of the concepts discussed in this chapter. It refers to the ability to leverage the vast quantities of internal and external data to improve an organization's efficiency, effectiveness, and agility.[1] During the last 30 years, the data available to businesses have increased exponentially. Technology innovation resulted in even more information becoming available in a greater variety of formats (emails, web pages, social media, wikis, apps, etc.). This information is accessible through a greater variety of media and communication channels, resulting in an increasingly complex and rich information environment.[2] Gartner expects that 80% of organizations have either rolled out internal data literacy initiatives to upskill their workforce or they intend to do so in the coming year. Reaping major rewards from data has become a critical organization issue, with data now being argued to be an even more important resource than oil.[3,4] Used effectively, the large volumes of internal and external data being created every minute provide organizations with great opportunities for breakthroughs in how they organize, operate, manage talent, create value, and scale their reach.[5] Effectively capturing, storing, organizing, integrating, protecting, analyzing, and making the most of their data requires an organization-wide team effort.[6] There are limited benefits to managing data in silos or restricting its management to a few experts in a technical function within the organization.[7] Given this, nontechnical stakeholders in every part of the organization also need to be literate and proficient with data.

It follows, then, that managers who supervise or oversee these stakeholders particularly need to be literate and proficient with data to ensure that data literacy and proficiency requirements are reflected in hiring, performance management, and firing decisions. But managers tend to avoid getting dragged into data issues, perhaps due to the technical terminology, the complex methodologies, the sheer scale of the data sets, and the lack of sufficient technical grounding in data management foundations.[8] This makes it tempting to "leave it to the experts."[9] But this can be a major mistake, as data issues are now quintessential business issues for managers at all levels of the organization.[10] It is managers who advocate, set the objectives for, and allocate resources for data management efforts. It is managers who determine how closely data analytics, data science, and business analytics specialists work with their team and other parts of the organization.[11] It is managers who have the domain expertise critical to the development of data products to optimize their part of the business.[12] It is managers who are the ultimate users or nonusers of data products and insights. It is managers who most need to understand what opportunities particular data, data sets, and data products offer, how to best develop them, how to remove barriers to their adoption, and how to make the most of them.[13]

In this chapter, we provide an introduction to data, data management, and data issues from a managerial perspective. Our intention is to provide a starting point to enable managers to understand the value of data and data management, the key data/data management concepts and terminologies, the manager's role in data management, and examples of common data management platforms and vendors.

Data

Data as the new oil

As it relates to digital technologies, the term data refers to a collection of the smallest units of information that can be stored, processed, or transmitted by a computer (datum is the singular form of data). What constitutes data can range from numbers and letters to pictures, sounds, and videos. Although we only see the video, for example, within digital technologies, data are represented as a series of binary digits or bits. (To be more specific, we should talk about data that "are," not data that "is," since data is the plural of datum,[14] but data used as a singular is more common in speaking about data. We use a mixture of both approaches throughout the book to balance technical accuracy with ease of comprehension.) The term "information assets" can also be used instead of data, as it is seen to encompassing data, information, and knowledge. We use data throughout this book to improve understandability, although as we use it we are referring to data, information, and knowledge. Further, with regard to data being represented as a series of binary digits or bits, each binary digit is either a one or zero, so that at the most basic level, all data are a bunch of ones and zeros referred to as binary data. This enables it to be stored, processed, and transmitted by computers. Data can be stored on a physical or virtual computer (e.g. virtual machine) and can be transmitted between computers via a network connection. It can also be stored on a physical storage device (e.g. USB, hard drive) and manually transferred onto another storage device or computer.

In the early days of computing, usable data was limited to the few internal information systems or software applications within an organization (e.g. accounting systems, HR systems, procurement systems) as well as limited external statistical data. But over time, there has been a proliferation in the number of devices and software applications collecting data. These include millions of devices with sensors, cameras, and audio recording; as well as the digitization and facilitation of more and more business processes and workflows through software applications. In addition to this, many of these devices, processes, and workflows are increasingly connected to the internet and therefore able to interact with each other, with physical or virtual computers, and with people. This results in vast amounts of data being created, stored, and available to use every second. The opportunities for organizations that are able to effectively manage this data are almost unlimited. For example, organizations can format, integrate, organize, analyze, and leverage insights from this data as a source of vast revenues (e.g. Google and Facebook), as a source of operational and strategic intelligence, to drive product innovation, to enhance customer experience, to form and better manage strategic partnerships, to disrupt industry offerings, and much more. Given this proliferation in available data and vast power possible from effectively leveraging it, some experts have contended that "data is the new oil" (i.e. that data may be an even greater source of global power and prosperity than oil).[15,16] Unverified data refers to data that managers are not sure is true or untrue. Trusting such data and making decisions based on it can be highly dangerous. For example, imagine having unverified data about customer preferences and investing in capabilities to satisfy those preferences, only to discover after the investment that the data was inaccurate and the preferences were completely wrong.

Types of data

Not all data are the same. Some data are readily usable and of great value. Other data are of little value or can't be used without undergoing extensive formatting, organizing, integration, analysis, and presentation. Hospitality and leisure managers may come across a range of terminologies relating to data types including structured data, unstructured data, machine data, open data, dark data, real-time data, spatiotemporal data, unverified data, and outdated data. Structured data are usually pre-formatted and highly organized, making analysis easy (e.g. credit card numbers, first names, or annual revenue figures). In contrast, unstructured data are not pre-formatted or organized, making collection, processing, and analysis challenging (e.g. audio files or Twitter conversations about a brand). Machine data are data created by machines such as airplanes, elevators, and traffic lights and by devices such as mobile phones and fitness-monitoring devices. This data can provide a real-time record of the behavior and activities of customers or other stakeholders (e.g. delays, difficulties, frustrations, hesitations, delights while using a service) and of the performance or effectiveness of machines and devices such as servers, networks, heating systems, and mobile devices. Open data refers to data that is free for anyone to use, without the usual copyright, privacy, or other legal restrictions. For example, government and international agencies may make available some of the data they collect as open data. Organizations may then be able to combine this open data with other external and internal data to optimize operational and strategic decisions. Dark data are data that is collected, processed, and stored through the normal course of business but not actually used;[17] making use of such data may open up great new opportunities for an organization. Real-time data can be used immediately, as it is created. For example, real-time customer experience data may reveal when a customer is getting frustrated, enabling a manager to intervene and override routine procedures that may have resulted in loss of repeat business from that customer. We mentioned earlier that unverified data is data that may or may not be incorrect, making information based on that data potentially dangerous. Information based on outdated data can be equally bad, if not worse. For example, imagine tourism service operators basing destination package information on customer experience satisfaction data from the 1970s. People will most likely want different things out of their holiday package today than they did in the 1970s.

This is not an exhaustive list of data types. Rather, we have touched on some of them to illustrate that when making decisions based on data, understanding the type of data that has been used is important. Similarly, understanding the nature of data and data issues is invaluable to managers when making decisions about whether to hire particular data specialists, who to hire in data roles, or whether to invest resources into data formatting, organizing, integration, analysis, and presentation projects. Figure 13.1 provides a visualization of some of the different types of data hospitality and leisure managers may come across.

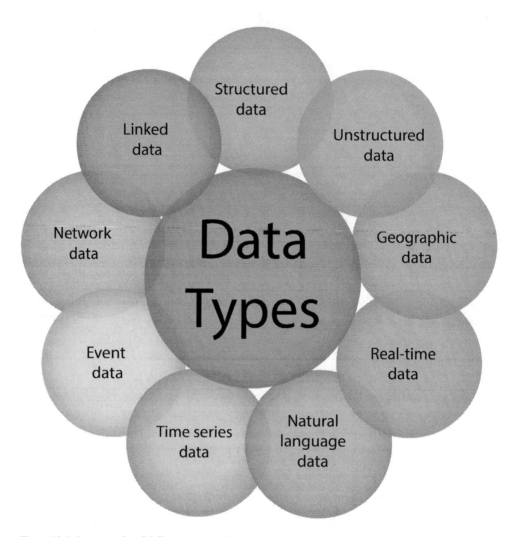

Figure 13.1 An example of different types of data

Data risks and other issues

The growing value and power in data also brings with it great and ever-growing risks. Dark organizations, groups, and individuals obtaining both authorized and unauthorized access to organizations' data can use it for dark purposes, including stealing their identity and their property,[18,19] selling customer data to criminal organizations, using customer data to interfere in elections[20,21,22] and stir up social unrest,[23,24] using customer data to take customers hostage, and much more. Early on, data-related risks were largely limited to storage, risk of loss, and data recovery challenges. But now, with almost all data being transmitted or stored online, the most important data-related risks include data security, user privacy, ethical collection, and ethical use of data. These issues have grown in prominence, as the main barrier between an organization's data and reckless, dark, or criminal entities are the measures that employees at all levels take to safeguard their organization's data. In their leadership, policy setting, hiring, and performance management decisions, hospitality and leisure managers play a crucial role in determining employees' attitude to, actions with, and responsible use of data. Other data-related issues typically focus on how to make the most of the mounting data organizations are collecting and have access to in order to enhance strategy and operations. Managers' roles in these issues focus on addressing questions such as how to format, organize, integrate, analyze, and present data to maximize the value derived from that data.

Big data

Big data is a term that refers to data sets that are so voluminous, so complex, and being created so fast that traditional data processing software and approaches cannot handle them. This data can include text, video, images, sounds, sensor data, and more (Figure 13.2 provides some examples of sources of big data). Six characteristics or dimensions of big data are often discussed: volume, velocity, variety, variability, veracity, and value. Volume simply refers to there being massive amounts of data to capture, organize, store, manage, and/or use. For example, there are more than 500 million tweets per day,[25] and it can be challenging for organizations to analyze a year's worth of Twitter data (e.g. in order to understand what is being said about their brand in tweets). Velocity refers to the fast rate at which data are received, processed, and need to be acted upon. For example, more than half a million comments and nearly 300,000 status updates are

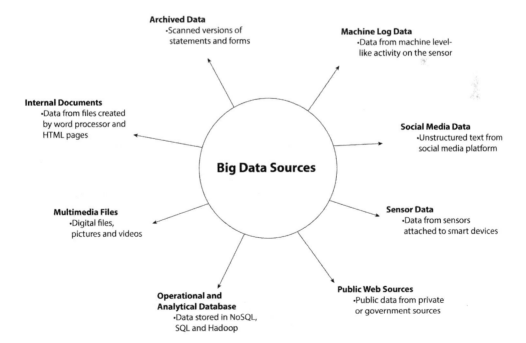

Figure 13.2 Example of sources of big data

received, analyzed, and stored in Facebook's databases every minute. Acting on the analyzed data, Facebook can respond to inappropriate comments in near real time. Variety refers to the many types of data sets. For example, there is traditional structured data, such as numbers and characters in a database, and unstructured data, such as text documents, images, videos, sounds, and emails. Variability refers to data whose meaning is constantly changing, and also changing rapidly. For example, in our earlier example of a brand analyzing tweets, the exact same tweets can have different meanings depending on the context (e.g. one tweet saying "Great, I love this brand!" may mean that person loves the brand, while another tweet saying "Great, I love this brand!" may be from someone being sarcastic who actually hates the brand). Veracity refers to the quality of the data. Not all the voluminous data sets that an organization has access to will be accurate. Also, those that are accurate are not likely to be in a format that can be used without significant effort to validate them, separate out what is useful and what is not, reformat them, integrate them with other data, and make them available in systems where they can be used for decision making. Some data sets are more reliable and easier to work with than others, making them of better quality. Finally, value is concerned with what benefits it is possible to derive from data sets (e.g. monetization, customer experience optimization, improved performance management).

In summary, the term big data relates to massive and rapidly expanding data sets from lots of different sources and in lots of different formats. The data are typically noisy, messy, and ever changing. The conversation about big data can be thought of as made up of two parts. One part is a conversation about the different voluminous data sets organizations can access, the quality of these data sets, and the potential value or riches that can be discovered in them. The other part is about approaches, practices, and methodologies to unlocking and leveraging the value of that data (e.g. methodologies and practices for capturing, storing, analyzing, transferring, presenting, and updating big data).

Data management

Given the value, power, and risks associated with data, it may not be surprising that a formal practice has evolved to ensure value derived from data is maximized while risks and costs are minimized. This practice is known as data management and is concerned with how to collect, validate, store, and use data most effectively.[26] Effective data management is a significant challenge for hospitality and leisure organizations given the avalanche of internal and external data to manage, and the growing sources of such data. For example, data can come from SaaS applications, ERP systems, legacy systems, databases, data warehouses, and data lakes. The data may also come from the web, social media platforms, open data datasets, and commercial data platforms. Alternatively, it may come from any number of devices including phones, computers, wearable devices, sensors, and monitoring devices. All this data must be collected safely, validated, stored safely, and formatted and presented so that different parts of the organization can access the right information at the right time and in the right format to make the best decisions. This requires that organizations have good technical leaders, capable technical specialists, the right technology platforms, and clear and enforced policies, procedures, and practices. The data management function typically plays a leadership role in issues such as data governance (who has what decision rights and accountability for data quality, data availability, and data accessibility), data architecture (what rules, policies, standards, and models are in place to determine what data are collected, how it is stored, how it is integrated, and how it is used), data modeling and design (defining and analyzing what data is required to support business processes), database and data storage management, and data security and data privacy. By having a working understanding of data management and effective data management practices, hospitality and leisure managers will be better positioned to hire the right leaders for the data management function, to hire the right operational staff to collaborate with the data management function, to support investment in the right data management technologies, to encourage the development of the right competencies to enable effective data management, and to not inadvertently undermine change efforts intended to deliver effective data management.

Business intelligence and business analytics

The vast amounts of data emanating from business operations are of little value if they are not used to improve operational and strategic decisions. Business intelligence (BI) is a term that refers to the collection, storing, and analyzing of this operational data in order to use it to improve operational and strategic decisions.[27,28] It can also refer to the methods and tools used to do so. BI focuses on descriptive analytics, showing "what" has happened in the past or what is currently happening and "how" it is happening.[29,30] So, for example, a BI dashboard may show us that food and beverage sales spiked to four times normal levels during the April–June quarter last year. As a result, we may need to decide whether to ramp up stock and staffing by three to four times normal levels for this quarter. Thus BI answers "what" and "how" questions to help us decide whether we should continue doing what we are doing, do more/less of what we are doing, or completely change what we are doing.[31] BI was once seen as an added utility, but this is no longer so. In the new data-driven environment, BI is critical to both competitiveness and survival.[32] The terms big data and business intelligence are closely related. Data are the underlying resource for BI, and the relationships existing between the two are often so close that it is difficult to separate them.[33]

Business analytics (BA) is a subset of business intelligence that focuses on predictive analytics.[34,35] That is, it focuses on the discovery, interpretation, and communication of meaningful patterns in data sets. Business analytics answers "why" questions or cause-and-effect determination questions.[36] Armed with answers about cause and effect, we can predict the outcomes of certain actions or failures to act. Whereas BI dashboards might indicate that food and beverage sales previously spiked in the April–June quarter, through BA we may discover that the spike happened because a big festival was relocated to our town for the next three years, bringing an influx of young and hip guests; we may get this from mining website traffic data and discovering that we had increased traffic due to a favorable influential blog post relating to the festival. Armed with this "why" information, we may decide not only to ramp up our stock and staffing levels during that period but also to send a thank-you gift to the influential blogger and a free hotel experience invitation to other influential bloggers.

Data analytics and data science

The term data analytics (also referred to just as "Analytics")[37] is an umbrella term referring to any form of analysis of data to uncover trends, patterns or anomalies or simply to measure performance.[38,39,40] It also includes interpretation, presentation, and communication of discovered patterns to improve decision making. Data analytics or analytics can also refer to one or more approaches, methodologies, and tools used to achieve the objectives of data analytics. Analytics approaches or methods include:

- Descriptive analytics – using historic or current data to determine "what" happened and "how" it happened.
- Predictive analytics – understanding the "why" or cause-and-effect relationships within data in order to be able to make accurate predictions.
- Prescriptive analytics – using algorithms to suggest optimal decisions based on the results of descriptive and predictive analytics.

Specialty applications of data analytics include value chain activities (e.g. marketing analytics, HR analytics, supply chain analytics), sectors (e.g. retail analytics, healthcare analytics), workflows (e.g. call analytics), data sources (e.g. video analytics, web analytics, speech analytics), and more.

Data science is a method for drawing insights from large data sets of structured and unstructured data.[41] It is a multidisciplinary field, meaning it draws on approaches, methods, techniques, and theories from varied disciplines such as mathematics, statistics, computer science, and information science. For example, it may draw on machine learning and deep learning techniques from the computer science field to learn from past decisions in order to improve the quality of automatically prescribed decisions, or it can draw on statistical methods such as regression analysis and structural equation modeling to improve the reliability of information used as a basis for prescribed decisions. The role of data scientists can include activities such as collecting data, cleaning data, organizing data, making statistical inferences, building/using machine learning or deep learning models, conducting online experiments, building customizable or personalized data products, visualizing data, communicating findings, and much more.[42,43] The value of data science to managers includes revenue growth (e.g. leveraging patterns in data to maximize sales opportunities), cost reduction (e.g. leveraging data insights to eliminate waste), improved customer experience (e.g. from combining customer analytics and big data insights), product innovation/new product development (e.g. discovering product shortcomings or unmet customer needs in big data), and improved agility and adaptability (e.g. sensing and preparing for effective adaptation to or benefiting from pending industry disruptions). Figure 13.3 shows that data science brings together operations and business function knowledge, math or statistics knowledge, and data management knowledge.

Data visualization

Data visualization refers to the communication of insights from data through visual representation.[45,46] The format of visual representation can vary from dashboards, infographics, and interactive charts to heat maps, network diagrams, cartograms, word clouds, videos, and more.[47,48] The insights discovered in data need to be communicated effectively and efficiently in order for potential users to make the most of them. This can be a challenging task when the interrelationships between data and the related insights are extensive, complex, or scenario dependent. Data visualization expands the repertoire of approaches and tools for communicating insights in the most efficient and impactful way. So, rather than a boring 30-minute PowerPoint slide presentation, a well-designed and interactive

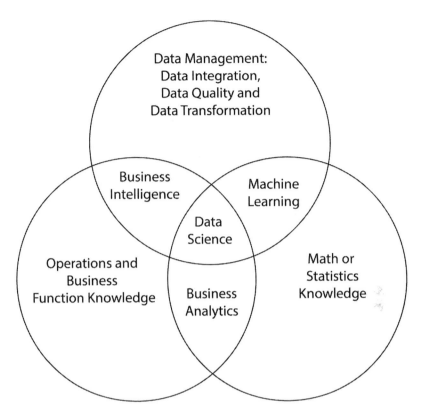

Figure 13.3 Data management, business intelligence, business analytics, and data science overlaps[44]

infographic may get the same information across much faster and with much greater impact. It is not just data specialists who can benefit from the use of data visualization methods, techniques, and tools; operating managers also spend much of their time communicating data insights to their direct reports, to stakeholders across the broader organization, and up and down the hierarchy. Data visualization proficiency can improve the efficiency and impact of their communications.

Implications for hospitality and leisure managers

Hospitality and leisure managers may be data-driven decision makers, functional data analysts, or analytics team managers/leaders. They will typically need to work with data systems architects and developers, and with data analysts and data scientists within or outside the organization. They may also be involved in hiring and line managing data and data management leaders and specialists. In either situation, their ability to work with data, to understand technical data issues, and to collaborate with data management specialists will be critical to their managerial performance. Figure 13.4 provides examples of data analytics and data science-related roles and the common job or position titles of employees performing those roles.

DSA Framework Category	Functional Role	Sample Occupations
Data Scientists & Advanced Analytics	Create sophisticated analytical models used to build new datasets and derive new insights from data	Data Scientist Economist
Data Analysts	Leverage data analysis and modeling techniques to solve problems and glean insight across functional domains	Data Analyst Business Intelligence Analyst
Data Systems Developers	Design, build and maintain organization's data and analytical infrastructure	Systems Analyst Database Administrator
Analytics Managers	Oversee analytical operations and communicate insights to executives	Chief Analytics Officer Marketing Analytics Manager
Functional Analysts	Utilize data and analytical models to inform specific functions and business decisions	Business Analyst Financial Analyst
Data-Driven Decision Makers	Leverage data to inform strategic and operational decisions	IT Project Manager Marketing Manager

Analytical Rigor

Figure 13.4 Data-related roles and type of expertise[52]

Google and reflect

Digital Capability	Common Terminology
Data	Raw data, clean data, metadata, structured data, unstructured data, semi-structured data, data quality
Big data	Database, data mart, data warehouse, data lake, data catalog, enterprise data hub, data fabric, operational data store, SaaS application, ERP system, legacy system, deployment platform, edge computing, data governance, data architecture, open data
Data management	Online analytical processing (OLAP), data mining, process mining, complex event processing, business performance management, benchmarking, text mining, descriptive analytics, prescriptive analytics, business analytics, business analyst, data analyst
Business intelligence	Business process management, corporate performance management, cube or data cube, dashboard, contextual data, balanced scorecard, slice and dice, snapshot, gap analysis, Key Performance Indicator (KPI), drill down, metrics, forecasting
Data analytics and data science	Machine learning, deep learning, neural networks, data mining, data set, data democratization, algorithm, natural language processing, machine vision, data anonymization, artificial intelligence, behavioral analytics, citizen data scientist, data classification, decision trees, multidimensional database (MDB) outlier, predictive modeling, Python, R (programming language), random forest, validity, reliability, decision science,[49] association analytics, sentiment analysis, time decomposition, cluster analysis
Data visualization	Charts, geospatial visualization, interactive visualization, climate change art, data art, data profiling, infographic, information visualization, interaction design, interaction techniques, scientific visualization, software visualization, statistical graphics, visual analytics, visual journalism, warming stripes, table or crosstab, distribution, flow, spatial, change over time, part to whole,[50] brainstorm, bubble chart, bubble map, circle packing, connection map, density plot, flow chart, flow map, heatmap, network diagram, population pyramid, radar chart, scatterplot, span chart, spiral plot, stacked area graph, stacked bar graph, stem and leaf plot, stream graph, sunburst diagram, tally chart, timeline, timetable, tree diagram, tree map, Venn diagram, violin plot, word cloud

Example tools and vendors

Digital Capability	Common Terminology
Data	GoSpotCheck, IBM Datacap, Mozenda, Octoparse, OnBase by Hyland, OpenRefine, Data Ladder, Cloudingo, IBM Infosphere Quality Stage
Big data	Amazon Redshift, Ataccama ONE, Cloudera, EnterWorks, Google BigQuery, Hortonworks Data Platform, IBM Db2 Hybrid Data Management Hadoop, Quoble, HPCC, Cassandra, MongoDB, Apache Storm, Rapidminer, Talend, Teradata, Apache Spark, Apache SAMOA, DataCleaner, Oracle Big Data Cloud, Oracle Big Data Cloud Service, Oracle Big Data SQL Cloud Service, Oracle NoSQL Database, SAP master data management software, SAS Data Management
Data management	Microsoft (Power BI), Google (e.g. Google Data Studio), Tableau, Qlik, ThoughtSpot, Sisense, Salesforce (e.g. Einstein Analytics), TIBCO Software, SAS BI, SAP (e.g. SAP business intelligence, SAP NetWeaver BW, SAP Business Objects), Oracle (e.g. Oracle BI, Oracle Enterprise BI Server, Oracle Hyperion System), IBM (e.g. IBM Cognos Intelligence), Birst, Yellowfin BI, Domo, Locker, MicroStrategy, GoodData, BOARD International, Logi Analytics, Information Builders, Pyramid Analytics

(Continued)

(Continued)

Digital Capability	Common Terminology
Business intelligence and business analytics	Microsoft (Power BI), Google (e.g. Google Data Studio), Tableau, Qlik, ThoughtSpot, Sisense, Salesforce (e.g. Einstein Analytics), TIBCO Software, SAS BI, SAP (e.g. SAP business intelligence, SAP NetWeaver BW, SAP Business Objects), Oracle (e.g. Oracle BI, Oracle Enterprise BI Server, Oracle Hyperion System), IBM (e.g. IBM Cognos Intelligence), Birst, Yellowfin BI, Domo, Locker, MicroStrategy, GoodData, BOARD International, Logi Analytics, Information Builders, Pyramid Analytics
Data analytics and data science	R, Python, C/C++, SQL, GoSpotCheck, IBM Datacap, Mozenda, Paxata, Trifacta, DataRobot, Feature Labs, Anaconda, Tableau, SAS, Alteryx, KNIME, RapidMiner, IBM Cognos, Hadoop, Hive, Pig, Spark,[51] Octoparse, OnBase by Hyland, Domino Data Lab, Informatica, KNIME Analytics Platform, Informatica, Anaconda Enterprise, Databricks, H20.ai
Data visualization	Tableau, Google Fusion Tables, JReport by Jinfonet, Google Charts, Microsoft Power BI, Infogram, Qlik, SAS, Cluvio, Visme

Discussion questions

Data

1   Do you agree that data is the new oil? Provide three arguments for and three arguments against the view that data can be regarded as the new oil.
2   What is the most high-profile data breach to have occurred to a hospitality and leisure organization that compromised the security and privacy of guest data? What guest information was accessed, and how many guests were affected?
3   What personal data are you emitting each day (e.g. via social media, search engines, mobile devices)?
4   What are some practical strategies for protecting your privacy?
5   What can hospitality managers do to minimize the risks to their employers' data?
6   Imagine you are a senior hospitality manager and you have the choice between two candidates to fill a vacant management position. One candidate has five years more experience, including time working for a well-respected competitor, but has minimal data smarts. Another candidate has five years less experience and has not worked at an organization as respected as your top competitor, but this candidate is very data literate (e.g. did a Master of Data Science with their hospitality management degree and spent three years working in the data management team at a leading bank while studying). Which candidate would you hire and why?

Big data

1   What is the difference between raw data, unstructured data, and structured data?
2   What is clean data, and what does the data cleansing process involve?
3   What is the difference between a database, a data warehouse, and a data lake?
4   If an organization has a data lake, can it do without a data warehouse?
5   What are five free open data sources that could be useful in the hospitality industry, and how could they be useful?
6   What are three open data use cases in the hospitality industry?

7 Briefly describe three ways you can use big data to improve your performance as a hospitality manager.

Business intelligence and business analytics

1 What is the difference between business intelligence and business analytics?
2 Which of the business intelligence tools under "Example Tools and Vendors" are open source tools?
3 Which of the business intelligence tools under "Example Tools and Vendors" are suited to enterprise-level customers, and which are suited to small/medium-sized business customers?

Data analytics and data science

1 What is the difference between data science and data analytics?
2 What is the difference between the roles of data analyst, business analyst, and data scientist?
3 As a hospitality manager, who would be more valuable to you: a data analyst, a business analyst, or a data scientist? Why?
4 Is it better to have a data scientist report to you as a hospitality manager or to someone in the IT team? Why?
5 Given a choice between hiring a data scientist with very strong statistical skills and knowledge of external data sets, but with no knowledge of the hospitality industry, and a data analyst who has been working in the hospitality industry for ten years, who would you rather hire and why?
6 What are the top five benefits to a hospitality manager of understanding data and data management terminology, tools, methods, and approaches?

Data visualization

1 As a hospitality manager, how could you benefit from being proficient in one or more data visualization tools?
2 As a hospitality manager, what can you do to benefit from data visualization tools if you are not proficient in them yourself?
3 Which of the data visualization tools in "Example Tools and Vendors" are open source tools?
4 Which of the data visualization tools in "Example Tools and Vendors" would be best suited for use in an enterprise-level organization, and which would be more suitable for use in a small to medium-sized business?

Notes

1 Brylad, M. (2019). Data Literacy: A Critical Skill for the 21st Century. Tableau Software. Retrieved December 17, 2019, from www.tableau.com/about/blog/2018/9/data-literacy-critical-skill-21st-century-94221
2 Mariani, M., Baggio, R., Fuchs, M., & Höepken, A. W. (2017). Business Intelligence and Big Data in Hospitality and Tourism: A Systematic Literature Review. *International Journal of Contemporary Hospitality Management*, 30(12), 3514–3554.
3 Vanian, J. (2016). Why Data is the New Oil. Fortune. Retrieved December 9, 2019, from https://fortune.com/2016/07/11/data-oil-brainstorm-tech/

4 Parkins, D. (2017). The World's Most Valuable Resource is No Longer Oil, But Data. Economist. Retrieved December 9, 2019, from www.economist.com/leaders/2017/05/06/the-worlds-most-valuable-resource-is-no-longer-oil-but-data

5 Mayhew, H., Saleh, T., & Williams, S. (2019). Making Data Analytics Work for You–Instead of the Other Way Around. McKinsey & Company. Retrieved December 17, 2019, from www.mckinsey.com/business-functions/mckinsey-digital/our-insights/making-data-analytics-work-for-you-instead-of-the-other-way-around

6 Mayhew, H., Saleh, T., & Williams, S. (2019). Making Data Analytics Work for You–Instead of the Other Way Around. McKinsey & Company. Retrieved December 17, 2019, from www.mckinsey.com/business-functions/mckinsey-digital/our-insights/making-data-analytics-work-for-you-instead-of-the-other-way-around

7 Mayhew, H., Saleh, T., & Williams, S. (2019). Making Data Analytics Work for You–Instead of the Other Way Around. McKinsey & Company. Retrieved December 17, 2019, from www.mckinsey.com/business-functions/mckinsey-digital/our-insights/making-data-analytics-work-for-you-instead-of-the-other-way-around

8 Mayhew, H., Saleh, T., & Williams, S. (2019). Making Data Analytics Work for You–Instead of the Other Way Around. McKinsey & Company. Retrieved December 17, 2019, from www.mckinsey.com/business-functions/mckinsey-digital/our-insights/making-data-analytics-work-for-you-instead-of-the-other-way-around

9 Mayhew, H., Saleh, T., & Williams, S. (2019). Making Data Analytics Work for You–Instead of the Other Way Around. McKinsey & Company. Retrieved December 17, 2019, from www.mckinsey.com/business-functions/mckinsey-digital/our-insights/making-data-analytics-work-for-you-instead-of-the-other-way-around

10 Mayhew, H., Saleh, T., & Williams, S. (2019). Making Data Analytics Work for You–Instead of the Other Way Around. McKinsey & Company. Retrieved December 17, 2019, from www.mckinsey.com/business-functions/mckinsey-digital/our-insights/making-data-analytics-work-for-you-instead-of-the-other-way-around

11 Oracle BrandVoice: How to Extract Business Value from Data Science: It's All About the Teamwork. (2019). Forbes.com. Retrieved December 17, 2019, from www.forbes.com/sites/oracle/2018/12/05/how-to-extract-business-value-from-data-science-its-all-about-the-teamwork/#4134870c651c

12 Oracle BrandVoice: How to Extract Business Value from Data Science: It's All About the Teamwork. (2019). Forbes.com. Retrieved December 17, 2019, from www.forbes.com/sites/oracle/2018/12/05/how-to-extract-business-value-from-data-science-its-all-about-the-teamwork/#4134870c651c

13 Oracle BrandVoice: How to Extract Business Value from Data Science: It's All About the Teamwork. (2019). Forbes.com. Retrieved December 17, 2019, from www.forbes.com/sites/oracle/2018/12/05/how-to-extract-business-value-from-data-science-its-all-about-the-teamwork/#4134870c651c

14 Bridgwater, A. (2018). The 13 Types of Data. Forbes. Retrieved from www.forbes.com/sites/adrianbridgwater/2018/07/05/the-13-types-of-data/#5a94baad3362

15 Parkins, D. (2017). The World's Most Valuable Resource is No Longer Oil, But Data. Economist. Retrieved December 9, 2019, from www.economist.com/leaders/2017/05/06/the-worlds-most-valuable-resource-is-no-longer-oil-but-data.

16 Vanian, J. (2016, July). Why Data is the New Oil. *Fortune.*

17 Dark Data. (2019). Gartner. Retrieved December 6, 2019, from www.gartner.com/en/information-technology/glossary/dark-data

18 Winder, D. (2018). Hack of Marriott Starwood Hotels Hits 500 Million Guests. ABC News. Retrieved December 7, 2019, from www.abc.net.au/news/2018-12-01/massive-data-breach-at-marriott-starwood-hotels/10573562

19 Winder, D. (2018). Hack of Marriott Starwood Hotels Hits 500 Million Guests. ABC News. Retrieved December 7, 2019, from www.abc.net.au/news/2018-12-01/massive-data-breach-at-marriott-starwood-hotels/10573562

20 Cadwalladr, C., & Graham-Harrison, E. (2018). Revealed: 50 Million Facebook Profiles Harvested for Cambridge Analytica in Major Data Breach. *The Guardian*, 17, 22.

21 Rafter, D. (2018). Cyberthreat Trends: 15 Cybersecurity Threats for 2020. Norton.Com. Retrieved September 20, 2020, from Norton.com website: https://us.norton.com/internetsecurity-emerging-threats-cyberthreat-trends-cybersecurity-threat-review.html

22 Cambridge Analytica Shuts All Operations After Facebook Scandal. (2018). Fortune. Retrieved December 7, 2019, from https://fortune.com/2018/05/02/cambridge-analytica-shutting-down/

23 Anderson, J. (2018). "Fake News" and Unrest in Nicaragua. The New Yorker. Retrieved December 7, 2019, from www.newyorker.com/magazine/2018/09/03/fake-news-and-unrest-in-nicaragua
24 Nast, C. (2018). The Co-Opting of French Unrest to Spread Disinformation. Wired. Retrieved December 7, 2019, from www.wired.com/story/co-opting-french-unrest-spread-disinformation/
25 58 Incredible and Interesting Twitter Stats and Statistics. (2019). Brandwatch. Retrieved December 10, 2019, from www.brandwatch.com/blog/twitter-stats-and-statistics/
26 "What is Data Management?" (2019). Oracle.Com. Retrieved December 9, 2019, from www.oracle.com/au/database/what-is-data-management/
27 Pratt, M., & Fruhlinger, J. (2019). What is Business Intelligence? Turning Data into Business Insights. CIO. Retrieved December 17, 2019, from www.cio.com/article/2439504/business-intelligence-definition-and-solutions.html
28 Comparing Business Intelligence, Business Analytics and Data Analytics. (2019). Tableau Software. Retrieved December 17, 2019, from www.tableau.com/learn/articles/business-intelligence/bi-business-analytics
29 Pratt, M., & Fruhlinger, J. (2019). What is Business Intelligence? Turning Data into Business Insights. CIO. Retrieved December 17, 2019, from www.cio.com/article/2439504/business-intelligence-definition-and-solutions.html
30 Comparing Business Intelligence, Business Analytics and Data Analytics. (2019). Tableau Software. Retrieved December 17, 2019, from www.tableau.com/learn/articles/business-intelligence/bi-business-analytics
31 Comparing Business Intelligence, Business Analytics and Data Analytics. (2019). Tableau Software. Retrieved December 17, 2019, from www.tableau.com/learn/articles/business-intelligence/bi-business-analytics
32 Mariani, M., Baggio, R., Fuchs, M., & Höepken, A. W. (2017). Business Intelligence and Big Data in Hospitality and Tourism: A Systematic Literature Review. *International Journal of Contemporary Hospitality Management*, 30(12), 3514–3554.
33 Mariani, M., Baggio, R., Fuchs, M., & Höepken, A. W. (2017). Business Intelligence and Big Data in Hospitality and Tourism: A Systematic Literature Review. *International Journal of Contemporary Hospitality Management*, 30(12), 3514–3554.
34 Business Intelligence vs. Business Analytics. (2018). Analytics.hbs.edu. Retrieved December 16, 2019, from https://analytics.hbs.edu/blog/business-intelligence-vs-business-analytics/
35 Ofori-Boateng, C. (2019). Data Analytics Versus Business Intelligence – And the Race to Replace Decision Making with Software. Forbes.com. Retrieved December 17, 2019, from www.forbes.com/sites/forbestechcouncil/2019/06/21/data-analytics-versus-business-intelligence-and-the-race-to-replace-decision-making-with-software/#29cab372612b
36 Comparing Business Intelligence, Business Analytics and Data Analytics. (2019). Tableau Software. Retrieved December 17, 2019, from www.tableau.com/learn/articles/business-intelligence/bi-business-analytics
37 Analytics. (2019). Gartner. Retrieved December 16, 2019, from www.gartner.com/en/information-technology/glossary/analytics
38 Comparing Business Intelligence, Business Analytics and Data Analytics. (2019). Tableau Software. Retrieved December 16, 2019, from www.tableau.com/learn/articles/business-intelligence/bi-business-analytics
39 Business Analytics: Everything You Need to Know. (2019). MicroStrategy. Retrieved December 16, 2019, from www.microstrategy.com/us/resources/introductory-guides/business-analytics-everything-you-need-to-know
40 Boulton, C. (2019). Data Analytics Examples: An Inside Look at 6 Success Stories. CIO. Retrieved December 17, 2019, from www.cio.com/article/3221621/6-data-analytics-success-stories-an-inside-look.html
41 Olavsrud, T. (2019). What is Data Science? Transforming Data into Value. CIO. Retrieved December 16, 2019, from www.cio.com/article/3285108/what-is-data-science-a-method-for-turning-data-into-value.html
42 Bowne-Anderson, H. (2018). What Data Scientists Really Do, According to 35 Data Scientists. Harvard Business Review. Retrieved December 17, 2019, from https://hbr.org/2018/08/what-data-scientists-really-do-according-to-35-data-scientists
43 What is Data Science? | Oracle. (2019). Oracle.com. Retrieved December 17, 2019, from www.oracle.com/data-science/what-is-data-science.html

44 Gao Institute of Management. (2020). Retrieved June 17, 2020, from www.gim.ac.in/content. php?name=ABOUT-PGDM-(BDA)&id=134

45 MicroStrategy. (2019). Data Visualization: What It is and Why We Use It. Retrieved December 17, 2019, from www.microstrategy.com/us/resources/introductory-guides/data-visualization-what-it-is-and-why-we-use-it

46 Data Visualization: What It is and Why It Matters. Sas.com. Retrieved December 17, 2019, from www.sas.com/en_au/insights/big-data/data-visualization.html

47 Data Visualization Beginner's Guide: A Definition, Examples, and Learning Resources. (2019). Tableau Software. Retrieved December 17, 2019, from www.tableau.com/learn/articles/data-visualization

48 Data Visualization: What It is and Why We Use It. (2019). MicroStrategy. Retrieved December 17, 2019, from www.microstrategy.com/us/resources/introductory-guides/data-visualization-what-it-is-and-why-we-use-it

49 Data Science Terminology: 26 Key Definitions Everyone Should Understand. (2019). Bernard Marr. Retrieved December 17, 2019, from www.bernardmarr.com/default.asp?contentID=1446

50 Glossary of Data Visualizations. (2019). Tableau Software. Retrieved December 17, 2019, from www.tableau.com/learn/articles/data-visualization/glossary

51 "Top Data Science Tools." (2019). James Cook University. Accessed December 17, 2019. https:// online.jcu.edu.au/canada/blog/top-data-science-tools

52 Gao Institute of Management. (2020). Retrieved June 17, 2020, from www.gim.ac.in/content. php?name=ABOUT-PGDM-(BDA)&id=134

14 Internet of things (IoT) technologies

Introduction

At the heart of the internet of things and related technologies or concepts is the use of connected sensors and algorithms to make things "smart" and or have them communicate with smarter things. These things can range from devices, equipment, and buildings to factories, biological processes, systems, and business processes. Long established, sensor technology has advanced to the point where there are sensors able to detect almost anything – from motion, voice, proximity, and touch to temperature, light, smoke, and much more. Although sensors have been capable of many of these things for a long time, what has changed is the ability to connect them to each other and to the internet. This enables them to share collected information with each other and with any other devices or things or people connected to the internet. All manner of things can now be connected to each other and to the internet. This connection enables these things to communicate the data they collect through built-in embedded sensors with each other. And through the use of software algorithms the things can analyze or have analyzed the collected information, use it to make decisions, and issue or follow instructions to and from each other or to and from people. The ability of things to perform activities like the latter, i.e. activities beyond merely sensing/capturing and sending/receiving data over an internet connection, makes them smart.

The sensing, connectivity, and smartness of things is set to profoundly alter how hospitality and leisure organizations create and deliver value. The ability of all things involved in hospitality and leisure organization workflows capable of being smart offers significant opportunities for novel new products/services and enhanced product/service offerings (e.g. while hotel staff may not be in a room with a guest at all times, certain smart devices are and these may be able to take guest service to new levels). It also offers vastly improved opportunities to improve efficiency (e.g. the vast array of data collected from all the different devices can be integrated and used to pinpoint wasted effort, bottlenecks, activities that could be automated, or costs that could be minimized) and effectiveness (e.g. concepts like smart workplaces and smart buildings can be leveraged to improve staff effectiveness). Other opportunities include the opportunity to improve adaptability and agility (e.g. through leveraging data on the things of strategic partners, governments, and the community, hospitality and leisure organizations may be able to better anticipate and adapt to crisis events, disruptions, and other changes). Hospitality and leisure managers play a critical role in ensuring their organizations recognize and seize the opportunities offered by the internet of things and related technologies and concepts. In order to play this role, they must understand the foundations, functioning, opportunities and threats, and use cases of the internet of things and related technologies and concepts. In the chapters that follow, our aim is to provide a basic introduction to key IoT concepts, functioning, use cases, and opportunities and threats. We hope hospitality and leisure managers find this introduction a useful building block to their ongoing efforts to understand and leverage the Internet of things to maximize value creation at their organizations.

Internet of things (IoT) and internet of everything (IoE)

Internet of things

The internet of things is a collection of connected or linked things (e.g. computers, devices, cars, industrial equipment, buildings) that are able to transfer data or communicate with each other, usually without requiring the input or intervention of a human being.[1] The things are usually connected, transfer information, and communicate with each other via a network (e.g. a small private network or a much bigger national or global network). At a global network level, you can think of it as the internet but with many more devices or things being connected than just computers (e.g. cars, phones, printers, traffic lights, bridges, planes, pillows, dust), and with these devices or things being able to communicate and transfer data and or instructions to each other. For example, this could be as simple as your fridge sending instructions to your phone for it to create a reminder for you to pick up some milk on the way home. On a more involved level, your fridge could go online to find a same-day milk delivery supermarket, order the milk, and notify your smart door lock to expect the delivery at a certain time and be ready to unlock the door once the milk arrives. If you have a robot in the home, the fridge or the lock could instruct the robot to pick up the milk from the front door and put it on a particular shelf in the fridge, so it is ready for you when you arrive home. The network connection between devices or things enables them to communicate or send data and instructions to each other (e.g. purchase order information, payment information, instructions for actions to take or places to go). These "things" also need to be able to read or sense themselves and/or their environment (e.g. the fridge has to be able to sense that the milk is running out, and when the milk has been replaced). Because of this, the devices or "things" are usually fitted with or have built-in or embedded sensors (e.g. touch sensors, proximity sensors, motion sensors, voice sensors, temperature sensors, liquid sensors, light sensors, heartbeat sensors, infrared sensors, gas sensors, smoke sensors, chemical sensors).[2] The job of the sensors is to collect information that things can communicate and or use. In addition, the things are usually also equipped with software systems or algorithms that can then analyze the sensed information and communicate the analysis or use the analysis it to issue corresponding instructions. For example, a sensor in a car may sense that a truck is coming at a particular speed toward the car; the built-in software system may analyze this data and determine the truck is about to collide with the car. The software system may issue instructions for the steering wheel and the brakes to perform actions that will prevent the accident. This is not so different from our eyes seeing that that the truck is speeding toward the car, our brain using this data to work out that an accident is going to eventuate, and our brain issuing our body parts instructions for actions to take (e.g. signal with our hands for the truck to stop or for the driver to get out of the way). Taken together, the combination of sensors, connectivity via a network, and software algorithms equip the things with significant ability to emulate or even transcend human ability in some activities. For example, it is more likely that your fridge can reliably ensure that you never run out of milk than you may be able to (e.g. you are less reliable as you may get distracted, forget, or be too tired, whereas this will not happen to the fridge).

With the right combination of sensors, netwoks, and software algorithms, almost all things can now be connected to the internet and become "smart" things with expanding potential for action; that is, things able to act on instructions from anywhere around the world or to act independently to serve us, protect us, enhance our performance, and much more.

Internet of everything (IoE)

The internet of everything extends the internet of things by connecting people, processes, data, and things (see visualization in Figure 14.1).[3] These are often referred to as the four pillars of the internet of everything (IoE). The IoE's expanded power is derived from the vastly expanded possibilities of everything coming online to share data/communicate, and interact in almost unlimited ways.[4] This differs from the internet of things, which is typically limited to the connection of physical things.[5] The people, process, data, and things aspects of the internet of everything can be thought of as pillars of the IoE. The people pillar refers to people's identity, interests and preferences, interaction, healthcare, work, address, payment, and other information being digitized, brought online, and being able to be interacted with. Once online, our virtual selves can interact with other people or with their virtual selves, with businesses, with business processes that are online, and with the things that are online (e.g. machines, devices). For example, such online things can customize products to suit us, they can intervene in activities we are undertaking if we are at risk (e.g. your car could sense, unbeknownst to you, that you are about to be hit by another car and either warn you to avoid it or take over the steering to avoid it – if legally authorized to do so). The process pillar refers to processes or aspects of processes being able to be done online, inputting into other online processes, or requiring outputs from other online processes. For instance, your connected car may send data to the car manufacturer's web based system about the condition of each part in your car, enabling the that web based system to know when critical car parts will be in poor condition. On receiving this information, the web based system may book you in for a change of brake pads at a service center that is walking distance from your workplace. In this case, information from you and your car has fed into and triggered the manufacturer's web based vehicle monitoring and servicing

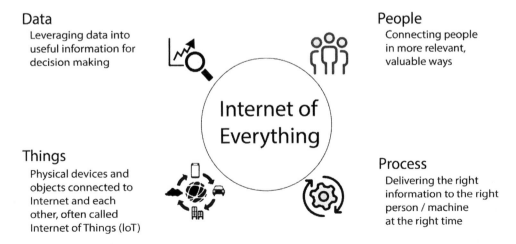

Data
Leveraging data into useful information for decision making

People
Connecting people in more relevant, valuable ways

Things
Physical devices and objects connected to Internet and each other, often called Internet of Things (IoT)

Process
Delivering the right information to the right person / machine at the right time

Figure 14.1 The internet of everything extends the internet of things by connecting people, processes, data, and things

processes. The data pillar relates to the collection, analysis, and use of data to facilitate and optimize processes. For example, in the case of our booking for a change of brake pads, it is the collection, analysis, and use of data from people (you and people like you), and things (your car and other similar cars) in addition to other data, that has enabled that process to occur and to occur at the optimal time. Finally, the things pillar is about the different physical things that are connected to each other and to everything else online (e.g. machines, devices, buildings, traffic lights, car parks). Bringing these pillars together, the IoE offers greater integration, automation, and "smarts" than has ever been possible. It is set to revolutionize how value is created and delivered.[6]

Connected vs. smart vs. autonomous

The terms connected, smart, and autonomous often come up in IoT-related topics. In addition to capturing and storing data (e.g. through the use of sensors), IoT devices are "connected" if they can send and receive information. This enables them to, for example, send sensor data that they've collected and to receive instructions. For example, your monitoring system may sense that someone is at the door and send you live video of that person. You may decide to send it instructions not to activate the alarm and, instead, to unlock the door because it is one of your relatives at the door dropping off something you forgot at their place. Without the connectivity (which may be via a mobile network such as 5G, or some other Wi-Fi network, or Bluetooth) the transfer of sensor data (video data in this case) and corresponding instructions (i.e to not trigger the alarm and instead unlock the front door) may be difficult. IoT devices are "smart" if, in addition to being connected, they can gather information about their environment, process it (e.g. perform computations), and respond to that information. So, for instance, an air conditioner is smart if it can sense the room temperature and adjust its output to ensure the room can remain at a comfortable temperature. An IoT device is autonomous to the extent that it can sense, understand, and appropriately respond to its environment and changes in its environment – thus eliminating or at least minimizing the need for human intervention. So for instance, a smart fridge would move up the autonomy continuum if it can sense (hear) that you are planning to have a large number of guests over, work out that you won't have enough milk to offer them all tea, and order the right amount of extra milk to be delivered in time so you don't run out of milk but also don't have excess milk left over. Even the smart air conditioner we described earlier has a level of autonomy if it works out on its own how to keep the temperature at a comfortable level for you. Sometimes these terms are interchangeably used through misunderstanding or through the boundaries between connection, smartness, and autonomy having some overlaps. There can be degrees to a device's connectivity, smartness, and autonomy such that one device may be smarter, more connected, and more autonomous than another.

IoT edge

While cloud architecture or "the cloud" offers almost unlimited storage and computation, a major shortcoming for some IoT-related uses is the time delay involved in sending sensor data to the cloud, and awaiting computation results or other data to be sent back prior to other actions being able to occur. Sean Bryson, vice president of Microsoft technology at Hitachi Consulting, gives the example of an autonomous vehicle traveling down a busy road. He points out that if that car has to stop immediately to prevent an accident, sending sensor data to the cloud and awaiting computation and sending back of the results is not viable – it will just take too long.[7] Edge computing provides a solution to this issue for IoT

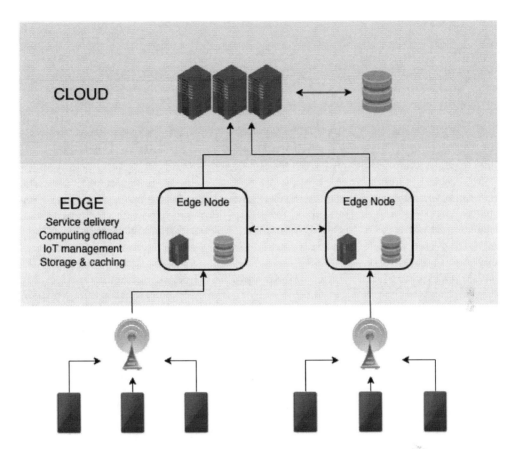

Figure 14.2 Edge computing brings computation and data storage to the locations where they are needed, instead of requiring sensor data to be sent to the cloud and waiting for the cloud to send the results of computation back to the location

devices. It is a form of distributed computing that brings cloud computing capabilities (i.e. computation and storage capabilities) to local devices.[8] These devices can then collect data via sensors, process it, and use the results for subsequent decisions and actions, instead of having to send sensor data to the cloud and awaiting the results of cloud computation. In the case of the autonomous vehicle needing to stop immediately to prevent an accident, Sean notes that the thousands of sensors within the vehicle can collect necessary data, assess the status of every piece of equipment and respond in fractions of a second.[9] Subsequent or nonurgent data can still be sent to the cloud for storage and computation (see visualization in Figure 14.2). Thus IoT edge refers to technologies or platforms that bring cloud capabilities locally to IoT devices, enabling them to sense, analyze, and respond in near real time. IoT edge technologies can minimize delays in processing, prevent delay-related product quality issues, and minimize financial risks and even fatality risks.

Industrial internet of things (IIoT)

The industrial internet of things (IIoT), also known as the industrial internet, is essentially the extension and use of the internet of things in industrial sectors and applications (e.g. in equipment/machine/device intensive industries such as oil and gas, power generation, manufacturing, aviation, logistics, food and beverage, and healthcare).[10] The ability of machines and devices to communicate with each other (also known as machine to machine or M2M communication), with people, and with processes, combined with big data and sophisticated analytics algorithms, offers the opportunity for industrial sector organizations to make unprecedented breakthroughs in reliability, efficiency, effectiveness, and agility.[11,12] Industrial machinery and operational processes can be monitored and optimized in ways that have not been possible before. For example, systems can monitor, collect, exchange, analyze, and deliver information on the condition of machines and equipment (e.g. detecting or predicting corrosion inside a refinery pipe). They can deliver information on the interaction of machines with each other and with people (e.g. detecting when one machine is limiting the productivity others), and they can deliver information on the status, efficiency, and effectiveness of processes (e.g. detecting errors and inefficiencies in the supply chain). Sophisticated algorithms can use the information being collected and analyzed to optimize processes and workflows (e.g. automatically scheduling on–call staff, laying off those who aren't improving, recommending who should receive bonuses, booking machine maintenance calls, recommending which vendors to continue buying equipment from). These things and more are made possible by real-time data from sensors, and the ability for data to be collected, analyzed, and routed between machines, people, and processes anywhere around the world in near real time. Hospitality and leisure managers may be involved in food and beverage, food processing and food technology processes or sectors, in which case IIoT use cases and innovations are likely to directly apply to them. If not, they may deal with industrial sector companies who may be vendors, strategic partners, or competitors. In either case, a good understanding of IIoT dynamics, use cases, and innovations can be invaluable. For example, such knowledge may enable a hospitality and leisure manager to go with a vendor who will have the best quality, safest, cheapest, most reliably delivered, and most integrable offering. Without such knowledge, the benefits of advances in the particular vendor's IIoT use may not receive the attention they ought to.

Cyber-physical systems, the Fourth Industrial Revolution, and Industry 4.0

Cyber-physical systems (CPS) are systems in which integrations of digital and physical things and processes enable the digital management of physical processes and environments (e.g. digital includes software and network connectivity, while physical includes hardware/species/biological/chemical elements). CPS are able to dynamically sense, adapt to, and manage changes in a physical process and in process' settings in real time.[13,14] They do this by collecting data from different sensors, combining it with data from a range of different systems, analyzing/interpreting this data, using the analysis/interpretations to make decisions (e.g. about how physical processes or environments need to change), and creating and relaying instructions for things and people to perform (e.g. turn up the temperature switch, activate the nurse call alarm, prepare a patient management plan).[15] Examples of CPS are abundant in a range of industries. In healthcare, CPS can be used to remotely monitor and manage a patient's health in real time.[16] For example, patient condition data can be collected via sensors in wearable healthcare technologies; this data can be analyzed/interpreted and combined with healthcare information system data to enable the right paramedics team (e.g. right location/station) to be called, for the patient to be taken to an emergency department with available capacity, and for the patient's general practitioner to preserve a booking spot to see that patient as soon as possible after they are discharged. This whole process is capable of occurring automatically, with only critical activities being performed by doctors, nurses, and paramedics. In manufacturing, CPS can be used to digitally manage particular manufacturing workflows at a plant, to manage entire plants or groups of plants, or to manage the entire manufacturing process across plants.[17] For manufacturing, Roberto Sabella, head of the Ericsson Research branch in Italy, invites people wanting to understand the power of CPS to imagine a situation in which robots, automated guided vehicles (AGVs), sensors, controllers, raw materials, products, and databases can communicate with one another, and where they can all be automatically orchestrated through a central intelligent system.[18] For an industry such as shipping/logistics, he invites people to imagine a port where cranes, vessels, AGVs, trucks, and containers can communicate with each other while being orchestrated by a central system aiming to optimize waiting time, damage rates, maintenance costs, environmental impact, safety, and so forth.[19] CPS and their elements can leverage technologies such as artificial intelligence, machine learning, and data analytics to be intelligent (or smart) and autonomous. For example, an "intelligent" cyber-physical system (or iCPS) may orchestrate all the activities of a "smart factory," automating and distributing different activity groups among different intelligent agents (e.g. intelligent sub-systems, intelligent things, intelligent processes, human beings).[20] CPS leverage the vastly expanded sensing, communication, analytics, automation, intelligence, autonomy, and other possibilities of digital-physical integration for breakthroughs in organization value creation, efficiency, agility, and adaptability.

The term "Fourth Industrial Revolution," sometimes interchangeably referred to as "industry 4.0" or "industrie 4.0", refers to the ushering in of cyber-physical systems and related technologies that are set to drastically change how organizations create and deliver value and, in turn, how societies function and how individuals live their lives.[21,22] This change is anticipated to be similar to, but of an even greater scale, than earlier industrial revolutions that drastically changed the functioning of businesses and societies.[23] For example,[24] the First Industrial Revolution ushered in the use of water and steam power to enable the creation of mechanical production facilities. The Second Industrial Revolution ushered in the use of electricity and enabled the division of labor, use of assembly lines, and the mass production of products. The Third Industrial Revolution ushered in IT systems to automate and better control production lines. In each revolution, the change in how organizations created value transformed the nature of work significantly. In turn, each revolution significantly transformed the functioning of cities and nation states and of how individuals lived their lives. For example, in the main, we are no longer subsistence farmers, factory laborers, or machine operators. We do more knowledge-oriented and creative work, earn much more, have much more free time, and live in cities and nation states that are very different from those in preceding industrial revolutions. In each revolution, the power and fortunes of individuals, organizations, and nation states leading or keeping up with the revolutions were drastically transformed.[25] For example, the First and Second Industrial Revolutions elevated the wealth and power of nation states like the United States and Japan.[26] It also elevated the fortunes of industrialists like Andrew Carnegie[27] and John Rockefeller.[28] And the Third Industrial Revolution has elevated nations like India and Japan and modern-day industrialists like Masayoshi Son, Jack Ma, N. R. Narayana Murthy, Bill Gates, and Sergey Brin. For individuals, organizations, and nation states that have not made sufficient effort to keep up with industrial revolutions, the revolutions have often diminished their wealth and power – if not marginalized them altogether.

Although the term Industry 4.0 (or Industrie 4.0) is sometimes used interchangeably with the Fourth Industrial Revolution, it was originally more specifically used to refer to the digital transformation of the manufacturing industry. Viewed this way, it is a subset of the Fourth Industrial Revolution. Whereas the Fourth Industrial Revolution is an all-encompassing term (i.e. referring to changes in how businesses produce products, in how cities/societies function, and in how individuals live), Industry 4.0 is is typically seen as being limited to digital transformation of the manufacturing industry, manufacturing organizations, and manufacturing processes (e.g. exploring how manufacturing industries, organizations, and processes can be transformed to make the most of the Fourth Industrial Revolution). Industry 4.0 considers issues such as what "smart manufacturing" and "smart factories" are, how they ought to work, and how to transform manufacturing and factories to be smart.

Smart buildings, smart workspaces, and smart homes

Smart buildings

In a nutshell, smart buildings are buildings that leverage the internet of things, cyber–physical systems, artificial intelligence, and other technologies to optimize the functioning, usability, and externalities of buildings. The functioning of buildings can be optimized through reduced energy costs, improved temperature and ventilation control, reduced maintenance costs, improved access control, improved useful life, improved safety, improved building condition/value, and more. Externalities, or impacts on communities and the environment, can be optimized through minimization of negative externalities (e.g. carbon emissions, energy consumption, hazardous waste) and maximization of positive externalities (e.g. negative emissions, positive impacts on community well-being). Usability can be optimized through improvements in the efficiency and effectiveness of the activities the building is being used for. Optimizations such as these are logical if we imagine, as an example, every component of a building being fitted with sensors, being online, being able to communicate with all other physical and digital components (e.g. devices, systems, processes), and being able to leverage artificial intelligence and data science to make autonomous smart decisions. As a result of all of this, a building would be able to know on its own who is in a building, where they are, what their comfort requirements are and how to meet them, what devices to activate and when, what video footage to analyze, who to notify if security anomalies are detected, what the conditions of a building's external environmental are, when there are likely to be disruptive issues with electrical grids and how to avoid the impact of those disruptions, and much more. Through integrations with workflow management systems, smart buildings may be able to drastically improve efficiency and effectiveness of work processes within organisations. For example, a smart building may be able to check which people entering the building have an appointment, automatically register their arrival in the visitor management system, send them an email or SMS confirmation sign-off upon arrival, direct them to skip the security cue and scan their QR code at the right door, and notify the person they are meeting to go down the elevator at the right time to greet them.

Smart workplaces

Smart workplaces combine concepts like smart buildings, the internet of things, cyber-physical systems, artificial intelligence, and other technologies with design and workflow management concepts to optimize the efficiency, effectiveness, and attraction of work settings. For example, smart buildings can be leveraged to ensure lighting, airflow, sunlight, and heating and air conditioning that anticipates and caters to workers' needs so as to enable them to do their best work efficiently and effectively (e.g. in regard to lighting, circadian rhythm lighting can optimize alertness, energy, and focus). IoT, data science, and artificial intelligence technologies can be leveraged to ensure that workplace conditions, equipment, tools, and resources automatically turn on and shut down in time to optimize accessibility and energy efficiency. The right data can be made available to the right devices and people, in the right format, in the right places, and at the right time – first time, every time. Smart buildings can communicate with other smart buildings, draw data from the external environment, pull in live traffic and public transportation data to ensure employees arrive and leave at the best times, maximize employees' breaks (e.g. best times to get lunch at their favorite cafes), avoid getting caught in the rain, and avoid areas most often associated with getting sick. Many more smart workplace use cases and best practices are continually emerging. Smart workplaces can be a potent attraction tool in the war for talent – for instance, consider the word of mouth and pulling power of Apple's and Google's work settings.

Smart homes

Smart homes are essentially like smart workplaces, except the focus is on maximizing efficiency, effectiveness, safety, security, livability, and comfort of a home's occupants. For example, smart solar systems, smart meters, and smart devices may ensure that power costs are kept at a minimum or that a household actually generates more electricity than it uses. Smart fridges, smart washing machines, smart air conditioners, and smart locks may autonomously take care of household tasks like food shopping, washing, climate control, and home access. Through Google's and Apple's connected or smart home platforms, home occupants can interact with devices at their home in real time from anywhere around the world. These devices can in turn interact with each other and with external systems and platforms. For example, a home monitoring system may automatically call police or an ambulance if it senses a security or safety threat within or outside the home.

Smart infrastructure, smart cities, and smart government

Smart infrastructure

Infrastructure refers to the physical structures and facilities needed for the effective functioning of society (e.g. roads, bridges, power lines, public buildings) and, sometimes, enterprise. Like other IoT things, infrastructure can also be connected, smart, and autonomous through leveraging concepts like smart buildings, the internet of things, cyber–physical systems, artificial intelligence, and other technologies.[29] Through leveraging these concepts and technologies, infrastructure can sense what is happening within itself and in the external environment. It can share the sensed information with other infrastructure (e.g. roads, traffic systems, street lights), with machines and devices (e.g. cars, smartphones, parking meters), with institutions (e.g. the fire department, the local emergency department, policing and intelligence agencies), and with information systems and workflows (e.g. government procurement systems, government healthcare systems, government emergency management systems, tender documents, ambulance diversion workflows). Infrastructure can also receive information from external systems and leverage artificial intelligence and data science, for example, to be self-aware and self-managing (e.g. sense the need for and coordinate its own maintenance depending on external weather conditions and government budget performance, anticipate and prevent public safety issues, coordinate with other infrastructure to limit traffic congestion, suggest/request changes to other infrastructure that may be creating bottlenecks or be the point of bottlenecks, prevent infrastructure abuse, limit the impact of public disorder events). The use cases for smart infrastructure are only limited by imagination and political/legal/social constraints. Diverse use cases can include letting swimmers know where it is safe to swim in real time in order to avoid shark attacks and drowning, anticipating wastewater overflow due to rain and coordinating preemptive action (e.g. to remove existing and emerging blockages), eliminating congestion from road networks by analyzing real-time data on the whereabouts of cars and redirecting them to alternate routes, recognizing criminals and stolen cars and directing police to their anticipated getaway routes, automatically analyzing video footage and alerting policing and public safety institutions to current and anticipated risks, optimizing infrastructure performance by pinpointing performance issues and limitations, and enabling real-time changing of public signage (e.g. street signs could automatically change speed limits and street accessibility). Governments that make smart infrastructure data publicly available enable businesses and consumers to leverage that data to improve available products/services and to improve the functioning of cities and regions. For example, when Transport for London shared public transportation data (e.g. what pickup spots and at what times), businesses and individuals used this data to create mobile apps or to integrate the data into existing apps so as to improve public transport accessibility.[30,31] Optimizing the performance and capacity of infrastructure can help meet challenges related to population growth, rising consumer/society expectations, and national productivity.

Smart cities

Smart cities are cities that enable and leverage smart infrastructure and the integration of smart infrastructure data with data collected from other things, from individuals, and from institutions to better govern and serve communities. For example, they can automatically source and integrate data from roads, bridges, buildings, transportation systems, water supply networks, drainage networks, police departments, citizens, schools, libraries, hospitals, social media platforms and other public services, assets, information systems, and platforms. They then leverage data analytics, data science, and artificial intelligence to better manage public service quality (e.g. availability of services, accessibility of services, timeliness, efficiency, safety, security), to reduce costs (e.g. city capital and operating costs), to reduce resource consumption (e.g. water, energy, labor), to improve community engagement, and to improve the quality of life satisfaction of citizens. As with smart infrastructure use cases and examples, smart city technology use cases and application examples are abundant. For example, on its continuing journey to becoming a smart city, the city of Barcelona implemented a network of optics throughout the city, enabling it to support IoT and to provide free high-speed Wi-Fi. This then enabled smart water, smart lighting, and smart parking management, saving the city over $98 million and creating 47,000 new jobs. In its continuing smart city journey, the city of Boston implemented smart trash cans that automatically determine when they need collection and the most efficient routes for sanitation workers to get to them. The city of Amsterdam has migrated to real-time monitoring of traffic flow, energy usage and public safety data to enable immediate adjustments to be made in relation to their management.[32] Figure 14.3 shows where a range of cities around the world are on the smart city maturity journey.

Smart government

Smart government extends the concepts of smart infrastructure and smart cities to optimize governance of democratic processes, the management of public service institutions, and the delivery of public services. Given their experiences with the business world, citizens expect responsive, efficient, and accountable government services and institutions. As their

City Name	Roadmap Designed	Smart City Department	Smart City Application Domains			
			Business	Citizen	Environment	Government
Bilbao	No	No	Yes	Yes	Yes	Yes
Birmingham	Yes	Yes	No	Yes	No	Yes
Bristol	Yes	Yes	Yes	Yes	Yes	Yes
Cape Town	No	No	No	Yes	Yes	Yes
Cleveland	Yes	No	No	Yes	Yes	Yes
Copenhagen	Yes	Yes	Yes	Yes	Yes	Yes
Fujisawa	Yes	Yes	Yes	Yes	Yes	Yes
Melbourne	No	No	No	Yes	No	Yes
Ottawa	Yes	Yes	Yes	Yes	Yes	Yes
Santander	No	No	No	Yes	No	Yes
Seattle	Yes	Yes	Yes	Yes	Yes	Yes
Seoul	Yes	Yes	No	Yes	No	Yes
Singapore	Yes	No	Yes	Yes	No	Yes
Stockholm	Yes	Yes	Yes	Yes	Yes	Yes
Toronto	Yes	No	No	Yes	Yes	Yes

Figure 14.3 Cities around the world and their smart city (SC) maturity (e.g. if they have a smart city roadmap, a smart city department, and have effected key smart city domains or application areas)[33]

expectations grow, they are becoming more intolerant of bureaucratic delays, lack of service availability, lack of service access, siloed government departments that don't talk to each other, and infrastructure that is not digitally enabled or able to interface with consumer devices. Examples of smart government initiatives include mobile apps that enable citizens to be community guardians (e.g. to capture and report incidents, to suggest improvements), they include single point sign-on to access all government services, they include leveraging business and consumer data to warn consumers about organizations misleading them,[34] and they include leveraging big data to anticipate security threats (e.g. leveraging travel/aviation data, traffic data, social media data, search engine and other data). They also include ensuring security and privacy of government information, enabling the use of digital IDs and digital government workflows, and enabling the secure integration of business and consumer systems and devices with government systems and devices.

Risks and other issues

As with many other digital technologies, key risks and issues of IoT-related technologies include privacy, security, ethics, and constantly changing technology standards. Examples of privacy-related issues include increased risks of unauthorized exposure of customer, citizen, or organization data. Examples of security risks include increased points of access to sensitive information to almost anyone around the world: whereas at one time a hacker was limited by availability of an internet connection, internet speed, lower availability of hacking targets, only computers as an access/breach point, and minimal online information to use – today all these things are almost unlimited). This creates a very big security challenge for organizations with regard to protecting all their people, things, systems, and processes.[35,36] Organizations and governments are expected to be ethically responsible in how they use the vast treasure troves of data available to them. This becomes a much bigger challenge with so many connected, smart, and autonomous devices. For example, it can be easy for artificial intelligence algorithms to create new information (by integrating and analyzing integrated data) but for it not to be acceptable for an organization to use or even access that data (e.g. it wouldn't be difficult for Google to create digital profiles of citizens and use artificial intelligence algorithms to comb the internet and internet-connected devices for extensive personal data about citizens – but this would likely be met with community outrage that could even lead to communities taking away Google's license to operate in particular communities). Finally, constantly changing technology standards mean that IoT-related technology users must always keep in mind that technology standards could change rapidly (e.g. from NFC to Bluetooth to 5G), and they ought to have platforms and devices that can accommodate new standards (e.g. that are able to adapt to new standards or cheap to replace).

Google and reflect

Licensing and entitlement management, IoT-enabled product as a service, things as customers, IoT-enabled applications, edge AI, infonomics, managed IoT services, IoT edge analytics, IoT cloud platform, mobile IoT (MIoT), IoT protocol, narrowband IoT (NB-IoT), quality of service (QoS), mesh network, telematics, IoT business solutions, digital business technology platform, digital twin, IoT security, digital ethics, IoT services, IoT platform, event stream processing, automotive, real-time data analytics, IoT edge architecture, LPWA, autonomous vehicles, low-cost development boards, commercial UAVs (drones), intelligent building automation systems, IT/OT alignment, asset performance management, managed machine-to-machine services, IoT integration, smart lighting, cloud MOM services (momPaaS), MDM of product data, MDM of "thing" data, internet of meat.

Example tools and vendors

Google Home voice-controlled speaker, Amazon Echo Plus, August Doorbell Cam, Nest Smoke Alarm, NETGEAR Orbi Ultra-Performance Whole Home Mesh Wi-Fi System, Kuri Mobile Robot, August Smart Lock, Arm Pelion, Bosch IoT Suite, Bosch Sensors, Cambium Networks cnReach Narrowband Wireless Solution, Cisco Intent-Based Networking (IBN) Solutions, Dell IoT Connected Bundles, Eaton PredictPulse, HP Enterprise Edgeline OT Link Platform, Intel OpenVINO, Intel IoT Market Ready Solutions, Lenovo ThinkSystem SE350, Particle IoT Rules Engine, Qualcomm Vision Intelligence Platform, Qualcomm 9205 LTE modem, Rigado Cascade Edge-as-a-Service, Roambee sensors and beacons, Roambee Honeycomb IoT API platform, Siemens/Alibaba MindSphere, Software AG Cumulocity IoT platform, Hitachi Lumada, PTC Thingworx, Nexiot Globehopper smart sensors, Huawei NB-IoT platform, SAP Leonardo, GE Predix, Ingenu RPMA device management platform, AWS IoT Core, Google Cloud IoT Core, Microsoft Azure IoT, Arundo Analytics, Bright Machines, Dragos, FogHorn, Iguazio, Preferred Networks, READY Robotics, SparkCognition, Element Analytics.[37,38]

Discussion questions

1   What is the best metaphor you can think of to explain how the internet of things works?
2   Is it possible for every single thing (living or nonliving) to be connected to the internet? For example, could dust, water, bacteria, diseases, plates, trees, and volcanoes be connected to the internet?
3   What do we mean when we say "things" can communicate with each other? What types of communication can they do?
4   What is a sensor? How is a connected sensor different?
5   What are ten different types of sensors?

6 What sensors could you attach to a chair to give it human–like senses?

7 What is the difference between the internet of things (IoT), the internet of every-thing (IoE), and the industrial internet of things (IIoT)?

8 What is the difference between a connected IoT device, a smart IoT device, and an autonomous IoT device?

9 What is edge computing? What is the IoT edge?

10 What is a cyber-physical system (CPS)? Are there different types of cyber-physical systems?

11 What is the difference between Industry 4.0, Industrie 4.0, and the Fourth Industrial Revolution?

12 Are Industry 4.0 and the Fourth Industrial Revolution possible without cyber-physical systems?

13 What is the difference between a smart building, a smart workplace, and a smart home?

14 Can you have smart workplaces and smart homes without smart buildings?

15 Which comes first: smart infrastructure, smart cities, or smart government?

16 What are five ways IoT and IoT-related technologies can compromise a person's privacy, security, and health?

Notes

1 Frangoul, A. (2017). The Internet of Things: Why It Matters. CNBC. Retrieved December 23, 2019, from www.cnbc.com/2017/10/23/the-internet-of-things-why-it-matters.html

2 What is a Sensor? Different Types of Sensors, Applications. (2017). Electronics Hub. Retrieved December 20, 2019, from www.electronicshub.org/different-types-sensors/

3 The Internet of Everything. (2019). Cisco.com. Retrieved December 20, 2019, from www.cisco.com/c/dam/en_us/about/business-insights/docs/ioe-value-at-stake-public-sector-analysis-faq.pdf

4 The Internet of Everything. (2019). Cisco.com. Retrieved December 20, 2019, from www.cisco.com/c/dam/en_us/about/business-insights/docs/ioe-value-at-stake-public-sector-analysis-faq.pdf

5 The Internet of Everything. (2019). Cisco.com. Retrieved December 20, 2019, from www.cisco.com/c/dam/en_us/about/business-insights/docs/ioe-value-at-stake-public-sector-analysis-faq.pdf

6 Seven Things You Need to Know about IIoT in Manufacturing. (2019). Forbes.com. Retrieved December 23, 2019, from www.forbes.com/sites/louiscolumbus/2019/06/02/seven-things-you-need-to-know-about-iiot-in-manufacturing_updated/#7de9c6095f56

7 Bryson, S. (2019). Internet of Things (IoT) – Five Components of IoT Edge Devices. Cisco. Retrieved December 30, 2019, from www.cisco.com/c/en/us/solutions/internet-of-things/iot-edge-devices.html

8 Bryson, S. (2019). Internet of Things (IoT) – Five Components of IoT Edge Devices. Cisco. Retrieved December 30, 2019, from www.cisco.com/c/en/us/solutions/internet-of-things/iot-edge-devices.html

9 Bryson, S. (2019). Internet of Things (IoT) – Five Components of IoT Edge Devices. Cisco. Retrieved December 30, 2019, from www.cisco.com/c/en/us/solutions/internet-of-things/iot-edge-devices.html

10 Everything You Need to Know about IIoT | GE Digital. (2019). Ge.com. Retrieved December 23, 2019, from www.ge.com/digital/blog/everything-you-need-know-about-industrial-internet-things

11 Industrial Internet of Things (IIoT) – Definition – Trend Micro USA. (2019). Trendmicro.com. Retrieved December 23, 2019, from www.trendmicro.com/vinfo/us/security/definition/industrial-internet-of-things-iiot

12 Everything You Need to Know about IIoT | GE Digital. (2019). Ge.com. Retrieved December 23, 2019, from www.ge.com/digital/blog/everything-you-need-know-about-industrial-internet-things

13 Sabella, R. (2018). Cyber Physical Systems for Industry 4.0. Ericsson.com. Retrieved December 30, 2019, from www.ericsson.com/en/blog/2018/10/cyber-physical-systems-for-industry-4.0

14 Sabella, R. (2018). Cyber Physical Systems for Industry 4.0. Ericsson.com. Retrieved December 30, 2019, from www.ericsson.com/en/blog/2018/10/cyber-physical-systems-for-industry-4.0

15 Sabella, R. (2018). Cyber Physical Systems for Industry 4.0. Ericsson.com. Retrieved December 30, 2019, from www.ericsson.com/en/blog/2018/10/cyber-physical-systems-for-industry-4.0

16 Sabella, R. (2018). Cyber Physical Systems for Industry 4.0. Ericsson.com. Retrieved December 30, 2019, from www.ericsson.com/en/blog/2018/10/cyber-physical-systems-for-industry-4.0

17 King, A. (2019). What are Cyber-Physical Systems? RMIT University. Rmit.edu.au. Retrieved December 30, 2019, from www.rmit.edu.au/industry/develop-your-workforce/tailored-workforce-solutions/c4de/articles/what-are-cyber-physical-systems

18 Sabella, R. (2018). Cyber Physical Systems for Industry 4.0. Ericsson.com. Retrieved December 30, 2019, from www.ericsson.com/en/blog/2018/10/cyber-physical-systems-for-industry-4.0

19 Sabella, R. (2018). Cyber Physical Systems for Industry 4.0. Ericsson.com. Retrieved December 30, 2019, from www.ericsson.com/en/blog/2018/10/cyber-physical-systems-for-industry-4.0

20 Sabella, R. (2018). Cyber Physical Systems for Industry 4.0. Ericsson.com. Retrieved December 30, 2019, from www.ericsson.com/en/blog/2018/10/cyber-physical-systems-for-industry-4.0

21 Wilson, B. (2016). What is the Fourth Industrial Revolution & How Will it Affect You? Blogs. oracle.com. Retrieved December 30, 2019, from https://blogs.oracle.com/oracleuniversity/what-is-the-fourth-industrial-revolution-how-will-it-affect-you

22 Schulze, E. (2019). Everything You Need to Know about the Fourth Industrial Revolution. CNBC. Retrieved December 30, 2019, from www.cnbc.com/2019/01/16/fourth-industrial-revolution-explained-davos-2019.html

23 Sabella, R. (2018). Cyber Physical Systems for Industry 4.0. Ericsson.com. Retrieved December 30, 2019, from www.ericsson.com/en/blog/2018/10/cyber-physical-systems-for-industry-4.0

24 Wilson, B. (2016). What is the Fourth Industrial Revolution & How Will it Affect You? Blogs. oracle.com. Retrieved December 30, 2019, from https://blogs.oracle.com/oracleuniversity/what-is-the-fourth-industrial-revolution-how-will-it-affect-you

25 Diamond, J. M. (1998). *Guns, Germs and Steel: A Short History of Everybody for the Last 13,000 Years.* Random House.

26 Porter, M. E. (2011). *Competitive Advantage of Nations: Creating and Sustaining Superior Performance.* Simon and Schuster.

27 Nasaw, D. (2007). *Andrew Carnegie.* Penguin.

28 Rockefeller, J. D., & Chernow, R. (1998). *Titan: The Life of John D. Rockefeller, Sr.* Random House

29 Siemens. (2020). Intelligent Infrastructure: How to Make a Smart Building More Profitable. Retrieved January 3, 2020, from https://assets.new.siemens.com/siemens/assets/api/uuid:396710f1-ea9e-4089-ae2f-8408528094c7/version:1560771253/cc-us-bt-cpp-intel-infrstrctr-wp.pdf

30 Macaulay, T. (2019). How Startups Aim to Transform Cycling with Enormous New TfL Dataset. Techworld. Retrieved January 3, 2020, from www.techworld.com/data/startups-aim-transform-urban-cycling-with-enormous-new-tfl-dataset-3701170/

31 Financial Times. (2020). Uber Integrates Transport for London Info Into App. Ft.com. Retrieved January 3, 2020, from www.ft.com/content/d557d9ec-6a8e-11e9-80c7-60ee53e6681d

32 Ellsmoor, J. (2019). Smart Cities: The Future of Urban Development. Forbes.com. Retrieved January 3, 2020, from www.forbes.com/sites/jamesellsmoor/2019/05/19/smart-cities-the-future-of-urban-development/#8ee0ae72f900

33 Sánchez-Corcuera, R., Nuñez-Marcos, A., Sesma-Solance, J., Bilbao-Jayo, A., Mulero, R., Zulaika, U., . . . & Almeida, A. (2019). Smart Cities Survey: Technologies, Application Domains and Challenges for the Cities of the Future. *International Journal of Distributed Sensor Networks*, 15(6). https://doi.org/10.1177/1550147719853984.

34 Grieve, C. (2019). Worst Performing Superannuation Funds Exposed by APRA "Heatmap." The Sydney Morning Herald. Retrieved January 3, 2020, from www.smh.com.au/business/banking-and-finance/worst-performing-superannuation-funds-exposed-by-apra-heatmap-20191210-p53ihq.html

35 Trendmicro. (2019). IIoT Security Risk Mitigation in the Industry 4.0 Era. trendmicro.com. Retrieved January 3, 2020, from https://documents.trendmicro.com/assets/rpt/IIoTsecurity-risk-mitigation-in-the-industry-4-era.pdf

36 Wood, E. (2019). It's Time to Secure the Internet of Everything: Regulations Rise as the IoT Continues to Expand. Forbes.com. Retrieved January 3, 2020, from www.forbes.com/sites/forbestechcouncil/2019/09/30/its-time-to-secure-the-internet-of-everything-regulations-rise-as-the-iot-continues-to-expand/#711b22f7fa44

37 Martin, D. (2019). 2019 Internet of Things 50: 15 Coolest IoT Hardware Companies. CRN. Retrieved January 5, 2020, from www.crn.com/slide-shows/internet-of-things/2019-internet-of-things-50-15-coolest-iot-hardware-companies/1

38 Staff, C. (2020). The Most Powerful IoT Companies in the World. Computerworld. Retrieved January 5, 2020, from www.computerworld.com/article/3412287/the-most-powerful-internet-of-things-iot-companies-to-watch.html#slide16

15 Artificial intelligence (AI) technologies

Introduction

The overarching theme of the digital technologies and concepts covered in this chapter is the design, use, and optimization of information systems and applications that can sense, comprehend, and recommend or take action. The design and use of such digital technologies and concepts are collectively referred to as artificial intelligence (AI). Artificial intelligence includes but extends far beyond familiar AI technologies like robots, smart devices, chatbots, and virtual assistants. AI is set to fundamentally transform how products and services are delivered and how the organizations delivering these products and services operate. Andrew Ng, co-founder of Coursera, AI Fund, Landing.AI, and Google Brain, uses the metaphor of the disruptive and transformative power of the internet to explain the disruptive and transformative power of AI.[1] The advent of the internet saw some companies aspire to become internet-enabled companies and others aspire to become true internet companies. While those aspiring to be internet-enabled companies focused on building and operating a website, those aspiring to be true internet companies focused on rearchitecting the whole company to fully leverage the new capabilities of the internet.[2] Many companies focusing on being internet enabled missed the point (i.e the point being the disruptive and transformative power of the internet) and were leapfrogged by true internet companies (e.g. Blockbuster vs. Netflix, Borders vs. Amazon). In the same way, today many companies may be aspiring to become AI-enabled companies when they really ought to be aspiring to become true AI companies (i.e rearchitecting the whole organization to fully leverage the new capabilities of AI).

AI technologies and related concepts offer organizations significant efficiency opportunities (e.g. using AI to perform routine tasks that can be automated through "if this – then – that" rules), significant effectiveness opportunities (e.g. using AI to augment human decision making and thus make better value delivery decisions), significant product and business model innovation opportunities (e.g. using AI to create new AI-based products and services such as automated analysts, digital assistants, robots, AI-augmented services, data management services), significant scalability opportunities (e.g. being able to offer automated AI-based services 24/7 worldwide), and significant adaptability and agility opportunities (e.g. leveraging AI's sensing and intelligence capabilities to anticipate disruptions and opportunities, better adapt to disruptions, or seize opportunities first). Early adopters of AI in the hospitality and leisure industry have used AI to improve service availability, to significantly reduce costs, to minimize human error, and to offer enhanced personalization. For example, FCM Travel Solutions created Sam, a travel intelligent chatbot able to interact with customers 24/7 like a skilled consultant. Taking the form of an app, Sam provides travelers with custom information on itineraries, restaurant recommendations, gates/travel time changes, upcoming weather conditions, driving directions, ridesharing tips, local tips, anticipatory service suggestions, and even receipt screenshot prompts.[3] Similarly, Hilton Hotels and Resorts (in partnership with IBM) has launched Connie, an AI robot able to speak with guests to discuss tourist information. Connie enhances her conversational understanding and speech by learning from every customer conversation.[4] Other hospitality and tourism organizations have leveraged real-time customer experience data for actionable predictive and prescriptive analytics. Leveraging such analytics, they've been able to offer superior customer experience relative to less AI-savvy competitors.

Transforming into an AI company is the responsibility of hospitality managers at all leadership levels, from top management strategic leaders to frontline leaders. Hospitality managers can play a critical role in shaping workforce attitudes toward AI, workforce AI capabilities, organization adoption of AI, and the scale and state of AI practice within an organization. To effectively play this role, they have to at least understand and keep up with AI terminologies and concepts. Although this is an iterative process of learning to keep up with digital technologies, in this chapter we provide a basic starting point. The chapter begins by introducing high-level AI and machine learning concepts. It then goes on to introduce interpretation, modeling, and learning and prediction tools and concepts that underpin the "intelligence" in artificial intelligence (e.g. natural language processing, speech recognition, computer vision, knowledge graphs, artificial neural networks, deep learning, expert systems). Finally, the chapter identifies some of the key AI-related issues and risks. Taken together, we hope readers will get a high-level understanding of AI and machine learning and of the interpretation, modeling, and learning and prediction tools and concepts underpinning AI. This will enable them to pursue self-directed follow-on learning with confidence so they can keep up with evolving AI developments and applications.

Artificial intelligence (AI) and machine learning (ML)

Artificial intelligence

Artificial intelligence (also referred to as machine intelligence, computational intelligence, or cognitive computing) is intelligence demonstrated by machines (e.g. computers, computer-based or computer-like machines). As a branch of computer science, it is the study of how intelligent agents (e.g. computer programs or computer-based machines) can best sense and adapt to changes in their environment to achieve their goals (e.g. winning a chess game, driving a car on a busy road, completing an obstacle course, dealing with a customer inquiry, or even taking out a military threat during a war). Artificial intelligence is often a foundational building block, enabler, catalyst, and/or extender of many other digital technologies and related concepts such as predictive and prescriptive data analytics, IoT smart devices, robotics, drones, and cyber-physical systems. The term artificial is used in contrast to natural human intelligence to signify that artificial intelligence (AI) attempts to mimic human intelligence or cognitive functions and behaviors such as attention, memory, learning, thinking, problem solving, decision making, natural language literacy, motor coordination, planning, manipulation, social intelligence, and creativity. When used, the term artificial intelligence (or its abbreviation AI) can be referring to the definition of AI (discussed earlier) or to the set of AI-based technologies and applications.

General AI vs. narrow AI

There are two broad types of AI: general AI and narrow AI. General AI (also referred to as artificial general intelligence [AGI], strong AI, full AI, or general intelligent action) is the type of adaptable and adaptive intelligence that humans are capable of, which enables them to autonomously perform a diverse range of actions by leveraging all human cognitive functions. This is the type of AI in Hollywood depictions of AI like *The Terminator*. Such depictions usually refer to general AI, or to super-intelligence, that is, artificial intelligence that exceeds human cognitive capabilities. New York University professor Meredith Broussard, who researches the role of artificial intelligence in journalism, proposes that general AI can be thought of as the equivalent of putting a human brain inside machines, thus enabling them to learn or be taught the full range of human capabilities (e.g. from empathizing and falling in love, to building a spreadsheet or a computer program, to raising children or leading a nation state).[5] Meredith contends that we are very far from achieving this type of AI, which is mostly fantasy. Although some artificial intelligence researchers contend it may be possible to achieve general AI at some point, others contend it is not possible for us to ever achieve it. Figure 15.1 shows the different types of AI, what they are capable of, and the performance implications resulting from their capability.

Narrow AI (also known as weak AI or applied AI) is what is actually commercial reality today. Narrow AI refers to programs or machines that can be taught or can learn to perform specific and well-defined tasks without explicitly being programmed to do so (e.g. analyze a data set of past winning and losing moves in chess, learn from them, and determine the optimal move to make in order to beat a chess grandmaster). Narrow AI can be thought of as AI that can perform a single activity or a narrow set of related activities that would typically require a human brain to be done. This is the type of AI in virtual assistants like Siri and Google Assistant, which can learn to decipher and respond to human speech in limited ways. It is also the type of AI used in purchase recommendation engines that suggest what other products you might like to buy based on your past purchase behavior or that of

Types of AI	Artificial Narrow Intelligence (ANI)	Artificial General Intelligence (AGI)	Artificial Super Intelligence (ASI)
What is it capable of?	Executive specific tasks without ability to self-expand functionality	Perform broad tasks, reason, and improve capabilities in a way that is comparable to humans.	Demonstrate intelligence beyond human capabilities.
What are the implications?	Outperform humans in specific repetitive functions like driving, medical diagnosis, games, etc.	Compete with humans on all fronts, such as earning university degrees, and convincing humans that it is human (Turing Test).	Outperform humans, helping to achieve societal objectives or threatening the human race.

Figure 15.1 Types of AI, their capabilities, and implications for human beings

others. Professor Broussard contends that narrow AI is really just beautiful mathematics, or computational statistics on steroids. That is, it is largely about machines being taught or learning to find patterns in data sets and then using these patterns as the basis for optimal recommendations, decisions, instructions, or actions. This type of AI is very different from the Hollywood stereotypes of machines like *The Terminator*, with broad human–like intelligence and capabilities. While narrow AI is limited to specific tasks, the number and range of specific tasks it can perform are almost limitless. Additionally, different types of tasks can be combined and built on each other to expand what is possible, so that narrow AI is not so narrow. For example, a range of specific tasks can be integrated and sequenced in such a way as to manage a smart home, a smart workplace, a smart factory, or even a smart city.

Bots

Bots are an application of narrow AI. A bot is a software application or program that runs/ performs an automated task (or a script). Bots usually operate over the internet and are hence sometimes referred to as internet robots or web robots. Bots can be taught or can learn to perform a vast array of processes, activities, and routines using business data sets and publicly available online data sets or search engine data. For example, chatbots are programs that interact with people in written or voice format to answer their questions, provide them services, or entertain them. Applications like Siri and Google Assistant are examples of voice-based chatbots. The range of bots available on the market is extensive and includes friend bots, digital assistants (like Siri), meeting planners, bot writers, language tutoring bots, legal bots (e.g. querying and refuting parking tickets), Q&A bots (e.g. customer service), therapy bots, survey bots, sales bots, and insurance claim bots. Although they can't solve all customer service/ support issues, bots enable 24/7 availability of a limited but improving level of service/support.

Machine learning

Machine learning (ML) is a subset of artificial intelligence. As a subset, it is artificial intelligence that focuses on algorithms for equipping machines with the ability to analyze and automatically learn from data sets and then use this learning as the basis for recommendations, decisions, instructions, or actions. This is not so different from the way a human being analyzes or reflects on their past experiences, learns from them, and uses this learning to guide future actions. Typically, machine learning involves machines being fed large amounts of historical data, and the ML algorithms using this data as "training data" (e.g. data from which to identify cause and effect patterns and make inferences based on statistical methods and mathematical optimization). Bots and recommendation engines are an example of machine learning technology application. It is machine learning algorithms in GPS maps that anticipate upcoming traffic and offer optimal routes to take, and it is machine learning that enables clinicians to be alerted by a wearable healthcare device that a patient is about to have a heart attack if there isn't an immediate intervention. In commercial uses, machine learning can also be referred to as predictive analytics.

Knowledge graphs, neural networks, and deep learning

Knowledge graphs

A knowledge graph is a graphical representation of the links between data and their meaning.[6] The links can be between different types of data in a data set (e.g. text, images, video), between data subgroups (e.g. homes in a particular country as a subgroup of homes in a data set), and/or between different data sets (e.g. databases, data stores, data lakes, external knowledge graphs and other information). The links and meaning are represented in a natural language–like format. The "graph" is usually in a network-like format, making it one of the most flexible formal data structures. This makes it easy to add on other data links or to modify a data link. Figure 15.2 shows part of a knowledge graph representing information about an aspect of the US election at a point in time. Knowledge graphs are data and thus require graph databases and related components (e.g. taxonomy and ontology editors, entity extractors, graph mappers, validation, visualization and search tools).[7] While technical specialists maintain knowledge graphs, nontechnical specialists can contribute their domain expertise to improve the quality and meaningfulness of the connections. There is huge power in having meaningful links between information that are constantly evolving as new data sets are added or as patterns are found in existing data sets. Both human beings and artificial intelligence algorithms can query this data using natural language or using graph-computing techniques and algorithms, like shortest-path computations or network analysis. Knowledge graphs bring together disparate data silos to provide an integrated view of the available information for problem solving, they link structured and unstructured data to illuminate relationships between them, and they provide a structured way to capture and store the insights of nontechnical domain experts (e.g. with regard to the links and meaning of links between a company's different data and information). In doing so, knowledge graphs enable better and faster decisions to be made, and to be made at scale (i.e. able to be made quickly 24/7 by people and machines anywhere in the world).

Neural networks and deep learning

Neural networks are a branch of machine learning. A neural network (also referred to as a neural net [NN] or an artificial neural network [ANN]) is an algorithm or set of algorithms that mathematically model the relationship between inputs and their outputs to enable accurate prediction to occur. The "neural" part of the term is derived from the neural networks approach having been inspired by, and attempting to mimic, the biological

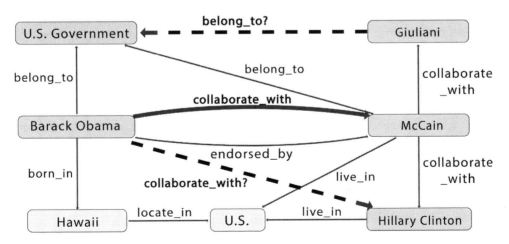

Figure 15.2 Part of a knowledge graph showing information about key figures in US politics at a point in time[8,9]

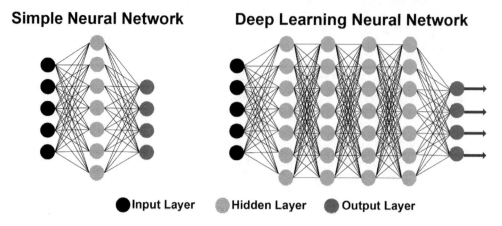

Figure 15.3 A simple neural network vs. a deep learning neural network

functioning of brains (e.g. brain neural pathways comprising connected neurons that communicate with each other and with other cells via a process called "neuronal firing"). The "network" part of the term is derived from the network-like connections. Although mimicking biological brain functioning in problem solving was the original inspiration, neural networks have deviated away from this somewhat, and moved more toward mathematical modeling. Still, artificial neural networks are made up of neurons as the basic computational unit that receives data, processes it, and sends signals to other neurons connected to it within the neural network structure. In this way, they still emulate a simplified form of brain functioning. Nevertheless, neural networks are still able to automatically learn from data and adapt signals and predictions to changing inputs. Business applications of neural networks are extensive and include evaluating loan applications (in banking), customer behavior modeling, facial recognition (e.g. in security and law enforcement), and medical image/scan analysis (e.g. in healthcare). Extending neural networks, deep learning (also referred to as deep structured learning, hierarchical learning, deep neural learning, or deep neural networks) is a machine learning method that uses multi-layer neural networks to solve complex problems. Figure 15.3 contrasts a simple neural network with a simple deep learning neural network.

Natural language processing, speech recognition, and computer vision

Natural language processing and speech recognition

Natural language processing (NLP), speech recognition, and computer vision are important subfields of artificial intelligence. NLP is concerned with how to get machines to understand and process natural human language (e.g. English, Chinese, Spanish, Arabic). Advances in natural language processing are enabling machines to understand instructions from us and to converse with us in our natural language. Natural language processing applications usually focus on enabling machines to understand and process speech and text (i.e. spoken language and written language). Applications of NLP include Google Assistant and Siri. Speech recognition is concerned with finding the best way to get machines to understand speech and translate it into machine readable format. Applications of speech recognition include call routing (e.g. when you call a bank or a phone company and are directed to the sales call centre based on you saying you want a new product), they include voice dialing (e.g. "call Jonathan"), and they include voice search (e.g. "OK, Siri, what is the weather tomorrow?"). Speech recognition and NLP are often used together in applications like Google Assistant and Siri. For example, speech recognition may hear what is being said and convert it to text, but then NLP is needed for machines to understand what the text actually means or what commands the person is actually issuing.

Computer vision

Finally, computer vision (and its subset, machine vision) are concerned with enabling machines to "see" by capturing, analyzing, and understanding captured images and video. Through image and video analysis, computer vision algorithms can detect faces of specific people or groups of people, shapes of objects, writing, movement, poses, motion, emotion, changes in objects, and changes in environments. Combined with additional information that a whole range of different sensors can detect, it is not hard to imagine how computer vision and machine vision can be very powerful. For example, they can provide machines such as robots and drones with vastly expanded possibilities (e.g. to fly through a dense and obstacle-filled rain forest at high speed, to recognize a suspect walking in a crowd and immediately call the police, to give robots human-like movement and body control). Figure 15.4 shows how computer vision can enable self-driving cars to "see" better than humans (e.g. simultaneous 360-degree sight, undistractable, better multitasking, faster processing/computation).

Expert systems

Expert systems were one of the early successful applications of AI. Essentially, they are systems that emulate the decision-making ability of human experts to solve complex

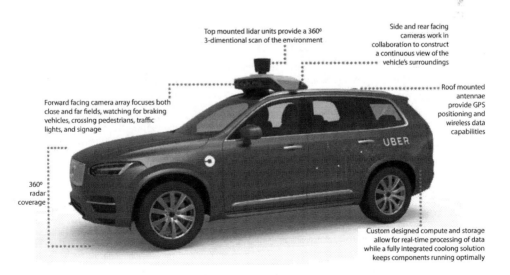

Figure 15.4 Computer vision can enable self-driving cars to "see" better than humans[10,11]

problems. Expert systems have built-in "if this – then – that" rules that enable them to make decisions based on a large number of inputs.[12] Expert systems are usually made up of an inference engine and a knowledge base. The inference engine applies the rules to the knowledge base (the knowledge base represents both the facts and the rules). Expert systems are used in healthcare for medical diagnosis (e.g. early diagnosis of cancer),[13] in banking to assess mortgage applications, and in engineering to diagnose the condition of infrastructure (e.g. dams).

Common AI issues and risks

Although AI has been around for a long time, it has gone through phases where it has been overhyped and subsequently under-delivered. In addition, it has often received negative media attention and warnings regarding its associated risks to society (e.g. potential loss of jobs, potential unintended consequences such as machines taking unethical actions or their intelligence outpacing the ability of humans to control them).[14,15] Because of background issues such as this, proposed AI ideas, projects, or strategies in organizations are sometimes met with disregard, skepticism, trivialization, passive-aggressiveness, or even hostility. Other AI-related issues or risks include data management issues (e.g. ingesting, sorting, linking, and properly using the vast amounts of data from sensors, devices, machines, people, media, and digital platforms – not managing this data properly limits the reliability of AI algorithms). Additional issues include technology and process issues (e.g. technical issues or process breakdowns resulting in AI malfunction such as oversights or incorrect decisions), privacy and security issues (e.g. hackers and fraudsters breaching stored data or data in transit resulting in violations in customer privacy and related legal issues), misguided AI models (e.g. incomplete or biased AI models making blatantly sexist or racist decisions), and interaction issues (e.g. empathy and social skill limitations of AI can ruin customer experience and brand credibility).[16]

Implications for hospitality and leisure managers

Hospitality and leisure organizations have large volumes of data available on existing and prospective customers, current and past employees, current and past suppliers, current and past products/services, and current and past events. In the past, human and financial resources limited the ability to leverage this information as a powerful competitive weapon. Artificial intelligence technologies can drastically reduce both the human and financial constraints. They provide powerful intelligence, automation, availability, scalability, efficiency, and effectiveness opportunities across digital and physical service channels. In the digital era, it is the critical role of hospitality and leisure managers to understand these digital technologies and their potential, and to be able to leverage them to redesign their organizations for game-changing breakthroughs in efficiency, differentiation, adaptability, and agility.

Google and reflect

Algorithm, heuristic programming, inductive reasoning, reinforcement learning, backpropagation, convolutional neural network (CNN), forward chaining, generative adversarial networks (GAN), unsupervised machine learning, Turing test,[17] bots/chatbots, cluster, cognitive science, image recognition, semantic analysis, supervised learning,[18] autonomous artificial intelligence, black box, transfer learning,[19] bias, semi-supervised learning, autonomic computing, classification algorithm, cognitive computing, game AI, genetic algorithm, logic programming, machine intelligence, recurrent neural network (RNN), swarm behavior,[20] AlphaGo, neuromorphic computing, spiking neural networks (SNN).

Example tools and vendors

Apple HomePod, Apple FaceID, Apple Siri, IBM Project Debater, Microsoft Cortana, Google Assistant, Amazon Alexa, Baidu Deep Voice, Facebook DeepFace, Alibaba City Brain, Google DeepMind, Waymo self-driving technology, Google Duplex, Amazon Go, Microsoft AIaaS, MATLAB, IBM Watson Machine Learning, IBM Watson Studio, Google Cloud AI Platform, Microsoft Azure Machine Learning Studio, Salesforce Einstein, Pega Platform, Amazon SageMaker, Microsoft Azure Machine Learning, TensorFlow, Box Skills, DataRobot, Deep Cognition, Anaconda Enterprise, Oracle Data Science Cloud Service, Azure Batch AI, IBM Watson Machine Learning Accelerator, Infosys Nia, H2O Driverless AI, Infor Coleman, Microsoft Cognitive Toolkit (CNTK), NVIDIA AI Platform for Developers, Apple Core ML 3, Apple Create ML, Apple A-series chips, Apple Neural Engine, Intel's OpenVINO Toolkit, CyberInt, HEALTH[at] SCALE Technologies, Algolux, Brodmann17, Dynamic Yield, SoundHound, AntWorks, Zimperium, Sensory TrulySecure, Awake Security, Security Knowledge Graph, Stardog enterprise knowledge graph platform, Franz Semantic Graph Database technology, Pilot. ai, Shazura, Nyris, 20 Billion Neurons, EVK, SpiNNaker, Intel Loihi.

Discussion questions

1 What is the difference between artificial intelligence, machine learning, and deep learning?
2 What is the difference between general AI and narrow AI?
3 Are there more applications of general AI or of narrow AI in hospitality management?
4 What is the difference between an artificial neural network and a deep neural network?
5 What is the difference between an AI-enabled company and a true AI company?
6 What are the top seven AI use cases in the hospitality and leisure industry?
7 What is the difference between a bot, a chatbot, and a robot?
8 What types of things can you do with a neural network that you can't do with a knowledge graph?
9 What is the difference between computer vision and machine vision?
10 What is an example of an expert system use case in the hospitality and leisure industry?
11 Rank the top six biggest risks and issues in relation to using artificial intelligence.
12 What organization capabilities do hospitality organizations need in order to become true AI companies?

Notes

1 Ng, A., & Chui, M. (2018). How Artificial Intelligence and Data Add Value to Businesses. McKinsey & Company. Retrieved January 13, 2020, from www.mckinsey.com/featured-insights/artificial-intelligence/how-artificial-intelligence-and-data-add-value-to-businesses
2 Ng, A., & Chui, M. (2018). How Artificial Intelligence and Data Add Value to Businesses. McKinsey & Company. Retrieved January 13, 2020, from www.mckinsey.com/featured-insights/artificial-intelligence/how-artificial-intelligence-and-data-add-value-to-businesses

3 Hospitality Net. (2020). Sam 2.0: Travel-Intelligent "Chatbot" Delivers New Live Chat, Expertise & Services to Travelers. Hospitality Net. Retrieved January 13, 2020, from www.hospitalitynet.org/news/4083807.html

4 Hilton Hotels and Resorts. (2016). Hilton and IBM Pilot "Connie", the World's First Watson-enabled Hotel Concierge. Youtube.com. Retrieved January 13, 2020, from www.youtube.com/watch?v=ifgf6bZhxiE&feature=youtu.be

5 Broussard, M., & Lowe, L. (2019) Author Discussion on Technology Series: Artificial Unintelligence. C-SPAN. Retrieved September 20, 2020, from C-SPAN.org website: https://www.c-span.org/video/?457638-2/artificial-unintelligence

6 Stichbury, J. (2017). WTF is a Knowledge Graph? Hackernoon.com. Retrieved January 9, 2020, from https://hackernoon.com/wtf-is-a-knowledge-graph-a16603a1a25f

7 Semantic Web Company. (2020). What is a Knowledge Graph – Transforming Data into Knowledge. PoolParty Semantic Suite. Retrieved January 9, 2020, from www.poolparty.biz/what-is-a-knowledge-graph

8 Anadiotis, G. (2019, March 18). Salesforce Research: Knowledge Graphs and Machine Learning to Power Einstein. Retrieved June 21, 2020, from ZDNet website: www.zdnet.com/article/salesforce-research-knowledge-graphs-and-machine-learning-to-power-einstein/

9 Lin, Y., Liu, Z., Luan, H., Sun, M., Rao, S., & Liu, S. (2015). Modeling Relation Paths for Representation Learning of Knowledge Bases 1506:00379. arXiv preprint arXiv. https://arxiv.org/abs/1506.00379

10 Tara, R. (2018). Technology vs. Humans. Engineers Seek Answers in Uber's Fatal Self Driving Car Accident. Retrieved June 21, 2020, from Engineering.com website: www.engineering.com/Hardware/ArticleID/16756/Technology-vs-Humans-Engineers-Seek-Answers-in-Ubers-Fatal-Self-Driving-Car-Accident.aspx

11 Burke, K. (2019). How does a Self-Driving Car See? Nvidia. Retrieved June 22, 2020, from https://blogs.nvidia.com/blog/2019/04/15/how-does-a-self-driving-car-see

12 Leonard-Barton, D., & Sviokla, J. (1988). Putting Expert Systems to Work. Harvard Business Review. Retrieved January 12, 2020, from https://hbr.org/1988/03/putting-expert-systems-to-work

13 Başçiftçi, F., & Avuçlu, E. (2018). An Expert System Design to Diagnose Cancer by Using a New Method Reduced Rule Base. *Computer Methods and Programs in Biomedicine*, 157, 113–120.

14 Clifford, C. (2018). Elon Musk: "Mark My Words – A.I. is Far More Dangerous than Nukes." CNBC. Retrieved January 8, 2020, from www.cnbc.com/2018/03/13/elon-musk-at-sxsw-a-i-is-more-dangerous-than-nuclear-weapons.html

15 Marr, B. (2018). Is Artificial Intelligence Dangerous? 6 AI Risks Everyone Should Know About. Forbes.com. Retrieved January 8, 2020, from www.forbes.com/sites/bernardmarr/2018/11/19/is-artificial-intelligence-dangerous-6-ai-risks-everyone-should-know-about/#3c5d4a942404

16 Cheatham, B., Javanmardian, K., & Samandari, H. (2020). Confronting the Risks of Artificial Intelligence. McKinsey & Company. Retrieved January 13, 2020, from www.mckinsey.com/business-functions/mckinsey-analytics/our-insights/confronting-the-risks-of-artificial-intelligence

17 Rosso, C. (2018). Defining Artificial Intelligence: A Glossary of Key AI Terms. Psychology Today. Retrieved January 13, 2020, from www.psychologytoday.com/au/blog/the-future-brain/201810/defining-artificial-intelligence-glossary-key-ai-terms

18 Kniahynyckyj, R. Artificial Intelligence: Terms Marketers Need to Know. Business.twitter.com. Retrieved January 13, 2020, from https://business.twitter.com/en/blog/artificial-intelligence-terms-marketers-need-to-know.html

19 Greene, T. (2017). A Glossary of Basic Artificial Intelligence Terms and Concepts. The Next Web. Retrieved January 13, 2020, from https://thenextweb.com/artificial-intelligence/2017/09/10/glossary-basic-artificial-intelligence-terms-concepts/

20 Davis, S. (2017). Artificial Intelligence Terms You Need to Know. DZone AI. dzone.com. Retrieved January 13, 2020, from https://dzone.com/articles/ai-glossary

16 Video analytics, computer vision, and virtual reality technologies

Introduction

The digital technologies discussed in this chapter enable organizations to leverage the growing troves of video data captured from a range of devices and stakeholders (e.g. CCTV, smartphones, online uploads), so as to offer new virtual products and services (e.g. virtual-world products and experiences or enhanced real-world products and experiences), to make new operational efficiency breakthroughs (e.g. drastically improving staff training and enhancing technology-based support for staff through the use of augmented and mixed reality), to craft novel marketing campaigns (e.g. novel virtual, augmented, or mixed reality marketing campaigns), to approach after-sales support differently (e.g. virtual, augmented, or mixed reality guided repairs performed by customers), and much more. Given the importance of customer experience, operational efficiency, and marketing innovations to the hospitality and leisure industry, these digital technologies are particularly important to the hospitality and leisure industry. As a result, a number of organizations are taking the lead in applying or experimenting with their application for a range of different purposes. These range from virtual tours of nearby tourist attractions, to enhanced facilities that leverage augmented reality, and to booking processes that allow customers to virtually experience what they are buying before booking it.[1] To realize the business value of these digital technologies requires hospitality and leisure managers to have a working understanding of how the technologies work, to understand the current and potential use cases for these technologies, and to understand how they can leverage these technologies to enhance efficiency, differentiation, and agility. In this chapter, we provide an introductory overview of the technologies, how they work, their business value, example use cases, common terminologies, and example vendors and platforms. The aim of the chapter is to provide a base-level overview of the technologies (i.e. of video analytics and computer vision, virtual reality, augmented reality, and mixed reality technologies) in order to enable hospitality and leisure managers to undertake their own self-directed, more in-depth, and ongoing learning. This is to keeping up with rapid developments in these technologies and their applications.

Video content analytics and computer vision

What is video analytics or video content analytics (VCA)?

Video analytics (also referred to as video content analysis, intelligent video analytics, video content analytics, or VCA) involves the use of software algorithms to analyze or check video data (e.g. recorded video footage or live streaming video) for particular objects, events, patterns, people, or issues. Once one or more particular issues, events, patterns, objects, or people are identified, the software can report it or generate automatic alerts, prescribe action, or take follow–on actions in response to what has been identified. For example, if the software recognizes a known criminal walking down the street, it can immediately alert police or request a police squad and direct it to the specific spot the criminal is about to walk to. The software may identify that vandalism occurred or that it routinely occurs at particular times of the day. Based on analysis of historical video footage, VCA software may even identify that theft is about to occur in a particular location and alert security or request police attendance (e.g. raising an urgent call request via the company's workflow management systems). VCA software may notice a confused or lost guest and request someone from guest services to check in on them. Alternatively, it might notice people entering a restricted area or that a guest room has not been made up in time for a guest's arrival. In either case, it can alert or request the right people to take action and even prescribe the optimal actions to take. Although lacking the benefit of different colors, Figure 16.1 shows VCA/computer vision software identifying different people, different cars, different crosswalks, road conditions, traffic conditions, and more.

How video content analytics works

Video analytics is a subset of computer vision, which in turn is a subset of artificial intelligence. Thus VCA works by leveraging image processing/image enhancement technologies and techniques like image sensors, image pixilation, image compression, image stabilization (reducing blurring associated with an imaging device), unsharp masking

Figure 16.1 An example of VCA/computer vision software developed by Voxel51[2]

(sharpening an image or making it more clear), super resolution (improving the resolution of an image), and other AI learning and prediction algorithms. A video is essentially just a series of image frames,[3] so analyzing video requires extracting and interpreting what is in image frames. An algorithm (e.g. a recurrent neural network algorithm) can be trained to do this. This involves providing it with lots of data that it can compare against what it is seeing in video image frames. In this case, the data would consist of a sequence of image frame descriptions. For example, we can provide an algorithm with a sequence of image frames for taking cleaning equipment to a room door, and label this sequence "room cleaning preparation." We can then provide it with a sequence of image frames for opening the room door for cleaning, and label it "room cleaning start." We can also provide it with a series of images for packing up cleaning equipment, and label it "room cleaning completion." We can then collectively label the three groups of images as "room cleaning." The algorithm is able to learn from these images and labels so that when new video data is fed into it, the algorithm can go through the video's image frames and identify any image, sequence of image frames, or group of sequences of image frames that it already knows. For example, it might notice a sequence of image frames corresponding to the existing sequence of image frames for "room cleaning" and, triangulating this with other data available to it, the algorithm may work out that the room has been cleaned or that cleaning is about to start and will be completed in time for a guest's arrival. The algorithm can learn from its calculations, conclusions, decisions, and mistakes and become more accurate over time. Video analytics can be used to detect faces of particular people or groups of people in videos, shapes of objects, writing, movement, poses, motion, emotion, particular events, changes in objects and environments, and much more. Figure 16.2 shows VCA/computer vision software recognizing people, their actions, and occurring events. The exponentially growing number of devices capturing or able to capture video, the exponentially growing availability of images and video footage available online, and the growing sophistication of VCA algorithms, make video footage a potently powerful source of value right now. Organizations are capturing

Figure 16.2 An example of VCA/computer vision software recognizing both people and actions/events[4]

some video data but they can capture much more, they can access vast troves of video data on the internet to train their VCA algorithms (e.g. YouTube video and associated chat history, Facebook video and associated chat history, LinkedIn video and associated chat history), and they can access sophisticated VCA platforms to make the most of all the internal and publicly available video data.

Relationship between VCA and computer vision

We noted earlier that VCA is a type of computer vision. More broadly, computer vision (also known as machine vision [MV]), is essentially the real-time recording of video/audio/other data and the leveraging of video content analytics and sophisticated pattern recognition algorithms to sense or understand the makeup of an environment (e.g. what objects are there, where are they, how are they moving).[5,6]

Business value of VCA and computer vision

The business value of VCA includes product innovation opportunities (offering new VCA-related products and services, like an industry-specific VCA platform), product/service enhancement opportunities (e.g. using VCA to anticipate and respond to guest issues before they occur, thus optimizing customer experience), business model innovation opportunities (e.g. video-based service delivery models), operational efficiency opportunities (e.g. using VCA to anticipate, prevent, or minimize disruptive events such as vandalism or theft that may slow down operational processes or result in higher costs), and risk mitigation opportunities (e.g. learning from VCA when or how particular security and other threats occur and taking action to prevent or minimize them). This business value can be expanded and significantly enhanced with real-time VCA that is combined with smart things[7] (e.g. devices, robots, bionics) to provide real-time, human-like sensing and responding.

Hospitality industry use cases of VCA and computer vision

Hospitality industry VCA use cases to date have included enhanced guest security through incident detection (e.g. identifying unattended objects in main lobbies or in car parks, identifying disruptive individuals, identifying camera tampering or minimizing footage tampering, identifying suspicious activity), through intrusion management (e.g. detecting unauthorized people in secure zones), through people/crowd counting (e.g. counting foot traffic and attendance to analyze patronage and conversion), through automatic number plate recognition (e.g. detecting unauthorized tailgating in secure car entrances), and through facial recognition (e.g. monitoring faces as they enter premises and high-risk areas, searching through faces for an investigation, searching for the location of particular individuals across a large facility). Hospitality and leisure industry VCA use cases have also included demand management (e.g. heat maps to understand guest traffic density and traffic choke points by time of day, understand guest traffic movement and areas of interest), and use cases have included demographic analytics (identifying the demographic profile of people entering, where they stay, how long they stay, where they go, what their mood is).[8,9,10,11] Some hospitality management organizations are integrating VCA with guest service and guest loyalty data to provide even better value for their most valuable guests. An example of VCA in action in the hospitality industry is the Hawaii Tourism Authority's "Discover Your Aloha" campaign, which analyzed the expressions of travelers' faces in video captured via webcams to determine what custom offers to push to them; it used facial recognition in videos and predictive analytics to identify the best offer for a traveler and to push it to them along with a booking link.[12] Similarly, Cherokee Nation Entertainment (CNE) used VCA across its ten casinos in Oklahoma to relieve its security team of the need to review video footage manually. As a result, they could focus on more proactive and preventative tasks. VCA analyzed camera footage from entrances and exits, from gaming machines, and from other areas, enabling CNE to have real-time visibility and alerts of traffic patterns, people counts, and any risky events or situations unfolding.[13] Although early use cases have focused on security and access control, VCA offers a lot of possibilities for understanding customers and for optimizing customer experiences, for enhanced operational insights, and for more effective operations management.

Virtual reality, augmented reality, and mixed reality

Virtual reality (VR), augmented reality (AR), and mixed reality (MR) represent continuing blurring of the boundary between the real world and the virtual world that enable enhanced or new experiences and enhanced or new business opportunities.[14]

Virtual reality (VR)

Virtual reality (VR) has been around since the 1930s as a technology for enabling users to experience a fully computer-generated or digital environment.[15] Once in the digital environment, users can see, hear, and interact with the digital environment. Although other senses can be incorporated to make the digital world experience more immersive, VR is not yet at the fully immersive, nerve-connected experiences depicted in movies like *The Matrix*. Still, VR can provide highly immersive experiences through great graphics, 360-degree visuals, binaural sound (i.e 3D stereo sound sensation that emulates hearing the full rich sound as though one were actually there), and tapping into other human senses.[16,17] Virtual worlds or environments can be unique digital creations that don't exist in the real world, they can recreations or emulations of the real world, or they can be somewhere in between. For example, virtual reality games can be played in fantasy digital worlds completely detached from reality, or they can be played in emulations of real-world conditions and rules, such as a World War II setting. In contrast to games, tourism operators may replicate the experience of navigating protected environments to enable tourists to "see" them without putting those environments and species at risk. Virtual reality experiences typically require specialized hardware such as VR headsets.[18,19,20] Depending on how immersive VR experience needs to be, other sensory optimization hardware like noise-cancelling headphones, cameras to track room space and boundaries, and motion capture technology may also be required.[21] VR is characterized by three elements: visualization, immersion and interactivity. Information can be retrieved in multi-sensory modalities by the users in a VR environment.[22,23]

Augmented reality (AR)

To augment means to make something greater by adding to it. Thus augmented reality (AR) refers to adding or superimposing digital data and/or images and animations on real-world elements to enhance them.[24] That is, it involves enhancing the real world with digital details that can, for example, improve understandability of the real world or engagement with the real world.[25,26,27] Augmented reality devices and applications can place digital objects in the real world. For example, Pokémon Go game creators enabled overlaying of the game's buildings and characters on real-world areas like streets and buildings in a town so players could play the game by navigating real-world streets and buildings. Augmented reality devices and applications can also overlay animations, information, or a combination of objects, animations and information.[28] AR-capable hardware includes mobile phones (e.g. AR apps are available in most apps stores), smart tablet devices (e.g. iPad), wearable AR devices (e.g. AR glasses like Epson MOVERIO or AR headsets like Oculus Go), and custom enterprise AR equipment. Figure 16.3 shows surgeons using AR to "see through" tissue to ease reconnnection blood vessels. AR offers hospitality and leisure organizations the opportunity to significantly expand customer engagement and customer experience through AR-enriched experiences, products, and services.[29]

Mixed reality (MR)

Drawing on next-generation sensing and imaging technologies, mixed reality "mixes" the real and virtual worlds and allows users to see, immerse themselves in, and interact with both worlds.[30,31] Users can manipulate the virtual world using their own hands, or

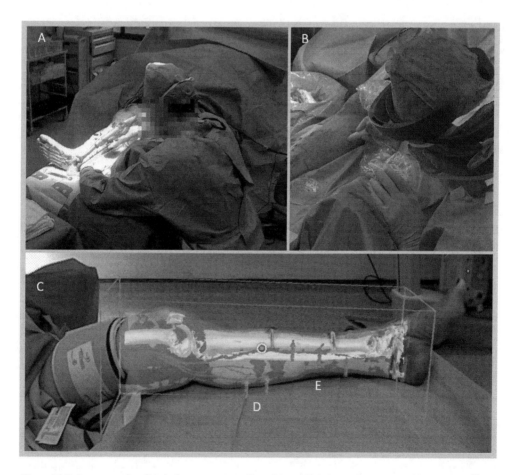

Figure 16.3 Augmented reality helps surgeons to "see through" tissue and reconnect blood vessels[32]

they can make changes to the real world guided by virtual objects or by making changes to virtual objects.[33] For example, surgeons at Imperial College London use Microsoft's HoloLens mixed reality devices to enable them to see "inside" a patient's body during an operation:[34] bones, blood vessels, and other body parts revealed in scans can be reconceptualized, animated, and superimposed on the patient's body so that surgeons can move them around as in a real surgery and see exactly where to cut or implant a device without obstructing the functioning of other body parts (e.g. see Figure 16.4). Perhaps less complex, a patient's blood vessels can be superimposed on their arm so that nursing staff can see exactly where the best spot to inject a needle is and trial the injection virtually in that spot before actually doing it.

Business value of VR, AR, and MR

Although VR, AR, and MR technologies are of value to all areas of business, they hold stand-out value in areas like product innovation, operational efficiency and effectiveness, marketing, HR, and after-sales support. In the product innovation area, they offer the opportunity to provide customers new or improved products (e.g. to create and offer virtual versions of any real-world environment or experience, to augment existing products and services with digital data and virtual objects, to create new products and services leveraging mixed reality). In the operational efficiency area, these technologies offer businesses the opportunity to provide their staff with the ability to see through opaque things and interact with them (e.g. underground infrastructure, cabling in walls, vessels in the brain, arteries in the body). This can result in faster repair times, minimization of costly errors, avoidance of equipment damaging actions, and more. And what is seen through this x-ray-like vision and interacted with is an increasingly more exact representation of the real thing thanks to connected IoT sensors and AI algorithms. For example, the superimposed blood vessel can expand or contract or burst in sync with and to the same

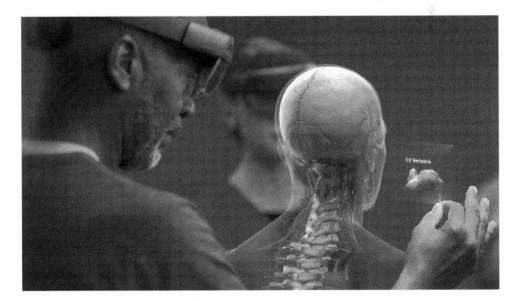

Figure 16.4 A healthcare worker looking at a C3 vertebra using a HoloLens 2 headset

degree as the real thing, enabling whoever is interacting with it to see, for example, the implications of shifting it one way or applying a little bit more pressure to it. AR and MR can also enable remote or automatic interaction with things, thanks to IoT and AI. For example, virtual versions of things can be linked to real versions so that a change in the virtual-world version automatically results in a change in the real-world version. Taken together, these abilities provide organizations with opportunities to redesign their workflows for greater efficiency and effectiveness (e.g. through greater possibilities for automation, and greater possibilities for remote supervision and management).

From an HR perspective, VR, AR, and MR can enable provision of real-time, on-site, interactive step-by-step training, guidance, or coaching that is superior to any manual or video. It could be used for better assessing aptitude prior to giving someone the responsibility for a task; that is, before undertaking a high-risk task in the real world, an employee may be required to first competently perform that task in the virtual world. Using analytics, employee's performance of such tasks in the virtual world could be contrasted to their performance in the real world to improve VR-based training. From a marketing perspective, VR, AR, and MR can be powerful marketing tools (e.g. enabling virtual experiences of products and services to drive sales, enabling customers to see how a product fits into their home setting, enabling gamification of marketing campaigns drawing on viral games like Pokémon Go). From an after-sales perspective, VR, AR, and MR can be used to enable customers to effectively make their own repairs, assemble items quicker, or coach customers through the repair process (e.g. imagine VR- or AR-guided assembly of IKEA furniture). Together, these different value propositions can transform how employees learn, the quality of the decisions they make, how they interact with customers, how they buy and who they buy from, how customers interact with a business' products, and much more.

Hospitality and leisure industry use cases of VR, AR, and MR

Early hospitality industry VR, AR, and MR use cases have included virtual travel tours, virtual booking processes, interactive hotel rooms, Pokémon Go–style gamified entertainment, and augmented hospitality environments.[35,36] An example of a virtual travel tour in action is the Atlantis Dubai, which provides a very inviting virtual tour of its premises. An example of virtual booking processes in action is Amadeus, which set up a virtual booking process that enables customers to enter a virtual world where they can look for flights, walk on the plane to inspect it and find the perfect seat, compare hotel prices, and look inside a hotel room before finally making a booking. On completion, Amadeus customers exit the virtual world but have made real-world bookings that they don't need to be anxious about – since they have experienced most aspects of the bookings.[37] An example of interactive hotel rooms is The Hub Hotel from Premier Inn in the United Kingdom, which used a combination of maps on hotel room walls and AR to enable guests to point their phones at different locations on the map to see additional information and places of interest in those locations, thus enhancing guest experience.[38,39] An example of gamification is hospitality organizations incorporating their sites or services in established AR games or creating their own VR or AR gaming apps for promotional purposes. An example of augmented hospitality environments is the Best Western Kelowna, which set up an Augmented Reality Quest for kids staying at the hotel to play alone or with other kids or with their parents.[40] To date, most use cases in the hospitality and leisure industry have focused on VR and AR applications for consumer engagement, but there are great possibilities for MR, especially in tourism. Also, VR, AR, and MR applications for workforce productivity, operational efficiency, and engagement of a broader set of stakeholders represent a great opportunity for hospitality and leisure organizations.

Google and reflect

CCTV, OpenCV, rule-based analytics, area of interest (AOI), region-of-interest, region-of-uninterest, smart surveillance engine, video management system, view group, dynamic masking, motion detection, shape recognition, object detection, tamper detection, video tracking, video error level analysis (VELA), object co-segmentation.

Immersive VR, virtual space, AR space, head-mounted display (HMD), haptics, VR head tracking, VR eye tracking, VR position tracking, VR field of view, VR blind spot, VR headset latency, VR headset interpupillary distance (or IPD), VR judder, VR headset refresh rate, 360 video, VR video stitching, VR sickness, low persistence, VR 1 to 1 movement, asynchronous time warp, spatial desync, VR ride.

Social VR platform, cinematic VR, fish tank VR, virtual theater, directional sound, motion platform/omnidirectional treadmill, discrete graphics processor, computer-aided design (CAD), extended reality (XR), GL transmission format (gITF), hologram, simultaneous localization and mapping (SLAM), six degrees of freedom (6DoF) tracking, visual-inertial odometry (VIO), waveguide displays, augmented face mesh, simulation-based learning, blended space, lifelike experience, multimodal interaction, simulated reality, supranet, telexistence, multiexperience development platform (MXDP), Google ARCore, PTC Vuforia, Augmentir, Amazon Sumerian, HP Reveal, SmartReality.

Example tools and vendors

Google Cloud Vision, Cloud Vision Intelligence, Agent Vi savVi, Agent Vi innoVi, NVIDIA DeepStream SDK, NVIDIA Jetson, NVIDIA Tesla, NVIDIA GPU Cloud (NGC),[41] Oculus Rift, HTC Vive, and PlayStation VR, Google Cardboard, Python Imaging Library (PIL), Open Source Computer Vision (OpenCV), Tensorflow, HTC Vive, iStaging LiveTour, Cupix, Viar360, BRIOVR, Scanta, Fishermen Labs, Groove Jones, Program-Ace, Xtrematic, Niantic Real World Platform, Windows Mixed Reality platform, Zappar ZapWorks platform, Lucyd Lab AR, Qualcomm Snapdragon platforms, Apple ARKit 3, Apple Reality Composer, Apple RealityKit, Magic Leap 1, PlayStation VR, FOVE Eye Tracking Virtual Reality Headset, Samsung Gear VR, Epson Drone Soar augmented reality app, Epson Moverio AR glasses, DAQRI Worksense, Bosch Common Augmented Reality Platform (CAP).

Discussion questions

1 What are the similarities and differences between VCA and other forms of data analytics?
2 What is a recurrent neural network? How is it different from other neural networks?
3 Where can organizations obtain the vast quantities of data required to train recurrent neural network algorithms to understand what they are seeing in video data?
4 Can VCA be applied to virtual reality, augmented reality, and mixed reality?
5 How can a hotel use VCA to improve its operational efficiency?
6 What is an example of an innovative new product leveraging VCA that a tourism operator could offer?

7 What are the top three enterprise-grade VCA platforms, and which is the best?
8 What are the top three SME-grade VCA platforms?
9 How can VCA be used to improve the quality of food and of customer experience in food and beverage settings?
10 Would adding real-world objects to a virtual reality setting fit the definition of augmented reality?
11 Would adding real-world objects to a virtual reality setting fit the definition of mixed reality?
12 How could tourism operators use augmented reality to improve real-life tours?
13 How could hotels use mixed reality to attract more guests?
14 What are the top five challenges to adopting and using VR, AR, and MR?
15 What are the top five risks associated with using VR, AR, and MR in hospitality and leisure?
16 What are the top three risks to not adopting or at least experimenting with VR, AR, and MR?
17 Within the example tools and vendors provided, identify three leading vendors and products in each of these product categories: virtual reality, immersive VR, augmented reality, mixed reality.
18 Within the example tools and vendors provided, identify three leading vendors and products in each of these product categories: consumer, small business, enterprise.
19 Within the example tools and vendors provided, identify three leading vendors and products in each of these product categories: gaming, marketing, healthcare, hospitality/tourism.
20 Group the example tools and vendors provided into the following categories: hardware products, software products, VR/AR/MR product development or service delivery platforms.

Notes

1 Huang, Y. C., Backman, K. F., Backman, S. J., & Chang, L. L. (2016). Exploring the Implications of Virtual Reality Technology in Tourism Marketing: An Integrated Research Framework. *International Journal of Tourism Research*, 18(2), 116–128.
2 NIST. (2019). Enhancing Public Safety Video Analytics with Computer Vision and Artificial Intelligence. Retrieved June 21, 2020, from NIST website: www.nist.gov/news-events/news/2019/11/enhancing-public-safety-video-analytics-computer-vision-and-artificial
3 Robinson, S. (2018). How Computer Vision Works. YouTube. Retrieved January 27, 2020, from www.youtube.com/watch?v=OcycT1Jwsns
4 NIST. (2019). Enhancing Public Safety Video Analytics with Computer Vision and Artificial Intelligence. Retrieved June 21, 2020, from NIST website: www.nist.gov/news-events/news/2019/11/enhancing-public-safety-video-analytics-computer-vision-and-artificial
5 PCMag. (2020). Definition of Computer Vision. PCMag. Retrieved June 17, 2020, from www.pcmag.com/encyclopedia/term/computer-vision
6 Schmelzer, R. (2020). Understanding the Recognition Pattern of AI. Forbes. www.forbes.com/sites/cognitiveworld/2020/05/09/understanding-the-recognition-pattern-of-ai/#3d30130621c7
7 Ganesan, V., Ji, Y., & Patel, M. (2020). Video Meets the Internet of Things. McKinsey & Company. www.mckinsey.com/industries/technology-media-and-telecommunications/our-insights/video-meets-the-internet-of-things
8 Hughes Systique Corp. (2019). The Role of Video Analytics in Tourism, Travel & Hospitality Industry. Retrieved January 27, 2020, from https://hsc.com/Blog/The-Role-of-Video-Analytics-in-Tourism-Travel-Hospitality-Industry
9 Agent Vi. (2020). Entertainment and Hospitality Solutions. Agentvi.com. Retrieved January 27, 2020, from www.agentvi.com/portfolio-items/entertainment-hospitality/?portfolioCats=19

10 Security Magazine. (2017). Securitymagazine.com. Retrieved January 27, 2020, from www. securitymagazine.com/articles/89083-using-video-analytics-to-create-efficiencies

11 UBAC Group. Face Recognition & Video Analytics for Campus & Retail Hospitality – UBAC Pte Ltd. Ubacgroup.com. Retrieved January 27, 2020, from https://ubacgroup.com/ face-recognition-data-analytics/intelligent-surveillance-face-detection/

12 Bhattacharjee, D., Seeley, J., & Seitzman, N. (2017). Advanced Analytics in Hospitality. McKinsey & Company. Retrieved January 27, 2020, from www.mckinsey.com/business-functions/ mckinsey-digital/our-insights/advanced-analytics-in-hospitality

13 Agentvi.com. Retrieved January 27, 2020, from https://agentvi.com/wp-content/uploads/2018/10/ Agent_Vi_Solutions_Entertainment_Hospitality-1.pdf

14 Intel. (2019). Virtual Reality Vs. Augmented Reality Vs. Mixed Reality. Retrieved January 30, 2020, from Intel website: www.intel.com.au/content/www/au/en/tech-tips-and-tricks/virtual-reality-vs-augmented-reality.html

15 Intel. (2019). Virtual Reality Vs. Augmented Reality Vs. Mixed Reality. Retrieved January 30, 2020, from Intel website: www.intel.com.au/content/www/au/en/tech-tips-and-tricks/virtual-reality-vs-augmented-reality.html

16 Intel. (2019). Virtual Reality Vs. Augmented Reality Vs. Mixed Reality. Retrieved January 30, 2020, from Intel website: www.intel.com.au/content/www/au/en/tech-tips-and-tricks/virtual-reality-vs-augmented-reality.html

17 Hackernoon.com. (2019). Augmented Reality vs. Mixed Reality vs. Virtual Reality. Retrieved January 30, 2020, from Hackernoon.com website: https://hackernoon.com/augmented-reality-vs-mixed-reality-vs-virtual-reality-ik8730gv

18 Tussyadiah, I. P., Wang, D., Jung, T. H., & Dieck, M.C.T. (2018). Virtual Reality, Presence, and Attitude Change: Empirical Evidence from Tourism. *Tourism Management*, 66, 140–154.

19 Mofokeng, N.E.M., & Matima, T. K. (2018). Future Tourism Trends: Virtual Reality based Tourism Utilizing Distributed Ledger Technologies. *African Journal of Hospitality, Tourism and Leisure*, 7(3), 1–14.

20 Huang, Y. C., Backman, K. F., Backman, S. J., & Chang, L. L. (2016). Exploring the Implications of Virtual Reality Technology in Tourism Marketing: An Integrated Research Framework. *International Journal of Tourism Research*, 18(2), 116–128.

21 Ambalina, L. (2019). Augmented Reality vs. Mixed Reality vs. Virtual Reality. Retrieved January 28, 2020, from Hackernoon.com website: https://hackernoon.com/augmented-reality-vs-mixed-reality-vs-virtual-reality-ik8730gv

22 Tussyadiah, I. P., Wang, D., Jung, T. H., & Dieck, M.C.T. (2018). Virtual Reality, Presence, and Attitude Change: Empirical Evidence from Tourism. *Tourism Management*, 66, 140–154.

23 Yung, R., & Khoo-Lattimore, C. (2019). New Realities: a systematic literature review on Virtual Reality and Augmented Reality in Tourism Research. *Current Issues in Tourism*, 22(17), 2056–2081.

24 Intel. (2019). Virtual Reality Vs. Augmented Reality Vs. Mixed Reality. Retrieved January 30, 2020, from Intel website: www.intel.com.au/content/www/au/en/tech-tips-and-tricks/virtual-reality-vs-augmented-reality.html

25 Lau, C.K.H., Chui, C.F.R., & Au, N. (2019). Examination of the Adoption of Augmented Reality: A VAM Approach. *Asia Pacific Journal of Tourism Research*, 24(10), 1005–1020.

26 Yung, R., & Khoo-Lattimore, C. (2019). New Realities: A Systematic Literature Review on Virtual Reality and Augmented Reality in Tourism Research. *Current Issues in Tourism*, 22(17), 2056–2081.

27 Hackernoon.com. (2019). Augmented Reality vs. Mixed Reality vs. Virtual Reality. Retrieved January 30, 2020, from Hackernoon.com website: https://hackernoon.com/augmented-reality-vs-mixed-reality-vs-virtual-reality-ik8730gv

28 Hackernoon.com. (2019). Augmented Reality vs. Mixed Reality vs. Virtual Reality. Retrieved January 30, 2020, from Hackernoon.com website: https://hackernoon.com/augmented-reality-vs-mixed-reality-vs-virtual-reality-ik8730gv

29 Lau, C.K.H., Chui, C.F.R., & Au, N. (2019). Examination of the Adoption of Augmented Reality: A VAM Approach. *Asia Pacific Journal of Tourism Research*, 24(10), 1005–1020.

30 Intel. (2019). Virtual Reality Vs. Augmented Reality Vs. Mixed Reality. Retrieved January 30, 2020, from Intel website: www.intel.com.au/content/www/au/en/tech-tips-and-tricks/virtual-reality-vs-augmented-reality.html

31 Marr, B. (2019). The Important Difference Between Augmented Reality and Mixed Reality. Retrieved January 30, 2020, from Bernard Marr website: https://bernardmarr.com/default.asp? contentID=1912

32 Imperial College London. (2018). Augmented Reality Helps Surgeons to "See Through" Tissue and Reconnect Blood Vessels. Retrieved June 21, 2020, from Medicalxpress.com website: https://medicalxpress.com/news/2018-01-augmented-reality-surgeons-tissue-reconnect.html

33 Hackernoon.com. (2019). Augmented Reality vs. Mixed Reality vs. Virtual Reality. Retrieved January 30, 2020, from Hackernoon.com website: https://hackernoon.com/augmented-reality-vs-mixed-reality-vs-virtual-reality-ik8730gv

34 Microsoft News Centre UK. (2018, February 8). Surgeons are Using HoloLens to "See Inside" Patients Before They Operate on Them. Retrieved from https://news.microsoft.com/en-gb/2018/02/08/surgeons-use-microsoft-hololens-to-see-inside-patients-before-they-operate-on-them/

35 Revfine.com. (2019). How Virtual Reality (VR) Can Enrich the Hospitality Industry. Retrieved January 30, 2020, from Revfine.com website: www.revfine.com/virtual-reality-hospitality-industry/

36 Revfine.com. (2019, August 8). How Augmented Reality is Transforming the Hospitality Industry. Retrieved January 30, 2020, from Revfine.com website: www.revfine.com/augmented-reality-hospitality-industry/

37 Revfine.com. (2019). How Virtual Reality (VR) Can Enrich the Hospitality Industry. Retrieved January 30, 2020, from Revfine.com website: www.revfine.com/virtual-reality-hospitality-industry/

38 Revfine.com. (2019). How Virtual Reality (VR) Can Enrich the Hospitality Industry. Retrieved January 30, 2020, from Revfine.com website: www.revfine.com/virtual-reality-hospitality-industry/

39 Revfine.com. (2019, August 8). How Augmented Reality is Transforming the Hospitality Industry. Retrieved January 30, 2020, from Revfine.com website: www.revfine.com/augmented-reality-hospitality-industry/

40 Revfine.com. (2019). How Virtual Reality (VR) Can Enrich the Hospitality Industry. Retrieved January 30, 2020, from Revfine.com website: www.revfine.com/virtual-reality-hospitality-industry/

41 MSV, J. (2019). Microsoft and NVIDIA Deliver Intelligent Video Analytics at the Edge. Forbes.com. Retrieved January 27, 2020, from www.forbes.com/sites/janakirammsv/2019/03/23/microsoft-and-nvidia-deliver-intelligent-video-analytics-at-the-edge/#16eba1927623

17 Robotics, drones, and 3D/4D printing technologies

Introduction

The overarching theme of the digital technologies discussed in this chapter is the ability to outsource surveillance (e.g. drone-based surveillance), physical actions or activities (e.g. robot-based action), and manufacturing (e.g. 3D printed objects) to smart machines (e.g. drones, robots, 3D printers). These capabilities of drones, robots, and 3D printers represent significant product innovation, cost saving, productivity improvement, operational effectiveness, risk mitigation, customer experience enhancement, staff engagement optimization, and organization agility opportunities. While initially seen by many as fads or playthings, commercial applications of these technologies are growing rapidly, and they are expected to impact almost every sector at a pace and scale not so different from that of personal computers and mobile phones. In the hospitality industry, robots like Hilton's robot concierge Connie are being used to complement or cover staff absences, taking actions like greeting guests, interacting with them, and answering their questions. At organizations like Alibaba's FlyZoo Future Hotel in China and the Huis Ten Bosch theme park in Japan, robot dinosaurs and robot waiters check in and serve guests. In hotels such as Timbre in Singapore and Yotel in Amsterdam, drone waiters are being trialed for providing table service, particularly at peak demand times. Other organizations are using drones for guided tours or virtual tours of local destinations that guests just can't get to. In Europe, restaurants like La Enoteca at Hotel Arts Barcelona use food printers to sculpt awe-inspiring dishes. Other organizations, like UK-based company Food Ink, 3D print their entire service including tables, chairs, menus, plates, cups, glasses, cutlery, and food. While some of these use cases for these digital technologies are exploratory, the commercial opportunities and speed of advancement is clear. It is the responsibility of hospitality and leisure managers to keep up with the advancements and use cases, and to find safe ways to experiment with and leverage the operational and strategic opportunities available from these technologies.

Robots and robotics

Robotics is the field of study concerned with how to best design, build, operate, and use robots. Robots are machines that can be programmed to physically interact with the world around them and can automatically carry out a series of actions/motions or a range of actions with varying levels of autonomy and intelligence.[1] Put differently, robots are artificially intelligent agents existing in a physical form that can take actions to affect the physical world.[2] Robots can be designed to carry out an astounding variety of tasks, particularly when they leverage sophisticated artificial intelligence algorithms. For example, robots can manufacture product parts, assemble cars, fill prescriptions, play with kids, provide customer service, fight wars, spy on others, and much more.

Building blocks of robots

Robots can differ greatly in their design, capabilities, and uses. For example, a robot for customer service is quite different from a robot for fighting wars or a robot for assembling cars. Despite this, they usually share common building blocks. At a very high level, they all have mechanical, electrical, and computer program elements. The mechanical element is the physical form, frame, or construct of the robot. The design of the mechanical element is usually based on the specific tasks or actions the robot will be performing; this could be a human-like form for a customer service robot or it could be a mechanical arm for welding car parts together. The electrical element is all the electrical and elec tronic components that operate in concert to power the robot, collect information via sensors from the robot's environment, enable controlled movement of the robot, and enable it to perform its task. The electrical element incorporates sub-elements like power supplies (batteries, solar, AC), motors/actuators (to convert electrical energy into movement), driving mechanisms (e.g. gears, chains, pulleys, belts, and gearboxes to enable movement in different directions and at different speeds), electronic controls (to control mechanical systems like brakes and suspension through switches), sensors (to sense things like proximity, sound, and light), and effectors (to effect a change on an object or the environment or to do the task the robot is meant to do, such as pick up a box or push an item in place). The computer program element is the embedded computer hardware and software code that either enables the robot to be instructed on what to do (e.g. through an internet-based software program) or to autonomously work out what to do (e.g. via artificial intelligence algorithms). As with other computer programs, there are specific programming languages used to write the software code or programs for robots to understand and act on. Examples of these languages include Variable Assembly Language (VAL), Robotic Markup Language (Robo ML), and Extensible Robot Control Language (XRCL).

How robots work

In a nutshell, you can think of the functioning of a robot in terms of an input, processing, and output system. The input involves the robot's sensors gathering information from its environment (e.g. images, object proximity, temperature, smoke, pressure, light, color, light and color intensity, touch), or it could be human-originated data entered via a keyboard, microphone, and/or a user interface. The collected sensor data is passed on to the embedded computer program, which interprets it, determines what specific objects are in front of the robot (for example), anticipates the actions and risks of those objects, determines how to best respond to them, and creates a set of response action instructions for the robot to take. The instructions are translated into electrical signals that are sent directly to the robot's hardware: e.g. switches might be turned on to activate particular wheels and move the robot into a particular position, then signals might be sent to move arms into a particular position so as to grab and then throw the object. The effect of the robot on the physical world (e.g. spinning wheels to move, picking up an object) is the output. During this whole input/processing/output process, the robot's sensors can still be picking up real-time information and passing it back to the computer program to do near real-time processing, thus enabling response instructions (and therefore the actions the robot takes) to be adapted as necessary.

Types of robots

There are many different types of robots. The different types are commonly classified by the environment in which they operate or by their application field. Other typologies focus on their level of autonomy or human resemblance. Classified by environment, there are fixed robots (e.g. operating in fixed and therefore well-defined environments, such as a robotic assembly line arm mounted on the ground) and there are mobile robots (e.g. operating in changing environments and therefore presenting additional challenges in accurately interpreting and operating in those different environments. Such mobile robots include mobile vacuum cleaners and self-driving cars). Mobile robots operate in diverse environments including underwater, in the air, in a dense jungle, or on the surface of the moon. These different environments may require robots to have one or more features such as wheels, legs, propellers, wings, or parachutes to enable them to navigate. Classified by field of application, there are industrial robots (e.g. large mounted robotic arms for assembling cars or mobile robots for moving inventory around in a warehouse) and there are service robots (robots that assist people to carry out tasks, especially dull, repetitive, and/or dangerous aspects of work). Service robots can be further classified into specific service areas or industries, such as healthcare/medical robots (e.g. surgical robots that perform surgeries requiring a very high degree of precision), home robots (e.g. robot vacuum cleaners, mobile webcam robots, robotic lawn mowers), defense or military robots (e.g. armed robotic vehicles or military drones), and educational robots (e.g. educational robokits such as the mBot-STEM Educational Robot Kit). Other types of robots include agricultural robots (robots that can perform agricultural activities such as fruit picking or farming activities like herding livestock or wildlife),[3,4,5] collaborative robots (robots designed to work safely with humans in a shared space), nanorobots (robots operating at the atomic or molecular level), swarm robots (the coordination of multiple robots to interact with each other and their environment so as to collectively achieve a particular task – similar to schools of fish or flocks of birds), and telepresence robots (robots that double as a person, are controlled remotely, and provide an alternative to physically being at a particular event or location).[6]

Business value and use cases of robotics

The business value of robotics includes cost savings, enhanced productivity, reduced risk, overcoming skill shortages, improved staff engagement, new or enhanced products, operational effectiveness, and more.[7] Robotics-related cost savings can come from robots performing activities previously performed by humans. Such activities can include repetitive but low-skill activities, high safety risk activities, or low error tolerance activities; for example, fast-food outlets like Wendy's and McDonalds have implemented automated order kiosks/robots to reduce staffing levels at particular outlets, and mining companies like Rio Tinto are leveraging robotics to remotely manage mining operations for autonomous drilling and autonomous haulage.[8,9] A robot replacement can work 24 hours a day, seven days a week without needing to take a break or experiencing stress and strain. It does not need line management to maximize its productivity once programmed appropriately, does not require privacy from monitoring, does not require leave, and does not get involved in costly political conflicts. In addition to the benefits just discussed, robotics-related productivity improvements can come from improved output per employee if organizations augment employees' work with the strengths of robots[10] (e.g. the da Vinci Surgical System improves the productivity of surgeons by enabling them to perform surgery using surgical robots and 3D vision systems).[11,12] In industries like manufacturing and logistics, companies such as beer and beverage maker Carlsberg use collaborative robots (or "cobots") in tandem with employees – robots do the heavy lifting or the unsafe work, leaving employees to do the tasks that necessitate human intelligence or input.[13]

Robots can be used in many different ways to reduce risks. For example, robots can perform tasks that are unsafe for humans (e.g. lifting back-straining loads, deactivating bombs, entering infectious areas to enforce infection control measures, welding intricate components at very high temperatures, entering terrorist zones). Robots can also mitigate or reduce risk by anticipating or spotting risks and either taking mitigating action or alerting people to take mitigating action; for example, in aged care robots are being used to anticipate and/or prevent patient falls.[14] Robots can be used to overcome skill shortages; for example, robots are being used to provide nursing and patient support services either in aged care facilities or in patients' own homes.[15] Robots can be used to provide companionship, ensure patients take their medications, facilitate patient exercise, and manage patient's daily routines,[16,17] thereby overcoming skill shortages in aged care. Robots can also be used to improve staff engagement and reduce absenteeism by taking over less desirable parts of a job and freeing employees to focus on the more desirable aspects. For example, robots can take over manual, repetitive, and time-consuming tasks and thus enable employees to do more creative or strategic work. This may even result in employees having more work/life balance flexibility, no longer bogged down with repetitive tasks that have to routinely occur at a set time in a set location.

Robotics can be leveraged for product innovation and/or business model innovation. On the product innovation front, robotics can be used to create new products/services or to enhance existing products/services. Disruptive new consumer, SME, and enterprise robotics products or services that leverage the capabilities of robotics are possible. Examples of robotics-driven product innovations in action are numerous across industries. In education, institutions are leveraging robots to innovate teaching delivery; for example, some educators are using Sphero's app-enabled robotic ball in classrooms to teach through play. In healthcare, companies are designing intelligent robots for hospitals and other care facilities; for example, Diligent Robotics designed Moxi, an autonomous robot that can independently navigate hospital hallways and tight spaces, find relevant medical equipment, set up patient rooms, and restock supply rooms. In agriculture and farming, specialty robots are being designed to perform or assist in the management of agricultural and farming processes. The increased use of robots in business operations and in homes creates a need for new software platforms, robotics support, and other services. Thus product innovation is possible from offering new robot forms, leveraging robots to carry out new forms of service delivery, leveraging robots to augment existing product or service offerings, and offering new services for robot users or owners. Robotics can also be leveraged to create entirely new business models or to enhance existing business models.[18,19,20] For example, some companies servicing the agricultural industry are shifting to a "robot as a service" (RaaS) business model (e.g. to provide robot-based weeding services that limit the need for their agricultural customers to purchase and manage robots for so many different farming activities). Other industries have started to develop similar RaaS offerings such as delivery RaaS, security RaaS, and cleaning RaaS.[21] For example, RaaS startup Robomart is trialing a driverless grocery-on-wheels service enabling people in the Boston area to grocery shop from their doorstep.[22] Finally, robotics can be leveraged to improve operational effectiveness. The combination of enhanced employee capability and the speed, precision, and 24/7 capabilities of robots can be leveraged to deliver better quality products and customer experiences.

Robotics use cases in the hospitality and leisure industry

To date, robotics applications and use cases in the hospitality and leisure industry have varied from supplementing aspects of customer experience to some level of staffing replacement to full staffing replacement. In hotels, for instance, an example of supplementing aspects of customer experience is the Hilton robot concierge Connie, who greets guests, interacts with them, and answers their questions.[23] And Alibaba's FlyZoo Future Hotel in China uses robot waiters. In contrast, the Huis Ten Bosch theme park in Japan uses life-like robot dinosaurs to check in and help its guests. Robots like these offer the hospitality and tourism industry the opportunity to interact with guests in novel ways and in different languages if deployed at the front desk or to provide room service. An example of full staff replacement is Japan's Henn-na Hotel, which replaced staff throughout the hotel with a variety of robots that leverage voice and facial recognition to check in guests, provide them with front desk services, store their luggage, interact with them, answer their questions, provide them with directions, and check them out.[24] Outside of the hotel industry, some companies are designing robotics products to make aspects of the travel experience easier. For example, TravelMate Robotics has created a robot suitcase that eliminates or at least minimizes the burden of carrying heavy luggage; the suitcase senses its environment and follows its owner around.[25] Busy travel agencies are using customer-interacting robots to resolve quick customer queries or to collect information and prequalify customers so that they can be served quickly and effectively by a human being once that person is free.[26] Airports and hospitality facilities are using security robots to autonomously scout, monitor, and detect safety risks such as concealed weapons or disruptive individuals.[27] These example use cases are just the beginning for the hospitality and leisure industry.[28]

Drones

What is a drone?

Drones, also known as unmanned/uncrewed aerial vehicles or systems (UAV or UAS), are aerial vehicles or aircraft that are remotely or autonomously piloted (i.e. not piloted by a human on board).[29,30,31] Their counterparts are unmanned or uncrewed ground vehicles (UGV), which are also remotely or autonomously driven with no human on board. Drones and UGVs can come in many sizes and have many different designs, depending on the task or activities they are designed to carry out.[32,33] For example, military-style drones and UGVs can be up to the size of commercial airplanes or bigger, whereas hobby-style drones are typically much smaller. In addition to having flight capability, drones can be fitted with a wide variety of sensors to gather information about their environment, and they can be equipped with robotic capabilities to take actions in that environment.[34] For example, drones for military purposes may be equipped with both computer vision and machine guns; drones for agricultural purposes may be equipped with different sensors and with crop spraying or crop harvesting mechanics; and drones for zoological purposes may have a combination of sensors and robotic features that enable them to enter species' territories, pretend to be one of the species, and fit into a species' social hierarchy[35] (e.g. for recording video footage of the social dynamics of species).[36]

Building blocks and functioning of drones

Like robots, drones can differ greatly in their design, capabilities, and uses,[37] but they all share some common high-level building blocks (see Figure 17.1 for a visualization of the common building blocks of a drone). All drones usually have a body or frame that is suited to the desired flight approach (e.g. fixed wing or rotary) and the types of tasks or activities the drone is to perform (e.g. surveillance, aerial photography, transporting people).[38] Fixed wing drones fly similar to or emulate the flight of normal planes. Therefore, they have a body very similar to normal planes, with rigid wings to generate lift and engines to generate thrust (e.g. to move the drone along the ground fast enough so air pressure can be generated below the wings for lift off). Rotary drones, on the other hand, have two or more rotor blades that not only turn on fixed masts and generate lift but also shape flight direction and speed as the blades rotate through the air. Drone body size, shape, and internal/external configuration are dependent on the task the drone is to do.[39] For example, a drone to spy on birds or bees may emulate the shape and appearance of the birds or bees being spied on,[40,41] whereas a drone to transport people may be designed to prioritize the safety and comfort of passengers and the aesthetics of the drone.[42,43] Drones usually have some sort of landing gear (e.g. helicopter-style gear for rotary drones and airplane-style gear for fixed wing drones). This landing gear may be an obvious part of the drone's body/frame or it may require activation. The design of the landing gear depends on the nature of the task to be performed by the drone and the constraints of the environment (e.g. landing on a stark ocean cliff face vs. a flat football field or a still river).

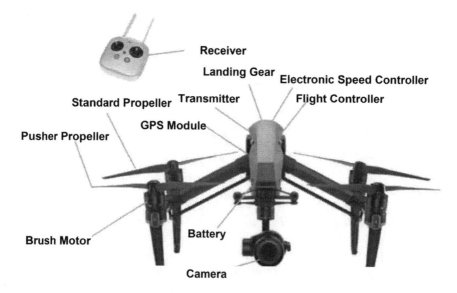

Figure 17.1 Components of a drone[44]

Drones usually have propellers, motors, and some form of power supply.[45] For fixed wing drones, propellers propel or provide the forward propulsion to enable the rigid wings to generate lift. For rotary drones, the propellers provide lift and enable speed and steering (e.g. a rotary drone with four propellers may have two standard propellers for lift and two pusher propellers for forward and backward thrust).[46] Motors spin the propellers to enable flight (typically a brushless motor,[47] but could be other types of motors or even a miniature engine).[48] A rotary drone with four propellers typically has a motor for each propeller, each of which draws on the drone's power supply (e.g. batteries, solar cells, hydro fuel cell, combustion engine, AC cable tethering, laser transmitter).[49] The power supply is usually encased in the body of the drone. Without the power supply, it would be difficult to activate all the onboard components (e.g. motors, sensors, cameras, computers, robot-like mechanics). Drones also have a flight controller and electronic speed controllers (ESC). A flight controller is an onboard computer that that receives control information from the pilot on the ground (e.g. instructions such as: more lift, more speed, change direction), from onboard sensors (e.g. information about objects in the way, wind speed and wind direction), and from the GPS module (e.g. specifying location in longitude, latitude, and elevation).[50] The flight controller combines this information to send instructions to the propellers (spin the forward propellers this direction, create this much lift). The electronic speed controllers connect the flight controller to the motors, so a four-propeller drone or quadcopter would need an ESC for each propeller motor.[51] The ESCs take instructions from the flight controller and power from the drone's power supply to make propeller motors spin a particular way.[52] Drones usually have a transmitter and receiver to enable communication with the drone. The transmitter is a remote-control device that the pilot on the ground or drone operator uses to send instructions (e.g. radio signals) to the receiver on the drone.[53] The job of the receiver is to receive the instructions or signals and pass them on to the flight controller.[54] The receiver may also pass data back to the transmitter for the pilot or operator on the ground to use. Drones usually have one or more onboard sensors, which can vary from drone to drone depending on what the drone will be used for.[55] Examples of onboard drone sensors include gyroscopes, barometers, accelerometers, GPS, magnetometers, range finders, obstacle sensors, distance sensors, thermal sensors, chemical sensors, and orientation sensors.

The components discussed thus far are found on most drones. Cameras, onboard computers, smartphone-like capabilities, and robotic capabilities are other less common components. Although less common, these components can significantly enhance the capabilities of drones and their business value. For example, sophisticated cameras and computation can enable sophisticated surveying and computer vision–based remote monitoring. Robotic capabilities and onboard computers can enable remote action (e.g. picking up and moving objects, taking out a terrorist, cleaning skyscraper windows). Adding sophisticated artificial intelligence algorithms can empower drones to take autonomous action (e.g. search and chase a person of interest while deploying and directing nearby police squads to capture them, rescue people from burning buildings, map a neighborhood or construction site, herd livestock, identify and remove dangerous obstacles, fight fires, find and destroy other drones).[56] Smartphone-like capabilities can enable remote voice-based instructions, the building of apps to expand the drone's capabilities, and more.[57,58] An important issue for many geographies is ensuring drones operate in an aerial space in which there they don't interfere with aircraft space, suburban infrastructure, and dwelling spaces (e.g. see Figure 17.2 for NASA's proposed space for drone operation).

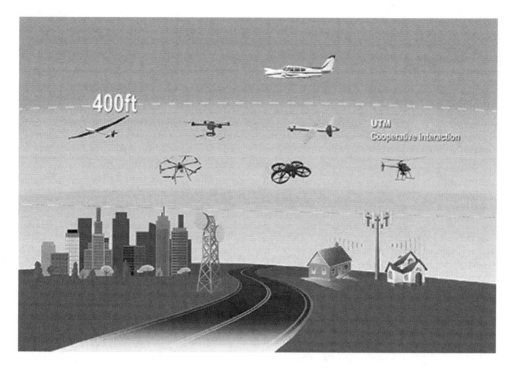

Figure 17.2 NASA's proposed space for drone operation: below aircraft space and above suburban infrastructure and dwellings[59]

Business value and use cases of drones

Drone use cases to date have included 3D mapping, delivery or transportation, inspection or monitoring, infrastructure maintenance, expanded internet connectivity, video data collection, search and rescue, firefighting/disaster response, filmmaking, lighting, inventory tracking, insurance, policing, and more.[60,61,62] For 3D mapping, drones have been used in industries such as agriculture, construction, and mining to survey sites, take photos, and create accurate contour maps that would otherwise be impossible or much less efficient to produce.[63,64] For delivery and transportation, drones have been used to deliver parcels; for example, Zipline is a US-based company that uses drones to deliver blood and vaccines to regions in developing countries still lacking infrastructure) and even deliver hot food much more efficiently than a driver.[65,66,67] And in some regions of the world, drone-based taxi or Uber services are being offered.[68] For inspection and monitoring, drones have been used to inspect site, building, and other infrastructure conditions.[69,70] For infrastructure maintenance, companies such as Aerones produce industrial drones that can remove ice buildup on wind turbines, clean skyscraper windows, stitch or fill cracks, clean drainage areas, and sand and paint.[71,72] For expanded internet connectivity, drones are being used to establish or amplify wireless internet connectivity during large-scale events or in regions where this previously was not possible without expensive infrastructure.[73,74,75,76,77] For video data collection, drones can be used to capture video footage in remote or hard to access locations and sensitive settings (e.g. silently and inconspicuously capturing wildlife interactions up close).[78,79,80] For search and rescue, drones have been used in a variety of challenges including monitoring beaches and dropping life buoys to swimmers in trouble, spotting shark threats and alerting swimmers, finding lost hikers, locating people in burning buildings, and assessing the status or impact of disaster events.[81,82] Filmmaking drones like the DJI Inspire 2 put cinema quality filming capabilities in the hands of the average person and provide film professionals with the opportunity to film using angles, stability, and focus types not possible with normal film cameras.[83] For lighting, drones can be used to create completely new spectacles at concerts, fireworks, and sporting events. For inventory tracking, drones with time-of-flight (ToF) sensors are used in industries like mining, agriculture, and forestry to measure amounts of soil, timber, stones, waste, and so forth.[84] For insurance, drones can fly over natural event or accident sites to assess damage severity and causes – which can help with claim applications.[85,86] Drones can be applied for a wide variety of policing uses such as helicopter replacements, self-directing monitoring devices, and crowd or population control devices (e.g. a drone could be used to inconspicuously follow a fugitive, leading police right to him without the commotion of a car or helicopter chase).[87] These example use cases are just the beginning; many more exist and even more will emerge each year as drone technologies impact every industry. Drones are not a fad; in fact, some observers have equated the evolution and impact of drones to that of personal computers and mobile phones – while their potential value was clear, the eventual pace, scale, and pervasiveness of their impact was hard to imagine.

Drone use cases in the hospitality and leisure industry

Hospitality and tourism industry use cases for drones are still in the very early stages. To date they have included using drones for mapping, for enhancing marketing campaigns, for guided tours or guided tour enhancement, for virtual tours, for transporting guests, and for covering staff shortages.[88] Using drones for mapping has included creating accurate maps of the interior of a site and its external surroundings so as to better guide guest navigation. Using drones for marketing has included creating impressive promotional images and videos to present hospitality facilities in the most attractive way (e.g. capturing facilities from angles and vantage points that were previously impossible).[89] In tourism marketing, drones offer the opportunity to capture irresistible shots of tourist attractions from a variety of angles and distances throughout the year that would have been previously impossible due to capability or resource constraints (e.g. capturing footage during day, at night, at sunset or sunrise, during particular wildlife events).[90] Drones can enhance guided tours with real-time video reflecting the interests of guests, or guests can go on virtual tours of local destinations from the comfort of their own hotel room.[91] Some hospitality organizations are trialing drone taxis or autonomous vehicles for picking up guests or dropping them off at different destinations.[92] Others are trialing using drone waiters to cover staff shortages or to scale staffing levels (e.g. hotels such as Timbre in Singapore and Yotel in Amsterdam have trialed drone waiters for table service and room service). Generic drone use cases such as infrastructure maintenance (e.g. window cleaning, painting, surface recoating), disaster response readiness, and facilities monitoring also represent guest attraction and operational efficiency opportunities.

3D and 4D printing

What are 3D and 4D printing?

The term 3D printing (also known as additive manufacturing or desktop fabrication) refers to the use of commercial or consumer equipment (or a printer) that, under computational control, deposits material layer by layer until a three-dimensional object is created in accordance with the specifications of a computer-aided design (CAD) model.[93] Origi-nally, the printed object may have been scanned with 3D object scanners or designed with CAD software. These 3D printers can recreate the object with superior precision, accuracy, and efficiency.[94] A 4D printer also builds 3D objects layer by layer but, unlike 3D printing, smart materials are used that enable an object to change its shape over time if exposed to water, heat, light, electric current, or magnetic fields – this change in shape is the "fourth dimension" that gives 4D printing its name. So 4D printing brings together 3D printing, smart materials (e.g. photo-polymeric liquid that hardens when exposed to light or photoresist material that decompose already solid polymers into liquids), and shape-changing design.

Building blocks and functioning of 3D and 4D printing

Although what they do is sophisticated, the common elements of 3D printers are straightforward (see Figure 17.3 for common elements of a basic 3D printer). 3D print-ers usually have a frame, power supply, and motion components. The frame houses all the components of the 3D printer. The frame design affects stability and durability of the machine and the size of what can be printed (assuming what is printed does not later expand). Some 3D printers have an open frame and others have a semi-closed or com-pletely enclosed frame. The benefits of an enclosed frame include temperature stability and protection from dust and other things that could get stuck in the 3D printer. The

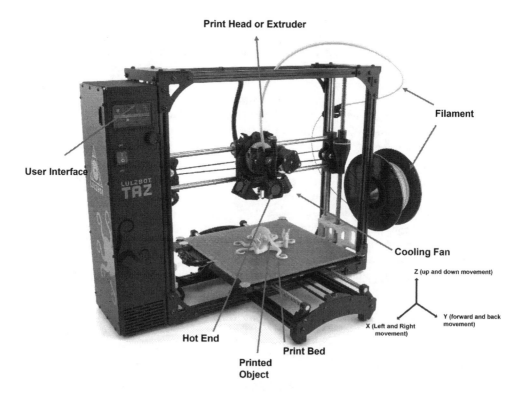

Figure 17.3 Anatomy of a basic 3D printer

power supply powers everything in the 3D printer. It is commonly encased together with the user interface and mounted on the frame. The power supply influences the temperature or heat the 3D printer can generate and thus the type of layering material (or filament) that it uses to print. The motion components are the combination of motors, belts, and other parts that ensure the nozzle depositing the layering material and/or the object being worked on are continuously moved into the right position along the three dimensions (e.g. the right combination of left and right, up and down, and forward and backwards). The motion components basically translate computational instructions into the right physical movement or positioning of the nozzle and object being worked on.

The 3D printer has a controller board and some form of user interface. The controller board (sometimes referred to as the motherboard, mainboard, or brain of the 3D printer) sends motion instructions to the motion components based on commands it receives from a computer and on information it gets from sensors (e.g. heat and motion sensors). The user interface is a screen that enables a user to receive status information and make adjustments (e.g. pause layering, reload layering material). The user interface is usually already built into the frame but can also be a separate unit. Either way, the user interface can be a basic LCD screen controlled with knobs, dials, and buttons or it could be a high-end touch screen.

For the layering process, 3D printers have filaments, print heads (or extruders), and a print bed. The filament is the material deposited in the layering process, or what the 3D printed objects are made out of. It is similar to ink for a normal 2D printer. There are many different types of filaments (e.g. made of different materials, different colors, different sizes/diameters). Filaments usually come on a spool (like those used to coil wire around), which is loaded on the 3D printer's spool holder. One end of the filament is inserted into the print head (or extruder) and gradually feeds into the print head at the rate the depositing is occurring. The print head is made up of cold end and hot end sections. The cold end clamps the filament and pushes it into the hot end. The hot end then melts the filament and deposits it or layers it (via the print head nozzle) as per the CAD model specifications of the object being printed. The sections of the print head have various drives, fans, and sensors to ensure that the filament is kept at the right temperature as it is fed from the spool and out the print head nozzle. Nozzles are interchangeable and come in different sizes depending on what is being printed and the desired print speed. A 3D printer can have a print head with more than one nozzle, or it can have more than one print head. In turn, the different print heads or nozzles can use different filaments at the same time, to enable printing of an object with more than one material. The print bed on 3D printers is the surface on which the layered printing of the object occurs. In Figure 17.3 you can see that the print bed moves the object being printed forward and back to have it in the required position for depositing. The print bed surface can be made of various materials that can influence how flat the surface is kept, how easy it is to remove the printed object, how easy it is to clean the surface, and more. A 3D printer may be connected to a network to enable remote control or monitoring of the printing process, and it may have one or more file transfer options (e.g. USB or SD card) so users can upload files for printing and initiate the print job using the available user interface.

Types of 3D printers

There are different types of 3D printers depending on their approach to 3D printing. Commonly, the types include fused deposition modeling (FDM) printers, stereolithography

(SLA) printers and laser sintering (SLS) printers. For FDM printers, the approach is as we have just described (i.e. filament is fed into a print head, melted, and extruded through the print head nozzle for layering). These types of printers are inexpensive (starting at a few hundred dollars), are widely used, and therefore have a wide variety of parts and materials available. In contrast, SLA printers start out with a liquid resin that is then hardened by a beam of UV light (i.e. instead of starting out with filament that needs to be melted). This type of printer is ideal for printing objects that contain great detail and require a smooth finish. Starting prices for this type of printer can be two to five times those of FDM printers. Finally, SLS printers work like SLA printers except that they start off with a powder instead of a liquid (e.g. nylon powder). This type of printer spreads a layer of the powder and then uses laser beams to sinter, or raise the temperature of specific parts of the powder layer so as to trace out and solidify a layer of the model. This process is repeated layer by layer until the physical object is fully printed. This type of printing enables printing using aluminum, nylon, sandstone, silver, and steel. It also enables very finely detailed objects to be made. Pricing for these types of printers start at around 40,000 to 50,000 times the price of SLA printers.

3D and 4D printing business value and use cases

Early value from 3D printing includes product innovation, business model innovation, efficiency, effectiveness, product/service differentiation, and improved customer experience. The emphasized value and use cases have varied from industry to industry.[95] For product innovation, a number of organizations in different industries are using 3D printing for cost-effective and faster prototyping of product designs. Yet other organizations are using 3D printers to create add-on components that significantly expand the usability of existing products used in day-to-day operations. For business model innovation, some organizations are offering completely new 3D printing–based business models that include licensing of 3D printing designs and 3D printing as a service (e.g. HP Inc. established HP 3D Printing Solutions as a new business that offers 3D printers, care services, lifecycle management, training, and optimization advisory services).[96,97] For efficiency, organizations in a range of industries are using 3D printing for low volume manufacturing of custom products and parts, thereby saving on costly engagement of high volume manufacturers (e.g. creating and using highly customized products that improve the efficiency of value chain processes or recreating a version of existing products/components that are too expensive via existing sourcing channels).[98] Some organizations are creating novel components to fit existing equipment, thus greatly expanding the usability of that equipment and therefore the efficiency of processes using it. For effectiveness, 3D printers are being used to plug component/part accessibility gaps for parts/components that are out of production but still required for a particular business' operations (e.g. it may be that the sole manufacturer has shut down or ceased making the part). In healthcare, this includes custom organs or other body parts for which there may not be enough human donors.[99] For product differentiation, some organizations are using 3D printers to create unique branded accessories and art that enhance brand awareness and value and enhance consumer experiences of particular settings. Products and parts that are 3D printed eliminate shipping costs, minimize inventory costs (e.g. by enabling 3D designs to be "stored in the cloud" so physical versions can be printed on demand),[100] eliminate product portability issues (e.g. the design can simply be emailed and printed, rather than needing to package and send to different locations), and more. As with other digital technologies we have covered, these use cases are just the beginning.[101]

Hospitality and leisure industry use cases of 3D and 4D printing

In hospitality and tourism, early 3D and 4D printing use cases have included enhancing customer experience through custom designed fixtures and fittings, enhancing branding through custom promotional items, on-demand production of components and spare/backup items, and enhanced food design. Regarding enhancement of customer experience through custom designed fixtures and fittings, innovative restaurants and hotels around the world have used 3D printers to print custom room fixtures and fittings and custom table settings so as to provide guests with themed experiences. Hospitality researchers at Cornell University demonstrated the efficacy of this by 3D printing an Italian-themed dinner set with column-style wine glasses, mask of Venice bowls, and Italian-style utensils and place-mats.[102,103] Custom designed fixtures, fittings, and dining sets can also be for custom ergonomic designs (e.g. for guests with disabilities). Regarding enhanced branding through custom promotional designs, hospitality organizations are able to custom design and 3D print on demand all manner of promotional materials (e.g. to use in the hospitality setting, to give away at promotional events, to give away to guests). Promotional materials and fixtures and fittings made using 3D printing technology have the added benefit of reducing supply chain risk (e.g. hospitality organizations can be sure about the design authenticity, environmental friendliness, and ethical production of the printed items). Regarding on-demand production of components and spare/backup items, hospitality organizations are using 3D printers and designs stored in the cloud to print lost or spare keys, spare items for consumers when they forget theirs (e.g. custom-fitting spare slippers, snorkels, or boots), and repair and maintenance components. Finally, with regard to food design, hospitality organizations are using 3D printers to create custom foods (e.g. fibrous plant–based meat that mimics the texture and nutritional values of normal meat)[104] and custom dish designs. For example, La Enoteca at Hotel Arts Barcelona uses a food printer and seafood puree to sculpt flower-like coral designs for the centerpiece, which is then embellished with an assortment of seafood such as sea urchin and caviar.[105] Other hospitality organizations like ChefJet and Foodini use 3D printers to add enhancements to existing dishes or to create perfect geometric configurations for confectionery and dessert dishes.[106] Taking it even further, UK-based company Food Ink 3D prints its entire service including tables, chairs, menus, plates, cups, glasses, cutlery, and food.[107]

3D and 4D printing issues and risks

While the digital technologies discussed in this chapter are evolving quickly and create significant efficiency, effectiveness, differentiation, and adaptability opportunities for organizations, they come with inherent risks. These include risks related to ambiguous and underdeveloped regulation, security and privacy risks, risks related to societal attitudes toward them, dependability and reliability risks, and risks related to availability of assurance and support services. Regarding regulations, it is easy for staff using drones or 3D printers, for example, to be unaware of and breach civil aviation safety laws (e.g. flying drones into prohibited areas) or duplicate copyrighted 3D/4D designs. It is also easy for staff to use these digital technologies for activities for which there is no restricting regulation as yet but that may be frowned on by society (e.g. robots or drones may capture and use sensitive video footage, causing community outrage). Regarding security and privacy, early versions of digital technologies are typically made by startup companies that may not address possible security breach and privacy risk flaws. As a result, the use of technologies may lead to unethical organizations accessing sensitive customer data. Social attitudes toward digital technologies also have to be considered; for instance, while robots may provide efficiency breakthroughs, organizations have to consider community concern about robots taking their jobs. If organizations don't consider such concerns, they may find communities boycotting their services. Finally, digital technologies go through hype and disillusionment cycles, and hospitality and leisure organizations have to ensure they don't get carried away with the hype (thus pushing the implementation of uses for technologies that aren't quite dependable/reliable yet) or disillusionment (thus turning a blind eye to technology adoption, only to become another Kodak or Blockbuster).

Google and reflect

Digital Technology	Common Terminology
Robotics	Robot axis/degrees of freedom, robot hand guiding, robot reach, robot repeatability, exoskeleton robot, social robots, robot payload, robot grip force, force limited robot, actuator, bionics, robot CPU, cloud robotics, cobots, cyborg, robot end effector, humanoid robot, gynoid robot, android robot, industrial robot, nanobot, RPA, robot uptime, adaptive motion control, robot path simulation, aerobot, combat robot, cruise missile, delta robot, forward chaining, haptic, robot hydraulics, service robot
Drones	Ready-to-fly (RTF) drone, almost-ready-to-fly (ARTF) drone, bind-and-fly (BNF) drone, quadcopter, octocopter, multicopter, drone flight time, gimbal, drone collision/obstacle avoidance, drone pitch, drone roll, drone yaw, UAS (unmanned aircraft system), drone frequency, drone S mode, drone P mode, A mode, dronie, field of view (FOV), drone firmware, FPV (first-person view) drone, geofencing, GLONASS, gyroscope, inertial measurement unit (IMU), infrared drone/UAV, photogrammetry, PIC (pilot in command), racing drone, drone return to home (RTH), target drone, decoy drone, reconnaissance drone, combat drone
3D/4D Printing	Acrylonitrile butadiene styrene (ABS), 3D printing G-code, polylactic acid (PLA), RepRap, 3D printer slicer, STL file format, 3D model slicer, heated print bed, Kapton tape, subtractive manufacturing, 3D print shell, 3D print raft, 3D print infill, 3D print curing, 3D sculpting, 3D printing overhang

Example tools and vendors

Digital Technology	Tools and Vendors
Robotics	iRobot Roomba 960, iRobot Braava 380T, GreyOrange Butler, GreyOrange Flexo, Arduino, Epson SCARA robots, Boston Dynamics, Boston Dynamics' ATLAS, Boston Dynamics' SPOT, Locus Robotics, SCHUNK, SCHUNK SVH, SCHUNK PGN–plus–E, ASI robots, ASI Chaos High Mobility Robot, ASI Forge Robotic Platform, Honda ASIMO, Softbank Robotics, Softbank's Pepper, Samsung Bot Retail, SamsungBot Care, SamsungBot Air, Sanbot by Qihan technology, Romeo by Softbank Robotics, by Blue Frog Robotics, Aibo by Sony, PIAGGIO "GITA" Cargo Bot, HRP-5P by AIST, Sphero, Diligent Robotics, Picknik Robotics, Sarcos, Bluefin Robotics, Petronics, AMP Robotics, Left Hand Robotics, Harvest Automation, Intuitive Surgical, Myomo, MakerBot Industries, Autodesk Fusion 360, ABB Robotics, Kuka industrial robots
Drones	DJI drones, GoPro Karma Drone, 3D Robotics IRIS+, Hubsan Zino, Lockheed Martin RQ-170 Sentinel, Parrot AR.Drone 2.0, Yuneec Typhoon Q500 quadcopter, EVO by Autel Robotics, ambulance drone by Delft Technical University, Plan Bee drone, Volocopter, Flirtey Eagle drone, SureFly, GimBall, PD-100 Black Hornet, Aerix Aerius, RoboBee X-Wing, DJI MG-1P Agricultural Spraying Drone, Neurala, Skycatch software, Alive software platform, Skydio drone

Digital Technology	Tools and Vendors
3D/4D Printing	Lulzbot Mini, Prusa i3 MK2, Formlabs Form 2, Anycubic Photon, Monoprice Maker Select Plus, Stratasys Fortus 250mc, MakerBot Replicator Z18, HP Jet Fusion 3D 4200 Printer, ProJet MJP 3600, Tronxy X5ST-500, BigRep ONE v3, Erectorbot EB 2076 LX, Builder Extreme 2000, BLB Industries THE BOX, Sciaky EBAM 110, AutoDesk Inventor, Autodesk 123D, Google SketchUp Make, Slic3r, Skeinforge, KISSlicer, HP 3D printing, Proto Labs, 3D Systems, Materialise 3D printing, Arcam AB, Autodesk, Stratasys Ltd, The ExOne Company, Hoganas AB, Optomec, Inc., Organovo Holdings, Inc., Ponoko Limited, Voxeljet AG, Formlabs 3D printers, Revolution 3D Printers, Airwolf 3D Printers

Discussion questions

Robotics

1 What is the difference between robots and robotics?
2 What is the difference between robotics and artificial intelligence?
3 What is the difference between a humanoid, an android, and a gynoid robot?
4 What is the most important part of a robot, and why?
5 What is the most common robotic programming language?
6 What is the best way to classify robots, and why?
7 What is the most important business value of robots?
8 How can using robots improve work satisfaction and engagement?
9 How can human beings best compete with robots in the workplace?
10 What five types of sensors can have the greatest impact on the capability of a robot, and how can a robot use the information from each type of sensor?
11 What is the most important ethical issue in relation to using robots?
12 How can robots be used to reduce business risk?
13 What are three examples of product innovation using robots?
14 What are three examples of business model innovation using robots?

Drones

1 What is the difference between a helicopter–sized drone, a helicopter, and a flying robot?
2 What is the most important sensor on a drone?
3 What is the smartest part of a drone?
4 What is the minimum and maximum number of propellers a drone can have?
5 How could artificial intelligence be used in a drone?
6 Could a drone be used to autonomously hedge trim a hedge? How could it work?
7 What is the biggest public concern about drones?
8 What is the biggest legal issue in relation to drones?
9 What is the most important business value of drones?

3D/4D printing

1 How is a 3D printer different from a 2D printer?
2 Can a 3D printer be used for 4D printing?
3 Which is the more important technology: 3D printing or additive manufacturing?

4 If you had an old machine for which there were no longer any repair parts being made, how would you go about using a 3D printer to solve that problem?
5 What is the cheapest type of 3D printing technology? What is the most expensive type?
6 Which 3D printing technology is best for making products out of metal?
7 Which 3D printing technology is best for making decorative glass products?
8 Are 3D-printed products as good as those manufactured traditionally?
9 Will 3D printing be bigger than the internet? Why?
10 What is the best 3D printer for consumer use, and why?
11 What is the best 3D printer for industrial use, and why?
12 What types of services are provided for 3D printing as a service (3daaS)?
13 What is the most serious strategic risk for businesses in relation to adopting 3D printing?

Notes

1 Nichols, G. (2018). Robotics in Business: Everything Humans Need to Know. Retrieved February 3, 2020, from ZDNet website: www.zdnet.com/article/robotics-in-business-everything-humans-need-to-know/
2 Simon, M. (2017, August 24). What is a Robot? Retrieved February 3, 2020, from Wired website: www.wired.com/story/what-is-a-robot/
3 Holley, P. (2019). New Zealand Farmers Have a New Tool for Herding Sheep: Drones that Bark Like Dogs. The Washington Post. Retrieved from www.washingtonpost.com/technology/2019/03/07/new-zealand-farmers-have-new-tool-herding-sheep-drones-that-bark-like-dogs/
4 Christian, J. (2019). This Drone is a Sheepdog. Retrieved February 11, 2020, from World Economic Forum website: www.weforum.org/agenda/2019/03/new-zealand-farmers-are-using-drones-to-herd-sheep/
5 Paranjape, A. A., Chung, S. J., Kim, K., & Shim, D. H. (2018). Robotic Herding of a Flock of Birds Using an Unmanned Aerial Vehicle. *IEEE Transactions on Robotics*, 34(4), 901–915.
6 Double Robotics – Telepresence Robot for Telecommuters. (2020). Doublerobotics.Com. Retrieved from www.doublerobotics.com/
7 Wolfgang, M., Vladimir, L., Sander, A., Martin, J., & Küpper, D. (2017). Gaining Robotics Advantage. www.bcg.com. Retrieved from www.bcg.com/en-au/publications/2017/strategy-technology-digital-gaining-robotics-advantage.aspx
8 Crozier, R. (2018). Rio Tinto to Build New "Intelligent" Mines. ITnews. Retrieved from www.itnews.com.au/news/rio-tinto-to-build-new-intelligent-mines-494651
9 Mining Global. (2014). Rio Tinto: Mine of the Future. Miningglobal.Com; Admin. Retrieved from www.miningglobal.com/operations/rio-tinto-mine-future
10 Wilson, H. J., & Daugherty, P. R. (2018). How Humans and AI are Working Together in 1,500 Companies. Harvard Business Review. Retrieved from https://hbr.org/2018/07/collaborative-intelligence-humans-and-ai-are-joining-forces
11 Siegel, E. R., McFadden, C., Monahan, K., Lehren, A. W., & Siniauer, P. (2018). The da Vinci Surgical Robot: A Medical Breakthrough with Risks for Patients. Retrieved February 4, 2020, from NBC News website: www.nbcnews.com/health/health-news/da-vinci-surgical-robot-medical-breakthrough-risks-patients-n949341
12 Wolfgang, M., Vladimir, L., Sander, A., Martin, J., & Küpper, D. (2017). Gaining Robotics Advantage. www.bcg.com. Retrieved from www.bcg.com/en-au/publications/2017/strategy-technology-digital-gaining-robotics-advantage.aspx
13 Francis, S. (2020). Carlsberg Reduces Risk of Accidents with Universal Robots. Retrieved February 4, 2020, from Robotics & Automation News website: https://roboticsandautomationnews.com/2020/01/06/carlsberg-reduces-risk-of-accidents-with-universal-robots/28215/
14 Maneeprom, N., Taneepanichskul, S., Panza, A., & Suputtitada, A. (2019). Effectiveness of Robotics Fall Prevention Program among Elderly in Senior Housings, Bangkok, Thailand: A Quasi-Experimental Study. *Clinical Interventions in Aging*, 14, 335–346. https://doi.org/10.2147/cia.s182336
15 Fischinger, D., Einramhof, P., Papoutsakis, K., Wohlkinger, W., Mayer, P., Panek, P., . . . & Vincze, M. (2016). Hobbit, a Care Robot Supporting Independent Living at Home: First prototype

and Lessons Learned. *Robotics and Autonomous Systems*, 75, 60–78. https://doi.org/10.1016/j.robot.2014.09.029

16 Bemelmans, R., Gelderblom, G. J., Jonker, P., & de Witte, L. (2012). Socially Assistive Robots in Elderly Care: A Systematic Review into Effects and Effectiveness. *Journal of the American Medical Directors Association*, 13(2), 114–120.e1. https://doi.org/10.1016/j.jamda.2010.10.002

17 DPS Publishing. (2016). The Future is Here – Robots in Aged Care. Retrieved February 5, 2020, from Aged Care Guide website: www.agedcareguide.com.au/talking-aged-care/the-future-is-here-robots-in-aged-care

18 PricewaterhouseCoopers. (2015). CEO Pulse: Pulse on Robotics: PwC. Retrieved February 14, 2020, from PwC website: www.pwc.com/gx/en/ceo-agenda/pulse/robotics.html

19 Accenture. (2018). Foster Innovation with Enterprise Robotics. Retrieved from www.accenture.com/_acnmedia/pdf-71/accenture-robotics-pov-web.pdf

20 AMFG. (2019). 5 Examples of How 3D Printing is Creating New Business Models. Retrieved February 14, 2020, from AMFG website: https://amfg.ai/2019/11/29/5-examples-of-how-3d-printing-is-creating-new-business-models/

21 PR Newswire. (2019). New Robotics: Shifting Business Models. Retrieved February 5, 2020, from Prnewswire.com website: www.prnewswire.com/news-releases/new-robotics-shifting-business-models-300818816.html

22 Dumont, J. (2019, January 17). Stop & Shop Will Pilot Driverless Delivery in Boston. Retrieved February 5, 2020, from Grocery Dive website: www.grocerydive.com/news/stop-shop-will-pilot-driverless-delivery-in-boston/546223/

23 Revfine.com. (2019). 8 Examples of Robots Being Used in the Hospitality Industry. Revfine.Com. Retrieved from www.revfine.com/robots-hospitality-industry/

24 Revfine.com. (2019). 8 Examples of Robots Being Used in the Hospitality Industry. Revfine.Com. Retrieved from www.revfine.com/robots-hospitality-industry/

25 Revfine.com. (2019). 8 Examples of Robots Being Used in the Hospitality Industry. Revfine.Com. Retrieved from www.revfine.com/robots-hospitality-industry/

26 Revfine.com. (2019). 8 Examples of Robots Being Used in the Hospitality Industry. Revfine.Com. Retrieved from www.revfine.com/robots-hospitality-industry/

27 Revfine.com. (2019). 8 Examples of Robots Being Used in the Hospitality Industry. Revfine.Com. Retrieved from www.revfine.com/robots-hospitality-industry/

28 Bowen, J., & Morosan, C. (2018). Beware Hospitality Industry: The Robots are Coming. *Worldwide Hospitality and Tourism Themes*, 10, 6.

29 Taking flight. (2016). The Economist. Retrieved from www.economist.com/technology-quarterly/2017-06-08/civilian-drones

30 Corrigan, F. (2019). How Do Drones Work and What is Drone Technology. DroneZon. Retrieved from www.dronezon.com/learn-about-drones-quadcopters/what-is-drone-technology-or-how-does-drone-technology-work/

31 Pierce, D. (2018). Drones: The Complete Guide. Retrieved February 11, 2020, from Wired website: www.wired.com/story/guide-drones/

32 Taking flight. (2016). The Economist. Retrieved from www.economist.com/technology-quarterly/2017-06-08/civilian-drones

33 Corrigan, F. (2019). How Do Drones Work and What is Drone Technology. DroneZon. Retrieved from www.dronezon.com/learn-about-drones-quadcopters/what-is-drone-technology-or-how-does-drone-technology-work/

34 Corrigan, F. (2019). How Do Drones Work and What is Drone Technology. DroneZon. Retrieved from www.dronezon.com/learn-about-drones-quadcopters/what-is-drone-technology-or-how-does-drone-technology-work/

35 Baggaley, K. (2019). Forget Props and Fixed Wings. New Bio-Inspired Drones Mimic birds, Bats and Bugs. Retrieved February 6, 2020, from NBC News website: www.nbcnews.com/mach/science/forget-props-fixed-wings-new-bio-inspired-drones-mimic-birds-ncna1033061

36 Mingle, J. (2019). Saving the Planet One Drone at a Time. Department of Zoology. Retrieved February 6, 2020, from Ox.ac.uk website: www.zoo.ox.ac.uk/article/saving-planet-one-drone-time

37 Corrigan, F. (2019). How Do Drones Work and What is Drone Technology. DroneZon. Retrieved from www.dronezon.com/learn-about-drones-quadcopters/what-is-drone-technology-or-how-does-drone-technology-work/

38 Corrigan, F. (2019). How Do Drones Work and What is Drone Technology. DroneZon. Retrieved from www.dronezon.com/learn-about-drones-quadcopters/what-is-drone-technology-or-how-does-drone-technology-work/

39 Corrigan, F. (2019). How Do Drones Work and What is Drone Technology. DroneZon. Retrieved from www.dronezon.com/learn-about-drones-quadcopters/what-is-drone-technology-or-how-does-drone-technology-work/

40 Baggaley, K. (2019). Forget Props and Fixed Wings. New Bio-Inspired Drones Mimic birds, Bats and Bugs. Retrieved February 11, 2020, from NBC News website: www.nbcnews.com/mach/science/forget-props-fixed-wings-new-bio-inspired-drones-mimic-birds-ncna1033061

41 New Scientist. (2005). Airborne Robotic Spycraft Inspired by Seagulls. Retrieved February 11, 2020, from New Scientist website: https://institutions.newscientist.com/article/mg18725155-900-airborne-robotic-spycraft-inspired-by-seagulls/

42 Flanagan, B. (2019, September 9). The Maker of Dubai's Flying Taxi Aims to Set Flight within the Next Three Years. Retrieved February 6, 2020, from WIRED Middle East website: https://wired.me/science/transportation/dubai-drone-flying-taxis-volocopter/

43 Blanchard, S., & Randall, I. (2019). Self-driving Flying Taxi with 18 Drone-like Propellers is Tested in the Skies of Singapore. Retrieved February 6, 2020, from Mail Online website: www.dailymail.co.uk/sciencetech/article-7599343/Hover-taxi-whizzes-Singapore-firm-eyes-Asian-push.html

44 Grind Drone. (2017). Drone Components and What They Do. Retrieved from http://grinddrone.com/drone-features/drone-components

45 Corrigan, F. (2019). How Do Drones Work and What is Drone Technology. DroneZon. Retrieved from www.dronezon.com/learn-about-drones-quadcopters/what-is-drone-technology-or-how-does-drone-technology-work/

46 Corrigan, F. (2019). How Do Drones Work and What is Drone Technology. DroneZon. Retrieved from www.dronezon.com/learn-about-drones-quadcopters/what-is-drone-technology-or-how-does-drone-technology-work/

47 Renesas Electronics. What are Brushless DC Motors. Retrieved February 11, 2020, from www.renesas.com/us/en/support/technical-resources/engineer-school/brushless-dc-motor-01-overview.html

48 Nichols, G. (2019). Why Don't Drones Use Small Versions of Commercial Aircraft Engines? ZDNet. Retrieved from www.zdnet.com/article/why-dont-drones-use-small-versions-of-commercial-aircraft-engines/

49 Arriansyah, A. (2016). The 6 Known Ways to Power a Drone. Techinasia.Com. Retrieved from www.techinasia.com/talk/6-known-ways-power-a-drone

50 Corrigan, F. (2019). How Do Drones Work and What is Drone Technology. DroneZon. Retrieved from www.dronezon.com/learn-about-drones-quadcopters/what-is-drone-technology-or-how-does-drone-technology-work/

51 Corrigan, F. (2019). How Do Drones Work and What is Drone Technology. DroneZon. Retrieved from www.dronezon.com/learn-about-drones-quadcopters/what-is-drone-technology-or-how-does-drone-technology-work/

52 Corrigan, F. (2019). How Do Drones Work and What is Drone Technology. DroneZon. Retrieved from www.dronezon.com/learn-about-drones-quadcopters/what-is-drone-technology-or-how-does-drone-technology-work/

53 Corrigan, F. (2019). How Do Drones Work and What is Drone Technology. DroneZon. Retrieved from www.dronezon.com/learn-about-drones-quadcopters/what-is-drone-technology-or-how-does-drone-technology-work/

54 Corrigan, F. (2019). How Do Drones Work and What is Drone Technology. DroneZon. Retrieved from www.dronezon.com/learn-about-drones-quadcopters/what-is-drone-technology-or-how-does-drone-technology-work/

55 Corrigan, F. (2019). How Do Drones Work and What is Drone Technology. DroneZon. Retrieved from www.dronezon.com/learn-about-drones-quadcopters/what-is-drone-technology-or-how-does-drone-technology-work/

56 Wyder, P. M., Chen, Y. S., Lasrado, A. J., Pelles, R. J., Kwiatkowski, R., Comas, E. O., . . . & Xiong, Z. (2019). Autonomous Drone Hunter Operating by Deep Learning and All-Onboard Computations in GPS-denied Environments. *PLoS ONE*, 14(11).

57 Daley, S. (2018). Fighting Fires and Saving Elephants: How 12 Companies are Using the AI Drone to Solve Big Problems. Retrieved February 10, 2020, from Built In website: https://builtin.com/artificial-intelligence/drones-ai-companies

58 Leswing, K. (2015). DJI's Powerful New Computer Will Lead to Better Drone Apps. Retrieved February 11, 2020, from Fortune website: https://fortune.com/2015/11/02/dji-manifold-computer/
59 McLellan, C. (2018, May 15). The New Commute: How Driverless Cars, Hyperloop, and Drones Will Change Our Travel Plans. Retrieved June 21, 2020, from TechRepublic website: www.techrepublic.com/article/the-new-commute-how-driverless-cars-hyperloop-and-drones-will-change-our-travel-plans/
60 McKinsey & Company. (2017). Commercial Drones are Here: The Future of Unmanned Aerial Systems. Retrieved from www.mckinsey.com/industries/capital-projects-and-infrastructure/our-insights/commercial-drones-are-here-the-future-of-unmanned-aerial-systems
61 Taking flight. (2016). The Economist. Retrieved from www.economist.com/technology-quarterly/2017-06-08/civilian-drones
62 Corrigan, F. (2019). What are Drones Used for from Business to Critical Missions. DroneZon. Retrieved from www.dronezon.com/drones-for-good/what-are-drones-used-for-and-best-drone-uses/
63 Taking flight. (2016). The Economist. Retrieved from www.economist.com/technology-quarterly/2017-06-08/civilian-drones
64 Corrigan, F. (2019). What are Drones Used for from Business to Critical Missions. DroneZon. Retrieved from www.dronezon.com/drones-for-good/what-are-drones-used-for-and-best-drone-uses/
65 Taking flight. (2016). The Economist. Retrieved from www.economist.com/technology-quarterly/2017-06-08/civilian-drones
66 Corrigan, F. (2019). What are Drones Used for from Business to Critical Missions. DroneZon. Retrieved from www.dronezon.com/drones-for-good/what-are-drones-used-for-and-best-drone-uses/
67 Amazon. (2019). Amazon.com: Prime Air. Amazon.Com. Retrieved from www.amazon.com/Amazon-Prime-Air/b?node=8037720011
68 Flanagan, B. (2019). The Maker of Dubai's Flying Taxi Aims to Set Flight within the Next Three Years. Retrieved February 11, 2020, from WIRED Middle East website: https://wired.me/science/transportation/dubai-drone-flying-taxis-volocopter/
69 Taking flight. (2016). The Economist. Retrieved from www.economist.com/technology-quarterly/2017-06-08/civilian-drones
70 Corrigan, F. (2019). What are Drones Used for from Business to Critical Missions. DroneZon. Retrieved from www.dronezon.com/drones-for-good/what-are-drones-used-for-and-best-drone-uses/
71 Heater, B. (2018). Aerones Makes Really Big Drones for Cleaning Turbines and Saving Lives. TechCrunch. Retrieved from https://techcrunch.com/2018/03/17/aerones-makes-really-big-drones-for-cleaning-turbines-and-saving-lives/
72 Aerones. (2018). Aerones. Retrieved from www.aerones.com/eng/wind_turbine_maintenance_drone/
73 Etherington, D. (2014). Google Acquires Titan Aerospace, The Drone Company Pursued By Facebook. TechCrunch. Retrieved from https://techcrunch.com/2014/04/14/google-acquires-titan-aerospace-the-drone-company-pursued-by-facebook/
74 Taking flight. (2016). The Economist. Retrieved from www.economist.com/technology-quarterly/2017-06-08/civilian-drones
75 Russell, J. (2019). Facebook is Reportedly Testing Solar-Powered Internet Drones Again – This Time with Airbus. TechCrunch. Retrieved from https://techcrunch.com/2019/01/21/facebook-airbus-solar-drones-internet-program/
76 Hickey, M. (2016). Report: Google Working on Awesome Solar-Powered Broadband Drones for 5G Wireless Internet. Forbes. Retrieved February 10, 2020, from www.forbes.com/sites/matthickey/2016/01/31/report-google-working-on-awesome-solar-powered-broadband-drones-for-5g-wireless-internet/#23e6c2f96a43
77 Hickey, M. (2016). Report: Google Working on Awesome Solar-Powered Broadband Drones for 5G Wireless Internet. Forbes. Retrieved from www.forbes.com/sites/matthickey/2016/01/31/report-google-working-on-awesome-solar-powered-broadband-drones-for-5g-wireless-internet/#1524f1ff6a43
78 Taking flight. (2016). The Economist. Retrieved from www.economist.com/technology-quarterly/2017-06-08/civilian-drones
79 Corrigan, F. (2019). What are Drones Used for from Business to Critical Missions. DroneZon. Retrieved from www.dronezon.com/drones-for-good/what-are-drones-used-for-and-best-drone-uses/
80 Baggaley, K. (2019). Forget Props and Fixed Wings. New Bio-Inspired Drones Mimic Birds, Bats and Bugs. Retrieved February 11, 2020, from NBC News website: www.nbcnews.com/mach/science/forget-props-fixed-wings-new-bio-inspired-drones-mimic-birds-ncna1033061

81 Taking flight. (2016). The Economist. Retrieved from www.economist.com/technology-quarterly/2017-06-08/civilian-drones

82 Corrigan, F. (2019). What are Drones Used for from Business to Critical Missions. DroneZon. Retrieved from www.dronezon.com/drones-for-good/what-are-drones-used-for-and-best-drone-uses/

83 Corrigan, F. (2019). What are Drones Used for from Business to Critical Missions. DroneZon. Retrieved from www.dronezon.com/drones-for-good/what-are-drones-used-for-and-best-drone-uses/

84 Corrigan, F. (2019). What are Drones Used for from Business to Critical Missions. DroneZon. Retrieved from www.dronezon.com/drones-for-good/what-are-drones-used-for-and-best-drone-uses/

85 Corrigan, F. (2019). What are Drones Used for from Business to Critical Missions. DroneZon. Retrieved from www.dronezon.com/drones-for-good/what-are-drones-used-for-and-best-drone-uses/

86 Taking flight. (2016). The Economist. Retrieved from www.economist.com/technology-quarterly/2017-06-08/civilian-drones

87 Corrigan, F. (2019). What are Drones Used for from Business to Critical Missions. DroneZon. Retrieved from www.dronezon.com/drones-for-good/what-are-drones-used-for-and-best-drone-uses/

88 Fetterling, J. (2018). 3 Ways Hotels are Creatively Using Drones. Prevue Meetings & Incentives. Retrieved from www.prevuemeetings.com/experiences/technology/3-ways-hotels-creatively-using-drones/

89 Alaska Adventure Charters & Aerial Photography. (2019). How Drones are Emerging as a Great Marketing Tool for Tourism Industry. Retrieved from www.alaskaadventurecharters.net/home/how-drones-are-emerging-as-a-great-marketing-tool-for-tourism-industry

90 Uaslogic.Com. (2016). Uses of Drones and UAS Vehicles for Tourism. Retrieved from https://uaslogic.com/drones-for-tourism.html

91 Mirk, D., & Hlavacs, H. (2014, July). Using Drones for Virtual Tourism. In *International Conference on Intelligent Technologies for Interactive Entertainment* (pp. 144–147). Springer.

92 Flanagan, B. (2019). The Maker of Dubai's Flying Taxi Aims to Set Flight within the Next Three Years. Retrieved February 11, 2020, from WIRED Middle East website: https://wired.me/science/transportation/dubai-drone-flying-taxis-volocopter/

93 Gewirtz, D. (2020). Everything You need to Know About 3D Printing and Its Impact on Your Business. Retrieved February 14, 2020, from ZDNet website: www.zdnet.com/article/everything-you-need-to-know-about-3d-printing-and-its-impact-on-your-business/

94 Gewirtz, D. (2020). Everything You Need to Know About 3D Printing and Its Impact on Your Business. Retrieved February 14, 2020, from ZDNet website: www.zdnet.com/article/everything-you-need-to-know-about-3d-printing-and-its-impact-on-your-business/

95 Conlin, B. (2018). More than Prototypes: A Look at the 3D Printing Industry. Retrieved February 14, 2020, from Business News Daily website: www.businessnewsdaily.com/9297-3d-printing-for-business.html

96 Hewlett Packard Inc. (2017). HP 3DaaS – 3D Printer Services, Supplies and Support | HP® Official Site. Retrieved February 12, 2020, from Hp.com website: www8.hp.com/us/en/printers/3d-printers/services/3daaS.html

97 Rayna, T., & Striukova, L. (2016). From Rapid Prototyping to Home Fabrication: How 3D Printing is Changing Business Model Innovation. *Technological Forecasting and Social Change*, 102, 214–224. https://doi.org/10.1016/j.techfore.2015.07.023

98 Graphic Display World. (2019). The New Business Case for 3D Printing. Retrieved February 14, 2020, from Graphicdisplayworld.com website: www.graphicdisplayworld.com/features/the-new-business-case-for-3d-printing

99 Starr, M. (2015). Cancer Patient Receives 3D-Printed Sternum and Ribs. Retrieved February 14, 2020, from CNET website: www.cnet.com/news/cancer-patient-receives-3d-printed-sternum-ribs/

100 Gannes, L. (2013). With KeyMe, an iPhone Pic Now Means You Can Always Print More House Keys Later. AllThingsD. Retrieved from http://allthingsd.com/20130808/with-keyme-an-iphone-pic-now-means-you-can-always-print-more-housekeys-later/

101 Columbus, L. (2018). The State of 3D Printing, 2018. Forbes. Retrieved from www.forbes.com/sites/louiscolumbus/2018/05/30/the-state-of-3d-printing-2018/#423edb287b0a

102 Lipton, J., Witzleben, J., Green, V., Ryan, C., & Lipson, H. (2015). Demonstrations of Additive Manufacturing for the Hospitality Industry. *3D Printing and Additive Manufacturing*, 2(4), 204–208. https://doi.org/10.1089/3dp.2015.0031

103 O'Neal, B. (2016). Set the Table & Let's Eat! Researchers Investigate Viability of 3D Printing in the Hospitality Industry. 3DPrint.com | The Voice of 3D Printing/Additive Manufacturing.

(2016, March 7). 3DPrint.Com | The Voice of 3D Printing/Additive Manufacturing. Retrieved from https://3dprint.com/122839/3d-print-hospitality-industry/

104 Montes, L., & Moynihan, R. (2018). This Meat Substitute Is Printed with a Pea and Rice Protein Paste and a 3D Printer. Business Insider. Retrieved February 11, 2020, from https://www.businessinsider.com/this-fake-meat-is-printed-in-a-lab-using-vegetables-and-a-3d-printer-2018-11?IR=T

105 Ahmed, R. (2017). 4 Famous Restaurants that Use 3D Printers. 3D Printing. Retrieved from https://3dprinting.com/food/4-famous-restaurants-that-use-3d-printers/

106 Ahmed, R. (2017). 4 Famous Restaurants that Use 3D Printers. 3D Printing. Retrieved from 3D Printing. https://3dprinting.com/food/4-famous-restaurants-that-use-3d-printers/

107 Ahmed, R. (2017). 4 Famous Restaurants that Use 3D Printers. 3D Printing. Retrieved from https://3dprinting.com/food/4-famous-restaurants-that-use-3d-printers/

18 Network and connectivity technologies

Introduction

The overarching theme of the digital technologies discussed in this chapter is connectivity. The digital technologies discussed play a critical role in the ability of people, systems, devices, and other things to pass and receive information from each other. It is this information, combined with computation, that is at the heart of and extends the power of other digital technologies like cloud computing, the internet of things, artificial intelligence, and robotics/drones. There is a range of connectivity technologies and standards, each offering strengths in areas like data transmission speed, transmission range, the amount of data that can be sent, connectivity reliability, connection security, connection availability, and connection portability. There are also limitations such as power consumption, high infrastructure setup and maintenance costs, durability, hackability, standard adoption, and connectivity equipment availability/reliability. In this chapter, we first provide an overview of cellular networks (6G, 5G, 4G, LTE, and others); then we provide an overview of global navigation satellite systems (e.g. those used by GPS devices) and low orbit satellite systems; and finally we provide an overview of low power wide area, low power wide area network, NFC, Smart Bluetooth, iBeacon, and other technologies that are at the heart of device-to-device connectivity. The range of available connectivity technologies/standards require hospitality and leisure managers to understand how different technologies/standards work and what their strengths and shortcomings are. It also requires them to make important choices about which standards to go with for what purpose, when to experiment with a particular technology/standard, when to cut the cord on an existing connectivity technology/standard, and when to undertake large scale adoption of a new standard. As previously mentioned, relying solely on in-house technical teams may limit the operational efficiency, product innovation, business model innovation, agility, and adaptability opportunities that are only possible by blending an understanding of customer needs, an understanding of operational processes, an understanding of the hospitality and leisure market and an understanding of hospitality and leisure operational staff. In this chapter, we provide a simplified introduction to these technologies. As with other technologies, this is meant to be a starting point to enable current and prospective managers to catch up, keep up with, and make the most of advancements in this group of digital technologies.

6G, 5G, 4G, LTE, and other cellular networks

Cellular networks and how they work

If you look in the top corner of your phone, you are likely to see a 5G, 4G, or 3G symbol (or, in the worst case, a 2G symbol). These symbols indicate the type of cellular or mobile network you are using to send and receive data to and from other devices and equipment. Cellular networks use land-based towers (also referred to as cell towers, cell sites, cellular base stations, or base transceiver stations) for sending and receiving data. Essentially, a cellular network divides up geographic areas into transmission areas called "cells." The cell towers or transceiver stations have all the necessary components to serve that cell (e.g. antennas, transceivers, control electronics, backup power, sheltering). The transceiver stations provide the network coverage that devices or equipment then use to send or receive different types of data. The bigger the geographic area requiring network coverage, the more transceiver stations need to be built and operated. There can be set up and maintenance costs, demand issues, environmental degradation issues, and other issues that limit the size and types of areas that can or cannot be covered. This is why you might suddenly lose the ability to send or receive data on your device in particular locations; you may be out of range of a transceiver station for your cellular network or the signal may be unable to reach you. Cellular networks can be contrasted with satellite networks, which transmit data through satellites orbiting the Earth. Unlike the relatively short range of transceiver stations and the large number of transceiver stations required to create a large cellular network, satellites can beam coverage to very large and even hard to reach areas, but satellites have traditionally still been much more costly to build, put in orbit, and maintain. Figure 18.1 provides a visualization of a cellular network and how cellular networks work together to enable connectivity/data exchange.

4G, LTE, and other cellular networks

The "G" in cellular network symbols stands for "generation"; subsequent generations (or increments) of the "G" symbol (e.g. from 1G and 2G to 3G and 4G to 5G and 6G) represent breakthroughs or expansions in the minimum speed, connectivity, and reliability of cellular networks as set by the International Telecommunication

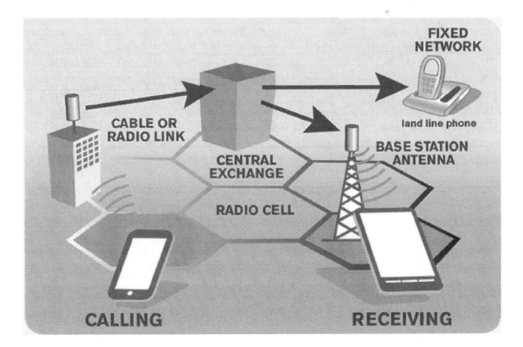

Figure 18.1 How cellular phones work[1]

Union Radiocommunication (or ITU-R) Sector. For example, while 1G enabled us to be able to talk to each other over a cellular network, 2G expanded the functionality to include the ability to send text messages and limited MMS (i.e. multimedia messages); 3G further expanded this functionality to include web pages, music, and videos. However, speeds were very slow relative to, say, a broadband internet connection; 4G and LTE extended cellular network speeds to more closely resemble the speed of a broadband internet connection. This enabled users to enjoy rich experiences on their mobile devices including streaming video, high-quality music, and multimedia apps – and all almost instantaneously, without long buffering times. The ITU-R set standards for 4G in early 2008, requiring any cellular service referred to as 4G to have peak speeds of at least 100 megabits per second for high-mobility communication (e.g. moving cars and trains) and 1,000 megabits per second (or 1 gigabit per second) for stationary or low-motion communication (e.g. walking or not moving). These standards represented a significant leap over existing speeds so that, despite significant investments, the cellular industry could not reach 4G standards. However, a new technology standard known as LTE (Long Term Evolution), first proposed in Japan in 2004, had evolved from proposal to successful trials to adoption in 2010. LTE became an international standard by 2011–2012. Although quite short of 4G standards, LTE offered significant improvements on 3G speeds.[2] Due to the significant improvements on 3G and perhaps also due to the challenges attaining 4G standards, the ITU-R allowed LTE to be called 4G. Cellular networks varied in whether they labeled their LTE offerings 4G LTE or just 4G. But in either case, it wasn't true 4G, as it wasn't up to the original ITU-R standards. Over time, improvements in LTE technology surprisingly resulted in LTE-Advanced (LTE-A) and LTE-Advanced Pro reaching and even surpassing the true 4G standards.

5G and 6G cellular networks

As good as 4G technology has been, advancements in IoT technologies and exponential growth in the number of connected things have pushed it to its limits (e.g. as of 2020 there were an estimated 20 billion connected devices). Fortunately, 5G technology has been in development and, as early as 2018 and 2019, most major economies had trialed or already started providing 5G network services. It is expected that 5G will have significantly greater capacity, with initial speeds of between 10 and 20 times faster than 4G, and potentially up to 100 times faster than 4G.[3] Among other things, it is expected to have greater latency (the time required for data to travel from one point to another) of 1 to 4 milliseconds, be more energy efficient, be able to support up to a million connected devices per square foot, and be able to work at greater speeds. It is expected to be a major step toward satisfying the connectivity requirements of advancements in technologies like the cloud, IoT, big data, artificial intelligence, augmented/mixed reality, and robotics/drones.[4] As 5G is being rolled out and improved, research on 6G has already begun to explore the types of use cases that won't be possible with 5G and that will require a 6G network. Such use cases identified to date include solving remaining accessibility problems (e.g. connecting all people, information, and things in ultra–real time irrespective of location), and improving communication between humans and things (e.g. ultra–high definition VR/AR/MR, ultra–real-time communication with things). Use cases also include an expanded communication environment (e.g. high-rise buildings, remote geographic areas, the sky, underwater, and space will all become high activity/communication areas), and increasingly sophisticated cyber-physical and bio–digital fusion (e.g. greater integration of cyberspace with human bodily functions, human thought, and human action).[5]

GPS III or GPS block III and low Earth orbit (LEO) satellites

GPS and GPS III and other global navigation satellite systems (GNSS)

The Global Positioning System (GPS) is a constellation of space-based satellites that orbit the Earth at an altitude of about 20,000 km. At regular intervals, the satellites transmit information about their position and the current time. These signals travel at the speed of light and can be intercepted by GPS receivers. GPS receivers can use the intercepted signals to provide precise location, navigation, and timing information. How do GPS receivers do this? At any point or location on the Earth, there is line visibility to at least four GPS satellites.[6] A GPS receiver is able to intercept the signal from each of these four satellites and use the signals to calculate how far away each satellite is (based on how long it takes for the signal to travel from the satellite to the receiver at the speed of light).[7,8] Once it knows how far away at least three of the satellites are, the GPS receiver can use a process called trilateration to pinpoint its exact location (or your location).[9] We use GPS almost daily, sometimes without even realizing it. We use it for directions, to provide pilots with real-time positioning information, to survey, to track the movement of things, for live recording, for military purposes, to avoid collision in shipping, for self-driving cars, and much more.[10] The GPS system was originally developed and is owned by the US Department of Defense, although anyone with a receiver can use it. But it isn't the only system used around the world. Europe has a similar system known as Galileo; China's system is known as BeiDou; and Russia's system is known as GLONASS (*Globalnaya navigatsionnaya sputnikovaya sistema*). Even though the term GPS is often used to refer to all these systems, GPS is technically only the US system; the better name to refer to all systems is global navigation satellite system (GNSS).[11]

GPS III refers to the next generation of GPS satellites designed and built by Lockheed Martin, with the first of these satellites launched in December 2018.[12] GPS III brings significant improvements in pinpointing location accuracy[13] (e.g. from within 3 meters to within 1 meter), significant improvements in signal strength (e.g. signals will be much easier to pick up even in obstructed areas like tree canopies and inside buildings), it brings significantly improved security and reliability (e.g. GPS signals will be much harder to maliciously or accidentally jam/obstruct), and it brings improved interoperability with other global navigation satellite systems. Advancements in GPS III hold a range of benefits for organizations including improved user experience, product innovation, and new market potential – as long as device makers have devices available to take full advantage of GPS III.[14] GPS III is anticipated to be fully capable by mid-2023 and to improve when another ten satellites go into orbit between 2026 and 2034.[15] Other global navigation satellite systems have also been working on upgrading their systems.

Low Earth orbit (LEO) satellites

Low Earth orbit satellites (or LEO) are satellites that orbit the Earth at a much lower altitude (about 400–2,000 km),[18] unlike conventional satellites that orbit at about 36,000 km and GNSS that orbit at about 20,000–26,000 km. There are several benefits to a low orbit, including better signal strength and less power to transmit the signal (as the satellite is near the Earth), lower propagation delay (good for applications requiring real-time data), and lower-priced satellite equipment. There are also disadvantages, including more satellites being needed to cover the Earth (as the lower a satellite is, the less area it can cover), regular maintenance requirement (due to having to continuously travel through the much denser atmosphere), and shorter life span. One aim of LEO satellites is to reach the more than 4 billion people who are without high-speed internet due to cellular infrastructure being too expensive.[19] Companies such as OneWeb are working on provision of Wi-Fi hotspots connected to their LEO satellites.[20] LEO satellites also offer new scientific exploration opportunities at significantly reduced cost (e.g. miniature satellite versions weighing between 1 g and 100 kg are now possible).[21] On the IoT front, LEO satellites offer a way to connect "things" no matter where they are on Earth. Their lower orbits (therefore higher detail) also enhance remote sensing capabilities of smart devices. Companies such as Iridium and Globalstar recently launched LEO satellites (64 and 24 satellites, respectively); Amazon intends to launch 3,236 LEO satellites to provide internet to areas without it; and SpaceX has sought permission to launch more than 30,000 satellites.[22,23] LPWAN technology companies like Semtech, the owner of LoRa technology, are experimenting with LEO satellite LoRa connectivity that covers the whole planet. Iridium has been working with Amazon to develop a satellite cloud-based solution with global coverage for IoT applications.[24] Figures 18.2 and 18.3 show the different types of orbits and their different uses.

NBIoT, LTE Cat-M1, LoRaWAN, and other low-power wide-area network (LPWAN) technologies

Devices using cellular networks use a lot of power to send a lot of data over medium distances, which is why they require constant power access or regular recharging. But

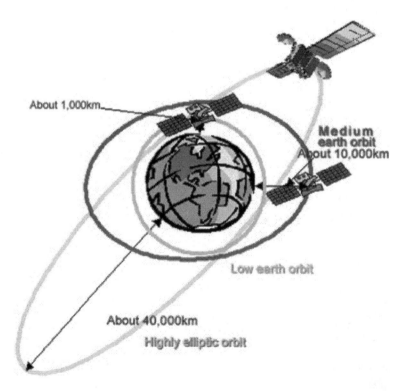

Figure 18.2 Low Earth orbit (LEO), medium Earth orbit (MEO), and geostationary orbit (GEO)[16,17]

Type of Use	Type of Orbit / Type of Satellite
Astronomy	Several orbits
Climate, weather forecast	LEO, GEO
Communications	GEO(low latitude), Molniya(high latitude)
Earth observation	GEO, LEO, global coverage
Global positioning, navigation	LEO, MEO, global coverage
Military	Several LEO orbits
Space environment	Several, including sounding rockets
Space station	LEO
Technology development	Several orbits

Note: Low Earth orbit(LEO), medium altitude Earth orbit(MEO), geostationary orbit(GEO).

Figure 18.3 Types of satellite or orbit, and what they are used for[25]

many IoT devices only need to send a little bit of data over much longer distances, they cannot be regularly recharged, and thus they need to make the most of battery life. Low-power wide-area (LPWA) and low-power wide-area network (LPWAN) technologies provide a solution to this. They are a type of wireless technology that allows for data to be sent at a low bit rate (e.g. 0.3–50 Kbps) over long distances (e.g. a few kilometers to tens of kilometers).[26] The technology for this type of network enables very low power consumption, so that an IoT device can use a standard AA battery for many years (contrast this to a battery-powered device using a cellular network; such a device typically needs to be recharged daily).[27] LPWA technologies' simpler, lightweight protocols translate into less complex/less costly hardware, less complex/less costly infrastructure requirements, and thus significantly reduced IoT connectivity costs (e.g. cents per device per month, as opposed to tens of dollars per month).[28] Thus the technologies provide the ability for IoT devices to transfer data to each other over significantly longer distances, at significantly lower power consumption, and significantly lower cost. This makes the idea of an organization connecting hundreds, thousands, or even hundreds of thousands of devices a much more realistic proposition. There is a range of LPWA and LPWAN technologies including LTE M, NBIoT, and LoRaWAN. These typically vary on dimensions such transmission speed, power consumption, latency, availability, mobility, extent of coverage, transmission distance, number of devices that can be connected per unit area, and cost. The right technology for an organization will depend on what the organization's use case is.

NBIoT

The narrowband internet of things (NBIoT) is a low-bandwidth LPWA cellular technology standard (low bandwidth meaning that very small amounts of data can be sent per second). NBIoT is classified as a 5G technology and has the proven security and privacy features of LTE mobile networks.[29,30] Key strengths of NBIoT over other standards include its super-low device power consumption, its capacity to have a massive number of devices connected per unit area, and its potential for ultra-cost-efficiency (it eliminates the need to aggregate sensor data before sending it to the primary server, thus reducing hardware costs).[31,32] Limitations of NBIoT include it being more suited to static devices than mobile ones, its low latency and its low speed (e.g. 26–159 Kbps). In fact, although low device power consumption is a strength of NBIoT, when large amounts of data have to be sent NBIoT can end up using more power, as a device has to be active for a longer period of time.[33,34] Given its current strengths and limitations, NBIoT has been viewed as being suited for use cases involving static devices that send minimal data and do so infrequently, thus maximizing battery life.[35] Examples of such use cases include smart power meters and battery-powered smart locks.

LTE-M

LTE-M (also commonly referred to as LTE Machine Type Communication [LTE MTC], enhanced Machine Type Communication [eMTC], and LTE Cat-M1) is another cellular LPWA standard for IoT and machine-to-machine communication.[36,37] Although NBIoT is stronger than LTE-M on the low device power consumption dimension, LTE-M is stronger than NBIoT on mobility, speed (e.g. up to six times that of NBIoT), and latency dimensions.[38] LTE-M is also backward compatible with existing 4G LTE networks, making it more likely than NBIoT to be available/accessible in certain parts of the world.[39] LTE-M is seen as being suited for use cases involving mobility, sending lots of data, and doing so frequently. LTE-M use cases include wearable devices, connectivity with devices in thick walls or deep basements, and asset tracking/monitoring.

LoRa/LoRaWAN

LoRa (long range) is an LPWAN technology, and LoRaWAN is a network protocol using LoRa that connects things (e.g. sensors) to the internet to enable bidirectional communication.[40,41] LoRa technology's key strengths are its long-range transmission (2–15 km) and low device power consumption, extending battery life by up to 10 years.[42] One of its limitations is the amount of data that can be sent per second (0.3–5 Kbps). As with NBIoT, this data transmission rate can result in high device power consumption if large amounts of data need to be sent. LoRa and LoRaWAN use cases include fleet tracking, livestock tracking, and sensors in very hard to reach places (e.g. in concrete or far away).[43,44]

Other LPWAN technologies

Other LPWAN technologies include Signfox and EC-GSM-IoT (extended coverage–GSM–internet of things). EC-GSM-IoT works over 4G, 3G, and even 2G mobile networks. This makes EC-GSM-IoT technology valuable in parts of the world that don't have access to the latest cellular networks. Still other technologies include Weightless, Wize, and Chirp.

NFC, Smart Bluetooth, iBeacon, and other communication protocols

What is NFC and how does it work?

NFC is short for near-field communication. It is a short-range wireless data transmission technology based on older RFID electromagnetic induction ideas. It enables two electronic devices to communicate with each other using electromagnetic waves when brought within 2–10 cm of each other.[45,46,47] NFC use cases include contactless payments (e.g. pay wave, pay pass, Apple Pay),[48] access control[49] (e.g. digital keys for smart locks), identification of objects via NFC tag scanning, speeding up pairing of Bluetooth objects, improved product authentication via scanning of NFC tags, provision of product on NFC tags, proof of compliance by checking if people with an NFC tag came in proximity with an area they were meant to inspect, and much more.[50] NFC technology enables devices or tags, or other things embedded with an NFC chip, to receive and/or transmit information that can be used in many different areas including customer engagement, product and supply chain management, marketing, asset management, and workflow management. Key benefits of NFC over similar technologies like Bluetooth or Wi-Fi is its much lower power consumption and ability to operate without a power source. A device with an NFC chip can create a magnetic field that is able to power or induce current in another NFC device, thus enabling that device to transmit data even if it has no power source of its own. This is referred to as inductive coupling. This is also how wireless chargers work (e.g. a charging device creates an electromagnetic field that induces charge in a wire connected to a rechargeable battery). An active NFC device (one with a power source and capable of both sending and receiving data, such as a smartphone) can interact with another active device so both can send and receive data. An active device can also interact with a passive device (one without a power source and only capable of transmitting data, such as an NFC tag or a tag embedded with an NFC chip). In this case, the active device powers the passive device (see Figure 18.4).

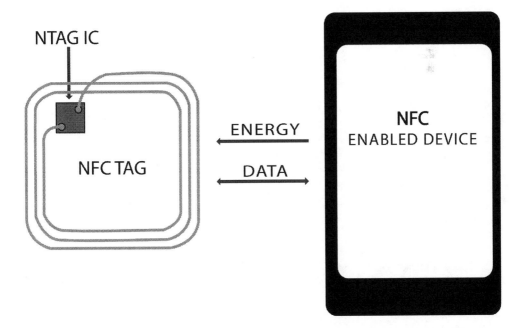

Figure 18.4 An NFC-enabled phone sets up a current, the NFC tag receives the "induced current," and – recognizing it is a valid signal – offers connection to the phone and begins data transfer[51]

NFC chips transmit data at up to 424 Kbps, which is significantly less than Bluetooth's 2.1 Mbps, but this is still adequate for sending text, photos, and even audio. NFC is also considered high security given the need for devices to be right next to each other. This limits the opportunity for others to eavesdrop or intercept the data transfer. Other benefits, as far as access control, include limiting the ability for people to lend their access to others or have it stolen (e.g. if NFC access is via a smartphone). Regarding efficiency, smartphone-enabled NFC access minimizes instances of people forgetting their keys or keycards (assuming they are less likely to forget their phone at home).

What are Bluetooth 5.0 and Bluetooth Low Energy (BLE), and how do they work?

Traditional or classic Bluetooth (Bluetooth 1.0 to 3.0) was often criticized for the difficulty in pairing devices and maintaining pairing, for slow transmission speeds, and for high device battery power consumption. Bluetooth 4.0 (also referred to as Bluetooth Smart or Smart Bluetooth) evolved as a response, offering high speed and low energy versions or categories of the technology. The low energy category (Bluetooth Low Energy, BLE, or Bluetooth LE) was designed for lower data rates (e.g. 1 Mbps) but much lower energy consumption. It allows Bluetooth devices to "sleep" while idle and only "wake up" or initiate Bluetooth functionality when data transmission is initiated. By reducing power consumption, BLE technology enables Bluetooth devices to operate for months or even years on a single coin cell battery. Reducing data transmission rates to lengthen battery life means that BLE is not suitable for devices that require a continuous stream of data (e.g. wireless headphones, speakers, radios). But the reduced transmission rate can work for devices that only need to send small bits of data or send data infrequently (e.g. wearable devices, periodic monitoring devices). Thus these devices can benefit from longer battery life without a compromised ability to send data. BLE-enabled devices are capable of multi-point data transmission and coworking with different Bluetooth specifications (e.g. earlier versions of Bluetooth or Bluetooth high speed).[52] So, a device with both BLE and a high-speed Bluetooth classic installed (Dual Mode Bluetooth) can switch between high-speed or low-energy uses as the situation demands. For example, if the device is a smartphone, BLE can take over the less intensive data tasks to preserve battery life, and classic Bluetooth can take over for tasks that require continuous connectivity or large data transmission.[53] As another example, if device is a sphygmomanometer (blood pressure measuring device), it can use BLE to record blood pressure status and then use classic Bluetooth to transmit images or other larger data.[54]

As at the time of writing this book, Bluetooth 5.0 was the latest evolution in the Bluetooth standard. This version doubles the data transmission rate, making audio transmission possible and edging closer toward video. It quadruples the transmission range from 50 meters to 200 meters, which is enough to cover all the devices in a house or office. It enables the selection of 2 Mbps, 1 Mbps, 500 Kbps, and 125 Kbps transmission rates, so device use can be optimized for data rate and/or data range. Finally, Bluetooth 5.0 brings eight times the broadcast capacity.[55] The improvements in data transmission rate, range, and broadcast capability expand the longevity and connection capabilities of IoT devices both indoors and outdoors.[56]

What is beacon technology and how does it work?

Beacons are small devices that use BLE to send you data or content based on where you are (e.g. information about a sale at your favorite store as you walk into a shopping center).[57,58] Beacons are usually mounted or stuck in the particular location targeted users are likely to pass, and thus where location-based content is best served for the particular purpose it is aimed at. Apps on a user's phone pick up the beacon signals and execute response actions (e.g. you might receive a push notification from your favorite store's app, if it is installed on your phone, offering 50% off select items if you visit the store today).[59] Beacon technology has been seen as ideal for indoor settings where GPS can't reach. Beacon use cases range from location-based or proximity marketing (e.g. Best Buy serves up different ads to customers depending on which section of the store they are in).[60] Access control (e.g. smart locks that automatically unlock when an authorized user walks up to the front door), automated check-in (e.g. once a guest passes the front desk or arrives in their room), location-based content delivery (e.g. delivering information or other resources like emergency warnings, PowerPoint slides, directions), resource tracking (e.g. people's presence in certain locations or availability of, assets), ticketing/passes (e.g. tickets or passes purchased on your phone automatically present themselves as you walk in saving search and presentation time), and much more.[61] iBeacon is the Apple standard version of beacons first introduced in 2013.

Google and reflect

Digital Technology	Common Terminology
Cellular networks	Hz/MHz/GHz, cellular bandwidth, cellular network latency, 4G LTE, 5G New Radio (5G NR), eMBB, mMTC, URLLC, 10-nanometer chip, 7-nanometer chip, cloud radio access network (cRAN), mmWave spectrum, 5G massive machine-type communication (mMTC), cellular network capacity, MIMO, network slicing, small-cell densification, licensed spectrum, unlicensed spectrum, 3GGP, carrier aggregation, cell tower, evolved packet system
GPS III and LEO satellites	GPS accuracy, GPS bearing, GPS coordinate systems, GPS navigation, NAVSTAR, Wide Area Augmentation System (WAAS), medium Earth orbit (MEO), geosynchronous equatorial orbit (GEO), picosatellite, microsatellite, minisatellite
LPWAN	Cellular LPWAN, cellular LPWA, EC-GSM-IoT, IoT stack, IoT gateway
NFC, Bluetooth Smart, and Beacons	NFC device, RFID, inductive coupling, proximity coupling device (PCD), host controller interface (HCI), inductive coupling, active NFC device, NFC tag, NFC card emulation, NFC encoding, ferrite sheet, passive NFC device, NFC forum, NFC-F, NFC-V, Bluetooth LE, Bluejacking,[62] Bluesnarfing, Bluespamming, Bluebugging, Bluecasting, Bluetooth douche, Bluetooth pairing, Bluetooth virus, Bluetooth personal area network, active slave broadcast (ASB), Bluetooth device address, Bluetooth host

Example tools and vendors

Digital Technology	Tools and Vendors
Cellular networks	Verizon 4G LTE, T-Mobile HSPA+, AT&T 5G+, Telstra 5G, Optus 5G, Deutsche Telekom, EE, Vodafone, China Mobile, SK Telecom
GPS III and LEO satellites	Else Astrocast LEO constellation for IoT communications, OneWeb satellites, Space Exploration Technologies Corp satellites, Iridium satellites, Virgin Orbit satellites, Amazon satellites, Eutelsat Communications SA satellites, Myriota
LPWA and LPWAN	Ingenu RPMA, Sigfox 0G network, LoRa Alliance, Weightless (SIG), Wize, Chirp, Huawei NBIoT, Ericsson cellular IoT, Vodafone NBIoT, LEAPIN Digital Keys' Smart Locks, iMETOS NB IoT
NFC, Bluetooth Smart and Beacons	Broadcom Topaz chip, DESFire MIFARE DESFire, NXP MIFARE Classic, Texas Instruments Bluetooth products, Nordic Semiconductor Bluetooth products, Silicon Labs Bluetooth products, Quuppa Bluetooth products, u-blox Bluetooth products, UnSeen Technologies Bluetooth products, Fanstel Bluetooth products, Laird Connectivity Bluetooth products

Discussion questions

Cellular Networks

1   Explain in plain language how a cellular network works.
2   What could you do with 2G that was not possible with 1G?
3   What can you do with 5G that you cannot do with 4G?
4   What is an example of a hospitality and leisure industry product innovation opportunity presented by 5G and 6G?
5   What is an example of a hospitality and leisure industry business model innovation opportunity presented by 5G and 6G?
6   What are the potential financial costs and risks of adopting 5G too early? What are the risks of adopting it too late?

GPS III and LEO Satellites

1   What is an example of a hospitality and leisure industry product innovation opportunity presented by GPS III or LEO satellites?
2   What is an example of a hospitality and leisure industry business model innovation opportunity presented by GPS III or LEO satellites?

LPWA and LPWAN

1   Which LPWA or LPWAN technology would you use if you frequently took guests on remote tours and relied on IoT devices to improve the guest experience?
2   Which LPWA or LPWAN is likely to be the most widely accepted, and why?

NFC, Bluetooth Smart, and Beacons

1   What is an example of a hospitality and leisure industry product innovation opportunity presented by NFC, Bluetooth Smart, or Beacons?
2   What is an example of a hospitality and leisure industry business model innovation opportunity presented by NFC, Bluetooth Smart, or Beacons?

Notes

1 Telstra. (2014). Mobile Base Stations and Health – Consumer Advice. Retrieved June 21, 2020, from Telstra.com website: www.telstra.com.au/consumer-advice/eme/base-stations

2 Segan, S. (2015, February 10). 3G vs. 4G: What's the Difference? PCMag. www.pcmag.com/news/3g-vs-4g-whats-the-difference

3 jameswhyte. (2018, March 14). What is the Difference between 4G and . . . Just Ask Gemalto. Retrieved from www.justaskgemalto.com/en/difference-4g-5g/

4 BBC News. (2020). What is 5G and What Will It Mean for You? Retrieved from www.bbc.com/news/business-44871448

5 NTT DOCOMO, INC. (2020). 5G Evolution and 6G. (n.d.). Retrieved March 2, 2020, from www.nttdocomo.co.jp/english/binary/pdf/corporate/technology/whitepaper_6g/DOCOMO_6G_White_PaperEN_20200124.pdf

6 Physics.Org. (2020). How Does GPS Work? Retrieved from www.physics.org/article-questions.asp?id=55

7 Physics.Org. (2020). How Does GPS Work? Retrieved from www.physics.org/article-questions.asp?id=55

8 Dempster, A. (2013, March 7). Explainer: What is GPS? The Conversation. Retrieved from https://theconversation.com/explainer-what-is-gps-12248

9 Physics.Org. (2020). How Does GPS Work? Retrieved from www.physics.org/article-questions.asp?id=55

10 Dempster, A. (2013, March 7). Explainer: What is GPS? The Conversation. Retrieved from https://theconversation.com/explainer-what-is-gps-12248

11 Dempster, A. (2013, March 7). Explainer: What is GPS? The Conversation. Retrieved from https://theconversation.com/explainer-what-is-gps-12248

12 Pappalardo, J. (2018, December 26). USAF's Next-Gen GPS Satellites Will Be a Huge Upgrade . . . Eventually. Popular Mechanics. Retrieved from www.popularmechanics.com/space/satellites/a25683704/gps-iii/

13 Lockheed Martin. (2018). Unbelievable Accuracy: GPS III. Retrieved from www.lockheedmartin.com/en-us/news/features/history/gps-iii.html

14 Cozzens, T. (2019, January 9). GPS III Finally Aloft, Benefits on the Way. GPS World. Retrieved from www.gpsworld.com/gps-iii-finally-aloft-benefits-on-the-way/

15 Cozzens, T. (2019, January 9). GPS III Finally Aloft, Benefits on the Way. GPS World. Retrieved from www.gpsworld.com/gps-iii-finally-aloft-benefits-on-the-way/

16 Borthomieu, Y. (2014). Satellite Lithium-Ion Batteries. Lithium-Ion Batteries, 311–344. https://doi.org/10.1016/b978-0-444-59513-3.00014-5

17 Meseguer, J., Pérez-Grande, I., & Sanz-Andrés, A. (2012). Keplerian Orbits. *Spacecraft Thermal Control*, 39–57.

18 Allain, R. (2015, September 15). What's So Special About Low Earth Orbit? WIRED. Retrieved from www.wired.com/2015/09/whats-special-low-earth-orbit/

19 Ritchie, G. (2019, August 9). Why Low-Earth Orbit Satellites are the New Space Race. Bloomberg. Retrieved from www.bloomberg.com/news/articles/2019-08-09/why-low-earth-orbit-satellites-are-the-new-space-race-quicktake

20 Ritchie, G. (2019, August 9). Why Low-Earth Orbit Satellites are the New Space Race. Bloomberg. Retrieved from www.bloomberg.com/news/articles/2019-08-09/why-low-earth-orbit-satellites-are-the-new-space-race-quicktake

21 Avnet Silica. (2019, June 27). Low-Earth-Orbit Satellites and IoT. Avnet Silica. Retrieved from www.avnet.com/wps/portal/silica/resources/article/low-earth-orbit-satellites-and-iot/

22 Ritchie, G. (2019, August 9). Why Low-Earth Orbit Satellites are the New Space Race. Bloomberg. Retrieved from www.bloomberg.com/news/articles/2019-08-09/why-low-earth-orbit-satellites-are-the-new-space-race-quicktake

23 Blackman, J. (2019, November 4). What is LEO, and How Will LEO Satellites Transform the IoT Sector? Enterprise IoT Insights. Retrieved from https://enterpriseiotinsights.com/20191104/channels/fundamentals/what-is-leo-and-how-will-leo-satellites-transform-iot

24 Blackman, J. (2019, November 4). What is LEO, and How Will LEO Satellites Transform the IoT Sector? Enterprise IoT Insights. Retrieved from https://enterpriseiotinsights.com/20191104/channels/fundamentals/what-is-leo-and-how-will-leo-satellites-transform-iot

25 Meseguer, J., Pérez-Grande, I., & Sanz-Andrés, A. (2012). Keplerian Orbits. *Spacecraft Thermal Control*, 39–57.

26 Wedd, M. (2018, September 26). What is LPWANs and the LoRaWAN Open Standard? IoT for All. Retrieved from www.iotforall.com/what-is-lpwan-lorawan/

27 Upale, A. (2018). LTE Cat M1 vs. NB-IoT vs. LoRa – Comparing LPWANs. Semiconductor store.Com. Retrieved from www.semiconductorstore.com/blog/2018/LTE-Cat-M1-vs-NB-IoT-vs-LoRa-Comparing-LPWANs-Symmetry-Blog/3496/

28 Wedd, M. (2018, September 26). What is LPWANs and the LoRaWAN Open Standard? IoT for All. Retrieved from www.iotforall.com/what-is-lpwan-lorawan/

29 Hwang, Y. (2020, January 17). Cellular IoT Explained – NB-IoT vs. LTE-M vs. 5G and More. IoT For All. Retrieved from www.iotforall.com/cellular-iot-explained-nb-iot-vs-lte-m/

30 Øyvann, S. (2017, January 26). From Parking to Farming, Applications for NB-IoT are Heading Out into the Real World. ZDNet. Retrieved from www.zdnet.com/article/from-parking-to-farming-applications-for-nb-iot-are-heading-out-into-the-real-world/

31 Hwang, Y. (2020, January 17). Cellular IoT Explained – NB-IoT vs. LTE-M vs. 5G and More. IoT For All. Retrieved from www.iotforall.com/cellular-iot-explained-nb-iot-vs-lte-m/

32 Gemalto.Com. (2020). Narrowband IoT Overview (NB-IoT). Retrieved from www.gemalto.com/iot/resources/innovation-technology/nb-iot

33 Hwang, Y. (2020, January 17). Cellular IoT Explained – NB-IoT vs. LTE-M vs. 5G and More. IoT For All. Retrieved from www.iotforall.com/cellular-iot-explained-nb-iot-vs-lte-m/

34 Øyvann, S. (2017, January 26). From Parking to Farming, Applications for NB-IoT are Heading Out into the Real World. ZDNet. Retrieved from www.zdnet.com/article/from-parking-to-farming-applications-for-nb-iot-are-heading-out-into-the-real-world/

35 Øyvann, S. (2017, January 26). From Parking to Farming, Applications for NB-IoT are Heading Out into the Real World. ZDNet. Retrieved from www.zdnet.com/article/from-parking-to-farming-applications-for-nb-iot-are-heading-out-into-the-real-world/

36 Hwang, Y. (2020, January 17). Cellular IoT Explained – NB-IoT vs. LTE-M vs. 5G and More. IoT For All. Retrieved from www.iotforall.com/cellular-iot-explained-nb-iot-vs-lte-m/

37 SierraWireless. (2018, April 3). LTE-M vs. NB-IoT: Make the Best Choice for Your Needs. Sierra-Wireless. Retrieved from www.sierrawireless.com/iot-blog/iot-blog/2018/04/lte-m-vs-nb-iot/

38 Hwang, Y. (2020, January 17). Cellular IoT Explained – NB-IoT vs. LTE-M vs. 5G and More. IoT For All. Retrieved from www.iotforall.com/cellular-iot-explained-nb-iot-vs-lte-m/

39 SierraWireless. (2018, April 3). LTE-M vs. NB-IoT: Make the Best Choice for Your Needs. Sierra-Wireless. Retrieved from www.sierrawireless.com/iot-blog/iot-blog/2018/04/lte-m-vs-nb-iot/

40 Wedd, M. (2018, September 26). What is LPWANs and the LoRaWAN Open Standard? IoT for All. Retrieved from www.iotforall.com/what-is-lpwan-lorawan/

41 I-SCOOP. (2015). LoRa and LoRaWAN: The Technologies, Ecosystems, Use Cases and Market. Retrieved from www.i-scoop.eu/internet-of-things-guide/lpwan/iot-network-lora-lorawan/

42 Maker.io Team. (2016, August 10). Introduction to LoRa Technology – The Game Changer. Digikey.Com; Maker.io. Retrieved from www.digikey.com/en/maker/blogs/introduction-to-lora-technology

43 Wedd, M. (2018, September 26). What is LPWANs and the LoRaWAN Open Standard? IoT for All. Retrieved from www.iotforall.com/what-is-lpwan-lorawan/

44 Pike, J. (2017, August 21). Understanding LoRa WAN Basics: A Non-Technical Explanation. Metova. Retrieved from https://metova.com/understanding-lora-basics-a-non-technical-explanation/

45 Triggs, R. (2019, June 30). What is NFC and How Does It Work. Android Authority. Retrieved from www.androidauthority.com/what-is-nfc-270730/

46 Joshi, C. (2019). What is NFC & How Does It Work? Beaconstac.Com. Retrieved from https://blog.beaconstac.com/2019/05/what-is-nfc-and-how-does-it-work/

47 Triggs, R. (2019, June 30). What is NFC and How Does It Work. Android Authority. Retrieved from www.androidauthority.com/what-is-nfc-270730/

48 Profis, S. (2014, September 9). Everything You Need to Know about NFC and Mobile Payments. CNET. Retrieved from www.cnet.com/how-to/how-nfc-works-and-mobile-payments/

49 Saritag. (2019). NFC Tag Authentication Explained. Seritag Learn NFC. Seritag.Com. Retrieved from https://learn.seritag.com/tech/nfc-tag-authentication-explained

50 Ratna, S. (2019). Best Use Cases of NFC to Implement in 2019: Proximity marketing without an app. Beaconstac.Com. Retrieved from https://blog.beaconstac.com/2019/01/proximity-marketing-without-an-app-best-use-cases-of-nfc-to-implement-in-2019/

51 Camperi, A. (2018). How to Use an NFC Reader. Retrieved June 21, 2020, from Getkisi.com website: www.getkisi.com/lessons/how-to-use-an-nfc-reader

52 Allion Labs. (2012). The Next Bluetooth Wave: High Speed & Low Energy Technology. Retrieved from www.allion.com/the-next-bluetooth-wave-high-speed-low-energy-technology/

53 Nguyen, A. (2018). When Would You Have BOTH Bluetooth Classic and Low Energy? Semi conductorstore.Com. Retrieved from www.semiconductorstore.com/blog/2018/When-Would-You-Have-BOTH-Bluetooth-Classic-and-Low-Energy-Symmetry-Blog/3110

54 Technical Direct (an Allion Labs site). (2012). The Next Bluetooth Wave: High Speed & Low Energy Technology. Retrieved from www.technical-direct.com/en/the-next-bluetooth-wave-high-speed-and-low-energy-technology/

55 Heukelman, C. (2017). Bluetooth 5 versus Bluetooth 4.2, What's the Difference? Semiconductor store.Com. Retrieved from www.semiconductorstore.com/blog/2017/Bluetooth-5-versus-Bluetooth-4-2-whats-the-difference/2080

56 Heukelman, C. (2017). Bluetooth 5 versus Bluetooth 4.2, What's the Difference? Semiconductor store.Com. Retrieved from www.semiconductorstore.com/blog/2017/Bluetooth-5-versus-Bluetooth-4-2-whats-the-difference/2080

57 Ranger, S. (2014, June 10). What is Apple iBeacon? Here's What You Need to Know. ZDNet. Retrieved from www.zdnet.com/article/what-is-apple-ibeacon-heres-what-you-need-to-know/

58 Maycotte, H. O. (2015, September 1). Beacon Technology: The Where, What, Who, How and Why. Forbes. Retrieved from www.forbes.com/sites/homaycotte/2015/09/01/beacon-technology-the-what-who-how-why-and-where/#4fd0c53e1aaf

59 Ranger, S. (2014, June 10). What is Apple iBeacon? Here's What You Need to Know. ZDNet. Retrieved from www.zdnet.com/article/what-is-apple-ibeacon-heres-what-you-need-to-know/

60 Lighthouse.io. (2019). The Beginners Guide to Beacons. Retrieved from https://lighthouse.io/beginners-guide-to-beacons/beacon-use-cases/

61 Lighthouse.io. (2019). The Beginners Guide to Beacons. Retrieved from https://lighthouse.io/beginners-guide-to-beacons/beacon-use-cases/

62 PCMAG. (2020). Definition of Bluetooth Glossary. Retrieved from www.pcmag.com/encyclopedia/term/bluetooth-glossary

19 Blockchain and other distributed ledger technologies

Introduction

Blockchain and other distributed ledger technologies offer new tamper-proof ways to verify identity and ownership, to make near-instant payments without the need for the involvement of third parties, to store value (e.g. through cryptocurrency), to facilitate peer-to-peer fundraising and lending (e.g. ICOs and STOs), to automate the execution of contractual agreements and related workflows (e.g. via smart contracts), to improve auditability, to distribute data storage, and to do all of this more securely.[1,2] The transformative impact of blockchain technologies has been equated to the advent of the internet. As with early applications of the internet, the applications of blockchain technologies are just in their infancy and have much more potential for growth in breadth and impact on business and society. The business value of these expanding blockchain applications includes expanded opportunities for product innovation (e.g. companies offering new or enhanced products and services enabled by use of blockchain technologies), business model innovation (e.g. finding more efficient, effective and profitable ways to serve existing and/or new customers), operational efficiency (e.g. automating workflows, removing third parties and related costs, reducing downtime and errors), and customer access (e.g. being able to remotely serve billions of customers in developing economies who previously couldn't be served due to lack of bank accounts, identity verification mechanisms, and high third-party costs). The business value of blockchain applications also include risk mitigation (e.g. enhanced security, privacy and auditability from blockchain's sophisticated cryptography, distributed consensus, immutability, and ability to shard data so it does not exist in complete form on any one node), and social change (e.g. enhanced transparency may lead to changes in customer behaviors that businesses can capitalize on or may need to adapt to).[3,4,5,6,7,8] It is the responsibility of hospitality and leisure managers to understand the business value and use cases of blockchain technology, to safely explore and experiment with its adoption at their organizations, and to lead the investment and implementation of tested and proven blockchain adoption decisions. Abdicating this responsibility may result in their organizations being outdone by competitors who might have first mover advantage, or it may result in being disrupted by a technology that seemed far-fetched or not relevant to them (e.g. in the same way Borders got disrupted by the internet and internet companies).

Distributed ledger technology (DLT)

In contrast to an accounting ledger (such as a general ledger, purchase ledger, or sales ledger), a digital ledger is a digital file, collection of files, or a database (a database is an organized collection of data or files). In contrast to a centralized database (i.e. a database that exists in a fixed location, like a particular computer or a cloud location), a distributed ledger (also referred to as a shared ledger or distributed ledger technology [DLT]) is a database that exists in several locations and among several participants (e.g. sites, institutions, geographies, computers, devices).[9,10] The term distributed (also referred to as decentralized) refers to this existence across several locations. Being distributed, any additions or updates to the ledger (the collection of files or the database) are synchronized or copied to all participants' version of the ledger almost instantly (in seconds or minutes). But before any additions or updates can occur, they have to be agreed on and accepted by other participants (i.e. authorized, validated, and accepted). The process of agreeing is referred to as distributed ledger consensus or a consensus mechanism. It is facilitated by sophisticated algorithms. Because of this consensus mechanism, no centralized agent (e.g. a bank, a government, a corporation, a person) is needed to authorize, validate, and accept proposed updates.[11,12] A peer-to-peer network is required in order for the distributed ledger to exist in several locations and among several participants; this peer-to-peer network could be as simple as two computers being connected via USB or as complex as several computers being connected by a network infrastructure. Distributed ledgers are immutable, meaning that once ledger records are created, they cannot be deleted or altered – instead, other records are added to correct errors, omissions, or improvements (e.g. if the record was a transaction where a $100 purchase was made, but it was meant to be $80, then a $20 refund transaction is added rather than altering the original transaction). All records or files in a distributed ledger are date/time stamped and have a unique cryptographic signature. This provides a verifiable and auditable history of record creation and any subsequent updates.

Brought together, all these features of distributed ledgers (i.e. existing in several locations via a peer-to-peer network, consensus mechanism algorithms to facilitate updates, record immutability, date/time stamping and cryptographic signature) offer new levels of efficiency (e.g. minimizing or eliminating the need for centralized monitoring, authorization, and updating activities and related infrastructure) and new levels of security (e.g. due to the decentralized nature, immutability, cryptographic signatures, and auditability).[13] For example, regarding security, distributed ledgers ensure that the record of a financial transaction is near impossible to fake, create without permission, delete, modify, or hide. Not only would this be near impossible to achieve on every computer (or node) on the peer-to-peer network, but an incriminating auditable trail would more than likely eventually catch up with the instigator.

Blockchain

What it is and how it works

Blockchain is one type of distributed ledger that consists of blocks of data linked or "chained" together using high-end cryptography (cryptography is concerned with how to best convert information into unintelligible codes to prevent it being decoded and accessed by unauthorized people or entities).[14,15] Each block in a blockchain stores information or data (e.g. transaction information like date, purchaser, seller, or payment amount). Each block also has a code called a "hash" that is unique to the information stored in that block. Figure 19.1 shows the elements of a block. If the information stored in a block is modified in any way, the block's hash also changes to a different code that is unique to the modified or changed information. In addition to the information or data

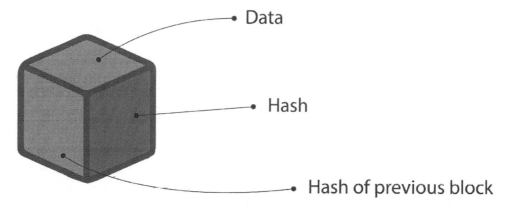

Figure 19.1 Each blockchain block contains some data, the hash of the block, and the hash of the previous block.

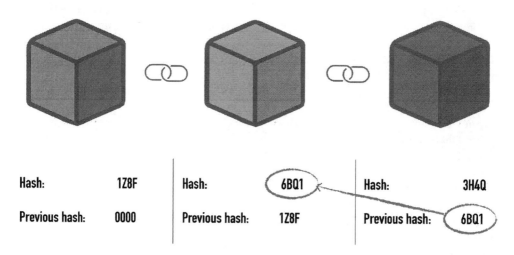

Figure 19.2 A chain of blocks, with each block other than the genesis block having the hash of the previous block.

stored in it, a block also contains a time stamp of when that information was created or edited. Each block also stores the hash (or unique code) of its previous block (see Figure 19.1). Before a new block can be added to the blockchain, it must correctly refer to the hash of the previous block; this cannot happen if the previous block has been modified, because its hash is different from what it should be. Storing the hash of its preceding block is how a block is linked or "chained" to preceding blocks. This link or chain between blocks is what makes blockchain so secure. Besides making tampering or modification of blocks nearly impossible (e.g. each must refer to the correct previous hash, which is copied across many nodes in the peer-to-peer network), blockchain provides a perfect audit trail or log of every change that occurred on the blockchain. Figure 19.2 shows a chain of blocks within blockchain, including the genesis block.

In addition to its linked block structure, blockchain functions with all the features of distributed ledgers (since it is a type of distributed ledger). That is, it operates over a peer-to-peer network, uses consensus mechanism algorithms to facilitate blockchain updates, uses date/time stamping and cryptographic signatures, and has immutable records). Blockchain technology platforms enable people to transact without the need for a central third party to assess and approve the authorization, validity, or security of the transaction (e.g. no need to pay, wait for, or trust the third party, no need to disclose personal information to the third party or be exposed to third-party risks), meaning cheap, instant, secure, anonymous and risk minimized transactions.

Other blockchain terminology

In addition to the distributed ledger and blockchain terminology discussed earlier, it is often difficult to discuss or read about blockchain without one or more of the following terminologies coming up.

Append-only data structure

This refers to the fact that you can only add new blocks to the blockchain, which then get chained to previous blocks; you can't alter or delete blocks once they've been added. This is one of the reasons blockchain is considered tamper proof and has an auditable history of record creation.

Permissionless vs. permissioned blockchain

A permissionless blockchain is one where anyone can join the network and perform certain actions on the network without requiring permission from anyone else on the network. In contrast, a permissioned network is one in which the network owner decides who can join a network and who can verify blocks. The consensus can be the same, or it can be tailored to the owner's preferences (e.g. it could be authority or credibility based).

Mining vs. miners

Mining is the process of verifying transactions to enable new blocks to be added to the blockchain network. Miners are blockchain nodes or participants that use their computers/computing power to perform this process. The process usually involves participants using mining programs for performing complex mathematical calculations to verify transactions and enable the creation of new blocks. In return, miners are usually paid a reward (e.g. on the Bitcoin blockchain, the reward is an amount of Bitcoin). Miners may compete to be the first to perform the mathematical calculations and verify the transaction, as only the first person to verify is paid the reward. It can cost miners money (e.g. cost of computing power or loss of deposit money they may pay to verify transactions in accordance with the rules). Some miners build a massive infrastructure (e.g. buildings or computing hardware and software) and hire large numbers of people to mine or verify blockchain transactions as a key source of income.

Proof of work

This is a widely used type of consensus algorithm for verifying transactions and adding new blocks to the blockchain. It involves miners competing with each other to be the first to solve the mathematical calculations required to verify transactions. Once the first miner solves the mathematical puzzle, it is broadcast to the network so other miners can confirm the solution is correct and so the block can be added to the blockchain. The first miner then receives a reward for being first to solve the mathematical puzzle and thus enable appending of the new block.

Public key vs. private key

To read or add data to the blockchain, you need a public key and a private key. A public key is like the address or location where the information is stored, and everyone knows its address. But although they may know where it is stored, it is encrypted (or locked) and can only be unlocked or decrypted with a private (or personal) key that authorizes reading or updating of the information stored in that location. A private key is what prevents other people from reading or updating your information and thus keeping it secure.

Genesis block

Also referred to as block zero, a genesis block is the first block created on a blockchain.

Smart contract

Smart contracts are legal contracts that self-execute on the blockchain once the terms and conditions of the contract have been satisfied. This is possible because the contract details (e.g. parties, terms and conditions) have already been agreed to and converted into self-executing code (e.g. if prospective purchasers meet the seller's criteria for sale of land plus the government's criteria for purchase of land and the seller pays the specified amount, then approve the transaction for title ownership over the land to the purchaser). This self-executing code sits on the blockchain, ready to be run or executed on the blockchain once triggered (by the satisfaction of the contract terms and condition). Once on the blockchain, a smart contract cannot be changed; it automatically happens without a third party once the triggering criteria are met. Being on the blockchain, the transaction can occur anonymously, it can occur without corruption, and it can occur without one or more of the parties coming back to muddy the meaning or interpretation of the contract terms.

Types of blockchain

There are four common types of blockchains, the types being differentiated by who can join, what type of access they can have, and how consensus is achieved. We provide a brief summary of each below.

Public blockchains

A public blockchain is a permissionless blockchain. It is public in that anyone can join this blockchain network with read and write permission; they do not need authorization from anyone else on the network. This is the main type of blockchain we have discussed so far, with features and advantages such as openness (anyone can join and view/add to it), distributed consensus, immutability (once a block is added, it can't be deleted or altered), scalability (existing on a large and ever-expanding network of nodes), and transparency. Disadvantages of public blockchains include difficulty changing the rules governing them and the risk that the blockchain can be compromised if the rules are not strictly enforced.

Private blockchains

A private blockchain is a permissioned blockchain, which is owned by an entity (e.g. a person, an organization or other group). That entity or its delegate decides who can access the blockchain, what type of access they can have (e.g. read, write, or audit), and how consensus will be achieved (e.g. who can mine and what rules apply). Private blockchains bring together some of the benefits of central control and some of the benefits of distributed ledgers, usually with aims such as reduced transaction cost, transaction efficiency, improved security, improved auditability, and the flexibility to change blockchain read, write, and audit rules. An example of a private or permissioned blockchain includes Hyperledger (a blockchain funded to enable industry collaboration for advancing blockchain-based distributed ledgers).

Consortium or federated blockchains

This type of blockchain is like a private blockchain, but instead of a single individual or company making all the decisions, a group of companies or their representative individuals make decisions collectively for the benefit of the whole blockchain network (e.g. decisions about who can access the blockchain, who can read/write to it, and what operating rules apply). Benefits of consortium or federated blockchains include pooling together of resources to establish and operate the blockchain network, better quality decisions from broader expertise of consortium members and representatives, and better security from curation of blockchain participants and their access rights. Examples of consortium blockchains include the R3 blockchain consortium (established as an invitation-only blockchain consortium for major banks like JP Morgan and Santander) and Energy Web Foundation (EWF; an enterprise grade blockchain for organizations in the energy industry including Mercados Electricos, FlexiDAO, Scytale Horizon, and Wirepas).

Hybrid blockchains

As their name indicates, hybrid blockchains aim to leverage the benefits of both public and private blockchains. Aspects of the network can be made private, so transactions with some types of stakeholders or things are permissioned, whereas other aspects of the network are public or open to anyone. For example, Facebook's proposed cryptocurrency Libra may need a hybrid blockchain composed of an open consumer-facing network and a private blockchain network for banks backing the currency.

Blockchain applications and use cases

Although many blockchain and other distributed ledger technology applications are still in their early stages, the applications are broadening rapidly and more and more applications are maturing.[16] For example, applications of blockchain technologies to cryptocurrency, smart contracts, bank settlement systems, and data storage are creating real customer and business value today.[17,18]

Cryptocurrency

Cryptocurrency is a type of digital currency or electronic money. Although it only exists in digital form, it can be converted into physical or government-issued currency via cryptocurrency exchanges (e.g. at the time of writing this paragraph, the cryptocurrencies Bitcoin and Ethereum were trading at USD $8,671 and $166, respectively). There are thousands of cryptocurrencies in existence, and with almost any organization or individual able to create their own currency, this number is likely to keep growing. Each cryptocurrency has unique features and benefits that influence its value, which is not too different from the unique features and benefits of different nations' currencies influencing their values. Examples of these features and benefits include supply limitations (e.g. there was a limited number of Bitcoins created, and this cannot be increased), transaction acceptability (e.g. Bitcoin has been the most widely accepted cryptocurrency for ordinary transactions, like buying a home or buying food), public interest (e.g. part of the reason behind Bitcoin's stellar price is that it is the most well-known and talked-about cryptocurrency), stability (e.g. the value of Bitcoin is generally seen as being more stable than lesser-known cryptocurrencies), and risk (e.g. during the boom and bust cycles of cryptocurrencies, some rose to price levels thousands of times their initial purchase price, only for prices to subsequently fall way below the initial purchase price and remain there; this was especially the case for lesser-known cryptocurrencies). Typically, anyone can purchase cryptocurrencies on a cryptocurrency exchange using real money, and they can exchange one cryptocurrency owned for another at the prevailing exchange rate. Although some fees are involved, these are minuscule compared to ordinary currency exchange rates. The benefits of cryptocurrencies over government-issued currencies include the ability to transact directly without third parties and third-party fees (e.g. banks, brokers, agents, legal representatives), the clear and permanent audit trail of each transaction, confidentiality (nobody needs to know who you are, where you come from, who you bank with, where you live, where you work, what your credit card number is, etc.), reduced privacy risks (if personal information isn't collected, it can't be accidentally accessed), faster transactions (a cryptocurrency transaction can happen almost instantly, while a similar bank transaction can take days), stronger security (the risk of someone discovering and using your private key is very low), and the ability to transact with people who previously couldn't be reached (e.g. people in some developing countries who previously had no access to a bank account). Disadvantages of cryptocurrency include complexity (although it is improving, a high level of technical expertise is still needed to purchase and use cryptocurrency), risk of loss (e.g. cryptocurrency exchanges have been breached resulting in cryptocurrency losses, and scammers have posed as cryptocurrency platform agents to steal money intended to purchase cryptocurrencies), price volatility (e.g. in one year the Bitcoin price rose to $22,000 and then crashed to $6,000 – and it is one of the less volatile cryptocurrencies), lack of regulation (e.g. there is as yet very little regulation of cryptocurrencies relative to government currencies. This often results in unwitting users being scammed: criminal enterprises have used cryptocurrency as a money laundering and criminal activity payment vehicle; people have lost large amounts of money speculating on future cryptocurrency price growth; and people have bought cryptocurrencies that are worthless).

Some organizations have had great success using cryptocurrency for fundraising purposes. Such organizations have used initial coin offerings (ICOs) as fundraising mechanisms in which they create and sell their own coins or tokens in much the same way that another company may sell its shares on a stock exchange to investors. For example, Block.one raised $4 billion via its 2018 ICO despite its blockchain development product not being fully launched and investors not being clear on exactly how the funds would be spent.[19] Government interventions in ICOs have reduced the number and size of ICOs, but they remain viable fundraising vehicles that can result in higher fundraising success (e.g. speed, amount, and cost of fundraising) than traditional fundraising channels (e.g. banks, professional investors, stock exchange listings). ICOs are increasingly being replaced by STOs (security token offerings), which are essentially the same thing but, thanks to government intervention, offer better protection against fraud, are based on real registered assets, comply with consumer financial safeguard laws, and are incorporated into the established securities market.

Smart contracts

We defined smart contracts earlier as contracts whose terms and conditions exist on the blockchain as self-executing algorithms.[20] Smart contracts have been applied to numerous types of contracts in different industries.[21,22] In trade finance, smart contracts have can be used to automate approval workflows and clearing calculations; in healthcare, smart contracts can be used to authorize access to patient records; in real estate, smart contracts can be used to automate property leasing and purchase agreements as well as related workflows (e.g. paying bond, holding bond, releasing bond, cooling off, title search, settlement, rent payment reconciliation);[23,24] in insurance, smart contracts can be used to automate claims processing; in government, smart contracts can be used to record election votes and announce the winner in a tamper-proof way; and obviously smart contracts can be used in peer-to-peer transactions.[25]

Banking

Banks are using or exploring using blockchain for clearing and settlement activities (e.g. the Australian stock exchange is exploring shifting its post-trade clearing and settlement onto a blockchain system to improve the efficiency and effectiveness of these activities), for payments (e.g. creating their own cryptocurrencies or utility tokens, such as UBS' utility settlement coin for financial markets, which works like other cryptocurrencies but is convertible into cash on deposit at central banks), to facilitate trade finance processes and authorization documents (e.g. bill of lading or letter of credit), to facilitate identity verification, and to facilitate syndicated loans.[26] Figure 19.3 shows the funds transfer process in a traditional digital ledger vs in a blockchain network.

Data storage

The application of blockchain technology to data storage is anticipated to disrupt cloud data storage.[27] Proponents of this application of blockchain technology (e.g. proponents such as FileStorm, Sia, Storj, and Maidsafe) propose that decentralized data storage (distributing data files across a large peer-to-peer node network) is much more secure, makes it harder to lose data, and will be cheaper than the current centralized cloud infrastructure approach.[28] In addition, blockchain-based data files can be split up and spread piecemeal across nodes all over the world, thus restricting who can see the full integrated file.[29]

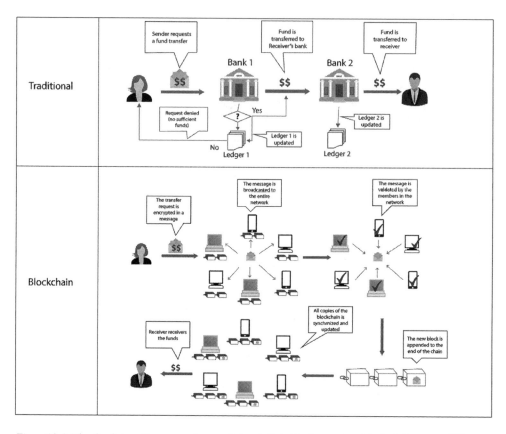

Figure 19.3 The funds transfer process in a traditional digital ledger vs in a blockchain network[30]

Other applications

Other blockchain applications include verification of the authenticity of goods through blockchain-enabled supply chains, notarization to ensure proof of existence, validity of intellectual property origins, and more. Blockchain use cases are rapidly expanding in diversity and realization of the business benefits they promise.[31,32]

Blockchain use cases in the hospitality industry

As noted at the start of this chapter, blockchain and distributed ledger technologies provide opportunities for product innovation, business model innovation, operational efficiency breakthroughs,[33] access to new markets, and mitigation of risks.[34] Early adopters of blockchain and distributed ledger technology in the hospitality industry have initially been focused on streamlined and more secure payments, identity validation, loyalty programs, inventory tracking, and supply chain management.[35] Streamlining payments and making them more secure has involved much the same approach as in other industries (e.g. exploring accepting cryptocurrency, creating or participating in private blockchains or blockchain consortiums to speed up payment settlement).[36] Identity validation has involved partnering with blockchain identification and document authorization service companies to simplify guest identification and authorization workflows. For example, using Shocard's blockchain-based platform, guests can upload their travel documents, which are encrypted and hashed on the Bitcoin blockchain.[37] Guests are then provided with a "single travel token," which can call up those documents for faster and frictionless authentication. Loyalty program applications of blockchain technology limit loyalty scheme fraud and better track use. For example, Trippki, a blockchain-based loyalty reward system, rewards customers with native "TRIP" tokens for staying at a hotel or using hotel amenities.[38] The administration and tracking of tokens and their use is almost automated on the blockchain. Tourism companies like TUI, the largest tourism company in the world, have implemented blockchain-based inventory management initiatives like "Bed-Swap" for real-time bed availability tracking across locations.[39,40] Other companies are using blockchain to track guest baggage movements. Yet other hospitality industry operators are building industry blockchain platforms.[41] For example, BeeToken's Beenest home-sharing platform connects customers with hosts with commission-free peer-to-peer transactions for payments.[42] Finally, blockchain technology can be leveraged to ensure that goods and services across the supply chain are what they are purported to be and come from where they are purported to come from (e.g. if food is safe for guests with certain allergies, then this can be verified on the blockchain; if food is halal, then this should be auditable).[43] Diversity in blockchain applications and use cases in the hospitality industry continue to grow at a rapid pace.[44]

Blockchain issues and risks

Early adopters of blockchain technology will have significant advantages for locking in key partnerships (e.g. consider Hilton and its partnership with IBM, or the way Microsoft locked in key distributors in the PC business), and significant advantages for locking in valuable customer segments (e.g. consider how Microsoft locked in enterprise customers, or consider that Bitcoin is more trusted than other cryptocurrencies). Early adopter advantages also include setting industry use case standards, and enjoying superior profits. But such firms have to take care not to overinvest or attempt to scale too early (e.g. before customers are ready or before the technology is ready for certain types of use cases).[45,46,47] Other blockchain issues include lack of regulation (e.g. unsuspecting customers may fall for scammer platforms pretending to be the real platform or people pretending to be representatives of your organization), they include significant power consumption and related environmental implications (e.g. the sophisticated blockchain calculations require significant power), and they include complexity (e.g. the benefits of blockchain products and services can be obscured by complex processes required to identify users and for users to use them). Other blockchain issues also include blockchain's potential slow and cumbersome nature (e.g. due to the complexity and sophistication of the calculations), and resistance from entrenched entities (e.g. wide-scale adoption of blockchain threatens to disrupt the existing order in much the same way that the internet disrupted business. As a result, entrenched entities may be incentivized to discredit or fight blockchain adoption). Early adopters must tread with care, as the aforementioned issues result in risks that could derail their efforts or bring harm to their organizations.

Google and reflect

Blockchain node, blockchain address, P2P network, blockchain block, block explorer, block height, chain linking, hash, hashing, hash rate, satoshi, altcoin, blockchain wallet, hot wallet, cold wallet, blockchain forking, hard fork, soft fork, dApp, nonce, proof-of-stake, proof-of-authority, lightning network, stale block, orphan block, uncle block, multi-signature, blockchain oracle, whitepaper, Byzantine fault-tolerance, cryptographic hash function (CHF), Merkle tree, cryptography, double spending problem, hashcash, computational trust, public key cryptography, Ripple currency (XRP), Litecoin currency, Libra currency, Monero currency, cryptocurrency exchange, blockchain sharding.

Example tools and vendors

IBM Blockchain, Ripple, Etherium, Hyperledger Fabric, Microsoft Azure Blockchain, Stellar, Quorum, Blockstream, NEO, Oracle Blockchain Cloud Service, Hyperledger Iroha, MultiChain, Tendermint, ConsenSys,[48] PixelPlex, Accubits, SoluLab, PATRON, Celsius Network, Hyperledger Sawtooth, R3 Corda, Menlo One, Gameflip, DACC, Goldilock, FCoin.[49]

Discussion questions

1 What is the difference between blockchain and a distributed ledger?
2 What are three different metaphors you could use to explain to your grandmother how blockchain works?
3 Is blockchain trustworthy? Why?
4 What is the difference between blockchain, Bitcoin, Ethereum, and Ripple (XRP)?
5 What is the difference between a public key and a private key?
6 What are the four main components of a blockchain ecosystem?
7 What are the different types of blockchain, and what is the value of each?
8 Identify and explain the six top features or properties of blockchains.
9 What is a blockchain block, and how is it created?
10 Can blockchain blocks be modified?
11 What type of data can be stored in a blockchain?
12 What is the double spending problem, and how does blockchain overcome it?
13 What is a consensus algorithm?
14 Identify and explain ten different types of consensus algorithms.
15 What are the top five platforms for developing blockchain applications?
16 How is a smart contract different from a normal contract?
17 How is a dApp different from a normal app?
18 Explain how cryptocurrency mining works.
19 What problems does blockchain sharding solve?
20 What are the top five blockchain applications or types of use cases?
21 What are the top five hospitality and leisure organizations successfully leveraging blockchain technology, and how are they using it?
22 What is the business value of blockchain? What six areas of business value have been identified in this chapter?
23 Of all the blockchain use cases, which offers the biggest opportunity for cost reduction in the hospitality industry?
24 Of all the blockchain use cases, which offers the best opportunity for business model innovation in the hospitality industry?
25 Of all the blockchain use cases, which offers the best opportunity for product innovation in the hospitality industry?

26 Of all the blockchain use cases, which offers the best opportunity for safeguarding the security and privacy of guest data in the hospitality industry?

27 Of all the blockchain use cases, which offers the best opportunity to enhance the adaptability and agility of hospitality and leisure organizations?

Notes

1 Finley, K., & Barber, G. (2019). Blockchain: The Complete Guide. Wired. Retrieved January 22, 2020, from www.wired.com/story/guide-blockchain/

2 Mearian, L. (2020). What is Blockchain? The Complete Guide. Computerworld. Retrieved January 22, 2020, from www.computerworld.com/article/3191077/what-is-blockchain-the-complete-guide.html?page=2

3 Bender, J. P., Burchardi, K., & Shepherd, N. (2019). Capturing the Value of Blockchain. www.bcg.com. Retrieved January 22, 2020, from www.bcg.com/en-au/publications/2019/capturing-blockchain-value.aspx

4 Bender, J. P., Burchardi, K., & Shepherd, N. (2019). Capturing the Value of Blockchain. www.bcg.com. Retrieved January 22, 2020, from www.bcg.com/en-au/publications/2019/capturing-blockchain-value.aspx

5 Panetta, K. (2019). The CIO's Guide to Blockchain. Gartner.com. Retrieved January 22, 2020, from www.gartner.com/smarterwithgartner/the-cios-guide-to-blockchain/

6 Carson, B., Romanelli, G., Walsh, P., & Zhumaev, A. (2018). Open Interactive Popup Blockchain beyond the Hype: What is the Strategic Business Value? McKinsey & Company. Retrieved January 22, 2020, from www.mckinsey.com/business-functions/mckinsey-digital/our-insights/blockchain-beyond-the-hype-what-is-the-strategic-business-value

7 Scribani, J. (2018). This is the Value of Blockchain to Different Industries. World Economic Forum. Retrieved January 22, 2020, from www.weforum.org/agenda/2018/12/the-business-value-of-the-blockchain/

8 Plansky, J., O'Donnell, T., & Richards, K. (2016). A Strategist's Guide to Blockchain. strategy+business. Retrieved January 22, 2020, from www.strategy-business.com/article/A-Strategists-Guide-to-Blockchain?gko=9d4ef

9 Finley, K., & Barber, G. (2019). Blockchain: The Complete Guide. Wired. Retrieved January 22, 2020, from www.wired.com/story/guide-blockchain/

10 Mearian, L. (2020). What is Blockchain? The Complete Guide. Computerworld. Retrieved January 22, 2020, from www.computerworld.com/article/3191077/what-is-blockchain-the-complete-guide.html?page=2

11 Finley, K., & Barber, G. (2019). Blockchain: The Complete Guide. Wired. Retrieved January 22, 2020, from www.wired.com/story/guide-blockchain/

12 Mearian, L. (2020). What is Blockchain? The Complete Guide. Computerworld. Retrieved January 22, 2020, from www.computerworld.com/article/3191077/what-is-blockchain-the-complete-guide.html?page=2

13 Mearian, L. (2020). What is Blockchain? The Complete Guide. Computerworld. Retrieved January 22, 2020, from www.computerworld.com/article/3191077/what-is-blockchain-the-complete-guide.html?page=2

14 Mearian, L. (2020). What is Blockchain? The Complete Guide. Computerworld. Retrieved January 22, 2020, from www.computerworld.com/article/3191077/what-is-blockchain-the-complete-guide.html?page=2

15 CompTIA. (2018). Harnessing the Blockchain Revolution – CompTIA's Practical Guide for the Public Sector. Default. Retrieved January 22, 2020, from www.comptia.org/content/research/harnessing-the-blockchain-revolution-comptia-s-practical-guide-for-the-public-sector

16 Blockchain-council.org. (2019). Top 10 Promising Blockchain Use Cases. Retrieved January 22, 2020, from www.blockchain-council.org/blockchain/top-10-promising-blockchain-use-cases/

17 Carson, B., Romanelli, G., Walsh, P., & Zhumaev, A. (2018). Open Interactive Popup Blockchain beyond the Hype: What is the Strategic Business Value? McKinsey & Company. Retrieved January 22, 2020, from www.mckinsey.com/business-functions/mckinsey-digital/our-insights/blockchain-beyond-the-hype-what-is-the-strategic-business-value

18 Bender, J. P., Burchardi, K., & Shepherd, N. (2019). Capturing the Value of Blockchain. www.bcg.com. Retrieved January 22, 2020, from www.bcg.com/en-au/publications/2019/capturing-blockchain-value.aspx

19 Silva, M. (2019). Crypto Companies are Settling with the SEC, But that's Not Stopping Them. Quartz. Retrieved January 20, 2020, from https://qz.com/1720295/after-4b-ico-block-ones-24m-sec-settlement-lets-it-keep-building/

    Rooney, K. (2018). A Blockchain Start-up Just Raised $4 Billion without a Live Product. CNBC. Retrieved January 20, 2020, from www.cnbc.com/2018/05/31/a-blockchain-start-up-just-raised-4-billion-without-a-live-product.html

20 Deloitte CFO Insights. (2016). Getting Smart about Smart Contracts. Retrieved January 22, 2020, from www2.deloitte.com/tr/en/pages/finance/articles/cfo-insights-getting-smart-contracts.html

21 Cheng-Shorland, C. (2018). Moving Beyond Smart Contracts: What are the Next Generations of Blockchain Use Cases? Retrieved January 22, 2020, from www.forbes.com/sites/forbestechcouncil/2018/12/05/moving-beyond-smart-contracts-what-are-the-next-generations-of-blockchain-use-cases/#259adfdb13e5

22 Ream, J., Chu, Y., & Schatsky, D. (2016). Upgrading Blockchains. Deloitte Insights. Retrieved January 22, 2020, from www2.deloitte.com/us/en/insights/focus/signals-for-strategists/using-blockchain-for-smart-contracts.html

23 Cheng-Shorland, C. (2018). How Technology is Changing the Real Estate Market. Forbes.com. Retrieved January 22, 2020, from www.forbes.com/sites/forbestechcouncil/2018/07/31/how-technology-is-changing-the-real-estate-market/#40ff325b6d06

24 Deloitte. (2018). Blockchain and Smart Contracts Could Transform Property Transactions. Retrieved January 20, 2020, from https://deloitte.wsj.com/cfo/2018/01/03/blockchain-and-smart-contracts-could-transform-property-transactions/

25 Ream, J., Chu, Y., & Schatsky, D. (2016). Upgrading Blockchains. Deloitte Insights. Retrieved January 22, 2020, from www2.deloitte.com/us/en/insights/focus/signals-for-strategists/using-blockchain-for-smart-contracts.html

26 Arnold, M. (2017). Five Ways Banks are Using Blockchain. Financial Times. Ft.com. Retrieved January 20, 2020, from www.ft.com/content/615b3bd8-97a9-11e7-a652-cde3f882dd7b

27 Nelson, P. (2019). How Data Storage will Shift to Blockchain. Network World. Retrieved January 22, 2020, from www.networkworld.com/article/3390722/how-data-storage-will-shift-to-block-chain.html

28 Nelson, P. (2019). How Data Storage will Shift to Blockchain. Network World. Retrieved January 22, 2020, from www.networkworld.com/article/3390722/how-data-storage-will-shift-to-block-chain.html

29 Nelson, P. (2019). How Data Storage will Shift to Blockchain. Network World. Retrieved January 22, 2020, from www.networkworld.com/article/3390722/how-data-storage-will-shift-to-block-chain.html

30 Liu, M., Wu, K., & Xu, J. J. (2019). How Will Blockchain Technology Impact Auditing and Accounting: Permissionless versus Permissioned Blockchain. *Current Issues in Auditing*, 13(2), A19–A29

31 CompTIA. (2018). Harnessing the Blockchain Revolution – CompTIA's Practical Guide for the Public Sector. Default. Retrieved January 22, 2020, from www.comptia.org/content/research/harnessing-the-blockchain-revolution-comptia-s-practical-guide-for-the-public-sector

32 Scribani, J. (2018). This is the Value of Blockchain to Different Industries. World Economic Forum. Retrieved January 22, 2020, from www.weforum.org/agenda/2018/12/the-business-value-of-the-blockchain/

33 Accenture.com. (2020). Unlock Trapped Value with blockchain. Retrieved January 22, 2020, from www.accenture.com/au-en/insight-blockchain-business-value

34 Carson, B., Romanelli, G., Walsh, P., & Zhumaev, A. (2018). Open Interactive Popup Block-chain beyond the Hype: What is the Strategic Business Value? McKinsey & Company. Retrieved January 22, 2020, from www.mckinsey.com/business-functions/mckinsey-digital/our-insights/blockchain-beyond-the-hype-what-is-the-strategic-business-value

35 Revfine.com. (2019). Blockchain Technology and Its Uses in the Hospitality Industry. Retrieved January 22, 2020, from www.revfine.com/blockchain-technology-hospitality-industry/

36 Revfine.com. (2019). Blockchain Technology and Its Uses in the Hospitality Industry. Retrieved January 22, 2020, from www.revfine.com/blockchain-technology-hospitality-industry/

37 Revfine.com. (2019). Blockchain Technology and Its Uses in the Hospitality Industry. Retrieved January 22, 2020, from www.revfine.com/blockchain-technology-hospitality-industry/

38 Revfine.com. (2019). Blockchain Technology and Its Uses in the Hospitality Industry. Retrieved January 22, 2020, from www.revfine.com/blockchain-technology-hospitality-industry/

39 Marr, B. (2018). The Awesome Ways TUI Uses Blockchain to Revolutionize the Travel Industry. Forbes.com. Retrieved January 22, 2020, from www.forbes.com/sites/bernardmarr/2018/12/07/the-amazing-ways-tui-uses-blockchain-to-revolutionize-the-travel-industry/#1972e6631e7f

40 Revfine.com. (2019). Blockchain Technology and Its Uses in the Hospitality Industry. Retrieved January 22, 2020, from www.revfine.com/blockchain-technology-hospitality-industry/

41 Cox, L. (2019). 7 Hospitality Companies Getting Behind Blockchain. DisruptionHub. Retrieved January 22, 2020, from https://disruptionhub.com/5-hospitality-companies-using-blockchain/

42 Revfine.com. (2019). Blockchain Technology and Its Uses in the Hospitality Industry. Retrieved January 22, 2020, from www.revfine.com/blockchain-technology-hospitality-industry/

43 Bhandarkar, K. (2018). Mindtree.com. Retrieved January 22, 2020, from www.mindtree.com/sites/default/files/2018-01/WEB-17.8-TTH-GLOB-Top-use-cases-for-blockchain%20in%20Hospitality-Thoughtpost_1.pdf

44 Intellectsoft Blockchain Lab. (2018). Will Hotels Leverage Blockchain? The Future of Hospitality Industry. Retrieved January 22, 2020, from https://blockchain.intellectsoft.net/blog/blockchain-hospitality-tourism-future/

45 Gartner. (2019). Gartner 2019 Hype Cycle for Blockchain Business Shows Blockchain Will Have a Transformational Impact across Industries in Five to 10 Years. Retrieved January 22, 2020, from www.gartner.com/en/newsroom/press-releases/2019-09-12-gartner-2019-hype-cycle-for-blockchain-business-shows

46 Panetta, K. (2019). The CIO's Guide to Blockchain. Gartner.com. Retrieved January 22, 2020, from www.gartner.com/smarterwithgartner/the-cios-guide-to-blockchain/

47 Raconteur. (2016). The Future of Blockchain in 8 Charts. Retrieved January 22, 2020, from www.raconteur.net/business-innovation/the-future-of-blockchain-in-8-charts

48 Gartner Peer Insights. (2020). Blockchain Platforms Reviews. Retrieved January 22, 2020, from www.gartner.com/reviews/market/blockchain-platforms

49 Rossow, A. (2020). 10 New Blockchain Companies to Watch for in 2018. Forbes.com. Retrieved January 22, 2020, from www.forbes.com/sites/andrewrossow/2018/07/10/top-10-new-blockchain-companies-to-watch-for-in-2018/#40d089705600

Index

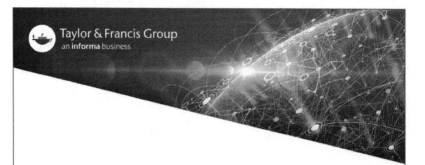